Board + CUET

CL MASTER SERIES

CBSE STUDY GUIDE

12th CLASS

with special focus on CUET examination

HISTORY

Includes

CUET Solved Paper 2022 &
CBSE Solved Papers 2022 (Term I and II)

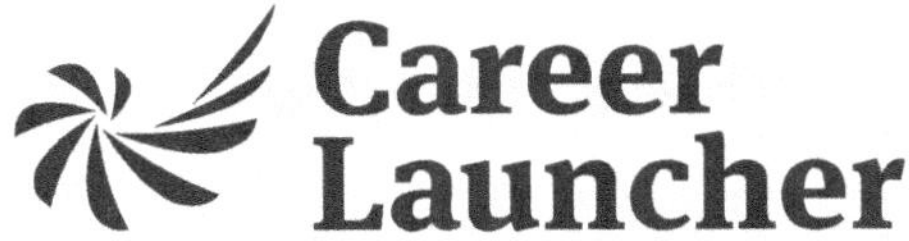

Title   : **CL Master Series :** CBSE Class XII - History (Study Guide)

Language   : English

Editor's Name : Dipak Abhishek

Copyright ©   : 2022 CLIP

No part of this book may be reproduced in a retrieval system or transmitted, in any form or by any means, electronics, mechanical, photocopying, recording, scanning and or without the written permission of the Author/Publisher.

Typeset & Published by :

Career Launcher Infrastructure (P) Ltd.

A-45, Mohan Cooperative Industrial Area, Near Mohan Estate Metro Station, New Delhi - 110044

Marketed by :

G.K. Publications (P) Ltd.

Plot No. 9A, Sector-27A, Mathura Road, Faridabad, Haryana-121003

ISBN   : **978-93-95101-44-8**

Printer's Details

For product information :

Visit ***www.gkpublications.com*** or email to ***gkp@gkpublications.com***

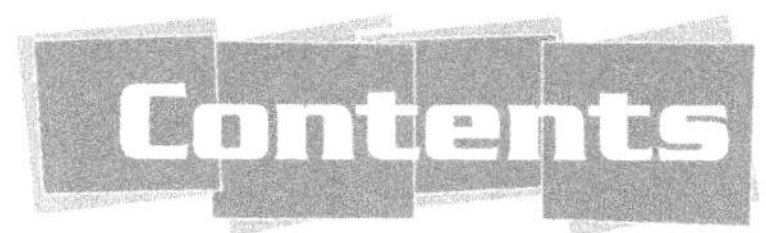

Contents

PART I

PART II

PART III

PART I

Bricks, Beads and Bones

The Harappan Civilisation

Beginning and Subsistence Strategies of the Harappan Civilisation

Summary

Harappan Civilisation

- The Indus valley civilisation is also called the Harappan culture.
- Harappa, the first site where this unique culture was discovered is dated between c. 2600 and 1900 BCE.
- There were earlier and later cultures, often called Early Harappan and Late Harappan, in the same area.
- The Harappan civilisation is sometimes called the Mature Harappan culture to distinguish it from these cultures.
- The Harappans ate a wide range of plant and animal products, including fish.
- Grains found at Harappan sites include wheat, barley, lentil, chickpea and sesame.
- Millets are found from sites in Gujarat. Traces of rice are relatively rare.
- Animal bones found at Harappan sites include those of cattle, sheep, goat, buffalo and pig. Animals were domesticated.
- Bones of wild species such as boar, deer and gharial are also found.
- Bones of fish and fowl are also found.

Agricultural Technologies

- Prevalence of agriculture is indicated by finds of grain.
- Representations on seals and terracotta sculpture indicate that the bull was known
- Oxen were used for ploughing.
- Terracotta models of the plough have been found at sites in Cholistan and at Banawali (Haryana).
- Evidence of a ploughed field at Kalibangan (Rajasthan), associated with Early Harappan levels. Two different crops were grown together.
- Most Harappan sites are located in semi-arid lands, where irrigation was probably required for agriculture.
- Traces of canals have been found at the Harappan site of Shortughai in Afghanistan
- Water reservoirs found in Dholavira (Gujarat) may have been used to store water for agriculture.

Mohenjodaro: A Planned Urban Centre

- The most unique feature of the Harappan civilisation was the development of urban centres.

- Mohenjodaro is the most well-known site (the first site to be discovered was Harappa)
- The settlement is divided into two sections, one smaller but higher(Citadel)and the other much larger but lower(Lower Town)

Citadel

- The Citadel owes its height to the fact that buildings were constructed on mud brick platforms.
- It was walled, which meant that it was physically separated from the Lower Town.

Citadel (used for special public purposes)

- Excavated at Mohenjo-daro in Sindh, Pakistan.
- This Citadel include the warehouse and the Great Bath.
- The Great Bath was a large rectangular tank in a courtyard surrounded by a corridor on all four sides.
- This huge deep bath could have been a place for ritual bathing or religious ceremonies.

Lower Town

- The Lower Town was also walled.
- Several buildings were built on platforms, which served as foundations.
- The settlement was first planned and then implemented accordingly.

Laying out drains

- One of the most distinctive features of Harappan cities was the carefully planned drainage system.
- In Lower Town roads and streets were laid out along an approximate "grid" pattern, intersecting at right angles.
- Drainage systems were not unique to the larger cities, but were found in smaller settlements as well.

Domestic architecture

- The Lower Town at Mohenjodaro provides examples of residential buildings.
- Many were centred on a courtyard, with rooms on all sides.

- Every house had its own bathroom paved with bricks, with drains connected through the wall to the street drains.
- Many houses had wells, often in a room that could be reached from the outside and perhaps used by passers-by.

Multiple Choice Questions [1 Marks]

Q.1. The Harappan seal Made of a _____ called steatite

(a) Metal   (b) Alloy

(c) Stone   (d) Copper

Ans. (c)

Q.2. The Harappan seal contain animal motifs and signs from a script which is

(a) Prakrit   (b) Kharoshti

(c) deciphered   (d) undeciphered

Ans. (d)

Q.3. Consider the following image

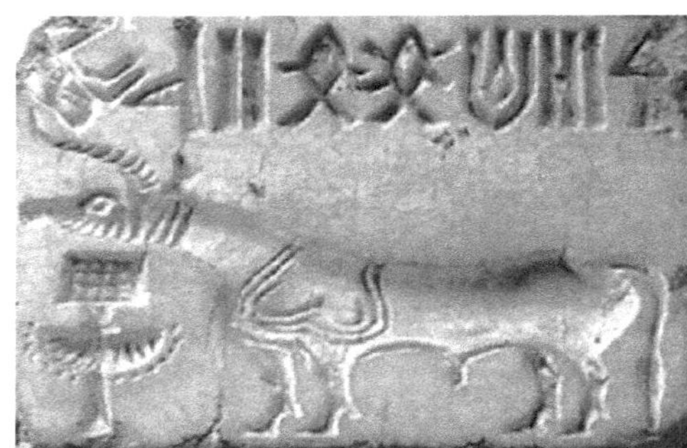

The above image represents a seal of which of the following civilization?

(a) Harappan   (b) Mesopotamia

(c) Tigris   (d) None of these

Ans. (a)

Q.4. A group of objects, distinctive in style, that are usually found together within a specific geographical area and period of time is called as

(a) Culture   (b) Civilization

(c) Society   (d) Nomads

Ans. (a)

Q.5. Seals, beads, weights, stone blades and baked bricks are distinctive objects of which of the following civilizations?

(a) Harappan   (b) Mesopotamia

(c) Tigris   (d) None of these

Ans. (a)

Q.6. The Harappan civilisation is sometimes called the

(a) Mature Harappan culture

(b) Early Harappan Civilization

(c) Late Harappan Civilization

(d) None of the above

Ans. (a)

Q.7. The below image represents which of the following distinctive objects of Harappan civilization?

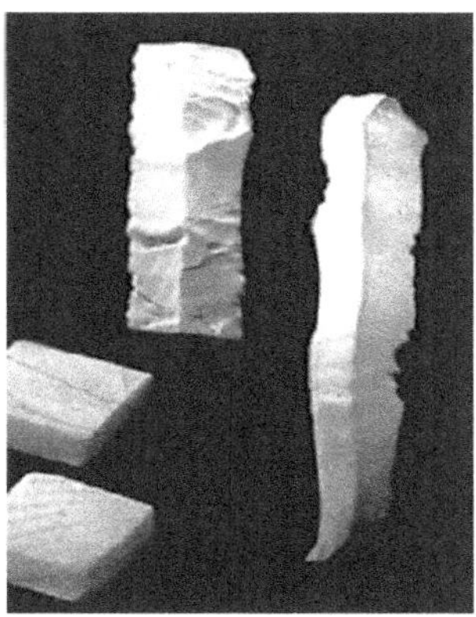

(a) beads   (b) stone blades

(c) baked bricks   (d) Both b and c

Ans. (d)

Q.8. The first site to be discovered was

(a) Mohenjodaro   (b) Harappa

(c) Lothal   (d) Kalibangan

Ans. (b)

Q.9. Millets are found from sites of which of the following regions?

(a) Gujrat   (b) Sindh

(c) Punjab   (d) Rajasthan

Ans. (a)

Q.10. Most of the Harappan sites were located in

(a) Semi-arid regions

(b) Arid regions

(c) Alluvial planes

(d) Doab belt

Ans. (a)

Very Short Answer Type   [1 Mark]

Q.1. BP, BCE and CE stands for

Ans. Before Present , Before Common Era and Common Era respectively

Q.2. With reference to the present political map, the Indus Valley Civilization settlements in Sindh and Cholistan belong to which of the following regions?

Ans. Pakistan

Q.3. Archaeological-botanist is an expert in which field?

Ans. Ancient plant remains.

Q.4. Mature Harappan culture developed in some areas occupied by which of the following culture?

Ans. Early Harappan cultures.

Q.5. How was the eating behaviour of the Harappan people?

Ans. The Harappans ate a wide range of plant and animal products, including fish.

Q.6. Mesopotamian texts datable to the third millennium BCE refer to copper coming from a region called Magan Here Magan represents which region?

Ans. Oman

Q.7. There was a single state, given the similarity in artefacts, the evidence for planned settlements, the standardised ratio of brick size, and the establishment of settlements near sources of raw material.

The above statement is talking about which civilization?

Ans. Harappan Civilization

Q.8. In the citadel, on which platform were the buildings constructed?

Ans. Buildings were constructed on mud brick platforms.

Short Answer Type - I [2 Marks]

Q.1. Name the places where special objects of Harappan civilization like seals, beads, weights, stone blades and baked bricks were found?

Ans. These objects were found from areas as far apart as Afghanistan, Jammu, Baluchistan (Pakistan) and Gujarat

Q.2. Give a brief note about the area before the mature Harappan period.

Ans. Cultures prior to the Mature Harappan were associated with distinctive pottery, evidence of agriculture and pastoralism, and some crafts. Settlements were generally small, and there were virtually no large buildings

Q.3. "There was a break between the Early Harappan and the Harappan civilisation" How can you validate the above fact?

Ans. There was a break between the Early Harappan and the Harappan civilisation, evident from large-scale burning at some sites, as well as the abandonment of certain settlements.

Q.4. Give a brief note about the Harappan seal

Ans. The Harappan seal is possibly the most distinctive artefact of the Harappan or Indus valley civilisation. Made of a stone called steatite, seals like this one often contain animal motifs and signs from a script that remains undeciphered.

Q.5. Define Culture?

Ans. It is defined as a group of objects, distinctive in style, that are usually found together within a specific geographical area and period of time.

Short Answer Type - II [3 Marks]

Q.1. How do archaeologists reconstruct the dietary habits of the Harappans?

Ans. The Harappans ate a wide range of plant and animal products, including fish. Archaeologists have been able to reconstruct dietary practices from finds of charred grains and seeds. These are studied by archaeo-botanists, who are specialists in ancient plant remains.

Q.2. What agricultural products and animal remains have been found at Harappan sites?

Ans. Grains found at Harappan sites include wheat, barley, lentil, chickpea and sesame. Millets are found from sites in Gujarat. Finds of rice are relatively rare. Animal bones found at Harappan sites include those of cattle, sheep, goat, buffalo and pig. Bones of wild species such as boar, deer and gharial are also found. Bones of fish and fowl are also found

Q.3. What were the different sources of irrigation during the Harappan period?

Ans. Most Harappan sites are located in semi-arid lands, where irrigation was probably required for agriculture. Traces of canals have been found at the Harappan site of Shortughai in Afghanistan. Water drawn from wells was used for irrigation. Besides, water reservoirs found in Dholavira (Gujarat) may have been used to store water for agriculture.

Q.4. What were the archaeological cultures like before the mature Harappan?

Ans. There were several archaeological cultures in the region prior to the Mature Harappan. These cultures were associated with distinctive pottery, evidence of agriculture and pastoralism, and some crafts. Settlements were generally small, and there were virtually no large buildings.

Q.5. Give a brief note about the findings of the studies conducted by archaeo-botanists

Ans. Archaeologists have been able to reconstruct dietary practices from finds of charred grains and seeds. These are studied by archaeo-botanists, who are specialists in ancient plant remains. Grains found at Harappan sites include wheat, barley, lentil, chickpea and sesame. Millets are found from sites in Gujarat. Finds of rice are relatively rare.

Long Answer Type   [5 Marks]

Q.1. Give a brief note about the findings of the studies conducted by archaeo-zoologists

Ans. Animal bones found at Harappan sites include those of cattle, sheep, goat, buffalo and pig. Studies done by archaeo-zoologists or zoo-archaeologists indicate that these animals were domesticated. Bones of wild species such as boar, deer and gharial are also found. No information whether the Harappans hunted these animals themselves or obtained meat from other hunting communities. Bones of fish and fowl are also found.

Q.2. Discuss about the agricultural practices and technologies used by Harappan people

[NCERT PRACTISE Questions]

Ans. While the prevalence of agriculture is indicated by finds of grain, it is more difficult to reconstruct actual agricultural practices. Representations on seals and terracotta sculpture indicate that the bull was known, and archaeologists extrapolate from this that oxen were used for ploughing. Moreover, terracotta models of the plough have been found at sites in Cholistan and at Banawali (Haryana). Archaeologists have also found evidence of a ploughed field at Kalibangan (Rajasthan), associated with Early Harappan levels .The field had two sets of furrows at right angles to each other, suggesting that two different crops were grown together.

Q.3. Discuss the precise system of weights used by the Harappana people

Ans. Exchanges were regulated by a precise system of weights, usually made of a stone called chert and generally cubical, with no markings. The lower denominations of weights were binary (1, 2, 4, 8, 16, 32, etc. up to 12,800), while the higher denominations followed the decimal system. The smaller weights were probably used for weighing jewellery and beads. Metal scale-pans have also been found.

Q.4. Discuss, how archaeologists reconstruct the past.   **[NCERT PRACTISE Questions]**

Ans. Archaeologists excavate the sites of the ancient past related to culture or civilization. They find out the art and craft such as seal, material, remains of houses, buildings, pots, ornaments, tools, coins, weights, measurements and toys, etc. Skulls, bones, jaws, teeth of the dead bodies and materials kept with these dead bodies are also helpful for archaeologists. With the help of the botanists, and zoologists, archaeologists study the plants and animal bones found at different places. Archaeologists try to find out the tools used in the process of cultivation and harvesting. They also try to find out traces of wells, canals, tanks, etc. as they served means of irrigation.

TOPIC 2

Planned Urban Centre Craft Production and Social Differences

Summary

Burials

- At burials in Harappan sites the dead were generally laid in pits.
- Some graves contain pottery and ornaments
- Jewellery has been found in burials of both men and women.
- In the excavations at the cemetery in Harappa in the mid-1980s, an ornament consisting of three shell rings, a jasper (a kind of semi-precious stone) bead and hundreds of micro beads was found near the skull of a male.
- In some instances the dead were buried with copper mirrors.
- Harappans did not believe in burying precious things with the dead.

Artefacts

- Rare objects made of valuable materials are generally concentrated in large settlements like Mohenjodaro and Harappa and are rarely found in the smaller settlements.
- For example, miniature pots of faience, perhaps used as perfume bottles, are found mostly in Mohenjodaro and Harappa, and there are none from small settlements like Kalibangan. (*Faience -a material made of ground sand or silica mixed with colour a nd a gum and then fired*)
- Gold too was rare, and as at present, probably precious - all the gold jewellery found at Harappan sites was recovered from hoards (*Hoards are objects kept carefully by people, often inside containers such as pots*)

Craft Production

- Chanhudaro is a tiny devoted to craft production, including bead-making, shell-cutting, metal-working, seal-making and weight-making.

- The variety of materials used to make beads is remarkable: stones like carnelian (of a beautiful red colour), jasper, crystal, quartz and steatite; metals like copper, bronze and gold; and shell, faience and terracotta or burnt clay.
- Some beads were made of two or more stones, cemented together, some of stone with gold caps.
- Specialised drills have been found at Chanhudaro, Lothal and more recently at Dholavira.
- Finished products (such as beads) from Chanhudaro and Lothal were taken to the large urban centres such as Mohenjodaro and Harappa
- Nageshwar and Balakot settlements are near the coast - These were specialised centres for making shell objects - including bangles, ladles and inlay, which were taken to other settlements.
- Craft production was undertaken in large cities such as Mohenjodaro and Harappa.

Multiple Choice Questions   [1 Mark]

Q.1. Which of the following Harappan sites is an example of a small settlement?

(a) Mohenjodaro   (b) Harappa

(c) Kalibangan   (d) None of these

Ans. (c) Mohenjodaro and Harappa were large settlements

Q.2. Miniature pots of faience, perhaps used as perfume bottles, are found mostly in which of the following sites?

(a) Mohenjodaro

(b) Harappa

(c) Kalibangan.

(d) Both (a) and (b)

Ans. (d) Mohenjodaro and Harappa

Q.3. Consider the following image?

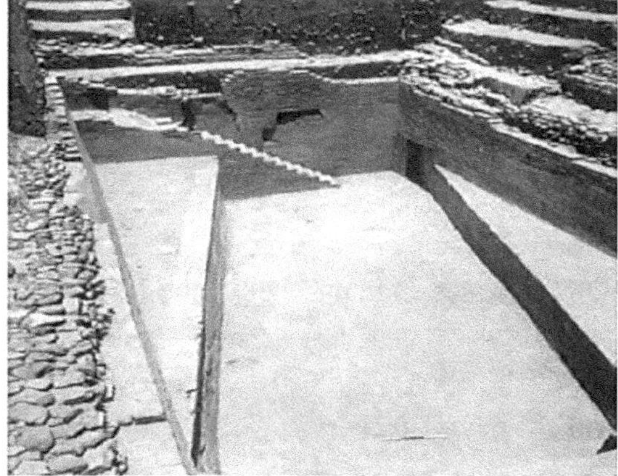

The above image represents

(a) Reservoir

(b) Granary

(c) Great Bath

(d) Citadel

Ans. (a) Reservoir at Dholavira

Q.4. Consider the following Harappan tools?

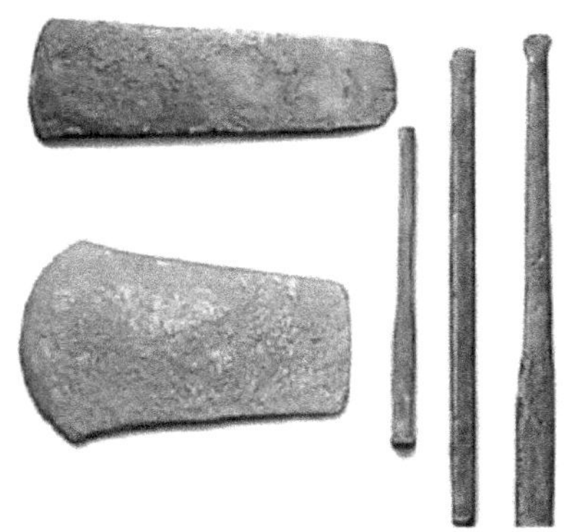

These tools are made up of ________

(a) Copper   (b) Bronze

(c) Iron   (d) Steatite

Ans. (a)

Q.5. Jasper is a kind of

(a) Precious stone

(b) semi-precious stone

(c) metal

(d) alloy

Ans. (b) Jasper - a kind of semi-precious stone

Q.6. Consider the following image

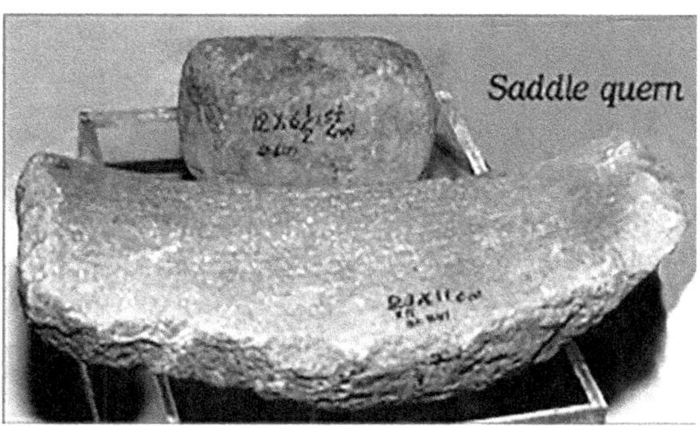

The above image represents the Saddle Quern excavated from which of the following Harappan sites?

(a) Mohenjodaro   (b) Lothal

(c) Kalibagan   (d) Harappa

Ans. (a)

Q.7. At burials in Harappan sites, some graves contain which of the following grave offerings?

(a) Pottery

(b) Ornaments

(c) Jewellery

(d) All of the above

Ans. (d) Some graves contain pottery and ornaments, perhaps indicating a belief that these could be used in the afterlife. Jewellery has been found in burials of both men and women.

Q.8. The roads and streets of which of the following settlements were laid out along an approximate "grid" pattern, intersecting at right angles.

(a) Lower Town

(b) Citadel

(c) great bath area of Mohenjodaro

(d) both (a) and (b)

Ans. (a)

Q.9. At burials, in Harappan sites the dead were generally laid in______

(a) Coffins   (b) bricks

(c) pits   (d) None of these

Ans. (c) At burials in Harappan sites the dead were generally laid in pits.

Q.10. Harappans did not believe in burying _________ with the dead.

(a) precious things

(b) artefacts

(c) semi-precious stone

(d) ornaments

Ans. (a) On the whole, it appears that the Harappans did not believe in burying precious things with the dead.

Q.11. Consider the image

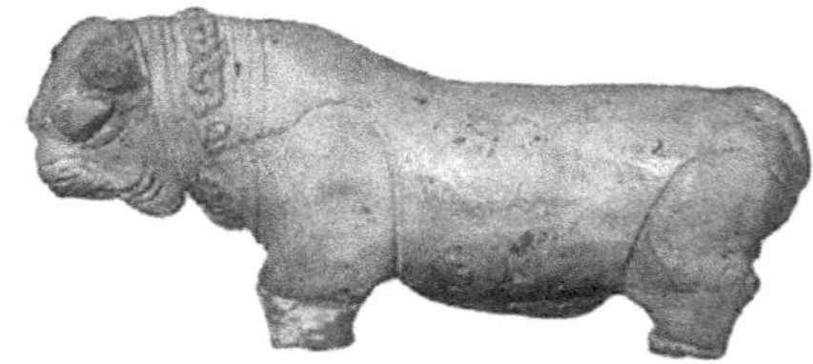

The above image represents _____

(a) Unicorn　　　　(b) Bull

(c) Lion　　　　(d) None of these

Ans. (b) A terracotta bull

 **Very Short Answer Type**　　　　**[1 Mark]**

Q.1. The pyramids of Egypt were contemporaneous with which of the following civilizations?

Ans. Harappan civilisation.

Q.2. Rare objects made of valuable materials were generally concentrated in which of the following areas?

Ans. large settlements like Mohenjodaro and Harappa

Q.3. Studying of burials by the archaeologists were used to find of which of the following differences amongst people living within a particular culture?

Ans. social or economic

Q.4. For which activity was Chanhudaro famous?

Ans. craft production

Q.5. Carnelian , jasper, crystal, quartz and steatite are examples of?

Ans. stones

Q.6. All the gold jewellery found at Harappan sites were recovered from ?

Ans. Hoards

Q.7. Nageshwar and Balakot settlements were the specific centers for which activity?

Ans. making shell objects

Q.8. In the Harappan civilization, exchanges were regulated by a precise system of weighing, usually made of which material?

Ans. stone called chert

Q.9. Into how many categories do archaeologists classify artifacts?

Ans. Archaeologists broadly classify artefacts as , utilitarian and luxuries.

Q.10. Define Hoards

Ans. Hoards are objects kept carefully by people, often inside containers such as pots.

Q.11. What color are the carnelian stones used to make beads?

Ans. red

Q.12. The Steatite material, which is used for making beads, is a

Ans. Soft Stone

Q.13. How many wells have been estimated by cholars in Mohenjodaro?

Ans. about 700.

 **Short Answer Type - I**　　　　**[2 Marks]**

Q.1. What was the most plausible theories assumed by archaeologists with respect to Harappan society?

Ans. The most plausible theory -There was a single state, given the similarity in artefacts, the evidence for planned settlements, the standardised ratio of brick size, and the establishment of settlements near sources of raw material

Q.2. How did carnelian get its red color?

Ans. The red colour of carnelian was obtained by firing the yellowish raw material and beads at various stages of production.

Q.3. Was the drainage system unique only to large cities?

Ans. No, the drainage systems were found in smaller settlements as well. At Lothal for example, while houses were built of mud bricks, drains were made of burnt bricks.

Q.4. How do archaeologists believe the objects were luxuries?

Ans. Archaeologists assume objects were luxuries if they are rare or made from costly, non-local materials or with complicated technologies.

Q.5. What are the factors that have led scholars to suggest that the Great Bath was for some kind of special ritual bath?

Ans. The uniqueness of the structure, as well as the context in which it was found (the Citadel, with several distinctive buildings), has led scholars to suggest that it was meant for some kind of a special ritual bath.

Short Answer Type - II   [3 Marks]

Q.1. What items were included in the utilitarian category of artifacts

Ans. It includes objects of daily use made fairly easily out of ordinary materials such as stone or clay. These include querns, pottery, needles, flesh-rubbers (body scrubbers), etc., and are usually found distributed throughout settlements.

Q.2. Describe the characteristics of Citadels

Ans. Citadel were used for special public purposes. These include the warehouse - a massive structure of which the lower brick portions remain, while the upper portions, probably of wood, decayed long ago - and the Great Bath.

Q.3. Was craft production also done in big cities?

Ans. Yes. Sometimes, larger waste pieces were used up to make smaller objects, but minuscule bits were usually left in the work area. These traces suggest that apart from small, specialised centres, craft production was also undertaken in large cities such as Mohenjodaro and Harappa.

Q.4. How is the Lower Town different from the Citadel?

Ans. The settlement is divided into two sections, one smaller but higher and the other much larger but lower. Archaeologists designate these as the Citadel and the Lower Town respectively. The Citadel owes its height to the fact that buildings were constructed on mud brick platforms. It was walled, which meant that it was physically separated from the Lower Town.

Q.5. What material was used to make the beads ?

Ans. A variety of materials were used to make the beads. Stones like carnelian (of a beautiful red colour), jasper, crystal, quartz and steatite; metals like copper, bronze and gold; and shell, faience and terracotta or burnt clay. Some beads were made of two or more stones, cemented together, some of stone with gold caps.

Long Answer Type   [5 Marks]

Q.1. What were the architectural features of the drainage system?

Ans. It is certainly the most complete ancient system as yet discovered. Every house was connected to the street drains. The main channels were made of bricks set in mortar and were covered with loose bricks that could be removed for cleaning. In some cases, limestone was used for the covers. House drains first emptied into a sump or cesspit into which solid matter settled while waste water flowed out into the street drains. Very long drainage channels were provided at intervals with sumps for cleaning.

Q.2. What were the characteristics of the Great Bath?

Ans. The Great Bath was a large rectangular tank in a courtyard surrounded by a corridor on all four sides. There were two flights of steps on the north and south leading into the tank, which was made watertight by setting bricks on edge and using a m ortar of gypsum. There were rooms on three sides, in one of which was a large well. Water from the tank flowed into a huge drain. Across a lane to the north lay a smaller building with eight bathrooms, four on each side of a corridor, with drains from each bathroom connecting to a drain that ran along the corridor.

Q.3. Write a brief note about the Domestic architecture of Harappan cites

Ans. The Lower Town at Mohenjodaro provides examples of residential buildings. Many were centred on a courtyard, with rooms on all sides. The courtyard was probably the centre of activities such as cooking and weaving, particularly during hot and dry weather. There were no windows in the walls along the ground level keeping the concern for privacy and the main entrance does not give a direct view of the interior or the courtyard

Q.4. Carefully planned drainage system was one of the distinctive features of Harappan cities? Support the statement   **[CBSE 2021]**

Ans. Harappa had a well-planned drainage system. It was distinctive and well developed. The roads and streets were laid out along an approximate "grid" pattern, intersecting at right angles. The streets with drains were laid out first and then houses built along them. Each house had one wall along a street so that domestic waste water can be flowed out into the drains. Thus a proper system of drainage was laid down so that no waste water gets collected on the streets. Hygiene and sanitation were its hallmarks.

TOPIC 3

Procuring Materials and the End of the Civilisation

Summary

Procurement of Materials used for craft production

- Clay were locally available
- stone, timber and metal had to be procured from outside the alluvial plain.
- Shortughai (Afghanista) - source of lapis lazuli, a blue stone that was apparently very highly valued
- Lothal which was near sources of carnelian (from Bharuch in Gujarat), steatite (from south Rajasthan and north Gujarat) and metal (from Rajasthan).
- Khetri region of Rajasthan (for copper) and south India (for gold).
- Copper was also probably brought from Oman
- Mesopotamian texts datable to the third millennium BCE refer to copper coming from a region called Magan, perhaps a name for Oman
- Mesopotamian texts mention contact with regions named Dilmun (probably the island of Bahrain), Magan and Meluhha, possibly the Harappan region.

Seals and sealings

- Seals and sealings were used to facilitate long-distance communication.
- Harappan seals usually have a line of writing, probably containing the name and title of the owner.
- The script remains undeciphered to date
- It is apparent that the script was written from right to left

Weights

- Exchanges were regulated by a precise system of weights, usually made of a stone called chert and generally cubical with no markings.

- The lower denominations of weights were binary (1, 2, 4, 8, 16, 32, etc. up to 12,800), while the higher denominations followed the decimal system.
- The smaller weights were probably used for weighing jewellery and beads.
- Metal scale-pans have also been found.

Ancient Authority -Theories assumed by archaeologists

1. Harappan society had no rulers, and that everybody enjoyed equal status.
2. There was no single ruler but several, that Mohenjodaro had a separate ruler, Harappa another, and so forth.
3. There was a single state, given the similarity in artefacts, the evidence for planned settlements, the standardised ratio of brick size, and the establishment of settlements near sources of raw material (the third theory seems the most plausible)

The End of the Civilisation

- There is evidence that by c. 1800 BCE most of the Mature Harappan sites in regions such as Cholistan had been abandoned.
- Several explanations have been put forward. These range from climatic change, deforestation, excessive floods, the shifting and/or drying up of rivers, to overuse of the landscape.

Discovering the Harappan Civilisation

- Cunningham, the first Director-General of the ASI, began archaeological excavations in the mid-nineteenth century
- Seals were discovered at Harappa by archaeologists such as Daya Ram Sahni in the early decades of the twentieth century
- Another archaeologist, Rakhal Das Banerji found similar seals at Mohenjodaro
- In 1924, John Marshall, Director-General of the ASI, announced the discovery of a new civilisation in the Indus valley to the world.

Techniques used for excavation

- Generally, the lowest layers are the oldest and the highest are the most recent. The study of these layers is called stratigraphy.
- Artefacts found in layers can be assigned to specific cultural periods and can thus provide the cultural sequence for a site.

Multiple Choice Questions [1 Mark]

Q.1. Mesopotamian texts mention trade and commerce with which of the following regions?

(a) Dilmun

(b) Magan

(c) Meluhha

(d) All of these

Ans. (d) Mesopotamian texts mention contact with regions named Dilmun (probably the island of Bahrain), Magan and Meluhha, possibly the Harappan region.

Q.2. Consider the following image

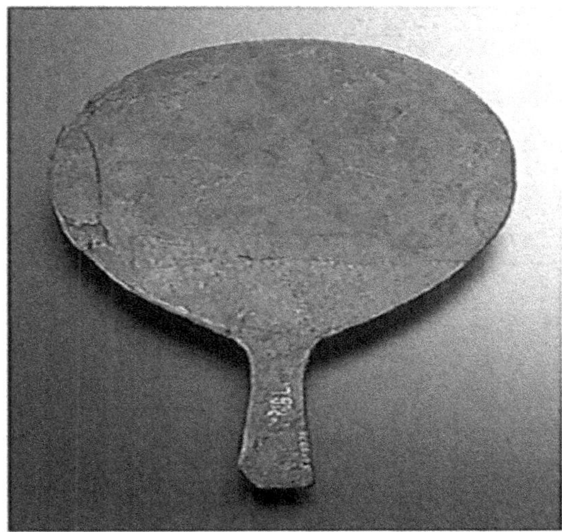

The given image represents a mirror made up of which of the following materials?

(a) Copper

(b) Bronze

(c) Iron

(d) Steatite

Ans. (a) A copper mirror

Q.3. Which of the following is the most plausible theories assumed by archaeologists?

    (a) Harappan society had no rulers, and that everybody enjoyed equal status.

    (b) There was no single ruler but several

    (c) There was a single state

    (d) None of the above

Ans. (c) The most plausible theory - There was a single state, given the similarity in artefacts, the evidence for planned settlements, the standardised ratio of brick size, and the establishment of settlements near sources of raw material

Q.4. Mesopotamian texts refer to copper coming from a region called Magan. Megan represents which of the following regions?

    (a) Egypt   (b) Oman

    (c) Bahrain   (d) Harappan region

Ans. (b) Mesopotamian texts datable to the third millennium BCE refer to copper coming from a region called Magan, perhaps a name for Oman

Q.5. Consider the following image

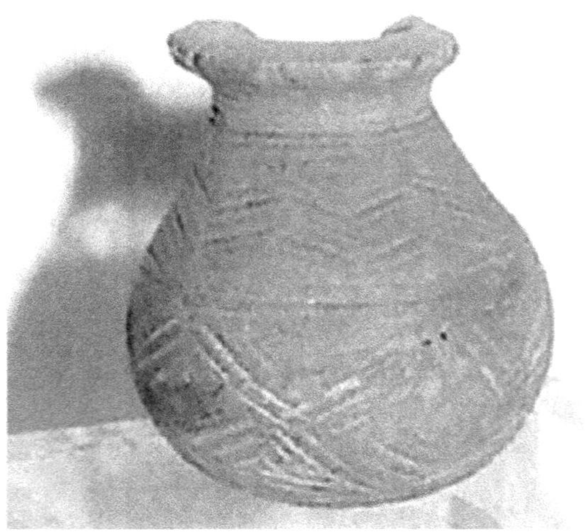

The above image is a little pot of faience which is considered as

    (a) utilitarian   (b) luxuries

    (c) precious   (d) grave offering

Ans. (c) little pots of faience (a material made of ground sand or silica mixed with colour and a gum and then fired) were probably considered precious because they were difficult to make.

Q.6. Which of the following materials for craft production was obtained from outside the alluvial plain?

    (a) Stone   (b) Timber

    (c) metal   (d) all of these

Ans. (d) A variety of materials was used for craft production. While some such as clay were locally available, many such as stone, timber and metal had to be procured from outside the alluvial plain.

Q.7. Consider the following image

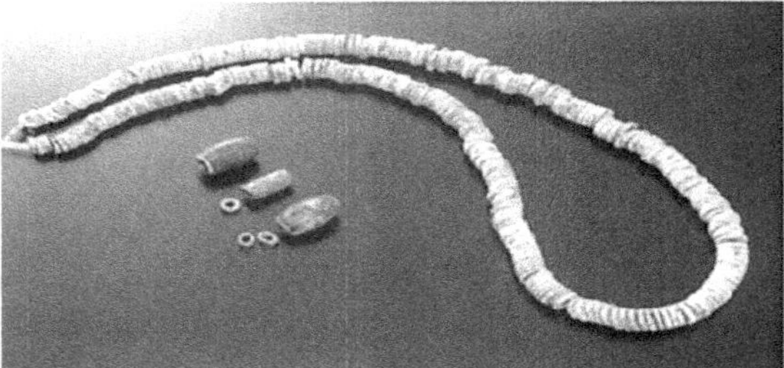

The above image represents

    (a) carnelian

    (b) beads

    (c) jasper

    (d) None of these

Ans. (b)

Q.8. The Harappans procured materials for craft production by using which of the following modes of transportations?

    (a) Land routes.

    (b) Riverine routes

    (c) Coastal routes

    (d) All of these

Ans. (d)

Q.9. What material was sourced from the Khetri region of Rajasthan

    (a) Copper

    (b) Blue Stone

    (c) Sandstone

    (d) Carnelian

Ans. (a)

Q.10. Consider the following figure

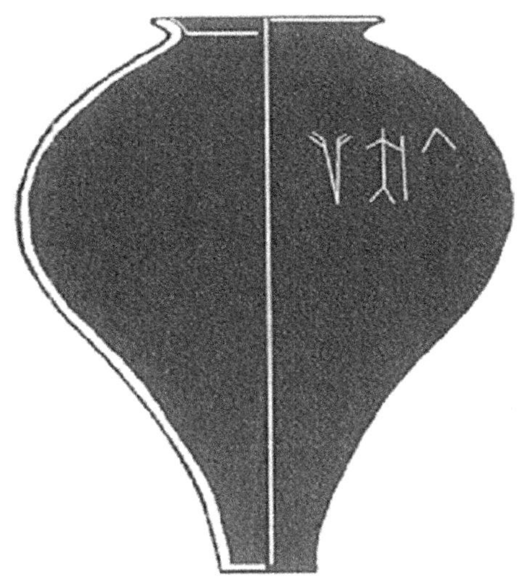

It is an Harappan jar found in which of the following regions?

(a) Dilmun   (b) Magan

(c) Oman   (d) Meluhha

Ans. (c)

Very Short Answer Type   [1 Mark]

Q.1. What was the important mode of transport of goods and people over land routes in the Harappan civilization?

Ans. bullock carts

Q.2. The Ganeshwar-Jodhpura culture represents which area?

Ans. Khetri area, Rajasthan

Q.3. The Harappans established settlements like Nageshwar and Balakot for easy procurement of which material?

Ans. shell

Q.4. The Shortughai site was the source of which material?

Ans. lapis lazuli, a blue stone

Q.5. Which harappan site was situated near sources of carnelian?

Ans. Lothal

Q.6. What material was sourced from south Rajasthan and north Gujarat for craft production?

Ans. steatite

Q.7. Name the region which had typical non-Harappan pottery and unusual wealth of copper objects

Ans. Ganeshwar-Jodhpura culture of Khetri area

Q.8. In which period did Cunningham, the first Director General of ASI, start archaeological excavations of Harappan sites?

Ans. mid- nineteenth century

Short Answer Type - I   [2 Marks]

Q.1. What material is used to make beads?

Ans. The variety of materials used to make beads is remarkable: stones like carnelian (of a beautiful red colour), jasper, crystal, quartz and steatite; metals like copper, bronze and gold; and shell, faience and terracotta or burnt clay.

Q.2. Give a brief note about Chanhudaro

Ans. Chanhudaro is a tiny settlement, almost exclusively devoted to craft production, including bead-making, shell-cutting, metal-working, seal-making and weight-making.

Q.3. What were the types of beads crafted?

Ans. Beads were made of two or more stones, cemented together, some of stone with gold caps. The shapes were numerous - disc- shaped, cylindrical, spherical, barrel-shaped, segmented. Some were decorated by incising or painting, and some had designs etched onto them.

Q.4. What was the method that allowed the bead to be made of different shapes?

Ans. Techniques for making beads differed according to the material. Steatite, a very soft stone, was easily worked. Some beads were moulded out of a paste made with steatite powder. This permitted making a variety of shapes, unlike the geometrical forms made out of harder stones.

Q.5. How did carnelian get its red colour?

Ans. The red colour of carnelian was obtained by firing the yellowish raw material and beads at various stages of production.

Q.6. Define stratigraphy?

Ans. In excavation , the lowest layers are the oldest and the highest are the most recent. The study of these layers is called stratigraphy.

Short Answer Type - II   [3 Marks]

Q.1. What does the study of distribution of artefacts signifies?

Ans. If we study the distribution of artefacts, we find that rare objects made of valuable materials are generally concentrated in large settlements like Mohenjodaro and Harappa and are rarely found in the smaller settlements. For example, miniature pots of faience, perhaps used as perfume bottles, are found mostly in Mohenjodaro and Harappa, and there are none from small settlements like Kalibangan.

Q.2. What were the Strategies for Procuring Materials ?

Ans. Variety of materials were used for craft production. While some such as clay were locally available, many such as stone, timber and metal had to be procured from outside the alluvial plain. Terracotta toy models of bullock carts suggest that this was one important means of transporting goods and people across land routes. Riverine routes along the Indus and its tributaries, as well as coastal routes were also probably used.

Q.3. Copper was probably brought from Oman, how can you confirm this fact?

Ans. Recent archaeological finds suggest that copper was also probably brought from Oman, on the south- eastern tip of the Arabian peninsula.

Chemical analyses have shown that both the Omani copper and Harappan artefacts have traces of nickel, suggesting a common origin.

Q.4. Write a shote note about this seal

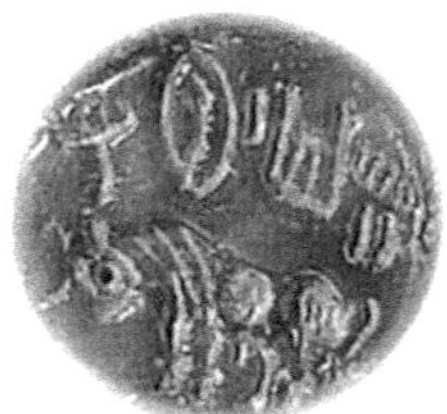

Ans. The round "Persian Gulf" seal found in Bahrain sometimes carries Harappan motifs. Interestingly, local "Dilmun" weights followed the Harappan standard.

Q.5. Consider the following image

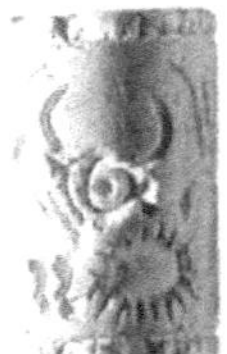 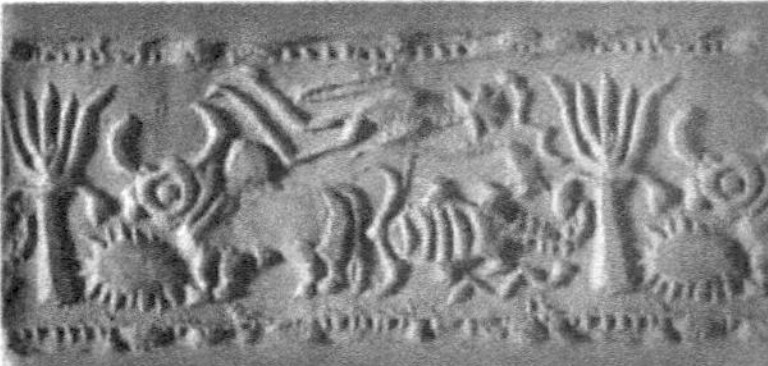

What is the similarity between these two seals?

Ans. This is a cylinder seal, typical of Mesopotamia, but the humped bull motif on it appears to be derived from the Indus region.

Long Answer Type   [5 Marks]

Q.1. How and from where the material for craft production was obtained by the Harappan civilization?

Ans. The Harappans procured materials for craft production in various ways. For instance, they established settlements such as Nageshwar and Balakot in areas where shell was available. Other such sites were Shortughai, in far-off Afghanistan, near the best source of lapis lazuli, a blue stone that was apparently very highly valued, and Lothal which was near sources of carnelian (from Bharuch in Gujarat), steatite (from south Rajasthan and north Gujarat) and metal (from Rajasthan). Another strategy for procuring raw materials may have been to send expeditions to areas such as the Khetri region of Rajasthan (for copper) and south India (for gold). These expeditions established communication with local communities.

Q.2. What are the methods adopted by archaeologists to identify the centers of craft production?

Ans. In order to identify centres of craft production, archaeologists usually look for the following: raw material such as stone nodules, whole shells, copper ore; tools; unfinished objects; rejects and waste material. In fact, waste is one of the best indicators of craft work. For instance, if shell or stone is cut to make objects, then pieces of these materials will be discarded as waste at the place of production Sometimes, larger waste pieces were used up to make smaller objects, but minuscule bits were usually left in the work area. These traces suggest that apart from small, specialised centres, craft production was also undertaken in large cities such as Mohenjodaro and Harappa.

Q.3. Discuss the End Harappan Civilisation

Ans. There is evidence that by c. 1800 BCE most of the Mature Harappan sites in regions such as Cholistan had been abandoned. In the few Harappan sites that continued to be occupied after 1900 BCE there appears to have been a transformation of material culture, marked by the disappearance of the distinctive artefacts of the civilisation - weights, seals, special beads. Overall, artefacts and settlements indicate a rural way of life in what are called "Late Harappan" or "successor cultures".

Q.4. Give a brief note about the Harappan script

Ans. Most inscriptions are short, the longest containing about 26 signs. Although the script remains undeciphered to date, it was evidently not alphabetical (where each sign stands for a vowel or a consonant) as it has just too many signs - somewhere between 375 and 400. It is apparent that the script was written from right to left as some seals show a wider spacing on the right and cramping on the left, as if the engraver began working from the right and then ran out of space.

Q.5. Discuss the Contacts of Harappan people with distant lands

Ans. The Harappan civilization people were in constant touch with other people across the sub continent. Recent archaeological finds suggest that copper was also probably brought from Oman. Chemical analyses have shown that both the Omani copper and Harappan artefacts have traces of nickel, suggesting a common origin. There are other traces of contact as well. A distinctive type of vessel, a large Harappan jar coated with a thick layer of black clay has been found at Omani sites . Mesopotamian texts datable to the third millennium BCE refer to copper coming from a region called Magan, perhaps a name for Oman, and interestingly enough copper found at Mesopotamian sites also contains traces of nickel. Mesopotamian texts mention contact with regions named Dilmun (probably the island of Bahrain), Magan and Meluhha, possibly the Harappan region.

Q.6. List the materials used to make beads in the Harappan Civilisation. Describe the process by which any one kind of bead was made.

[Outside Delhi 2019]

Ans. Making beads was an important craft of the Harappan people. It was mainly prevalent in Chanhudaro. Materials for making beads included beautiful red coloured stone-like camelian, jasper, crystal, quartz and steatite. Besides these, use of copper, bronze, gold, shell, faience, terracotta or burnt clay was also used. Process of making beads Making of beads differed as per the materials used. Beads had variety of shapes. They did not make geometrical shapes like one made of harder stones. Nodules were to be chipped for making rough shapes. They were finally flaked into the final form. By firing the yellowish raw material, the red colour of camelian was obtained. Grinding, polishing and drilling constituted the last phase. Chanhudaro, Lothal and Dholavira were famous for specialized drilling.

Chapter Practice

Multiple Choice Questions [1 Mark]

Q.1. Which of the following settlement is located near the coast.

(a) Chanhudaro (b) Dholavira (c) Nageshwar (d) Mohenjodaro

Q.2. Which of the following statements is true about Citadels?

(a) The settlements were smaller but higher than Lower Town

(b) Citadels were not physically separated from the Lower Town.

(c) The buildings in citadels were constructed on wooden platforms

(d) All statements are true

Q.3. Traces of canals have been found at which of the following Harappan sites?

(a) Shortughai (Afghanistan) (b) Punjab or Sind

(c) Banawali (Haryana). (d) Kalibangan (Rajasthan)

Very Short Answer Type [1 Mark]

Q.4. Mesopotamian texts datable to the third millennium BCE refer to copper coming from which region?
[CBSE 2018]

Q.5. Which was the important means of transporting goods and people across land routes in Harappan civilization?

Short Answer Type - I [2 Marks]

Q.6. Give a brief note about Saddle querns.

Q.7. Mention any source of irrigation used by Harappans for agriculture. [CBSE 2021]

Short Answer Type - II [3 Marks]

Q.8. How the Exchanges were regulated in Harappa civilization? [CBSE 2018]

Q.9. John Marshall's stint as Director General of the Archaeological Survey of India marked a major change in Indian Archaeology. Explain the statement. [CBSE 2019 - Outside Delhi]

Long Answer Type [5 Marks]

Q.10. The most unique feature of the Harappan civilization was the development of domestic architecture." Substantiate the statement. [CBSE 2019 - Outside Delhi]

CHAPTER 2

Kings, Farmers and Towns

Early States and Economies (c. 600 BCE-600 CE)

TOPIC 1

Inscriptions and Mahajanapadas

Summary

Inscriptions

- Inscriptions are writings engraved on hard surfaces such as stone, metal or pottery.
- They usually record the achievements, activities or ideas of those who commissioned them
- James Prinsep, an officer in the mint of the East India Company, deciphered Brahmi and Kharosthi, two scripts used in the earliest inscriptions and coins.
- Most of these mentioned a king referred to as Piyadassi - meaning "pleasant to behold"
- The earliest inscriptions were in Prakrit, a name for languages used by ordinary people.
- Ajatasattu and Asoka, known from Prakrit texts and inscriptions
- Pali, Tamil and Sanskrit, were also used to write inscriptions and texts.

The sixteen mahajanapadas

- Early Buddhist and Jaina texts mention, amongst other things, sixteen states known as mahajanapadas.
- Most mahajanapadas were ruled by kings, some, known as ganas or sanghas, were oligarchies,where power was shared by a number of men, often collectively called rajas. Both Mahavira and the Buddha belonged to such ganas.

- Each mahajanapada had a capital city, which was often fortified.
- Janapada means the land where a jana (a people, clan or tribe) sets its foot or settles. It is a word used in both Prakrit and Sanskrit.
- From c. sixth century BCE onwards, Brahmanas began composing Sanskrit texts known as the Dharmasutras.
- These laid down norms for rulers (as well as for other social categories), who were ideally expected to be Kshatriyas

First amongst the sixteen: Magadha

- Between the sixth and the fourth centuries BCE, Magadha (in present-day Bihar) became the most powerful mahajanapada.
- Magadha was a region where agriculture was especially productive.
- Elephants, an important component of the army, were found in forests in the region.
- Also, the Ganga and its tributaries provided a means of cheap and convenient communication.
- Initially, Rajagaha (the Prakrit name for present- day Rajgir in Bihar) was the capital of Magadha. Rajagaha was a fortified settlement, located amongst hills.
- Later, in the fourth century BCE, the capital was shifted to Pataliputra, present-day Patna

Sources to reconstruct the history of the Mauryan Empire

- Megasthenes (a Greek ambassador to the court of Chandragupta Maurya)
- Arthashastra (composed by Kautilya or Chanakya, traditionally believed to be the minister of Chandragupta.)
- The Mauryas are mentioned in later Buddhist, Jaina and Puranic literature, as well as in Sanskrit literary works.
- The inscriptions of Asoka

Administrative System

- There were five major political centres in the empire - the capital Pataliputra and the provincial centres of Taxila, Ujjayini, Tosali and Suvarnagiri, all mentioned in Asokan inscriptions.
- Megasthenes mentions a committee with six subcommittees for coordinating military activity.

Multiple Choice Questions [1 Mark]

Q.1. *Rigveda* was composed by people living along the Indus and its tributaries in which of the following period?

(a) 1500 - 1000 BC   (b) 1000 BC - 500 BC

(c) 1200 BC - 1000 BC (d) 500 BC - 300 BC

Ans. (a)

Q.2. Epigraphy is the study of

(a) Inscriptions   (b) Coins

(c) Burials   (d) Metals

Ans. (a)

Q.3. James Prinsep, an officer in the mint of the East India Company, deciphered which of the following scripts?

(a) Brahmi

(b) Kharosthi

(c) Piyadassi

(d) Both a and b

Ans. (a)

Q.4. Rigveda was composed by people living along which of the following rivers?

(a) Indus

(b) Ganga

(c) Kaveri

(d) Godavari

Ans. (a)

Q.5. Most of the earliest inscriptions mentioned a king referred to as Piyadassi.

Piyadassi was referred as

(a) Asoka

(b) Ajatsatru

(c) Bimbisaar

(d) Bindusaar

Ans. (a)

Q.6. The coins of which of the following kings have the names of the kings written in Greek and Kharoshthi scripts?

(a) Kings of Gupta empire

(b) Kushans

(c) Indo-Greek kings

(d) None of the above

Ans. (c)

Q.7. James Prinsep, who deciphered Brahmi and Kharosthi scripts was a ___

(a) Officer of ASI

(b) Officer of East India Company

(c) Traveller

(d) Historian

Ans. (b)

Q.8. Most of inscriptions mentioned a king referred to as ___

(a) Piyadassi

(b) Krishnasarah

(c) Devanampriya

(d) Rajkiye

Ans. (a)

Q.9. Consider the map of early states

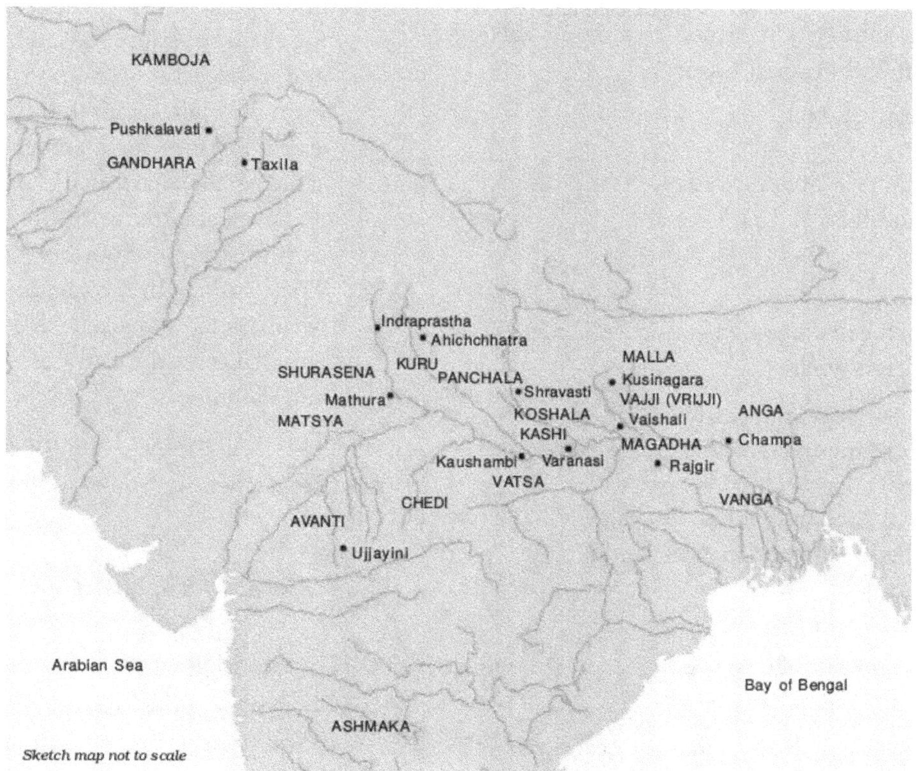

Which was the strongest state among all the Mahajanapadas?

(a) Vatsa   (b) Magadh   (c) Koshala   (d) Anga

Ans. (b)

Q.10. Which of the following rulers was known from Prakrit texts and inscriptions?

(a) Ajatasattu

(b) Asoka

(c) Chandragupt Maurya

(d) Both a and b

Ans. (d) Ajatasattu and Asoka, known from Prakrit texts and inscriptions.

Q.11. Janapada means the land where

(a) People settles

(b) King settles

(c) Jansabha called by the king

(d) None of the above

Ans. (a)

Q.12. The sixth century BCE is associated with which of the following events?

(a) Growing use of iron

(b) Development of coinage

(c) Early Buddhist and Jaina texts

(d) All of the above

Ans. (d)

Q.13. Who among the following rulers appointed Dhamma Mahamattas to spread the message?

(CBSE 2021)

(a) Chandragupta Maurya

(b) Kanishka

(c) Vikramaditya

(d) Ashoka

Ans. (d)

Very Short Answer Type [1 Mark]

Q.1. Which century is regarded as a major turning point in early Indian history?

Ans. sixth century BCE

Q.2. How many Mahajanapadas are mentioned in early Buddhist and Jain texts?

Ans. Sixteen

Q.3. Some of the *mahajanapadas* were oligarchies that symbolized what?

Ans. It symbolises that power was shared by a number of men, often collectively called *rajas*.

Q.4. In which mahajanpadas, the rajas collectively controlled resources such as land?

Ans. Vajji sangha

Q.5. In which period did Magadha become the most powerful Mahajanapada?

Ans. Between the sixth and the fourth centuries BCE

Q.6. The Mauryan Empire was lasted for how many years?

Ans. about 150 years

Q.7. Special officers, known as the dhamma mahamatta, were appointed to spread the message of?

Ans. dhamma.

Q.8. Who was the first ruler who inscribed his messages to his subjects and officials on stone surfaces?

Ans. Asoka

Q.9. The growth of Magadha culminated in the emergence of which ruler?

Ans. Mauryan Empire.

Q.10. Chandragupta Maurya, who founded the empire (c. 321 BCE), extended control as far northwest as ?

Ans. Afghanistan and Baluchistan

Q.11. Consider the following excerpt –

of the great officers of state, some ... superintend the rivers, measure the land, as is done in Egypt, and inspect the sluices by which water is let out from the main canals into their branches, so that every one may have an equal supply of it. The same persons have charge also of the huntsmen, and are entrusted with the power of rewarding or punishing them according to their deserts. They collect the taxes, and superintend the occupations connected with land; as those of the woodcutters, the carpenters, the blacksmiths, and the miners.

This is an excerpt from the account of ?

Ans. Megasthenes

Short Answer Type - I [2 Marks]

Q.1. Define Oligarchy

Ans. Oligarchy refers to a form of government where power is exercised by a group of men.

Q.2. What does Janapada mean?

Ans. Janapada means the land where a jana (a people, clan or tribe) sets its foot or settles. It is a word used in both Prakrit and Sanskrit.

Q.3. Describe the inscriptions of Asoka.

Ans. Asoka was the first ruler who inscribed his messages to his subjects and officials on stone surfaces - natural rocks as well as polished pillars. He used the inscriptions to proclaim what he understood to be dhamma. This included respect towards elders, generosity towards Brahmanas.

Q.4. Discuss about the Languages and scripts of the Harappan Civilization?

Ans. Most Asokan inscriptions were in the Prakrit language while those in the northwest of the subcontinent were in Aramaic and Greek. Most Prakrit inscriptions were written in the Brahmi script; however, some, in the northwest, were written in Kharosthi. The Aramaic and Greek scripts were used for inscriptions in Afghanistan.

Short Answer Type - II   [3 Marks]

Q.1. Describe the physical and political structure of mahajanapadas.

Ans. Early Buddhist and Jaina texts mention, amongst other things, sixteen states known as mahajanapadas. Most mahajanapadas were ruled by kings, some, known as ganas or sanghas, were oligarchies, where power was shared by a number of men, often collectively called rajas. Each mahajanapada had a capital city, which was often fortified

Q.2. How did Ashoka propagate the Dhamma?

Ans. Asoka tried to hold his empire together by propagating dhamma. Special officers, known as the dhamma mahamatta, were appointed to spread the message of dhamma.

Q.3. In which languages other than Prakrit were inscriptions and texts written?

Ans. The earliest inscriptions were in Prakrit, a name for languages used by ordinary people. Ajatasattu and Asoka, known from Prakrit texts and inscriptions. Pali, Tamil and Sanskrit, were also used to write inscriptions and texts.

Q.4. Describe the six subcommittees for coordinating military activities as outlined by Megasthenes.

Ans. Megasthenes mentions a committee with six subcommittees for coordinating military activity. Of these, one looked after the navy, the second managed transport and provisions, the third was responsible for foot-soldiers, the fourth for horses, the fifth for chariots and the sixth for elephants.

Q.5. Give a brief description about the capital of Magadh

Ans. Initially, Rajagaha (the Prakrit name for present-day Rajgir in Bihar) was the capital of Magadha. Rajagaha was a fortified settlement, located amongst hills. Later, in the fourth century BCE, the capital was shifted to Pataliputra, present-day Patna

Q.6. Discuss the developments of Indian epigraphy.

Ans. James Prinsep, an officer in the mint of the East India Company, deciphered Brahmi and Kharosthi, two scripts used in the earliest inscriptions and coins. Most of these mentioned a king referred to as Piyadassi - meaning "pleasant to behold" There were a few inscriptions which also referred to the king as Asoka, one of the most famous rulers known from Buddhist texts.

Long Answer Type   [5 Marks]

Q.1. Describe the role of the political centers of the Magadha Empire?

Ans. There were five major political centres in the empire - the capital Pataliputra and the provincial centres of Taxila, Ujjayini, Tosali and Suvarnagiri, all mentioned in Asokan inscriptions. It is likely that administrative control was strongest in areas around the capital and the provincial centres. These centres were carefully chosen, both Taxila and Ujjayini being situated on important long-distance trade routes, while Suvarnagiri was possibly important for tapping the gold mines of Karnataka.

Q.2. What norms were laid down Dharmasutras.?

Ans. From c. sixth century BCE onwards, Brahmanas began composing Sanskrit texts known as the Dharmasutras. These laid down norms for rulers (as well as for other social categories), who were ideally expected to be Kshatriyas . Rulers were advised to collect taxes and tribute from cultivators, traders and artisans. Raids on neighbouring states were recognised as a legitimate means of acquiring wealth.

Q.3. Discuss the spread of social and political structure in 6th century BCE?

Ans. The sixth century BCE is an era associated with early states, cities, the growing use of iron, the development of coinage, etc. It also witnessed the growth of diverse systems of thought, including Buddhism and Jainism. Early Buddhist and Jaina texts mention, amongst other things, sixteen states known as mahajanapadas. Most mahajanapadas were ruled by kings, some, known as ganas or sanghas, were oligarchies,where power was shared by a number of men, often collectively called rajas. In the case of the Vajji sangha, the rajas probably controlled resources such as land collectively. Each mahajanapada had a capital city, which was often fortified.

Q.4. What sources were used by historians to reconstruct the history of the Maurya Empire?

Ans. Historians have used a variety of sources to reconstruct the history of the Mauryan Empire.

These include archaeological finds, especially sculpture ,contemporary works, such as the account of Megasthenes, which survives in fragments. Another source that is often used is the *Arthashastra*, parts of which were probably composed by Kautilya or Chanakya, traditionally believed to be the minister of Chandragupta. Besides, the Mauryas are mentioned in later Buddhist, Jaina and Puranic literature, as well as in Sanskrit literary works. The inscriptions of Asoka on rocks and pillars are often regarded as amongst the most valuable sources.

TOPIC 2

New Notions of Kingship and Changing Countryside

Summary

New Notions of Kingship

- By the second century BCE, new kingdoms emerged in the Deccan and further south, including the chiefdoms of the Cholas, Cheras and Pandyas in Tamilakam (the name of the ancient Tamil country, which included parts of present-day Andhra Pradesh and Kerala, in addition to Tamil Nadu)

Divine King

- One means of claiming high status was to identify with a variety of deities. This strategy is best exemplified by the
- Kushanas (c. first century BCE- first century CE), who ruled over a vast kingdom extending from Central Asia to northwest India.
- The Kushanas considered themselves godlike.
- Many Kushana rulers also adopted the title devaputra, or "son of god"

Gupta Empire

- By the fourth century there is evidence of larger states, including the Gupta Empire.

- Many of these depended on samantas, men who maintained themselves through local resources including control over land.
- They offered homage and provided military support to rulers.
- Powerful samantas could become kings: conversely, weak rulers might find themselves being reduced to positions of subordination.
- Source - literature, coins and inscriptions - The Prayaga Prashasti

A Changing Countryside

- Source of information - Jatakas (written in Pali around the middle of the first millennium CE) and the Panchatantra.
- Relationship between a king and his subjects (villagers)
- Kings frequently tried to fill their coffers by demanding high taxes

Terminologies

Gahapati

- A gahapati was the owner, master or head of a household, who exercised control over the women, children, slaves and workers who shared a common residence.

- He was also the owner of the resources - land, animals and other things - that belonged to the household.

Manusmrti

- It is one of the best-known legal texts of early India, written in Sanskrit and compiled between c. second century BCE and c. second century CE.

Agrahara

- An agrahara was land granted to a Brahmana, who was usually exempted from paying land revenue and other dues to the king, and was often given the right to collect these dues from the local people.

Periplus

- "Periplus" is a Greek word meaning sailing around and "Erythraean" was the Greek name for the Red Sea

Numismatics

- It is the study of coins, including visual elements such as scripts and images, metallurgical analysis and the contexts in which they have been found.

Towns and Trade

Emergence of new Urban centres (sixth century BCE) - All major towns were located along routes of communication.

- Pataliputra - riverine routes.
- Ujjayini - land routes
- Puhar - near the coast
- Mathura were bustling centres of commercial, cultural and political activity.

Trade in the subcontinent and beyond

- From the sixth century BCE, land and river routes criss-crossed the subcontinent and extended in various directions

- Successful merchants, designated as masattuvan in Tamil and setthis and satthavahas in Prakrit, could become enormously rich.

Coins and kings

- Punch-marked coins made of silver and copper (c. sixth century BCE onwards) were amongst the earliest to be minted and used.

- Numismatists have studied these and other coins to reconstruct possible commercial networks.

- The first coins to bear the names and images of rulers were issued by the Indo-Greeks, who established control over the north-western part of the subcontinent c. second century BCE.

- The kushanas, however, issued the largest hoards of gold coins first gold coins c. first century CE.

- Coins (Copper coins)were also issued by tribal republics such as that of the Yaudheyas of Punjab and Haryana (c. first century CE).

- Some of the most spectacular gold coins were issued by the Gupta rulers.

Multiple Choice Questions   [1 Mark]

Q.1. Satavahanas ruled over parts of _________ and _________ India

(a) Western and Central

(b) Southern and Central

(c) Central and Eastern

(d) Southern and Western

Ans. (a) Satavahanas ruled over parts of western and central India (*c.* second century BCE-second century CE)

Q.2. What was the origin of the Shakas?

(a) Central Asian

(b) Europe

(c) Middle East

(d) Indian sub-continent

Ans. (a) The Shakas, a people of Central Asian origin who established kingdoms in the north-western and western parts of the subcontinent, derived revenues from long-distance trade

Q.3. 'dhamma mahamatta', were appointed in Asokan empire to spread the message of

(a) Peace

(b) Buddha's Preaching

(c) Tipitaka's

(d) dhamma

Ans. (d) Special officers, known as the *dhamma mahamatta*, were appointed to spread the message of *dhamma*.

Q.4. The __________ lays down minute details of administrative and military organisation of the Mauryan Kingdom

(a) Jatakas

(b) Panchatantra.

(c) Arthashastra

(d) None of the above

Ans. (c)

Q.5. Read the following excerpt

Guards of elephant forests, assisted by those who rear elephants, those who enchain the legs of elephants, those who guard the boundaries, those who live in forests, as well as by those who nurse elephants, shall, with the help of five or seven female elephants to help in tethering wild ones, trace the whereabouts of herds of elephants by following the course of urine and dung left by elephants.

The above paragraph tells about the method of capturing elephants which has been mentioned in which of the following book?

(a) Indica

(b) Manusmriti

(c) Arthashastra

(d) Vishnupuran

Ans. (c) The new kingdoms emerged in the Deccan and further south, including the chiefdoms of the Cholas, Cheras and Pandyas in Tamilakam

Q.6. Which of the following present state is/are included in Tamilakam?

(a) Andhra Pradesh

(b) Kerala

(c) Tamil Nadu

(d) All of the above

Ans. (d) The new kingdoms that emerged in the Deccan and further south, including the chiefdoms of the Cholas, Cheras and Pandyas in Tamilakam (the name of the ancient Tamil country, which included parts of present-day Andhra Pradesh and Kerala, in addition to Tamil Nadu), proved to be stable and prosperous.

Q.7. Which of the following rulers adopted the title devaputra

(a) Kushana rulers

(b) Parthian

(c) Cholas

(d) Pandyas

Ans. (a) Many Kushana rulers adopted the title *devaputra*, or "son of god", possibly inspired by Chinese rulers who called themselves sons of heaven.

Q.8. The Shakas, a people of Central Asian origin who established kingdoms in the north-western and western parts of the subcontinent, derived revenues from __________

(a) Agriculture

(b) Domestic trade

(c) Mansabdari

(d) Long-distance trade.

Ans. (d)

Q.9. Read the following excerpt

(When he visited the forest) people came down the mountain, singing and dancing ... just as the defeated show respect to the victorious king, so did they bring gifts - ivory, fragrant wood, fans made of the hair of deer, honey, sandalwood, red ochre, antimony, turmeric, cardamom, pepper, etc. ... they brought coconuts, mangoes, medicinal plants, fruits, onions, sugarcane, flowers, areca nut, bananas, baby tigers, lions, elephants, monkeys, bear, deer, musk deer, fox, peacocks, musk cat, wild cocks, speaking parrots, etc. ...

The above excerpt has been taken from which of the following epic

(a) Silappadikaram   (b) Manimekalai

(c) Valaiyapadhi   (d) Kundalakesi

Ans. (a)

Q.10. Find the incorrect statement about the chief

(a) A chief is a powerful man whose position is always hereditary.

(b) He derives support from his kinfolk.

(c) His functions also include performing special rituals

(d) He receives gifts from his subordinates

Ans. (a) A chief is a powerful man whose position may or may not be hereditary.

Q.11. Consider the following image

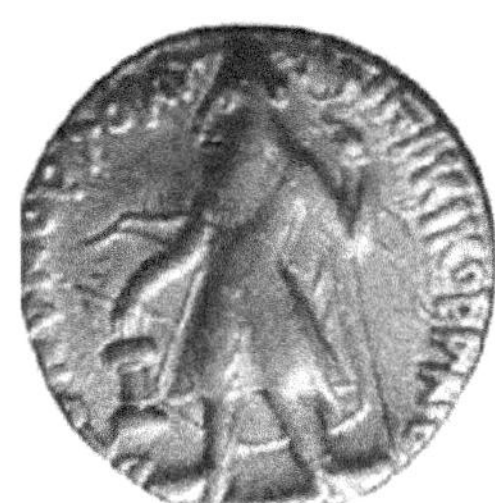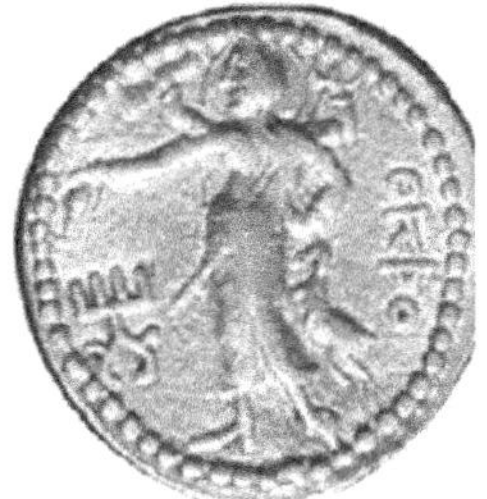

The above image represents ______

(a) Kushana coin   (b) Gupta coins

(c) Samantas coins   (d) None of the above

Ans. (a)

Q.12. Who among the following rulers issued spectacular gold coins in ancient India ?

(CBSE 2021)

(a) Mauryas

(b) Yaudheyas

(c) Guptas

(d) Kushanas

Ans. (c)

Very Short Answer Type   [1 Mark]

Q.1. One means of claiming high status was to identify with a variety of deities. This strategy was best exemplified by which ruler?

Ans. Kushanas

Q.2. Colossal statues of which rulers have been found installed in a shrine at Mat near Mathura (Uttar Pradesh).

Ans. Kushana rulers

Q.3. The *Jatakas* were written around the middle of the first millennium CE in which language?

Ans. Pali

Q.4. "Periplus" is a Greek word which means ____

Ans. sailing around

Q.5. "Erythraean" was the Greek name for which sea?

Ans. Red Sea.

Q.6. Prabhavati Gupta was the daughter of which ruler?

Ans. Chandragupta II

Q.7. The Aramaic and Greek scripts were used for inscriptions in which country?

Ans. Afghanistan.

Q.8. Read the following excerpt from the Prayaga Prashasti:

He was without an antagonist on earth; he, by the overflowing of the multitude of (his) many good qualities adorned by hundreds of good actions, has wiped off the fame of other kings with the soles of (his) feet; (he is) Purusha (the Supreme Being), being the cause of the prosperity of the good and the destruction of the bad (he is) incomprehensible; (he is) one whose tender heart can be captured only by devotion and humility; (he is) possessed of compassion; (he is) the giver of many hundred-thousands of cows; (his) mind has received ceremonial initiation for the uplift of the miserable, the poor, the forlorn and the suffering; (he is) resplendent and embodied kindness to mankind; (he is) equal to (the gods) Kubera (the god of wealth), Varuna (the god of the ocean), Indra (the god of rains) and Yama (the god of death)...

The above excerpt of Prayag Prashasti was written in the praise of which ruler?

Ans. Samudragupta

Q.9. Which story indicates, the relationship between a king and his subjects?

Ans. Gandatindu Jataka

Q.10. What does the picture below represent?

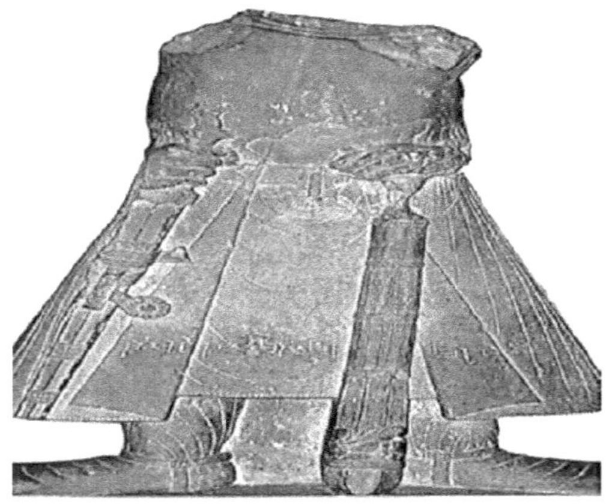

Ans. It is a Sandstone sculpture of a Kushana king

Short Answer Type - I   [2 Marks]

Q.1. Which text advises the king to do:

Seeing that in the world controversies constantly arise due to the ignorance of boundaries, he should ... have ... concealed boundary markers buried - stones, bones, cow's hair, chaff, ashes, potsherds, dried cow dung, bricks, coal, pebbles and sand. He should also have other similar substances that would not decay in the soil buried as hidden markers at the intersection of boundaries.

Ans. The Manusmrti is one of the best-known legal texts of early India, written in Sanskrit and compiled between c. second century BCE and c. second century CE.

Q.2. Who was gahapati?

Ans. A gahapati was the owner, master or head of a household, who exercised control over the women, children, slaves and workers who shared a common residence. He was also the owner of the resources - land, animals and other things - that belonged to the household.

Q.3. What was Manusmrti ?

Ans. It is one of the best-known legal texts of early India, written in Sanskrit and compiled between c. second century BCE and c. second century CE.

Q.4. Define the term Agrahara?

Ans. An *agrahara* was land granted to a Brahmana, who was usually exempted from paying land revenue and other dues to the king, and was often given the right to collect these dues from the local people.

Q.5. Which was the first coins to bear the names and images of rulers ?

Ans. The first coins to bear the names and images of rulers were issued by the Indo-Greeks, who established control over the north-western part of the subcontinent *c.* second century BCE.

Q.6. Define Numismatics

Ans. It is the study of coins, including visual elements such as scripts and images, metallurgical analysis and the contexts in which they have been found.

Short Answer Type - II   [3 Marks]

Q.1. Who composed Harshacharita?

Ans. The Harshacharita is a biography of Harshavardhana, the ruler of Kanauj composed in Sanskrit by his court poet, Banabhatta

Q.2. Who were samantas?

Ans. By the fourth century there is evidence of larger states, including the Gupta Empire. Many of these depended on *samantas*, men who maintained themselves through local resources including control over land. They offered homage and provided military support to rulers. Powerful *samantas* could become kings: conversely, weak rulers might find themselves being reduced to positions of subordination.

Q.3. What were the urban centres that emerged in several parts of the subcontinent from *c.* sixth century BCE. ?

Ans. The emerging urban centres from *c.* sixth century BCE. were capitals of *mahajanapadas*. All major towns were located along routes of communication. Some such as Pataliputra were on riverine routes. Others, such as Ujjayini, were along land routes, and yet others, such as Puhar, were near the coast, from where sea routes began. Many cities like Mathura were bustling centres of commercial, cultural and political activity.

Q.4. What was the use of iron-tipped ploughshare in agriculture?

Ans. The iron-tipped ploughshare was used to turn the alluvial soil in areas which had high rainfall. Moreover, in some parts of the Ganga valley, production of paddy was dramatically increased by the introduction of transplantation, although this meant back-breaking work for the producer. While the iron ploughshare led to a growth in agricultural productivity, its use was restricted to certain parts of the subcontinent

Long Answer Type   [5 Marks]

Q.1. How the history of Gupta rulers has been reconstructed by historians?

Ans. Histories of the Gupta rulers have been reconstructed from literature, coins and inscriptions, including *prashastis*, composed in praise of kings in particular, and patrons in general, by poets. While historians often attempt to draw factual information from such compositions, those who composed and read them often treasured them as works of poetry rather than as accounts that were literally true. The *Prayaga Prashasti* (also known as the Allahabad Pillar Inscription) composed in Sanskrit by Harishena, the court poet of Samudragupta, arguably the most powerful of the Gupta rulers (*c.* fourth century CE), is a case in point.

Q.2. Who were the people associated with the construction and repair of sudarshan Lake?

Ans. The Sudarshana lake was an artificial reservoir. We know about it from a rock inscription (c. second century CE) in Sanskrit, composed to record the achievements of the Shaka ruler Rudradaman. The inscription mentions that the lake, with embankments and water channels, was built by a local governor during the rule of the Mauryas. However, a terrible storm broke the embankments and water gushed out of the lake. Rudradaman, who was then ruling in the area, claimed to have got the lake repaired using his own resources, without imposing any tax on his subjects. Another inscription on the same rock (c. fifth century) mentions how one of the rulers of the Gupta dynasty got the lake repaired once again.

Q.3. How the Situation of Prabhavati Gupta was exceptional?

Ans. Prabhavati Gupta was the daughter of one of the most important rulers in early Indian history,

Chandragupta II . She was married into another important ruling family, that of the Vakatakas, who were powerful in the Deccan . According to Sanskrit legal texts, women were not supposed to have independent access to resources such as land. However, the inscription indicates that Prabhavati had access to land, which she then granted. This may have been because she was a queen and her situation was therefore exceptional. It is also possible that the provisions of legal texts were not uniformly implemented.

Q.4. Pataliputra had a history of its own, Discuss.

Ans. Pataliputra, began as a village known as Pataligrama. Then, in the fifth century BCE, the Magadhan rulers decided to shift their capital from Rajagaha to this settlement and renamed it. By the fourth century BCE, it was the capital of the Mauryan Empire and one of the largest cities in Asia. Subsequently, its importance apparently declined. When the Chinese pilgrim Xuan Zang visited the city in the seventh century CE, he found it in ruins, and with a very small population.

Q.5. Discuss the salient features of Punch-marked coins.

Ans. Punch-marked coins made of silver and copper (*c.* sixth century BCE onwards) were amongst the earliest to be minted and used. These have been recovered from excavations at a number of sites throughout the subcontinent. Attempts made to identify the symbols on punch- marked coins with specific ruling dynasties, including the Mauryas, suggest that these were issued by kings. It is also likely that merchants, bankers and townspeople issued some of these coins.

Q.6. Discuss the trade in the subcontinent and beyond.

Ans. From the sixth century BCE, land and river routes criss-crossed the subcontinent and extended in various directions. Rulers often attempted to control these routes, possibly by offering protection for a price. Those who traversed these routes included peddlers who probably travelled on foot and merchants who travelled with caravans of bullock carts and pack-animals. Also, there were seafarers, whose ventures were risky but highly profitable. Successful merchants, designated as masattuvan in Tamil and setthis and satthavahas in Prakrit, could become enormously rich. A wide range of goods were carried from one place to another.

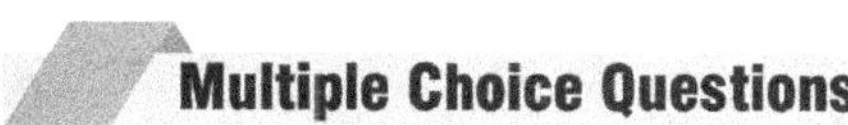

Chapter Practice

Multiple Choice Questions [1 Mark]

Q.1. The Prayaga Prashasti was composed in Sanskrit by Harishena, the court poet of which of the following rulers?

(a) Chandragupta Maurya

(b) Samudragupta

(c) DhanaNanda

(d) Ashoka

Q.2. Find the incorrect statement about Sudarshana lake

(a) The lake, was built by a local governor during the rule of the Mauryas

(b) It was repaired twice by Gupta dynasty.

(c) It was an artificial reservoir.

(d) The lake is situated in Gujrat

Q.3. Find the False statement with respect to the developments after the end of the Harappan civilisation

(a) The dead were buried with a rich range of iron tools and weapons.

(b) Evidence of pastoral populations in the North

(c) Making of elaborate stone structures known as megaliths

(d) Emergence of early states, empires and kingdoms.

Very Short Answer Type [1 Mark]

Q.4. Who was the owner, master or head of a household?

Q.5. Most of the Asokan inscriptions are in which language?

Short Answer Type - I [2 Marks]

Q.6. What was Agrahara?

Q.7. What are inscriptions?

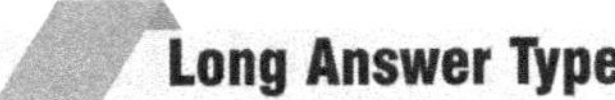 **Short Answer Type - II** [3 Marks]

Q.8. How do historians reconstruct the lives of ordinary people? [NCERT Practise Question]

Q.9. Describe the sources historians have used to reconstruct the history of the Mauryan Empire.

[CBSE Delhi 2019]

Long Answer Type [5 Marks]

Q.10. Discuss the notions of kingship that developed in the post-Mauryan period.

[NCERT Practise Question]

Kinship, Caste and Class

Early Societies (c. 600 BCE-600 CE)

Kinship Marriage and Social Differences

Summary

Ideal of patriliny

- Under patriliny, sons could claim the resources (including the throne in the case of kings) of their fathers when the latter died.
- Most ruling dynasties (c. sixth century BCE onwards) claimed to follow this system
- The patriliny had existed prior to the composition of the epic
- *Mahabharata* reinforced the idea that it was valuable.

Rules of marriage

- Sons were important for the continuity of the patrilineage, daughters were viewed rather differently within this framework.
- Daughters had no claims to the resources of the household.
- Marrying them into families outside the kin was considered desirable. This system, called exogamy

Codes of social behaviour

- The Brahmanas laid down the codes of social behaviour
- These were meant to be followed by Brahmanas in particular and the rest of society in general.

- From c. 500 BCE, these norms were compiled in Sanskrit texts known as the Dharmasutras and Dharmashastras.
- The most important of such works, the Manusmriti, was compiled between c. 200 BCE and 200 CE.
- The influence of Brahmanas was by no means all-pervasive.
- The Dharmasutras and Dharmashastras recognised as many as eight forms of marriage.
- Of these, the first four were considered as "good" while the remaining were condemned.
- It is possible that these were practised by those who did not accept Brahmanical norms.

The gotra of women

- Brahmanical practice(from c. 1000 BCE onwards was to classify people (especially Brahmanas) in terms of gotras.
- Each gotra was named after a Vedic seer, and all those who belonged to the same gotra were regarded as his descendants.
- Two rules about gotra were particularly important: women were expected to give up their father's gotra and adopt that of their husband on marriage and members of the same gotra could not marry.

Terminologies

- *Patriliny* means tracing descent from father to son, grandson and so on.

  Matriliny is the term used when descent is traced through the mother

- Sanskrit texts use the term kula to designate families and jnati for the larger network of kinfolk.

- The term vamsha is used for lineage

- Endogamy refers to marriage within a unit - this could be a kin group, caste, or a group living in the same locality.

- Exogamy refers to marriage outside the unit.

- Polygyny is the practice of a man having several wives.

- Polyandry is the practice of a woman having several husbands.

Social Differences: Within and Beyond the Framework of Caste

- Caste - set of hierarchically ordered social categories.

- The ideal order was laid down in the Dharmasutras and Dharmashastras.

- Brahmanas - ranked first

- Shudras and "untouchables" at the very bottom of the social order.

- Positions within the order were supposedly determined by birth.

The "right" occupation

- The Dharmasutras and Dharmashastras also contained rules about the ideal "occupations" of the four categories or *varnas*.

- Brahmanas - to study and teach the Vedas, perform sacrifices and get sacrifices performed, and give and receive gifts.

- Kshatriyas -to engage in warfare, protect people and administer justice, study the Vedas, get sacrifices performed, and make gifts.

- The last three "occupations" were assigned to the Vaishyas, who were in addition expected to engage in agriculture, pastoralism and trade.

- Shudras were assigned only one occupation - that of serving the three "higher" *varnas*.

Jatis and social mobility

- In Brahmanical theory, jati, like varna, was based on birth.

- However, while the number of varnas was fixed at four, there was no restriction on the number of jatis.

- In fact, whenever Brahmanical authorities encountered new groups - for instance, people living in forests such as the nishadas - or wanted to assign a name to occupational categories such as the goldsmith or suvarnakara, which did not easily fit into the fourfold varna system, they classified them as a jati.

- Jatis which shared a common occupation or profession were sometimes organised into shrenis or guilds.

Beyond the four *varnas*: Integration

- Categories such as the *nishada* were not influenced by Brahmanical ideas

- They are often described as odd, uncivilised, or even animal-like.

- Brahmanas considered them outside the system

- Others who were viewed with suspicion included populations such as nomadic pastoralists

- Sometimes those who spoke non-Sanskritic languages were labelled as *mlechchhas* and looked down upon.

Beyond the four *varnas* Subordination and conflict

- Brahmanas also developed a sharper social divide by classifying certain social categories as "untouchable".

- Some activities were regarded as particularly "polluting". These included handling corpses and dead animals.

- Those who performed such tasks, designated as *chandalas*, were placed at the very bottom of the hierarchy.

- The *Manusmriti* laid down the "duties" of the *chandalas*.

- The Chinese Buddhist monk Fa Xian (*c.* fifth century CE) and a Chinese pilgrim, Xuan Zang (*c.* seventh century) wrote about untouchables

Multiple Choice Questions   [1 Mark]

Q.1. Buddha founded -------------- an organization for monks -

(a) Sangha   (b) Temples

(c) kanaqhas   (d) Church

Ans. (a)

Q.2. From which of the following regions did the Shakas come to India?

(a) Central Asia   (b) Egypt

(c) South East Asia   (d) Mongolia

Ans. (a)

Q.3. Read the following excerpt of a mantra

I free her from here, but not from there. I have bound her firmly there, so that through the grace of Indra she will have fine sons and be fortunate in her husband's love.

The above paragraph is an excerpt of a mantra from which of the following epic?

(a) Mahabharata

(b) Rigveda

(c) Adi Parvan

(d) Kanyadana

Ans. (b) I free her from here, but not from there. I have bound her firmly there, so that through the grace of Indra she will have fine sons and be fortunate in her husband's love.

Q.4. Indra was, a god of

(a) Valour   (b) Warfare

(c) Rain   (d) All of the above

Ans. (d) Indra was one of the principal deities, a god of valour, warfare and rain.

Q.5. Adi Parvan is the first section of which of the following epic?

(a) Mahabharata   (b) Manusmriti

(c) Devdootam   (d) Sangam text

Ans. (a)

Q.6. Fill in the blank by considering the following map

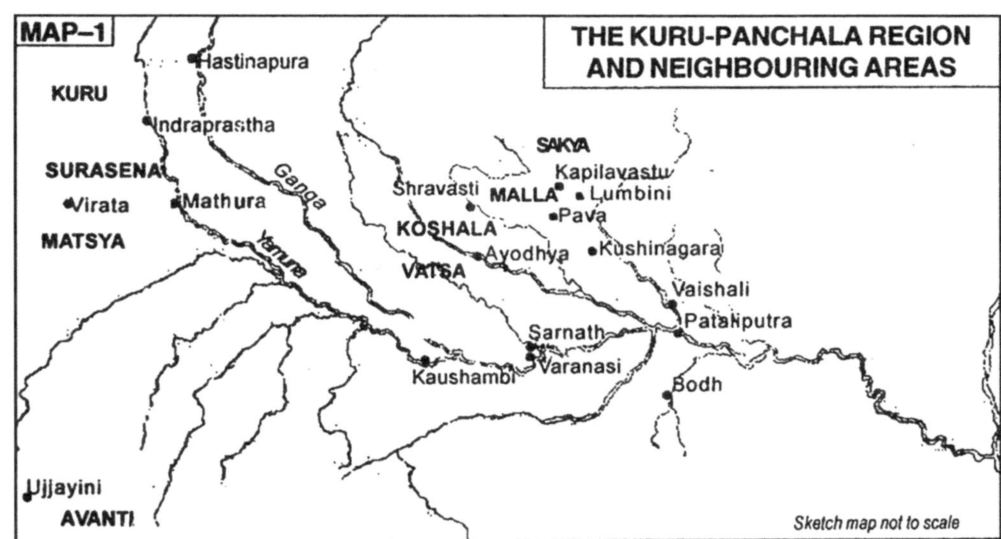

Kauravas and the Pandavas, who belonged to a single ruling family, that of the ______

(a) Sakya   (b) Malla   (c) Avanti   (d) Kurus

Ans. (d) The Kauravas and the Pandavas, who belonged to a single ruling family, that of the Kurus, a lineage dominating one of the *janapadas*

Q.7. Which Upanishad contains a list of successive generations of teachers and students, many of whom were designated by metronymics. ?

(a) Brihadaranyaka   (b) Vedanta

(c) Chhandogya   (d) Kalpa

Ans. (a)

Q.8. Which of the following texts recognised as many as eight forms of marriage

(a) Dharmasutras   (b) Dharmashastras

(c) Manusmriti   (d) None of the above

Ans. (d)

Q.9. Which parts of India were ruled by the Satavahanas during the 2nd century BCE - 2nd century CE.

(a) Western India   (b) Central India

(c) The Deccan   (d) Both (a) and (c)

Ans. (d)

Q.10. He was called as 'Devanampiya' and Piyadassi'. He ruled the Indian subcontinent from c. 268 to 232 BCE. He is remembered for the propagation of Dhamma. Who among the following ruler has been described in the above information?

(a) Ashoka

(b) Chandragupta Maurya

(c) Samudra Gupta

(d) Ajatshatru

Ans. (a)

Q.11. The code of social behaviour was determined by which of the following social categories?

(a) Brahmanas   (b) Kshatriyas

(c) Vaishyas   (d) Both (a) and (b)

Ans. (a)

Q.12. The codes of social behaviour were compiled in Sanskrit texts and referred as

(a) Dharmasutras   (b) Dharmashastras.

(c) Vedic seer   (d) Both (a) and (b)

Ans. (d)

Q.1. Sanskrit texts use the term kula to designate

____

Ans. families

Q.2. Sanskrit texts use jnati for the larger network of?

Ans. Sanskrit texts use jnati for the larger network of kinfolk.

Q.3. The term vamsha is used for ________

Ans. lineage.

Q.4. What was the name of the women who succeeded the thrown in a very exceptional circumstance?

Ans. Prabhavati Gupta succeeded the thrown

Q.5. Most of the ruling dynasties claimed to follow the system of patriliny from

Ans. c. sixth century BCE onwards

Q.6. Patriliny had existed prior to the composition of the epic called

Ans. The Mahabharata

Q.7. Who prepared the critical edition of the *Mahabharata*. ?

Ans. V.S. Sukthankar prepared the critical edition of the Mahabharata

Q.8. In early societies it was easier for historians to obtain information for which class of people?

Ans. In early societies it was easier for historians to obtain information for elite families

Q.9. The Mahabharata story describes a feud over?

Ans. The *Mahabharata* describes a feud over land and power

Q.10. What does the Kuru lineage represent?

Ans. It is a lineage dominating one of the janapadas

Q.11. The central story of the *Mahabharata* reinforced the idea that it was valuable.

The above statement is talking about which valuable thing?

Ans. Patriliny

Q.12. Define the term Matriliny

Ans. It is the term used when descent is traced through the mother

Q.13. Define the term Polyandry

Ans. Polyandry is the practice of a woman having several husbands.

Q.14. Define the term patriliny

Ans. Under patriliny, sons could claim the resources (including the throne in the case of kings) of their fathers when the latter died.

Short Answer Type - I   [2 Marks]

Q.1. What did the Chinese Buddhist monk Fa Xian write about the untouchables?

Ans. The Chinese Buddhist monk Fa Xian (*c.* fifth century CE) wrote that "untouchables" had to sound a clapper in the streets so that people could avoid seeing them.

Q.2. Name the people who were considered outside the system by the brahmins

Ans. There were populations whose social practices were not influenced by Brahmanical ideas. They are often described as odd, uncivilised, or even animal-like. Categories such as the *nishada, mlechchhas*, nomadic pastoralists are examples of this.

Q.3. What is narrative and didactic?

Ans. Historians usually classify the contents of the present text under two broad heads - sections that contain stories, designated as the *narrative*, and sections that contain prescriptions about social norms, designated as *didactic*.

Q.4. How was the ancestral property divided in the context of Manusmriti?

Ans. According to the *Manusmriti*, the paternal estate was to be divided equally amongst sons after the death of the parents, with a special share for the eldest. Women could not claim a share of these resources.

Q.5. Who emerged as a social actors in different parts of the subcontinent?

Ans. Slaves, landless agricultural labourers, hunters, fisherfolk, pastoralists, peasants, village headmen, craftspersons, merchants and kings emerged as social actors in different parts of the subcontinent. Their social positions were often shaped by their access to economic resources.

Short Answer Type - II   [3 Marks]

Q.1. What was the way to find out whether the *gotra* system was generally followed or not in the early Vedic period?

Ans. One way to find out whether this was commonly followed is to consider the names of men and women, which were sometimes derived from gotra names. These names are available for powerful ruling lineages such as the Satavahanas who ruled over parts of western India and the Deccan (*c.* second century BCE-second century CE).

Q.2. What was caste system and its framework ?

Ans. Caste, refers to a set of hierarchically ordered social categories. The ideal order was laid down in the Dharmasutras and Dharmashastras. Brahmanas claimed that this order, in which they were ranked first, was divinely ordained, while placing groups classified as Shudras and "untouchables" at the very bottom of the social order. Positions within the order were supposedly determined by birth.

Q.3. What were the strategies adopted by the Brahmanas to enforce the social norms?

Ans. The Brahmanas evolved two or three strategies for enforcing these norms. One, as we have just seen, was to assert that the *varna* order was of divine origin. Second, they advised kings to ensure that these norms were followed within their kingdoms. And third, they attempted to persuade people that their status was determined by birth.

Q.4. What were the duties of the chandalas

Ans. The *Manusmriti* laid down the "duties" of the *chandalas*. They had to live outside the village, use discarded utensils, and wear clothes of the dead and ornaments of iron. They could not walk about in villages and cities at night. They had to dispose of the bodies of those who had no relatives and serve as executioners.

Q.5. Discuss the types of marriages?

Ans. 1. Endogamy refers to marriage within a unit - this could be a kin group, caste, or a group living in the same locality.

2. Exogamy refers to marriage outside the unit.

3. Polygyny is the practice of a man having several wives.

4. Polyandry is the practice of a woman having several husbands.

Q.6. For which class or people of the society were the codes of social behavior laid down by the Brahmins?

Ans. The Brahmanas laid down codes of social behaviour in great detail. These were meant to be followed by Brahmanas in particular and the rest of society in general. From *c.* 500 BCE, these norms were compiled in Sanskrit texts known as the Dharmasutras and Dharmashastras. The most important of such works, the *Manusmriti,* was compiled between *c.* 200 BCE and 200 CE.

Q.1. What are the right occupations of the four categories of *varnas*?

Ans. The Dharmasutras and Dharmashastras contained rules about the ideal "occupations" of the four categories or *varnas*. Brahmanas were supposed to study and teach the Vedas, perform sacrifices and get sacrifices performed, and give and receive gifts. Kshatriyas were to engage in warfare, protect people and administer justice, study the Vedas, get sacrifices performed, and make gifts. The last three "occupations" were also assigned to the Vaishyas, who were in addition expected to engage in agriculture, pastoralism and trade. Shudras were assigned only one occupation - that of serving the three "higher" *varnas*.

Q.2. Give an example of rulers who countered the ideal of exogamy and gotras as recommended in the Brahmanical texts.

Ans. An examination of the names of women who married Satavahana rulers indicates that many of them had names derived from *gotras* such as Gotama and Vasistha, their father's *gotras*. They evidently retained these names instead of adopting names derived from their husband's *gotra* name as they were required to do according to the Brahmanical rules. Some of these women belonged to the same *gotra*. This ran counter to the ideal of exogamy recommended in the Brahmanical texts. In fact, it exemplified an alternative practice, that of endogamy or marriage within the kin group

Q.3. How were people classified on the basis of gotra and what were the two basic rules of gotra?

Ans. One Brahmanical practice, evident from *c.* 1000 BCE onwards, was to classify people (especially Brahmanas) in terms of *gotras*. Each *gotra* was named after a Vedic seer, and all those who belonged to the same *gotra* were regarded as his descendants. Two rules about gotra were particularly important: women were expected to give up their father's *gotra* and adopt that of their husband on marriage and members of the same *gotra* could not marry.

Q.4. Who were the Non-Kshatriya kings?

Ans. According to the Shastras, only Kshatriyas could be kings. However, several important ruling lineages probably had different origins. The social background of the Mauryas, who ruled over a large empire, has been hotly debated. While later Buddhist texts suggested they were Kshatriyas, Brahmanical texts described them as being of "low" origin. The Shungas and Kanvas, the immediate successors of the Mauryas, were Brahmanas. Other rulers, such as the Shakas who came from Central Asia, were regarded as *mlechchhas* (outsiders by the Brahmanas)

Q.5. Which activities were regarded as polluting by the Brahmanas

Ans. In sharp contrast to the purity aspect, some activities were regarded as particularly "polluting". These included handling corpses and dead animals. Those who performed such tasks, designated as *chandalas*, were placed at the very bottom of the hierarchy. Their touch and, in some cases, even seeing them was regarded as "polluting" by those who claimed to be at the top of the social order.

TOPIC 2

Beyond Birth , Social Differences and The Mahabharata

Summary

Gendered access to property

- According to the *Manusmriti*, the paternal estate was to be divided equally amongst sons after the death of the parents, with a special share for the eldest.

- Women could not claim a share of these resources.

- However, women were allowed to retain the gifts they received on the occasion of their marriage as *stridhana*

- This could be inherited by their children, without the husband having any claim on it.

- At the same time, the *Manusmriti* warned women against hoarding family property, or even their own valuables, without the husband's permission.

- For men, the Manusmriti declares, there are seven means of acquiring wealth: inheritance, finding, purchase, conquest, investment, work, and acceptance of gifts from good people.

- For women, there are six means of acquiring wealth: what was given in front of the fire (marriage) or the bridal procession, or as a token of affection, and what she got from her brother, mother or father.

- She could also acquire wealth through any subsequent gift and whatever her "affectionate" husband might give her.

Varna and access to property

- According to the Brahmanical texts, another criterion (apart from gender) for regulating access to wealth was *varna*.

- The only "occupation" prescribed for Shudras was servitude, while a variety of occupations were listed for men of the first three *varnas*.

- If these provisions were actually implemented, the wealthiest men would have been the Brahmanas and the Kshatriyas.

- Even as the Brahmanical view of society was codified in the Dharmasutras and Dharmashastras, other traditions developed critiques of the *varna* order.

- The Buddhists recognised that there were differences in society, but did not regard these as natural or inflexible.

- They also rejected the idea of claims to status on the basis of birth.

The Critical Edition of the Mahabharata

- Prepared by (1919) - A team comprising dozens of scholars under the leadership of a noted Indian Sanskritist, V.S. Sukthankar

- Objective - Collecting Sanskrit manuscripts of the text, written in a variety of scripts, from different parts of the country.

- The project took 47 years to complete.

Outcome

- Our understanding of these processes is derived primarily from texts written in Sanskrit by and for Brahmanas.

- Everything that was laid down in these texts was not actually practised.

- The ideas contained in normative Sanskrit texts were on the whole recognised as authoritative

- They were also questioned and occasionally even rejected.

The Mahabharata

- A colossal epic running in its present form into over 100,000 verses with depictions of a wide range of social categories and situations

- It was composed over a period of about 1,000 years (*c.* 500 BCE onwards)

- The Mahabharata describes a feud over land and power between two groups of cousins, the Kauravas and the Pandavas, who belonged to a single ruling family, that of the Kurus, a lineage dominating one of the janapadas

- Ultimately, the conflict ended in a battle, in which the Pandavas emerged victorious.

- After that, patrilineal succession was proclaimed

Multiple Choice Questions [1 Mark]

Q.1. Who laid the Codes of social behaviour?

(a) Brahmanas   (b) Aranyakas

(c) Vedangas   (d) None of the following

Ans. (a)

Q.2. *Manusmriti*, was compiled between

(a) *c.* 400 BCE and 200 CE.

(b) *c.* 200 BCE and 200 CE.

(c) *c.* 100 BCE and 100 CE.

(d) *c.* 200 BCE and 100 CE.

Ans. (b)

Q.3. From _______ Dharmasutras and Dharmashastras norms were compiled in Sanskrit texts

(a) *c.* 500 BCE

(b) *c.* 1000 BCE

(c) *c.* 400 BCE

(d) *c.* 200 BCE

Ans. (a)

Q.4. Sanskrit texts and inscriptions used the term _______ to designate merchants.

(a) Tandya

(b) Gopath

(c) Vanik

(d) Nirukta

Ans. (c)

Q.5. Read the following information given carefully:

1. She was a Rajput princess from Merta in Marwar.

2. She considered Lord Krishna as her lover

Identify the name of the devotee of Saguna Bhakti from the following options

(a) Andal

(b) Gargi

(c) MeeraBai

(d) Maitreyi

Ans. (c)

Q.6. Consider the following image

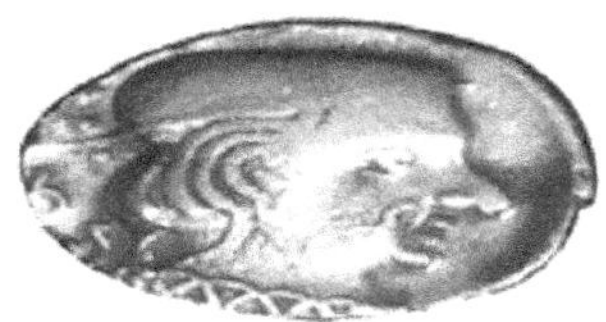

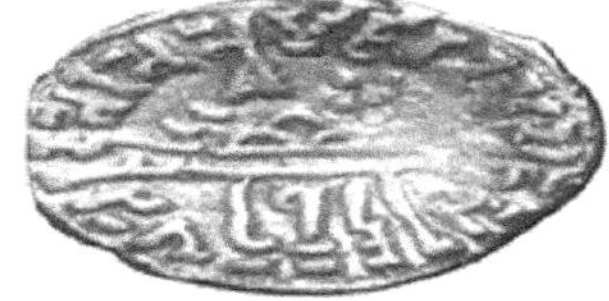

The above figure of silver coin represents a fourth century ruler.

(a) Indo- Greek Ruler (b) Shaka ruler

(c) Kushans (d) Meander

Ans. (b)

Q.7. With reference to Mahabharata, read the following paragraph carefully and answer the MCQs by choosing the most appropriate option.

By making peace you honour your father and me, as well as your well-wishers ... it is the wise man in control of his senses who guards his kingdom. Greed and anger drag a man away from his profits; by defeating these two enemies a king conquers the earth ... You will happily enjoy the earth, my son, along with the wise and heroic Pandavas ... There is no good in a war, no law (*dharma*) and profit (*artha*), let alone happiness; nor is there (necessarily) victory in the end - don't set your mind on war ...

In the above paragraph Gandhari is making an appeal to

(a) Arjuna (b) Duryodhana

(c) Dhritirashtra (d) Bhima

Ans. (b)

Q.8. A play called the' Mrichchhakatika' written in fourth century CE by which of the following community?

(a) Brahmana (b) Sarthavaha

(c) Shudraka (d) Kshatriya

Ans. (c)

Q.9. Identify the character of Mahabharata with the help of the following information.

1. Belonged to the Rakshasa clan

2. Married with Bheema

3. Mother of Ghatotkacha

(a) Hidimba (b) Subhadra

(c) Draupadi (d) Gandhari

Ans. (a)

Q.10. Identify the character of Mahabharata with the help of the following information.

1. Guru or Mentor of Kaurvas and Pandvas

2. Did not accept Eklavya as his disciple

(a) Guru Vashsishtha

(b) Guru Vyasa

(c) Guru Sandeepni

(d) Guru Dronacharya

Ans. (d)

Very Short Answer Type [1 Mark]

Q.1. Which rulers were identified through metronymics?

Ans. Satavahana rulers were identified through metronymics

Q.2. Who propounded the code of social behaviour?

Ans. Brahmanas propounded the code of social behaviour

Q.3. Dharmasutras and Dharmashastras were compiled in which language?

Ans. Dharmasutras and Dharmashastras were compiled in Sanskrit language

Q.4. What does metronomics represent?

Ans. Names derived from that of the mother

Q.5. What was the nature of succession to the throne among the Satavahana rulers?

Ans. The nature of succession to the throne among the Satavahana rulers were patrilineal.

Q.6. In which texts the duties of Chandalas are mentioned?

Ans. The *Manusmriti* laid down the "duties" of the *chandalas*.

Q.7. The hierarchically ordered social categories of castes were supposedly determined by

Ans. The hierarchically ordered social categories of castes were supposedly determined by birth

Q.8. Which deity is mentioned in the Rigveda as the chief god of valor, war and rain?

Ans. Indra is mentioned in the Rigveda as the chief god of valor, war and rain

Q.9. In which text eight forms of marriage are mentioned?

Ans. In Manusmriti text eight forms of marriage are mentioned

Q.10. The term puta is a Prakrit word which means?

Ans. puta is a Prakrit word which means son

Q.11. Some rulers of which dynasty were polygamous

Ans. Satavahana rulers were polygamous

Q.12. Which traveler saw that the executioners and scavengers were forced to live outside the city?

Ans. Chinese pilgrim, Xuan Zang (*c.* seventh century)

Q.13. Which ruler entered into a marriage alliance with the kin of Rudradaman?

Ans. Gotami-puta Siri-Satakani

Q.14. Eklavya is considered to belong to which category?

Ans. Eklavya belonged to *nishada*

Short Answer Type - I [2 Marks]

Q.1. Which rulers were considered as Mlechhas?

Ans. Rulers, such as the Shakas who came from Central Asia, were regarded as mlechchhas, barbarians or outsiders by the Brahmanas

Q.2. Which upnishad contains a list of successive generations of teachers and students?

Ans. The Brihadaranyaka Upanishad, one of the earliest Upanishads contains a list of successive generations of teachers and students, many of whom were designated by metronymics.

Q.3. For whom did the brahmanas laid down the codes of social behaviour?

Ans. Brahmanas laid the codes of social behaviour. These were meant to be followed by Brahmanas in particular and the rest of society in general.

Q.4. Define Vamsha

Ans. The term vamsha is a Sanskrit word that means 'family, lineage'

Q.5. Which foreign travellers wrote about the untouchables?

Ans. The Chinese Buddhist monk Fa Xian (*c.* fifth century CE) and a Chinese pilgrim, Xuan Zang (*c.* seventh century) wrote about untouchables

Q.6. What are the terms for family and kin used in Sanskrit texts

Ans. Sanskrit texts use the term kula to designate families and jnati for the larger network of kinfolk. The term vamsha is used for lineage.

Q.7. Define the term kinfolk.

Ans. Families are usually parts of larger networks of people defined as relatives, or kinfolk.

Short Answer Type - II [3 Marks]

Q.1. What type of marriage was considered desirable.

Ans. Marrying daughters into families outside the kin was considered desirable. This system, called exogamy (literally, marrying outside), meant that the lives of young girls and women belonging to families that claimed high status were often carefully regulated to ensure that they were married at the "right" time and to the "right" person.

Q.2. Define Jatis

Ans. Jatis were based on birth. However, while the number of varnas was fixed at four, there was no restriction on the number of jatis. Jatis which shared a common occupation or profession were sometimes organised into shrenis or guilds.

Q.3. The Mahabharata is a story that describes a feud between whom over land and power?

Ans. It describes a feud over land and power between two groups of cousins, the Kauravas and the Pandavas, who belonged to a single ruling family, that of the Kurus, a lineage dominating one of the *janapadas*

Q.4. What were the differences in the practice of the patriarchal framework used by the ruling dynasties from the 6th century BC onwards

Ans. Most ruling dynasties (*c.* sixth century BCE onwards) claimed to follow this system, although there were variations in practice: sometimes there were no sons, in some situations brothers succeeded one another, sometimes other kinsmen claimed the throne, and, in very exceptional circumstances, women such as Prabhavati Gupta exercised power.

Q.5. How could men and women acquire wealth?

Ans. For men, the Manusmriti declares, there are seven means of acquiring wealth: inheritance, finding, purchase, conquest, investment, work, and acceptance of gifts from good people. For women, there are six means of acquiring wealth: what was given in front of the fire (marriage) or the bridal procession, or as a token of affection, and what she got from her brother, mother or father. She could also acquire wealth through any subsequent gift and whatever her "affectionate" husband might give her.

Q.6. What was Buddhists alternative understanding of social inequalities ?

Ans. The Buddhists also developed an alternative understanding of social inequalities, and of the institutions required to regulate social conflict.

In a myth found in a text known as the *Sutta Pitaka* they suggested that originally human beings did not have fully evolved bodily forms, nor was the world of plants fully developed. All beings lived in an idyllic state of peace, taking from nature only what they needed for each meal.

Long Answer Type　　　　　　　[5 Marks]

Q.1. What were the factors that gave rise to the belief that *kanyadana* was an important religious duty of the father?

Ans. Daughters had no claims to the resources of the household and marrying them into families outside the kin was considered desirable. This system, called exogamy (literally, marrying outside), meant that the lives of young girls and women belonging to families that claimed high status were often carefully regulated to ensure that they were married at the "right" time and to the "right" person. This gave rise to the belief that *kanyadana* or the gift of a daughter in marriage was an important religious duty of the father.

Q.2. How VS Sukathankar and his team validate the epic Mahabharata by preparing a critical version of the Mahabharata?

Ans. VS Sukathankar and team worked out a method of comparing verses from each manuscript. They selected the verses that appeared common to most versions and published these in several volumes, running into over 13,000 pages. The project took 47 years to complete. Two things became apparent: there were several common elements in the Sanskrit versions of the story, evident in manuscripts found all over the subcontinent, from Kashmir and Nepal in the north to Kerala and Tamil Nadu in the south. Also evident were enormous regional variations in the ways in which the text had been transmitted over the centuries. These variations were documented in footnotes and appendices to the main text.

Q.3. Explain why patriliny may have been particularly important among elite families.

Ans. 1. Patriliny is the system through which descent from father to son and grandson is traced.

Reasons why Patriliny was important among elite families.

2. As per the Dharmashastras, it was an established belief that the son carried forward the dynasty. That was the main reason that the families wished for sons not for daughters.

3. In royal families, the acquisition of throne was included in the inheritance. After the death of a king, his eldest son was supposed to inherit the throne. After the death of the parents, the property was to be equally divided among all the sons. In fact, parents avoided disputes in the family after their death. Most of the royal families followed the patriliny since 600 B.C. But sometimes this system had exceptions also.

Q.4. Why The Mahabharata is called a Dynamic Text

Ans. The growth of the Mahabharata did not stop with the Sanskrit version. Over the centuries, versions of the epic were written in a variety of languages through an ongoing process of dialogue between peoples, communities, and those who wrote the texts. Several stories that originated in specific regions or circulated amongst certain people found their way into the epic. At the same time, the central story of the epic was often retold in different ways. And episodes were depicted in sculpture and painting. They also provided themes for a wide range of performing arts - plays, dance and other kinds of narrations.

Q.5. Discuss whether the Mahabharata could have been the work of a single author.

Ans. The Mahabharta is a colossal epic, comprising about one lakh verses. This enormous composition is traditionally attributed to Sage Vyas. However, historians are of the view that the Mahabharta was composed over a period of 1000 years, so it can not be the work of a single author. Large didactic section resembling the manuscript was added during the period between 200C and 400CE. This outburst made Mahabharata an epic consisting of 100,000 verses.The historian assume that the original story was composed by charioteer bards known as "Sutas", who generally accompanied Kshatriyas warriors to the battle field and composed poems celebrating their victories and other achievements. Then from 500 B.C.E. Brahmanas took over the story and began to commit it to writing, Subsequently between C.200 and 400 C.E didactic sections resembling the Manusmriti were added to the Mahabharata. All this shows that Mahabharata could not be the work of a single author.

Chapter Practice

Multiple Choice Questions [1 Mark]

Q.1. Find the correct statement
   (a) The Shungas and Kanvas, were the immediate successors of the Mauryas
   (b) The Shungas and Kanvas were Brahmanas.
   (c) The Shakas came from Central Asia
   (d) All of the above

Q.2. Find the incorrect statement about Jatis
   (a) There were certain restriction on the number of jatis.
   (b) It was based on birth.
   (c) Jatis were sometimes organised into shrenis or guilds.
   (d) None of the above

Very Short Answer Type [1 Mark]

Q.3. Differentiate between Endogamy and Exogamy. [CBSE 2021]

Q.4. Identify any two occupations to be performed by Kshatriyas as per Varna Order. [CBSE 2017]

Short Answer Type - I [2 Marks]

Q.5. What is in Brihadaranyaka Upanishad? [CBSE 2016]

Q.6. What was the profession of Brahmins?

Short Answer Type - II [3 Marks]

Q.7. State whether gender differences were really important in the early societies. from c. 600 BCE to 600 CE. [CBSE 2018]

Q.8. Explain how you will prove that the text of Mahabharata was a dynamic one. [CBSE 2018]

Q.9. Explain the language and content of Mahabharata. [CBSE 2017]

Long Answer Type [5 Marks]

Q.10. What do you know about the authors and the period when Mahabharata was compiled ? Explain. [CBSE 2017]

CHAPTER 4

Thinkers, Beliefs and Buildings

Cultural Developments (c. 600 BCE - 600 CE)

Sacrificial Tradition and Beyond Worldly Pleasures - Buddhism and Jainism

Summary

The sacrificial tradition

- Several pre-existing traditions of thought, religious belief and practice, including the early Vedic tradition, known from the *Rigveda*, compiled between *c.*1500 and 1000 BCE.

- The *Rigveda* consists of hymns in praise of a variety of deities, especially Agni, Indra and Soma.

- Many of these hymns were chanted when sacrifices were performed, where people prayed for cattle, sons, good health, long life, etc.

- At first, sacrifices were performed collectively.

- Later (*c.* 1000 BCE-500 BCE onwards) some were performed by the heads of households for the well-being of the domestic unit.

- More elaborate sacrifices, such as the *rajasuya* and *ashvamedha*, were performed by chiefs and kings who depended on Brahmana priests to conduct the ritual.

How Buddhist texts were prepared and preserved

- The Buddha (and other teachers) taught orally - through discussion and debate.

- None of the Buddha's speeches were written down during his lifetime.

- After his death (c. fifth-fourth century BCE) his teachings were compiled by his disciples at a council of "elders" or senior monks at Vesali (Pali for Vaishali in present-day Bihar).

- These compilations were known as Tipitaka - literally, three baskets to hold different types of texts.

- The Vinaya Pitaka included rules and regulations for those who joined the sangha or monastic order

- The Buddha's teachings were included in the Sutta Pitaka

- The Abhidhamma Pitaka dealt with philosophical matters.

- Each pitaka comprised a number of individual texts.

- Later, commentaries were written on these texts by Buddhist scholars.

- Other texts such as the Dipavamsa (literally, the chronicle of the island) and Mahavamsa (the great chronicle) were written, containing regional histories of Buddhism.

The Message of Mahavira

- Mahavira was preceded by 23 other teachers or *tirthankaras*

- The most important idea in Jainism is that the entire world is animated: even stones, rocks and water have life.

- Non-injury to living beings, especially to humans, animals, plants and insects, is central to Jaina philosophy.

- According to Jaina teachings, the cycle of birth and rebirth is shaped through karma.

- Asceticism and penance are required to free oneself from the cycle of karma.

- This can be achieved only by renouncing the world; therefore, monastic existence is a necessary condition of salvation.

- Jaina monks and nuns took five vows: to abstain from killing, stealing and lying; to observe celibacy; and to abstain from possessing property.

The Buddha and the Quest for Enlightenment

- Siddhartha, as the Buddha was named at birth, was the son of a chief of the Sakya clan.

- He had a sheltered upbringing within the palace, insulated from the harsh realities of life. One day he persuaded his charioteer to take him into the city.

- His first journey into the world outside was traumatic.

- He was deeply anguished when he saw an old man, a sick man and a corpse.

- He realised in that moment that the decay and destruction of the human body was inevitable.

- He also saw a homeless mendicant, who, it seemed to him, had come to terms with old age, disease and death, and found peace.

- Siddhartha decided that he too would adopt the same path.

- Soon after, he left the palace and set out in search of his own truth.

- Siddhartha explored several paths including bodily mortification which led him to a situation of near death.

- Abandoning these extreme methods, he meditated for several days and finally attained enlightenment.

- After this he came to be known as the Buddha or the Enlightened One.

- For the rest of his life, he taught dhamma or the path of righteous living.

- Buddha's message spread across the subcontinent and beyond - through Central Asia to China, Korea and Japan, and through Sri Lanka, across the seas to Myanmar, Thailand and Indonesia.

The Teachings of the Buddh

- The Buddha's teachings have been reconstructed from stories, found mainly in the Sutta Pitaka.

- According to Buddhist philosophy, the world is transient (anicca) and constantly changing; it is also soulless (anatta) as there is nothing permanent or eternal in it.

- Within this transient world, sorrow (dukkha) is intrinsic to human existence.

- It is by following the path of moderation between severe penance and self-indulgence that human beings can rise above these worldly troubles.

- In the earliest forms of Buddhism, whether or not god existed was irrelevant.

- The Buddha regarded the social world as the creation of humans rather than of divine origin.

Followers of the Buddha

- Buddha founded a sangha, an organisation of monks who too became teachers of dhamma. These monks lived simply, possessing only the essential requisites for survival

- As they lived on alms, they were known as bhikkhus.

- Initially, only men were allowed into the sangha, but later women also came to be admitted. This was made possible through the mediation of Ananda, one of the Buddha's dearest disciples, who persuaded him to allow women into the sangha.

- The Buddha's foster mother, Mahapajapati Gotami was the first woman to be ordained as a bhikkhuni.

- The Buddha's followers were regarded as equal, having shed their earlier social identities on becoming bhikkhus and bhikkhunis.

- The internal functioning of the sangha was based on the traditions of ganas and sanghas, where consensus was arrived at through discussions.

The Therigatha

- This unique Buddhist text, part of the Sutta Pitaka, is a collection of verses composed by bhikkhunis.
- It provides an insight into women's social and spiritual experiences.

Multiple Choice Questions   [1 Mark]

Q.1. Consider the following verses

The nature of the self

This self of mine within the heart, is smaller than paddy or barley or mustard or millet or the kernel of a seed of millet. This self of mine within the heart is greater than the earth, greater than the intermediate space, greater than heaven, greater than these worlds.

The true sacrifice

This one (the wind) that blows, this is surely a sacrifice ... While moving, it sanctifies all this, therefore it is indeed a sacrifice.

These are the two verses of which of the following Upanishads?

(a) Chhandogya

(b) Brahadaranyak

(c) Aranyakas

(d) None of the above

Ans. (a)

Q.2. Which one of the following teaching is not associated with the teachings of Mahavira or Jaina Philosophy?   **[CBSE 2021]**

(a) The entire world is animated.

(b) Ahimsa (Non-Violence)

(c) The cycle of birth and rebirth is not related to Karma.

(d) Monastic existence is a necessary condition of salvation

Ans. (b)

Q.3. Which one of the following statements related to Buddhism is not correct?   **[CBSE 2021]**

(a) Pilgrims such as Fa Xian and Xuan Zang travelled from China to India for knowledge.

(b) Bodisattas were perceived as deeply compassionate beings.

(c) Bodhisattas accumulated merit through their efforts and used it to attain *Nibbana*

(d) Mahayana literally means the 'great vehicle'

Ans. (c) Bodhisattas were perceived as deeply compassionate beings who accumulated merit through their efforts but used this not to attain *nibbana* and thereby abandon the world, but to help others.

Q.4. Thinkers such as Zarathustra, Kong Zi, Socrates, Plato and Aristotle tried to understand the mysteries of existence and the relationship between human beings and the _________

(a) Social order   (b) Cosmic order

(c) Cultural order   (d) None of the above

Ans. (b)

Q.5. Supporters of Mahayana regarded other Buddhists as followers of _________

(a) Hinayana   (b) theravadins

(c) theras   (d) None of the above

Ans. (a) Supporters of Mahayana regarded other Buddhists as followers of Hinayana.

Q.6. Socrates, Plato and Aristotle were thinkers of which of the following countries?

(a) Greece   (b) Iran

(c) China   (d) Portuguese

Ans. (a) Mid-first millennium BCE was the turning point in world history where we saw emergence of thinkers such as Zarathustra in Iran, Kong Zi in China, Socrates, Plato and Aristotle in Greece, and Mahavira and Gautama Buddha in India.

Q.7. The teachings of Buddha were compiled by one of his disciples who was known by the name of

(a) Vinaya Pitaka   (b) Sutta Pitaka

(c) Abhidhamma Pitaka (d) Tipitaka

Ans. (d) 1. After his death (c. fifth-fourth century BCE) his teachings were compiled by his disciples at a council of "elders" or senior monks at Vesali (Pali for Vaishali in present-day Bihar).

    2. These compilations were known as Tipitaka - literally, three baskets to hold different types of texts.

Q.8. Several pre-existing traditions of thought, religious belief and practice, including the early Vedic tradition, were known from which of the following texts?

    (a) Yajurveda   (b) *Rigveda*

    (c) Upanishads   (d) *Tipitaka*

Ans. (b) Several pre-existing traditions of thought, religious belief and practice, including the early Vedic tradition, known from the *Rigveda*, compiled between *c.*1500 and 1000 BCE.

Q.9. Rajasuya and *Ashvamedha* sacrifices were performed by who among the following ?

    (a) Chiefs   (b) Kings

    (c) Priests   (d) Both (a) and (b)

Ans. (d) More elaborate sacrifices, such as the *rajasuya* and *ashvamedha*, were performed by chiefs and kings who depended on Brahmana priests to conduct the ritual.

Q.10. The Buddha and other teachers taught to their disciples _

    (a) Through Vinaya Pitaka

    (b) Through Sutta Pitaka

    (c) Through debate and discussion

    (d) Through Written speeches of Buddha

Ans. (d) 1. The Buddha (and other teachers) taught orally - through discussion and debate.

    2. None of the Buddha's speeches were written down during his lifetime.

Q.11. Consider the following story when a grief-stricken woman whose child had died came to the Buddha, he gently convinced her about the inevitability of death rather than bring her son back to life.

The above story found in which Pitaka?

Ans. Sutta Pitaka.

Q.12. Consider the following two verses

Bring, O strong one, this sacrifice of ours to the gods, O wise one, as a liberal giver. Bestow on us, o priest, abundant food. Agni, obtain, by sacrificing, mighty wealth for us.

Procure, O Agni, for ever to him who prays to you (the gift of) nourishment, the wonderful cow. May a son be ours, offspring that continues our line ...

These are two verses from the _______ invoking Agni, the god of fire, often identified with the sacrificial fire, into which offerings were made so as to reach the other deities

    (a) Yajurveda   (b) Samaveda

    (c) Rigveda   (d) Atharveda

Ans. (c)

Very Short Answer Type   [1 Mark]

Q.1. Followers of the older tradition described themselves as ?

Ans. the older tradition described themselves as theravadins

Q.2. What is the literal meaning of Mahayana?

Ans. The great vehicle

Q.3. The literal meaning of Mahavamsa is

Ans. The great chronicle

Q.4. The literal meaning of Dipavamsa is

Ans. The chronicle of the island

Q.5. W hat is the literal meaning of Hinayana

Ans. lesser vehicle

Q.6. Which concept was perceived as deeply compassionate beings who accumulated merit through their efforts but used this not to attain *nibbana* and thereby abandon the world, but to help others.

Ans. Bodhisatta

Q.7. The Rigveda consists of hymns in praise of?

Ans. Variety of deities especially Agni, Indra and Soma.

Q.8. From which Veda do the early Vedic traditions know?

Ans. The early vedic traditions known from the *Rigveda*

Q.9. Shahjehan Begum was the ruler of?

Ans. She was the ruler of Bhopal state

Q.10. Sultan Jehan was the successor of which ruler?

Ans. Sultan Jehan was the successor of Shahjehan Begum

Q.11. In which language was the Chandogya Upanishad composed?

Ans. Sanskrit

Short Answer Type - I　　　[2 Marks]

Q.1. How was the sacrifice done in the beginning?

Ans. Initially, sacrifices were performed collectively. Later (*c.* 1000 BCE-500 BCE onwards) some were performed by the heads of households for the well- being of the domestic unit.

Q.2. Who performed the Rajasuya and Ashwamedha Yagya?　　　**[CBSE 2017]**

Ans. Elaborate sacrifices, such as the *rajasuya* and *ashvamedha*, were performed by chiefs and kings who depended on Brahmana priests to conduct the ritual.

Q.3. What are the five vows of jainism?

Ans. Jaina monks and nuns took five vows: to abstain from killing, stealing and lying; to observe celibacy; and to abstain from possessing property.

Q.4. How the teachings of Mahavira were compiled?

Ans. The teachings of Mahavira were also recorded by his disciples. These were often in the form of stories, which could appeal to ordinary people.

Q.5. What is Hagiography?　　　**[CBSE 2018]**

Ans. *Hagiography* is a biography of a saint or religious leader. Hagiographies often praise the saint's achievements, and may not always be literally accurate. They are important because they tell us about the beliefs of the followers of that particular

Q.6. What is the most important idea of Jainism?

Ans. The most important idea in Jainism is that the entire world is animated: even stones, rocks and water have life.

Short Answer Type - II　　　[3 Marks]

Q.1. Why is the middle of the first millennium BC often considered a turning point in world history?　　　**[CBSE 2017]**

Ans. The mid-first millennium BCE is often regarded as a turning point in world history as it saw the emergence of thinkers such as Zarathustra in Iran, Kong Zi in China, Socrates, Plato and Aristotle in Greece, and Mahavira and Gautama Buddha, among many others, in India.

Q.2. How do teachers convince others about the validity of their philosophy?

Ans. Teachers travelled from place to place, trying to convince one another as well as laypersons, about the validity of their philosophy or the way they understood the world. Debates took place in the *kutagarashala* - literally, a hut with a pointed roof - or in groves where travelling mendicants halted. If a philosopher succeeded in convincing one of his rivals, the followers of the latter also became his disciples. So support for any particular sect could grow and shrink over time.

Q.3. Discuss the philosophy of Jaina　**[CBSE 2019]**

Ans. Non-injury to living beings, especially to humans, animals, plants and insects, is central to Jaina philosophy. The principle of ahimsa, emphasised within Jainism, has left its mark on Indian thinking as a whole. According to Jaina teachings, the cycle of birth and rebirth is shaped through karma. Asceticism and penance are required to free oneself from the cycle of karma. This can be achieved only by renouncing the world; therefore, monastic existence is a necessary condition of salvation.

Q.4. Why John Marshall dedicated his important volumes on Sanchi to rulers of Bhopal?

Ans. The rulers of Bhopal, Shahjehan Begum and her successor Sultan Jehan Begum, provided money for the preservation of the ancient site. She funded the museum that was built there as well as the guesthouse where he lived and wrote the volumes. She also funded the publication of the volumes.

Q.5. How do we know about the Buddha's teachings?

Ans. Buddha's teachings have been reconstructed by carefully editing, translating and analysing the Buddhist texts. Historians have also tried to reconstruct details of his life from hagiographies. Many of these were written down at least a century after the time of the Buddha, in an attempt to preserve memories of the great teacher.

Q.6. Discuss Buddhist philosophy **[CBSE 2019]**

Ans. According to Buddhist philosophy, the world is transient (*anicca*) and constantly changing; it is also soulless (*anatta*) as there is nothing permanent or eternal in it. Within this transient world, sorrow (*dukkha*) is intrinsic to human existence. It is by following the path of moderation between severe penance and self-indulgence that human beings can rise above these worldly troubles. In the earliest forms of Buddhism, whether or not god existed was irrelevant.

Long Answer Type [5 Marks]

Q.1. Discuss the sacrificial tradition of early Vedic period.

Ans. There were several pre-existing traditions of thought, religious belief and practice, including the early Vedic tradition, known from the *Rigveda*, compiled between *c.*1500 and 1000 BCE. The *Rigveda* consists of hymns in praise of a variety of deities, especially Agni, Indra and Soma. Many of these hymns were chanted when sacrifices were performed, where people prayed for cattle, sons, good health, long life, etc. At first, sacrifices were performed collectively. Later (*c.* 1000 BCE-500 BCE onwards) some were performed by the heads of households for the well- being of the domestic unit. More elaborate sacrifices, such as the *rajasuya* and *ashvamedha*, were performed by chiefs and kings who depended on Brahmana priests to conduct the ritual.

Q.2. Discuss the details of Buddha's life?

Ans. Siddhartha, as the Buddha was named at birth, was the son of a chief of the Sakya clan. He had a sheltered upbringing within the palace, insulated from the harsh realities of life. One day he persuaded his charioteer to take him into the city. His first journey into the world outside was traumatic. He was deeply anguished when he saw an old man, a sick man and a corpse. He realised in that moment that the decay and destruction of the human body was inevitable. He also saw a homeless mendicant, who, it seemed to him, had come to terms with old age, disease and death, and found peace. Siddhartha decided that he too would adopt the same path. Soon after, he left the palace and set out in search of his own truth.

Q.3. How Buddhist texts were prepared and preserved ?

Ans. After the death of Buddha(c. fifth-fourth century BCE) his teachings were compiled by his disciples at a council of "elders" or senior monks at Vesali (Pali for Vaishali in present-day Bihar). These compilations were known as Tipitaka - literally, three baskets to hold different types of texts. They were first transmitted orally and then written and classified according to length as well as subject matter. Buddhist texts were preserved in manuscripts for several centuries in monasteries in different parts of Asia. Modern translations have been prepared from Pali, Sanskrit, Chinese and Tibetan texts

TOPIC 2

Stupas, Sculptures and New Religious Traditions

Summary

Mid-first millennium BCE

- Turning point in world history

- Emergence of thinkers such as Zarathustra in Iran, Kong Zi in China, Socrates, Plato and Aristotle in Greece, and Mahavira and Gautama Buddha in India.

Stupas

- From earliest times, people tended to regard certain places as sacred.

- These included sites with special trees or unique rocks, or sites of awe- inspiring natural beauty.

- These sites, with small shrines attached to them, were sometimes described as chaityas.

- Buddhist literature mentions several chaityas.

- It also describes places associated with the Buddha's life - where he was born (Lumbini), where he attained enlightenment (Bodh Gaya), where he gave his first sermon (Sarnath) and where he attained nibbana (Kusinagara).

- Gradually, each of these places came to be regarded as sacred.

- About 200 years after the time of the Buddha, Asoka erected a pillar at Lumbini to mark the fact that he had visited the place.

About Stupas

- Relics of the Buddha such as his bodily remains or objects used by him were buried there.

- These were mounds known as stupas.

- The tradition of erecting stupas may have been pre-Buddhist, but they came to be associated with Buddhism.

- According to a Buddhist text known as the Ashokavadana, Asoka distributed portions of the Buddha's relics to every important town and ordered the construction of stupas over them.(eg Bharhut, Sanchi and Sarnath)

Stupa at Sanchi

- One of the most important Buddhist centres

- The discovery of Sanchi has vastly transformed our understanding of early Buddhism.

- The rulers of Bhopal, Shahjehan Begum and her successor Sultan Jehan Begum, provided money for the preservation of the ancient site.

How Were Stupas Built

- donations made by kings such as the Satavahanas

- donations were made by guilds (eg. ivory workers who financed part of one of the gateways at Sanchi)

- Bhikkhus and bhikkhunis also contributed towards building these monuments.

The Structure of the Stupa

- The stupa (a Sanskrit word meaning a heap) originated as a simple semi-circular mound of earth, later called anda.

- Gradually, it evolved into a more complex structure, balancing round and square shapes.

- Above the anda was the harmika, a balcony- like structure that represented the abode of the gods.

- Arising from the *harmika* was a mast called the *yashti*, often surmounted by a *chhatri* or umbrella.

- Around the mound was a railing, separating the sacred space from the secular world.

Amaravati and Sanchi Stupa

Why did Sanchi survive while Amaravati did not ?

- *in situ* preservation was not adopted for Amaravati but in the case of Sanchi, it was adopted by the British authoritues

- Amaravati was discovered before scholars understood the value of the finds and realised how critical it was to preserve things where they had been found instead of removing them from the site.

- When Sanchi was "discovered" in 1818, three of its four gateways were still standing, the fourth was lying on the spot where it had fallen and the mound was in good condition.

New Religious Traditions

The development of Mahayana Buddhism

- By the first century CE, there is evidence of changes in Buddhist ideas and practices.

- Early Buddhist teachings had given great importance to self-effort in achieving *nibbana*.

- Besides, the Buddha was regarded as a human being who attained enlightenment and *nibbana* through his own efforts.

- However, gradually the idea of a saviour emerged.

- It was believed that he was the one who could ensure salvation.

- Simultaneously, the concept of the Bodhisatta also developed.

- Bodhisattas were perceived as deeply compassionate beings who accumulated merit through their efforts but used this not to attain nibbana and thereby abandon the world, but to help others.

- The worship of images of the Buddha and Bodhisattas became an important part of this tradition.

- This new way of thinking was called Mahayana - literally, the "great vehicle".

- Those who adopted these beliefs described the older tradition as Hinayana or the "lesser vehicle".

- Supporters of Mahayana regarded other Buddhists as followers of Hinayana.

- However, followers of the older tradition described themselves as theravadins, that is, those who followed the path of old, respected teachers, the theras.

The growth of Puranic Hinduism

- The notion of a saviour was not unique to Buddhism.

- Similar ideas being developed in different ways within traditions that we now consider part of Hinduism.

- These included Vaishnavism (a form of Hinduism within which Vishnu was worshipped as the principal deity) and Shaivism (a tradition within which Shiva was regarded as the chief god), in which there was growing emphasis on the worship of a chosen deity.

- In such worship the bond between the devotee and the god was visualised as one of love and devotion, or bhakti.

Building temples

- The early temple was a small square room, called the garbhagriha, with a single doorway for the worshipper to enter and offer worship to the image.

- Gradually, a tall structure, known as the *shikhara*, was built over the central shrine.

- Temple walls were often decorated with sculpture.

- Later temples became far more elaborate - with assembly halls, huge walls and gateways, and arrangements for supplying water

- One of the unique features of early temples was that some of these were hollowed out of huge rocks, as artificial caves.

- The tradition of building artificial caves was an old one.

- Some of the earliest of these were constructed in the third century BCE on the orders of Asoka for renouncers who belonged to the Ajivika sect.

Multiple Choice Questions [1 Mark]

Q.1. Fa Xian and Xuan Zang travelled all the way from China to India in search of _______

(a) Peace

(b) Philosophical research

(c) Texts

(d) Culture

Ans. (c) When Buddhism spread to East Asia, pilgrims such as Fa Xian and Xuan Zang travelled all the way from China to India in search of texts.

Q.2. Find the incorrect statement about Sanchi Stupa

(a) British government provided money for the preservation of the ancient site.

(b) *In situ* preservation was not adopted for Sanchi Stupa

(c) It was one of the most important Buddhist centres

(d) It was discovered in 1818

Ans. (a) 1. The discovery of Sanchi has vastly transformed our understanding of early Buddhism.

2. The rulers of Bhopal, Shahjehan Begum and her successor Sultan Jehan Begum, provided money for the preservation of the ancient site.

Q.3. Find the correct statement about Stupas

(a) Relics of the Buddha were buried there.

(b) The stupa originated as a simple semi-circular mound of earth

(c) The tradition of erecting stupas started with Buddhism.

(d) (a) and (b) only

Ans. (d) 1. Relics of the Buddha such as his bodily remains or objects used by him were buried there.

2. These were mounds known as stupas.

3. The tradition of erecting stupas may have been pre-Buddhist, but they came to be associated with Buddhism.

Q.4. Ashokavadana text belongs to which of the following religions?

(a) Buddhism   (b) Hinduism

(c) Vaishnavism   (d) Shaivism

Ans. (a) According to a Buddhist text known as the Ashokavadana, Asoka distributed portions of the Buddha's relics to every important town and ordered the construction of stupas over them.(eg Bharhut, Sanchi and Sarnath)

Q.5. Which of the following group of people contributed towards building stupas

(a) Bhikkhus and bhikkhunis

(b) Guilds

(c) Kings

(d) All of the above

Ans. (d)

Q.6. In the structure of the stupa, harmika represents

(a) abode of the gods (b) umbrella.

(c) secular world   (d) balancing shapes.

Ans. (a) 1. The stupa (a Sanskrit word meaning a heap) originated as a simple semi-circular mound of earth, later called anda.

2. Gradually, it evolved into a more complex structure, balancing round and square shapes.

3. Above the anda was the harmika, a balcony- like structure that represented the abode of the gods.

Q.7. Find the correct statement about sacrifices

(a) Sacrifices were performed collectively in all periods

(b) Hymns were chanted when sacrifices were performed

(c) In Sacrifices people prayed for wealth and marriages

(d) None of the above

Ans. (b) Many of these hymns were chanted when sacrifices were performed, where people prayed for cattle, sons, good health, long life, etc.

Q.8. Jaina monks and nuns took which of the following vows:

1. Abstain from killing
2. stealing
3. lying
4. observe celibacy
5. abstain from possessing property.

Choose the correct answer from the codes given below

(a) 1, 3, 4 and 5   (b) 2, 3, 4 and 5

(c) 1, 3, 4 and 5   (d) 1, 2, 3, 4 and 5

Ans. (d) Jaina monks and nuns took five vows: to abstain from killing, stealing and lying; to observe celibacy; and to abstain from possessing property.

Q.9. Which of the following statement does not come under Jaina philosophy or teachings?

[CBSE 2021]

(a) Non-injury to living and non living being, is central to Jaina philosophy.

(b) The cycle of birth and rebirth is shaped through karma.

(c) Asceticism and penance are required to free oneself from the cycle of karma.

(d) Monastic existence is a necessary condition of salvation in Jainism

Ans. (a)

Q.10. Find the incorrect statement about Pitaka

(a) The Vinaya Pitaka included rules and regulations for those who joined the monastic order

(b) Buddha's teachings were included in the Sutta Pitaka

(c) The Abhidhamma Pitaka dealt with philosophical matters.

(d) Each pitaka comprised a number of discussions and debates.

Ans. (d) Each pitaka comprised a number of individual texts.

Q.11. Find the False statement about Buddha's sangha

(a) It was an organisation of monks who too became teachers of dhamma.

(b) Monks were known as bhikkhus and bhikkhunis.

(c) Both men and Women were allowed into the sangha

(d) Buddha's mother who gave him birth, Mahapajapati Gotami, was the first bhikkhuni.

Ans. (d)

The Buddha's foster mother, Mahapajapati Gotami was the first woman to be ordained as a bhikkhuni.

Q.12. A Prakrit text known as the Uttaradhyayana Sutta, describes, how a queen named Kamalavati tried to persuade her husband to renounce the world

The above story compiled under the teaching of ____

(a) Mahavira

(b) Budddha

(c) Satakarni

(d) Ananda

Ans. (a)

Q.13. Which of the following pitika describes the conversation between King Ajatashatru, the ruler of Magadha, and the Buddha?

(a) Sutta Pitaka

(b) Vinaya Pitaka

(c) Abhidhamma Pitaka

(d) Dhamma

Ans. (a)

Very Short Answer Type   [1 Mark]

Q.1. According to Jaina teachings, the cycle of birth and rebirth is shaped through?

Ans. The cycle of birth and rebirth is shaped through Karma

Q.2. About 200 years after the time of the Buddha, which ruler erected a pillar at Lumbini to mark the fact that he had visited the place?

Ans. Ashoka erected a pillar at Lumbini to mark the fact that he had visited the place

Q.3. Dipavamsa and Mahavamsa contain regional histories of which religions?

Ans. Dipavamsa and Mahavamsa contain regional histories of Buddhism.

Q.4. From earliest times, people tended to regard certain places as sacred which include sites with special trees or unique rocks, with small shrines attached to them. These were sometimes described as?

Ans. Chaityas were regarded as sacred which include sites with special trees or unique rocks, with small shrines attached

Q.5. What is the essential condition of salvation according to Jainism?

Ans. Monastic existence is the essential condition of salvation according to Jainism

Q.6. The Buddha's teachings have been reconstructed from stories, found mainly in which Pitakas

Ans. Buddha's teachings have been reconstructed from stories, found mainly in Sutta Pitaka

Q.7. According to Jainism which two conditions are required to be free from the cycle of karma?

Ans. Asceticism and penance are required to be free from the cycle of karma

Q.8. The Therigatha is a collection of verses composed by

Ans. Therigatha is a collection of verses composed by bhikkhunis.

Q.9. Jaina scholars produced a wealth of literature in which languages?

Ans. Jaina scholars produced a wealth of literature in a variety of languages - Prakrit, Sanskrit and Tamil.

Q.10. What is the tradition of the Ajivikas?

Ans. They have often been described as fatalists: those who believe that everything is predetermined.

Q.11. What is the tradition of the Lokayatas?

Ans. Lokayatas, usually described as materialists.

Short Answer Type - I [2 Marks]

Q.1. What events deeply hurt Gautam Buddha?

Ans. Siddhartha, as the Buddha was named at birth, was the son of a chief of the Sakya clan. He was deeply anguished when he saw an old man, a sick man and a corpse.

Q.2. What is therigatha?

Ans. It is a unique Buddhist text, part of the Sutta Pitaka, is a collection of verses composed by bhikkhunis. It provides an insight into women's social and spiritual experiences.

Q.3. What are the places associated with the life of Buddha?

Ans. Places associated with the Buddha's life - where he was born (Lumbini), where he attained enlightenment (Bodh Gaya), where he gave his first sermon (Sarnath) and where he attained nibbana (Kusinagara).

Q.4. How did the debate take place in the 6th century BC?

Ans. Debates took place in the *kutagarashala* - literally, a hut with a pointed roof - or in groves where travelling mendicants halted. If a philosopher succeeded in convincing one of his rivals, the followers of the latter also became his disciples.

Q.5. Discuss the role of the begums of Bhopal in preserving the stupa at Sanchi.

Ans. Begums of Bhopal made a great contribution to the preservation of the Stupa of Sanchi. Shahejahan Begum and her successor Sultan Jahan Begum of Bhopal were the rulers of Bhopal, who made generous grants to the preservation of the Stupa of Sanchi. They also contributed financially to built a museum near the stupa

Short Answer Type - II [3 Marks]

Q.1. Why do you think women and men joined the sangha?

Ans. Men and women joined sanghas because

1. Many of them wanted to renounce the worldly pleasures.

2. They could study the Buddhist literature and philosophy by staying in the company of other monks.

3. Many people entered sanghas to become priests and teachers of Buddhism.

4. All were considered equal and the previous social identity was to be renounced.

5. The environment of sanghas was democratic. The decision making within sanghas was based on voting.

The above features attracted many and they took to the life of sanghas

Q.2. How Siddhartha attained enlightenment ?

Ans. Siddhartha explored several paths including bodily mortification which led him to a situation of near death. Abandoning these extreme methods, he meditated for several days and finally attained enlightenment. After this he came to be known as the Buddha or the Enlightened One. For the rest of his life, he taught *dhamma* or the path of righteous living

Q.3. How do teachers convince others about the validity of their philosophy?

Ans. Teachers travelled from place to place, trying to convince one another as well as laypersons, about the validity of their philosophy or the way they understood the world. Debates took place in the *kutagarashala* - literally, a hut with a pointed roof - or in groves where travelling mendicants halted. If a philosopher succeeded in convincing one of his rivals, the followers of the latter also became his disciples. So support for any particular sect could grow and shrink over time.

Q.4. How do the principles of Jainism influence Indian thinking ? [CBSE 2019]

Ans. Jainism is an ancient religion and it has its own philosophy which has been influencing Indian thought. Jainism thinks that the world is real, and the spirit is also real. It has a theory of karma which explains the interaction between soul and nature. It also preaches Ahimsa (non-violence) and aparigraha (non-storage). It has also influenced the Shaiva and Vaishnava cults. Jainism preaches intellectual tolerance and has a practical appreciation of all living..

Q.5. Mention any two features of gotra as per the Brahmanical practice. What evidences do we get from the Satavahanas inscriptions regarding the inheriance of gotra ? Explain. [CBSE 2014]

Ans. Every gotra was named after a Vedic seer. All those who belonged to the same gotra were considered as his descendants. Women were expected to give up their father's gotra and adopt that of their husband on marriage and members of the same gotra could not marry. Many inscriptions of the Satavahanas have been recovered, which allow historians to trace family bonds. Some of the women who married Satavahana rulers had names of their father's gotras that is Gotama and Vasistha. They retained these names instead of adopting names derived from their husband's gotra.

Long Answer Type [5 Marks]

Q.1. Explain the process of development of Mahayana Buddhism

Ans. By the first century CE, there is evidence of changes in Buddhist ideas and practices. Early Buddhist teachings had given great importance to self-effort in achieving *nibbana*. Besides, the Buddha was regarded as a human being who attained enlightenment and *nibbana* through his own efforts. However, gradually the idea of a saviour emerged. It was believed that he was the one who could ensure salvation. Simultaneously, the concept of the Bodhisatta also developed.

Bodhisattas were perceived as deeply compassionate beings who accumulated merit through their efforts but used this not to attain *nibbana* and thereby abandon the world, but to help others. The worship of images of the Buddha and Bodhisattas became an important part of this tradition. This new way of thinking was called Mahayana - literally, the "great vehicle". Those who adopted these beliefs described the older tradition as Hinayana or the "lesser vehicle".

Q.2. Discuss the development in sculpture and architecture associated with the rise of Vaishnavism and Shaivism.

Ans. Vaishnavism and Shaivism are the two branches of Hinduism. In case of Vaishnavism, Lord Vishnu was regarded as the chief deity. In case of Shaivism Lord Shiva was regarded as the chief deity. Both traditions were part of the Bhakti movement. This tradition of Vaishnavism and Shaivism also impacted the tradition of architecture and sculpture. The temples developed the house deities. The initial temples were small and simple. It was a small room called Garbhagriha. Later it expanded, a tall structure was built on the garbhagriha. It was called Shikhara. The walls of the temple were decorated with suitors. Soon temples were built that had huge entrance and big halls for the comfort of visitors.

Q.3. Trace out the growth of Buddhism. Explain the main teachings of Buddha. **[CBSE 2018]**

Ans. Buddhism grew rapidly both during the lifetime of the Buddha and after his death. Buddhism grew due to Buddhist text-Tipitaka (the Vinaya Pitaka, Sutta Pitaka, Abhidhamma Pitaka), the Dipavamsa and Mahavamsa, Ashokavadana, Jatakas and Buddhist hagiography. Buddhist Sanghas, Bhikkhus and Bhikkhunis spread the message.

Teachings of Buddha

1. The world is transient (anicca) arid changing constantly.

2. It is soulless (anatta) as there is nothing permanent or eternal.

3. In the transient world, sorrow is intrinsic to human existence. It is by following the path of moderation between severe penance and self-indulgence that human beings can rise above these wordly troubles.

4. Buddha emphasised individual agency and righteous action as the means to escape from the cycle of re-birth and attain self-realisation.

5. Extinguish ego and desire to end the cycle of suffering.

Chapter Practice

Multiple Choice Questions   [1 Mark]

Q.1. Consider the following image

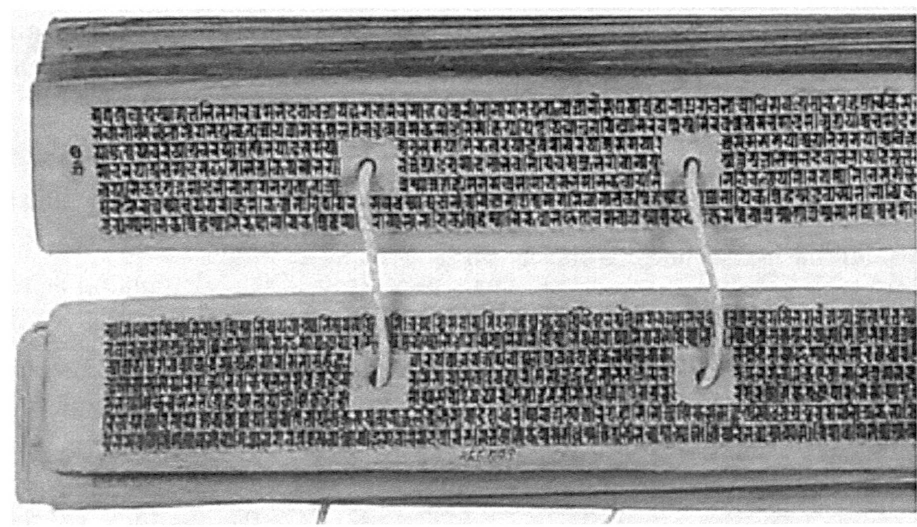

The above image represents a *Buddhist manuscript* in

(a) Pali   (b) Sanskrit   (c) Chinese   (d) Tibetan

Q.2. Which of the following country sought Shahjehan Begum's permission to take away the eastern gateway of Sanchi stupa?

(a) France   (b) Portuguese   (c) United Kingdom   (d) None of the above

Very Short Answer Type   [1 Mark]

Q.3. Consider the following paragraph

'**They**' emphasised individual agency - suggesting that men and women could strive to attain liberation from the trials and tribulations of worldly existence. This was in marked contrast to the Brahmanical position, wherein, as we have seen, an individual's existence was thought to be determined by his or her birth in a specific caste or gender.

In the above paragraph '**They**' represents

(a) Mahavira   (b) Buddha   (c) Kar   (d) Both (a) and (b)

Q.4. What ideas were found in the Upanishads?

Q.5. What was kutagarashala?

Q.6. Who questioned the authority of Vedas?

Q.7. Correct the following statement and rewrite it in your answer book.   [CBSE 2021]

"Mahayana and Hinayana are the sects of Jainism"

Q.8. Write the name of place where Buddha attained Nibbana.   [CBSE 2021]

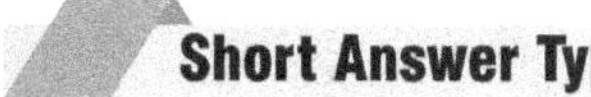 **Short Answer Type - I**   **[2 Marks]**

Q.9. Discuss Buddhist text Dipavamsa and Mahavamsa.

Q.10. What was the Buddha's method of teaching?

Short Answer Type - II   **[3 Marks]**

Q.11. What were the three baskets containing different types of texts?

Long Answer Type   **[5 Marks]**

Q.12."Buddhism grew rapidly both during the lifetime of the Buddha and after his death". Justify the statement with suitable arguments.   [CBSE 2019]

PART II

Through The Eye of Travelers
(c. 600 BCE - 600 CE)

TOPIC 1

Personal details about the travelers who had came to India

Summary

Al-Biruni

- Al-Biruni was born in 973, in Khwarizm in present day Uzbekistan.

- He was well versed in several languages: Syriac, Arabic, Persian, Hebrew and Sanskrit.

- In 1017, when Sultan Mahmud invaded Khwarizm, he took several scholars and poets back to his capital, Ghazni; Al-Biruni was one of them.

- He arrived in Ghazni as a hostage, but gradually developed a liking for the city, where he spent the rest of his life until his death at the age of 70. It was in Ghazni that Al-Biruni developed an interest in India.

- Al-Biruni spent years in the company of Brahmana priests and scholars, learning Sanskrit, and studying religious and philosophical texts. While his itinerary is not clear, it is likely that he travelled widely in the Punjab and parts of northern India.

- Al-Biruni's *Kitab-ul-Hind*, written in Arabic, is simple and lucid. It is a voluminous text, divided into 80 chapters on subjects such as religion and philosophy, festivals, astronomy, alchemy, manners and customs, social life, weights and measures, iconography, laws and metrology.

Ibn Battuta

- This Moroccan traveller was born in Tangier into one of the most respectable and educated families known for their expertise in Islamic religious law or shari'a.

- Unlike most other members of his class, Ibn Battuta considered experience gained through travels to be a more important source of knowledge than books.

- He just loved travelling, and went to far-off places, exploring new worlds and peoples. Before he set off for India in 1332-33, he had made pilgrimage trips to Mecca, and had already travelled extensively in Syria, Iraq, Persia, Yemen, Oman and a few trading ports on the coast of East Africa.

- Travelling overland through Central Asia, Ibn Battuta reached Sind in 1333. He had heard about Muhammad bin Tughlaq, the Sultan of Delhi, and lured by his reputation as a generous patron of arts and letters, set off for Delhi, passing through Multan and Uch.

- The Sultan was impressed by his scholarship, and appointed him the *qazi* or judge of Delhi. He remained in that position for several years, until he fell out of favour and was thrown into prison. Once the misunderstanding between him and the Sultan was cleared, he was restored to imperial service, and was ordered in 1342 to proceed to China as the Sultan's envoy to the Mongol ruler.

- Ibn Battuta was an inveterate traveller who spent several years travelling through north Africa, West Asia and parts of Central Asia (he may even have visited Russia), the Indian subcontinent and China, before returning to his native land, Morocco. When he returned, the local ruler issued instructions that his stories be recorded.

Francois Bernier

- François Bernier was the French jeweler.
- François Bernier, a Frenchman, was a doctor, political philosopher and historian.
- He was in India for twelve years, from 1656 to 1668, and was closely associated with the Mughal court, as a physician to Prince Dara Shukoh, the eldest son of Emperor Shah Jahan, and later as an intellectual and scientist, with Danishmand Khan, an Armenian noble at the Mughal court.
- He dedicated his major writing to Louis XIV, the king of France, and many of his other works were written in the form of letters to influential officials and ministers.
- Bernier's works were published in France in 1670-71 and translated into English, Dutch, German and Italian within the next five years.

Other traveler who came to India

- Marco Polo (from Italy), Abd al-Razzaq Kamal al-Din ibn Ishaq al- Samarqandi (from Samarqand), Afanasii Nikitich Nikitin (fifteenth century, from Russia), Duarte Barbosa, d.1521 (from Portugal), Peter Mundy (from England) etc.

Multiple Choice Questions [1 Mark]

Q.1. It was in Ghazni that Al-Biruni developed an interest in India. This was not unusual. Al-Biruni was born in-

    (a) 453 AD   (b) 782 AD

    (c) 973 AD   (d) 1017 AD

Ans. (c)

Q.2. Al-Biruni spent years in the company of Brahmana priests and scholars, learning Sanskrit, and studying religious and philosophical texts. Where was the Al-Biruni died?

    (a) Khwarizm   (b) Punjab

    (c) Kabul   (d) Ghazni

Ans. (d)

Q.3. Ibn Battuta's book of travels, called Rihla. Rihla was written in which language?

    (a) Arabic   (b) Greek

    (c) Sanskrit   (d) Persian

Ans. (a)

Q.4. Like many others, he came to the Mughal Empire in search of opportunities. François Bernier particularly fascinated with the trading conditions in India, and compared India to-

    (a) Britain   (b) Iran

    (c) Ottoman empire   (d) Both (b) and (c)

Ans. (d)

Q.5. Bernier's works were published in France in 1670-71 and translated into English, Dutch, German and Italian within the next five years. François Bernier is a-

    (a) Doctor

    (b) Political philosopher

    (c) Historian

    (d) All of the above

Ans. (d)

Q.6. Once the Portuguese arrived in India in about 1500, a number of them wrote detailed accounts regarding Indian social customs and religious practices. Duarte Barbosa came to India in which century?

    (a) Fourteen century

    (b) Fifteen century

    (c) Sixteen century

    (d) Seventeen century

Ans. (c)

Q.7. As we have seen, travellers often compared what they saw in the subcontinent with practices with which they were familiar. Seydi Ali Reis was from which country?

    (a) Iran   (b) Morocco

    (c) Italy   (d) Turkey

Ans. (d)

Q.8. You may have noticed that travellers' accounts provide us with a tantalising glimpse of the lives of men and women during these centuries. Marco Polo came to India in-

    (a) 1292-1294   (b) 1518

    (c) 1458   (d) 1123-1226

Ans. (a)

Q.9. Generally (though not always),he adopted a distinctive structure in each chapter, beginning with a question, following this up with a description based on Sanskritic traditions, and concluding with a comparison with other cultures. Given statement is true for which writer?

    (a) Al-Biruni   (b) Ibn Battuta

    (c) Marco Polo   (d) None of the above

Ans. (a)

Q.10. Al-Biruni spent years in the company of Brahmana priests and scholars, learning Sanskrit and studying religious and philosophical texts. Al Biruni was mostly writing in which language?

    (a) Arabic   (b) Sanskrit

    (c) Persian   (d) English

Ans. (a)

Very Short Answer Type   [1 Mark]

Q.1. Kitab-ul-Hind was written by?

Ans. It was written by Al-Biruni

Q.2. Ibn Battuta was from?

Ans. He was from Morocco

Q.3. Who worked as a physician to Prince Dara Shukoh?

Ans. François Bernier worked as a physician to Prince Dara Shukoh

Q.4. In fifteen century which Russian traveler came to India?

Ans. Afanasii Nikitich Nikitin came to India in the 5th century

Q.5. Seydi Ali Reis died in which year?

Ans. Seydi Ali Reis (from Turkey) died in 1518.

Q.6. Marco Polo was originally from which country?

Ans. He was from Italy

Q.7. Who gave warning to European king through their writings?

Ans. François Bernier.

Q.8. How many chapters in Al-Biruni's Kitab-ul-Hind?

Ans. There are 80 chapters in. Kitab-ul-Hind

Q.9. In which year Ibn Battuta reached Sind?

Ans. He reached Sindh in 1333

Q.10. Ibn Battuta returned to home after how many years?

Ans. After 30 years in 1354

Short Answer Type - I   [2 Marks]

Q.1. What are the objectives of Al-Biruni's work?

Ans. Al-Biruni described his work as: a help to those who want to discuss religious questions with them (the Hindus), and as a repertory of information to those who want to associate with them.

Q.2. Ibn Battuta's book of travels, called Rihla, was about?

Ans. *Ibn Battuta's book of travels, called Rihla,* written in Arabic, provides extremely rich and interesting details about the social and cultural life in the subcontinent in the fourteenth century.

Q.3. Who was the ruler of India when Ibn Battuta came to India?

Ans. Muhammad bin Tughlaq was the sultan of Delhi when Ibn Battuta acme to India.

Q.4. When Ibn Battuta visited China?

Ans. He was ordered in 1342 to proceed to China as the Sultan's envoy to the Mongol ruler.

Q.5. Zaytun was situated in which country?

Ans. Zaytun (now known as Quanzhou) was the port town of China which was visited by Ibn Battuta.

Q.6. According to Ibn Battuta how many days took to travel Multan to Delhi?

Ans. According to Ibn Battuta, it took forty days to travel from Multan to Delhi and about fifty days from Sind to Delhi. The distance from Daulatabad to Delhi was covered in forty days, while that from Gwalior to Delhi took ten days.

Q.7. For how many years François Bernier was in India?

Ans. He was in India for twelve years, from 1656 to 1668, and was closely associated with the Mughal court, as a physician to Prince Dara Shukoh, the eldest son of Emperor Shah Jahan, and later as an intellectual and scientist, with Danishmand Khan, an Armenian noble at the Mughal court.

Q.8. Uluq word is related to?

Ans. In India the postal system is of two kinds. The horsepost, called uluq, is run by royal horses stationed at a distance of every four miles.

Q.9. "a strange nation", term is given by which writer to which place?

Ans. The travelogue of Abdur Razzaq written in the 1440s is an interesting mixture of emotions and perceptions. On the one hand, he did not appreciate what he saw in the port of Calicut (present-day Kozhikode) in Kerala, which was populated by "a people the likes of whom I had never imagined", describing them as "a strange nation".

Short Answer Type - II   [3 Marks]

Q.1. How did Al-Biruni came to India?

Ans. In 1017, when Sultan Mahmud invaded Khwarizm, he took several scholars and poets back to his capital, Ghazni; Al-Biruni was one of them. It was in Ghazni that Al-Biruni developed an interest in India. When the Punjab became a part of the Ghaznavid empire, contacts with the local population helped create an environment of mutual trust and understanding.

Q.2. What makes Ibn-Battuta different from members of their class?

Ans. Unlike most other members of his class, Ibn Battuta considered experience gained through travels to be a more important source of knowledge than books. He just loved travelling, and went to far-off places, exploring new worlds and peoples. Before he set off for India in 1332-33, he had made pilgrimage trips to Mecca, and had already travelled extensively in Syria, Iraq, Persia, Yemen, Oman and a few trading ports on the coast of East Africa.

Q.3. How did Ibn Battuta got Qazi rank under the sultan of Delhi?

Ans. Travelling overland through Central Asia, Ibn Battuta reached Sind in 1333. He had heard about Muhammad bin Tughlaq, the Sultan of Delhi, and lured by his reputation as a generous patron of arts and letters, set off for Delhi, passing through Multan and Uch. The Sultan was impressed by his scholarship, and appointed him the *qazi* or judge of Delhi.

Q.4. Give some detail about the François Bernier.

Ans. François Bernier was the French jeweller who travelled to India at least six times. He was particularly fascinated with the trading conditions in India, and compared India to Iran and the Ottoman empire. François Bernier, a Frenchman, was a doctor, political philosopher and historian. Like many others, he came to the Mughal Empire in search of opportunities. He was in India for twelve years, from 1656 to 1668, and was closely associated with the Mughal court, as a physician to Prince Dara Shukoh, the eldest son of Emperor Shah Jahan, and later as an intellectual and scientist, with Danishmand Khan, an Armenian noble at the Mughal court.

Q.5. Who followed the footsteps of Ibn Battuta?

Ans. Among the best known of these writers were Abdur Razzaq Samarqandi, who visited south India in the 1440s, Mahmud Wali Balkhi, who travelled very widely in the 1620s, and Shaikh Ali Hazin, who came to north India in the 1740s.

Q.6. What was the specialty in Al Biruni's writings?

Ans. Generally (though not always), Al-Biruni adopted a distinctive structure in each chapter, beginning with a question, following this up with a description based on Sanskritic traditions, and concluding with a comparison with other cultures. Some present-day scholars have argued that this almost geometric structure, remarkable for its precision and predictability, owed much to his mathematical orientation. Al-Biruni, who wrote in Arabic, probably intended his work for peoples living along the frontiers of the subcontinent. He was familiar with translations and adaptations of Sanskrit, Pali and Prakrit texts into Arabic - these ranged from fables to works on astronomy and medicine.

Q.7. What was the description of Paan according to Ibn Battuta?

Ans. Ibn Battuta's description of the paan: The betel is a tree which is cultivated in the same manner as the grape-vine; … The betel has no fruit and is grown only for the sake of its leaves … The manner of its use is that before eating it one takes areca nut; this is like a nutmeg but is broken up until it is reduced to small pellets, and one places these in his mouth and chews them. Then he takes the leaves of betel, puts a little chalk on them, and masticates them along with the betel.

Q.8. What was the opinion of Al Biruni for the Sanskrit language?

Ans. Al-Biruni described Sanskrit as follows: If you want to conquer this difficulty (i.e. to learn Sanskrit), you will not find it easy, because the language is of an enormous range, both in words and inflections, something like the Arabic, calling one and the same thing by various names, both original and derivative, and using one and the same word for a variety of subjects, which, in order to be properly understood, must be distinguished from each other by various qualifying epithets.

Q.9. "Ibn Battuta found cities in the Indian subcontinent full of exciting opportunities."

Explain the statement with reference to the city of Delhi.   **[CBSE 2018]**

Ans. Ibn Battuta found cities in the Indian subcontinent full of exciting opportunities, especially the city of Delhi:

1. Delhi covers a wide area and has a dense population.

2. There is a rampart round the city that is without parallel. The breadth of its wall is eleven cubics and inside it, there are houses for the night sentry and gatekeepers.

3. Inside the ramparts, there are storehouses for storing edibles, magazines, ammunition, ballistas and siege machines.

4. There are twenty eight gates in the city which are called darwaza in which, Budaun Darwaza is the biggest.

5. In Gul Darwaza there is an orchard. It has fine cemetery in which graves have domes over them and those that do not have a dome, have an arch for sure.

Long Answer Type   [5 Marks]

Q.1. Give a brief note about the Kitab-ul-Hind.

Ans. Al-Biruni's *Kitab-ul-Hind*, written in Arabic, is simple and lucid. It is a voluminous text, divided into 80 chapters on subjects such as religion and philosophy, festivals, astronomy, alchemy, manners and customs, social life, weights and measures, iconography, laws and metrology. Generally (though not always), Al-Biruni adopted a distinctive structure in each chapter, beginning with a question, following this up with a description based on Sanskritic traditions, and concluding with a comparison with other cultures. Some present-day scholars have argued that this almost geometric structure, remarkable for its precision and predictability, owed much to his mathematical orientation.

Q.2. Give some information about Ibn Battuta's book and his travel experiences.

Ans. Ibn Battuta's book of travels, called Rihla, written in Arabic, provides extremely rich and interesting details about the social and cultural life in the subcontinent in the fourteenth century. This Moroccan traveller was born in Tangier into one of the most respectable and educated families known for their expertise in Islamic religious law or shari'a. He just loved travelling, and went to far-off places, exploring new worlds and peoples. Before he set off for India in 1332-33, he had made pilgrimage trips to Mecca, and had already travelled extensively in Syria, Iraq, Persia, Yemen, Oman and a few trading ports on the coast of East Africa. Travelling was also more insecure: Ibn Battuta was attacked by bands of robbers several times. In fact he preferred travelling in a caravan along with companions, but this did not deter highway robbers. While travelling from Multan to Delhi, for instance, his caravan was attacked and many of his fellow travellers lost their lives; those travellers who survived, including Ibn Battuta, were severely wounded.

Q.3. Give a brief note on the writings of François Bernier.

Ans. Bernier travelled to several parts of the country, and wrote accounts of what he saw, frequently comparing what he saw in India with the situation in Europe. He dedicated his major writing to Louis XIV, the king of France, and many of his other works were written in the form of letters to influential officials and ministers. In virtually every instance Bernier described what he saw in India as a bleak situation in comparison to developments in Europe. As we will see, this assessment was not always accurate. However, when his works were published, Bernier's writings became extremely popular. Bernier's works were published in France in 1670-71 and translated into English, Dutch, German and Italian within the next five years. Between 1670 and 1725 his account was reprinted eight times in French, and by 1684 it had been reprinted three times in English. This was in marked contrast to the accounts in Arabic and Persian, which circulated as manuscripts and were generally not published before 1800.

TOPIC 2

Travelers Perception of Indian Society

Summary

Al Biruni's

- According to him, Sanskrit was so different from Arabic and Persian that ideas and concepts could not be easily translated from one language into another.

- He discussed several "barriers" that he felt obstructed understanding.

- Al-Biruni tried to explain the caste system by looking for parallels in other societies.

- He attempted to suggest that social divisions were not unique to India.

- In spite of his acceptance of the Brahmanical description of the caste system, Al-Biruni disapproved of the notion of pollution.

- However, in real life the system was not quite as rigid. For instance, the categories defined as *antyaja* (literally, born outside the system) were often expected to provide inexpensive labour to both peasants and zamindars.

Ibn Battuta

- By the time Ibn Battuta arrived in Delhi in the fourteenth century, the subcontinent was part of a global network of communication that stretched from China in the east to north-west Africa and Europe in the west.

- Some of the best examples of Ibn Battuta's strategies of representation are evident in the ways in which he described the coconut and the *paan*, two kinds of plant produce that were completely unfamiliar to his audience.

- Ibn Battuta found cities in the subcontinent full of exciting opportunities for those who had the necessary drive, resources and skills.

- Ibn Battuta described Delhi as a vast city, with a great population, the largest in India. Daulatabad (in Maharashtra) was no less, and easily rivalled Delhi in size.

- Ibn Battuta informs us that certain varieties of fine muslin were so expensive that they could be worn only by the nobles and the very rich.

- The bazaars were not only places of economic transactions, but also the hub of social and cultural activities.

- In India the postal system is of two kinds. The horsepost, called uluq, is run by royal horses stationed at a distance of every four miles. The foot-post has three stations per mile; it is called dawa.

Francois Bernier

- Bernier's *Travels in the Mughal Empire* is marked by detailed observations, critical insights and reflection.

- He constantly compared Mughal India with contemporary Europe, generally emphasising the superiority of the latter.

- According to Bernier, one of the fundamental differences between Mughal India and Europe was the lack of private property in land in the former.

- He was a firm believer in the virtues of private property, and saw crown ownership of land as being harmful for both the state and its people.

- As an extension of this, Bernier described Indian society as consisting of undifferentiated masses of impoverished people, subjugated by a small minority of a very rich and powerful ruling class. This, then, is how Bernier saw the Mughal Empire - its king was the king of "beggars and barbarians";

- Bernier's descriptions influenced Western theorists from the eighteenth century onwards.

- While Bernier's preoccupation with projecting the Mughal state as tyrannical is obvious, his descriptions occasionally hint at a more complex social reality.

- Bernier described Mughal cities as "camp towns", by which he meant towns that owed their existence, and depended for their survival, on the imperial camp.

Women, Slaves, Sati and Laborers

- It appears from Ibn Battuta's account that there was considerable differentiation among slaves. Some female slaves in the service of the Sultan were experts in music and dance, and Ibn Battuta enjoyed their performance at the wedding of the Sultan's sister. Female slaves were also employed by the Sultan to keep a watch on his nobels.

- Slaves were generally used for domestic labour, and Ibn Battuta found their services particularly indispensable for carrying women and men on palanquins or dola.

- However, women's lives revolved around much else besides the practice of sati. Their labour was crucial in both agricultural and non-agricultural production.

Multiple Choice Questions   [1 Mark]

Q.1. Who translated the Patanjali's book on grammar into Arabic?

    (a) Al Biruni   (b) Ibn Battuta

    (c) Marco Polo   (d) Francois Bernier

Ans. (a)

Q.2. According to Al Biruni caste system in India was-

    (a) As same as Europe   (b) Unique to India

    (c) Not unique to India (d) As same as Islam

Ans. (c)

Q.3. Ibn Battuta arrived in Delhi in which century?

(a) Thirteen century   (b) Fourteen century

(c) Fifteen century   (d) Sixteen century

Ans. (b)

Q.4. Which is the biggest city in India according to Ibn Battuta?

(a) Mumbai   (b) Daulatabad

(c) Patna   (d) Delhi

Ans. (d)

Q.5. The foot-post has ------- per mile; it is called dawa.

(a) Two stations   (b) Eight stations

(c) Three stations   (d) Five stations

Ans. (c)

Q.6. According to Bernier during sixteen century landownership was in hand of-

(a) Nobels   (b) King

(c) Peasants   (d) Foreigners

Ans. (b)

Q.7. During the seventeenth century about what percent of the population lived in towns?

(a) 10   (b) 15

(c) 20   (d) 40

Ans. (b)

Q.8. In the ancient times slaves were used as-

(a) Spy   (b) For homework

(c) As a gift   (d) All of the above

Ans. (d)

Q.9. Bernier saw a child sati in which city?

(a) Delhi

(b) Lahore

(c) Kabul

(d) Patna

Ans. (b)

Very Short Answer Type [1 Mark]

Q.1. Metrology is define as-

Ans. Metrology is the science of measurement.

Q.2. Who was deputed to write what Ibn Battuta dictated?

Ans. Ibn Juzayy was deputed to write what Ibn Battuta dictated

Q.3. According to Ibn Battuta which cities is not less than Delhi?

Ans. Daulatabad was not less than Delhi

Q.4. Tarababad is famous for?

Ans. In Daulatabad there is a market place for male and female singers, which is known as Tarababad.

Q.5. Who saw the Mughal Empire- its king was the king of "beggars and barbarians"?

Ans. Francois Bernier

Q.6. Define the term Sheth.

Ans. In western India merchants groups were called mahajans, and their chief called the sheth.

Q.7. Who used the Bernier description for his work?

Ans. French philosopher Montesquieu.

Q.8. Pelsaert was from which country?

Ans. He was from Netherland.

Short Answer Type - I [2 Marks]

Q.1. For whom Al Biruni translated the work of Euclid into Sanskrit?

Ans. For his Brahmana friends, he translated the works of Euclid (a Greek mathematician) into Sanskrit.

Q.2. According to Rihla what are the problems through which a traveler suffer?

Ans. Robbers were not the only hazard on long journeys: the traveler could feel homesick, or fall ill.

Q.3. On which point Al Biruni disapproved with Brahmans of India?

Ans. In spite of his acceptance of the Brahmanical description of the caste system, Al-Biruni disapproved of the notion of pollution.

Q.4. Define the term Uluq and Dawa.

Ans. In India the postal system is of two kinds. The horsepost, called uluq, is run by royal horses stationed at a distance of every four miles. The foot-post has three stations per mile; it is called dawa, that is one-third of a mile.

Q.5. For whom Ibn Battuta purchased slaves?

Ans. When Ibn Battuta reached Sind he purchased "horses, camels and slaves" as gifts for Sultan Muhammad bin Tughlaq.

Q.6. Who are called nagarsheth?

Ans. Merchants often had strong community or kin ties, and were organized into their own caste-cum occupational bodies. In western India these groups were called mahajans, and their chief, the sheth. In urban centers such as Ahmedabad the mahajans were collectively represented by the chief of the merchant community who was called the nagarsheth.

Q.7. Who describes the land revenue as "remunerations of sovereignty"?

Ans. Abu'l Fazl, the sixteenth-century official chronicler of Akbar's reign, describes the land revenue as "remunerations of sovereignty".

Q.8. What was the view of Pelsaert for Indian Society?

Ans. Pelsaert, a Dutch traveller, visited the subcontinent during the early decades of the seventeenth century. Like Bernier, he was shocked to see the widespread poverty, "poverty so great and miserable that the life of the people can be depicted or accurately described only as the home of stark want and the dwelling place of bitter woe".

Short Answer Type - II   [3 Marks]

Q.1. Define the term Hindu?

Ans. The term "Hindu" was derived from an Old Persian word, used c. sixth-fifth centuries BCE, to refer to the region east of the river Sindhu (Indus). The Arabs continued the Persian usage and called this region "al-Hind" and its people "Hindi". Later the Turks referred to the people east of the Indus as "Hindu", their land as "Hindustan", and their language as "Hindavi". None of these expressions indicated the religious identity of the people. It was much later that the term developed religious connotations.

Q.2. What was the Al-Biruni's description of the caste system in India?   **[CBSE 2019]**

Ans. Al-Biruni tried to explain the caste system by looking for parallels in other societies. He noted that in ancient Persia, four social categories were recognised: those of knights and princes; monks, fire-priests and lawyers; physicians, astronomers and other scientists; and finally, peasants and artisans. In other words, he attempted to suggest that social divisions were not unique to India.

Q.3. What are the perceptions of Ibn Battuta for Indian cities?

Ans. Ibn Battuta found cities in the subcontinent full of exciting opportunities for those who had the necessary drive, resources and skills. They were densely populated and prosperous, except for the occasional disruptions caused by wars and invasions. It appears from Ibn Battuta's account that most cities had crowded streets and bright and colourful markets that were stacked with a wide variety of goods.

Q.4. What was the importance of Bazaars in ancient times?

Ans. The bazaars were not only places of economic transactions, but also the hub of social and cultural activities. Most bazaars had a mosque and a temple, and in some of them at least, spaces were marked for public performances by dancers, musicians and singers.

Q.5. What was system of Communication during the Fourteen century?

Ans. The state evidently took special measures to encourage merchants. Almost all trade routes were well supplied with inns and guest houses. Ibn Battuta was also amazed by the efficiency of the postal system which allowed merchants to not only send information and remit credit across long distances, but also to dispatch goods required at short notice. The postal system was so efficient that while it took fifty days to reach Delhi from Sind, the news reports of spies would reach the Sultan through the postal system in just five days.

Q.6. What was the view of Bernier for the Indian society?

Ans. Bernier described Indian society as consisting of undifferentiated masses of impoverished people, subjugated by a small minority of a very rich and powerful ruling class. Between the poorest of the poor and the richest of the rich, there was no social group or class worth the name. Bernier confidently asserted: "There is no middle state in India." This, then, is how Bernier saw the Mughal Empire - its king was the king of "beggars and barbarians"; its cities and towns were ruined and contaminated with "ill air"; and its fields, "overspread with bushes" and full of "pestilential marishes". And, all this was because of one reason: crown ownership of land.

Q.7. Write a short note about the visit of Abdur Razzaq to India?

Ans. The travelogue of Abdur Razzaq written in the 1440s is an interesting mixture of emotions and perceptions. On the one hand, he did not appreciate what he saw in the port of Calicut (present-day Kozhikode) in Kerala, which was populated by "a people the likes of whom I had never imagined", describing them as "a strange nation". Later in his visit to India, he arrived in Mangalore, and crossed the Western Ghats.

Q.8. What were the conditions of towns during Bernier visits to India?

Ans. In fact, during the seventeenth century about 15 per cent of the population lived in towns. This was, on average, higher than the proportion of urban population in Western Europe in the same period. In spite of this Bernier described Mughal cities as "camp towns", by which he meant towns that owed their existence, and depended for their survival, on the imperial camp. He believed that these came into existence when the imperial court moved in and rapidly declined when it moved out. He suggested that they did not have viable social and economic foundations but were dependent on imperial patronage.

Q.9. Give a short note about the Karkhanas during sixteen century.

Ans. Bernier is perhaps the only historian who provides a detailed account of the working of the imperial karkhanas or workshops: Large halls are seen at many places, called karkhanas or workshops for the artisans. In one hall, embroiderers are busily employed, superintended by a master. In another, you see the goldsmiths; in a third, painters; in a fourth, varnishers in lacquer-work; in a fifth, joiners, turners, tailors and shoe-makers; in a sixth, manufacturers of silk, brocade and fine muslins … The artisans come every morning to their karkhanas where they remain employed the whole day; and in the evening return to their homes.

Q.10. What were the conditions of women in sixteen century? **[CBSE 2017]**

Ans. Contemporary European travellers and writers often highlighted the treatment of women as a crucial marker of difference between Western and Eastern societies. Not surprisingly, Bernier chose the practice of sati for detailed description. He noted that while some women seemed to embrace death cheerfully, others were forced to die. However, women's lives revolved around much else besides the practice of sati. Their labour was crucial in both agricultural and non-agricultural production. Women from merchant families participated in commercial activities, sometimes even taking mercantile disputes to the court of law. It therefore seems unlikely that women were confined to the private spaces of their homes.

Long Answer Type   [5 Marks]

Q.1. According to Al Biruni what are the barriers to understanding the societies and people?

Ans. Each traveler adopted distinct strategies to understand what they observed. Al-Biruni, for instance, was aware of the problems inherent in the task he had set himself. He discussed several "barriers" that he felt obstructed understanding. The first amongst these was language. According to him, Sanskrit was so different from Arabic and Persian that ideas and concepts could not be easily translated from one language into another. The second barrier he identified was the difference in religious beliefs and practices. The self-absorption and consequent insularity of the local population according to him, constituted the third barrier. What is interesting is that even though he was aware of these problems, Al-Biruni depended almost exclusively on the works of Brahmanas, often citing passages from the Vedas, the Puranas, the Bhagavat Gita, the works of Patanjali, the Manusmriti, etc., to provide an understanding of Indian society.

Q.2. Write a short note on the caste system during the Al Biruni visits to India, according to him?

Ans. Al-Biruni tried to explain the caste system by looking for parallels in other societies. He noted that in ancient Persia, four social categories were recognised: those of knights and princes; monks, fire-priests and lawyers; physicians, astronomers and other scientists; and finally, peasants and artisans. In other words, he attempted to suggest that social divisions were not unique to India. In spite of acceptance of the Brahmanical description of the caste system, Al-Biruni disapproved of the notion of pollution. He remarked that everything which falls into a state of impurity strives and succeeds in regaining its original condition of purity. The sun cleanses the air, and the salt in the sea prevents the water from becoming polluted. If it were not so, insisted Al-Biruni, life on earth would have been impossible.

Q.3. How was the Delhi during Fourteen century? Give some detail according Ibn Battuta.?

[CBSE 2016]

Ans. Ibn Battuta described Delhi as a vast city, with a great population, the largest in India. Here is an excerpt from Ibn Battuta's account of Delhi, often spelt as Dehli in texts of the period ;The city of Dehli covers a wide area and has a large population ... The rampart round the city is without parallel. The breadth of its wall is eleven cubits; and inside it are houses for the night sentry and gatekeepers. Inside the ramparts, there are store-houses for storing edibles, magazines, ammunition, ballistas and siege machines. The grains that are stored (in these ramparts) can last for a long time, without rotting ... In the interior of the rampart, horsemen as well as infantrymen move from one end of the city to another. The rampart is pierced through by windows which open on the side of the city, and it is through these windows that light enters inside. The lower part of the rampart is built of stone; the upper part of bricks. It has many towers close to one another. There are twenty eight gates of this city which are called darwaza, and of these, the Budaun darwaza is the greatest; inside the Mandwi darwaza there is a grain market; adjacent to the Gul darwaza there is an orchard. The city of Dehli has a fine cemetery in which graves have domes over them, and those that do not have a dome, have arch, for sure. In the cemetery they sow flowers such as tuberose, jasmine, wild rose, etc.; and flowers blossom there in all seasons.

Q.4. What are the perceptions of Ibn Battuta for trade and agriculture in India?

Ans. While Ibn Battuta was not particularly concerned with explaining the prosperity of towns, historians have used his account to suggest that towns derived a significant portion of their wealth through the appropriation of surplus from villages. Ibn Battuta found Indian agriculture very productive because of the fertility of the soil, which allowed farmers to cultivate two crops a year. He also noted that the subcontinent was well integrated with inter-Asian networks of trade and commerce, with Indian manufactures being in great demand in both West Asia and Southeast Asia, fetching huge profits for artisans and merchants. Indian textiles, particularly cotton cloth, fine muslins, silks, brocade and satin, were in great demand. Ibn Battuta informs us that certain varieties of fine muslin were so expensive that they could be worn only by the nobles and the very rich.

Q.5. Give a short note on the landownership during sixteen century?

Ans. According to Bernier, one of the fundamental differences between Mughal India and Europe was the lack of private property in land in the former. He was a firm believer in the virtues of private property, and saw crown ownership of land as being harmful for both the state and its people. He thought that in the Mughal Empire the emperor owned all the land and distributed it among his nobles, and that this had disastrous consequences for the economy and society. Curiously, none of the Mughal official documents suggest that the state was the sole owner of land. For instance, Abu'l Fazl, the sixteenth-century official chronicler of Akbar's reign, describes the land revenue as "remunerations of sovereignty", a claim made by the ruler on his subjects for the protection he provided rather than as rent on land that he owned.

Q.6. Examine why Bernier described the Mughal towns as the 'Camp Towns'.   **[CBSE 2016]**

Ans. During the seventeenth century about 15 percent of the population lived in the towns. This was on average, higher than the proportion of urban population in Western Europe in the same period. In spite of this, Bernier described the Mughal cities as 'Camp towns', by which he meant towns that owed their existence and depended for their survival, on the imperial camp.

He believed that these came into existence when the imperial court moved in and rapidly declined when it moved out. He suggested that they did not have viable social and economic foundations but were dependent on imperial patronage.

Bernier was drawing an over simplified picture.

There were all kinds of towns : manufacturing towns, trading towns, port-towns, sacred centres, pilgrimage towns, etc. Their existence is an index of the prosperity of merchant communities and professional classes.

Chapter Practice

Multiple Choice Questions [1 Mark]

Q.1. The term "Hindu" was derived from an Old Persian word that referred to the region which lied to the east of which of the following rivers ?

(a) Sindhu

(b) Sone

(c) Ganges

(d) Saraswati

Q.2. Find the false statements:

(a) Al-Biruni and Ibn Batuta were written in Arabic

(b) Al-Biruni had written Kitab-ul-Hind

(c) Rihla was written by Ibn Batuta

(d) Al-Biruni Kitab-ul-Hind and Rihla were biographies

Q.3. Accounts of which of the following two travellers are compared with respect to the information related to China?

(a) Ibn Batuta and Marco Polo

(b) Marco Polo and Bernier

(c) Duarte Barbosa and Fa Hien

(d) Bernier and Jean-Baptiste Tavernier

Very Short Answer Type [1 Mark]

Q.4. Who's work was reprinted many times?

Q.5. Which traveler disapproved of the notion of pollution?

Short Answer Type - I [2 Marks]

Q.6. Define antyaja? [CBSE 2020]

Q.7. State the inherent problems faced by Al-Baruni in the task of understanding Indian Social and Brahamanical practices. Mention any two sources that provided him the support. [CBSE 2017]

Short Answer Type - II   [3 Marks]

Q.8. Why was Rihla called a remarkable book of Ibn Battuta ? Give two reasons.   [CBSE 2019]

Q.9. What were the elements of the practice of sati that drew the attention of Bernier?   [CBSE 2020]

Long Answer Type   [5 Marks]

Q.10. Describe Bernier's description of land ownership in India and also describe its influence on Western theorists from 18th century onwards.   [CBSE 2019]

Q.11. Describe the experiences of Al-Biruni in the Indian Subcontinent.   [CBSE 2019]

Q.12. "India had a unique system of communication during the fourteenth century." Examine the statement of Ibn Batuta.   [CBSE 2017]

CHAPTER 6

Bhakti - Sufi Traditions

Bhakti Cults and Their Upgradation in North and South India

Summary

- In the course of the evolution of these forms of worship, in many instances, poet-saints emerged as leaders around whom there developed a community of devotees.

- At a different level, historians of religion often classify bhakti traditions into two broad categories: saguna (with attributes) and nirguna (without attributes).

- Some of the earliest bhakti movements (c. sixth century) were led by the Alvars (literally, those who are "immersed" in devotion to Vishnu) and Nayanars (literally, leaders who were devotees of Shiva). They travelled from place to place singing hymns in Tamil in praise of their gods.

- Some historians suggest that the Alvars and Nayanars initiated a movement of protest against the caste system and the dominance of Brahmanas or at least attempted to reform the system.

- one of the major anthologies of compositions by the Alvars, the Nalayira Divyaprabandham, was frequently described as the Tamil Veda, thus claiming that the text was as significant as the four Vedas in Sanskrit that were cherished by the Brahmanas.

- Perhaps one of the most striking features of these traditions was the presence of women. For instance, the compositions of Andal, a woman Alvar, were widely sung (and continue to be sung to date). Andal saw herself as the beloved of Vishnu; her verses express her love for the deity.

- one of the major themes in Tamil bhakti hymns is the poets' opposition to Buddhism and Jainism.

- Historians have attempted to explain this hostility by suggesting that it was due to competition between members of other religious traditions for royal patronage.

- The twelfth century witnessed the emergence of a new movement in Karnataka, led by a Brahmana named Basavanna (1106-68) who was a minister in the court of a Kalachuri ruler. His followers were known as Virashaivas (heroes of Shiva) or Lingayats (wearers of the linga).

- The Lingayats challenged the idea of caste and the "pollution" attributed to certain groups by Brahmanas. They also questioned the theory of rebirth.

- Our understanding of the Virashaiva tradition is derived from vachanas (literally, sayings) composed in Kannada by women and men who joined the movement.

- Baba Guru Nanak (1469-1539) was born in a Hindu merchant family in a village called Nankana Sahib near the river Ravi in the predominantly Muslim Punjab. He trained to be an accountant and studied Persian.

- The message of Baba Guru Nanak is spelt out in his hymns and teachings. These suggest that he advocated a form of nirguna bhakti.

- Mirabai (c. fifteenth-sixteenth centuries) is perhaps the best-known woman poet within the bhakti tradition.

Multiple Choice Questions   [1 Mark]

Q.1. Often associated with the goddess were forms of worship that were classified as Tantric. Many of these ideas influenced-

(a) Shaivism   (b) Buddhism

(c) Both (a) and (b)   (d) None of the above

Ans. (c)

Q.2. At a different level, historians of religion often classify bhakti traditions into two broad categories: saguna (with attributes) and nirguna (without attributes). The former included traditions that focused on the worship of-

(a) Shiva   (b) Vishnu

(c) Goddess or Devi   (d) All of the above

Ans. (d)

Q.3. Some of the earliest bhakti movements (c. sixth century) were led by the Alvars and Nayanars. In these two forms Alvars are those who worships-

(a) Vishnu   (b) Shiva

(c) Devi   (d) Buddha

Ans. (a)

Q.4. The Nalayira Divyaprabandham, was frequently described as the Tamil Veda, thus claiming that the text was as significant as the four Vedas in Sanskrit that were cherished by the Brahmanas. Who composed this text?

(a) Alvars   (b) Nayanars

(c) Buddhists   (d) None of the above

Ans. (a)

Q.5. Which chola ruler had consecrated metal images of Appar, Sambandar and Sundarar in a Shiva temple? These were carried in processions during the festivals of these saints.

(a) Pranataka 1   (b) Rajraja 1

(c) Aditya 1   (d) Uttama chola

Ans. (a)

Q.6. Baba Guru Nanak (1469-1539) was born in a Hindu merchant family in a village called Nankana Sahib near the river Ravi in the predominantly Muslim Punjab. He advocated which form of bhakti?

(a) Saguna   (b) Nirguna

(c) Advaita   (d) Sufism

Ans. (b)

Q.7. Baba Guru Nanak organised his followers into a community. He set up rules for congregational worship (sangat) involving collective recitation. He appointed one of his disciples. Who was his successor?

(a) Angad

(b) Arjan singh

(c) Guru Govind singh

(d) None of the above

Ans. (a)

Very Short Answer Type   [1 Mark]

Q.1. The terms great and little traditions were coined by a sociologist named Robert Redfield in the twentieth century. It is describe the cultural practices of which society?

Ans. Peasant societies

Q.2. Some of the most magnificent Shiva temples, including those at Chidambaram, Thanjavur and Gangaikondacholapuram, were constructed under the patronage of which rulers?

Ans. Chola rulers.

Q.3. Who was founder of Virashaivas (heroes of Shiva) or Lingayats?

Ans. Basavanna (1106-68).

Q.4. Which sect believes that on death the devotee will be united with Shiva and will not return to this world?

Ans. Lingayats

Q.5. In which century lingayats originate?

Ans. Twelfth century.

Q.6. Baba Guru Nanak was born at which place?

Ans. Nankana Sahib near the river Ravi.

Q.7. Basavna was a minister in which ruler?

Ans. Kalachuri ruler.

Short Answer Type - I [2 Marks]

Q.1. Most striking features of bhakti traditions were the presence of women. Andal was a woman. She was devotee of?

Ans. Perhaps one of the most striking features of these traditions was the presence of women. For instance, the compositions of Andal, a woman Alvar, were widely sung (and continue to be sung to date). Andal saw herself as the beloved of Vishnu.

Q.2. Who was Karaikkal Ammaiyar?

Ans. Karaikkal Ammaiyar, a devotee of Shiva, adopted the path of extreme asceticism in order to attain her goal. Her compositions were preserved within the Nayanar tradition.

Q.3. One of the major themes in Tamil bhakti hymns is the poets' opposition to Buddhism and Jainism. What is the main reason behind this?

Ans. This is particularly marked in the compositions of the Nayanars. Historians have attempted to explain this hostility by suggesting that it was due to competition between members of other religious traditions for royal patronage.

Q.4. Define Gurbani?

Ans. The fifth preceptor, Guru Arjan, compiled Baba Guru Nanak's hymns along with those of his four successors and other religious poets like Baba Farid, Ravidas (also known as Raidas) and Kabir in the Adi Granth Sahib. These hymns, called "gurbani", are composed in various languages.

Short Answer Type - II [3 Marks]

Q.1. Define Saguna and Nirguna?

Ans. At a different level, historians of religion often classify bhakti traditions into two broad categories: saguna (with attributes) and nirguna (without attributes). The former included traditions that focused on the worship of specific deities such as Shiva, Vishnu and his avatars (incarnations) and forms of the goddess or Devi, all often conceptualized in anthropomorphic forms. Nirguna bhakti on the other hand was worship of an abstract form of god.

Q.2. What are the attitudes of alvaras and nayanars towards caste?

Ans. Some historians suggest that the Alvars and Nayanars initiated a movement of protest against the caste system and the dominance of Brahmanas or at least attempted to reform the system. To some extent this is corroborated by the fact that bhaktas hailed from diverse social backgrounds ranging from Brahmanas to artisans and cultivators and even from castes considered "untouchable".

Q.3. What was the view of lingayats on caste system?

Ans. The Lingayats challenged the idea of caste and the "pollution" attributed to certain groups by Brahmanas. They also questioned the theory of rebirth. These won them followers amongst those who were marginalised within the Brahmanical social order. The Lingayats also encouraged certain practices disapproved in the Dharmashastras, such as post-puberty marriage and the remarriage of widows.

Q.4. Give some detail about Mirabai?

Ans. Mirabai (c. fifteenth-sixteenth centuries) is perhaps the best-known woman poet within the bhakti tradition. Biographies have been reconstructed primarily from the bhajans attributed to her, which were transmitted orally for centuries. According to these, she was a Rajput princess from Merta in Marwar who was married against her wishes to a prince of the Sisodia clan of Mewar, Rajasthan.

Q.5. Define the term Great and Little tradition?

Ans. The terms great and little traditions were coined by a sociologist named Robert Redfield in the twentieth century to describe the cultural practices of peasant societies. In fact, many beliefs and practices were shaped through a continuous dialogue between what sociologists have described as "great" Sanskritic Puranic traditions and "little" traditions throughout the land.

Long Answer Type   [5 Marks]

Q.1. Give a short note on the Virshaiva tradition of Karnataka?

Ans. The twelfth century witnessed the emergence of a new movement in Karnataka, led by a Brahmana named Basavanna (1106-68) who was a minister in the court of a Kalachuri ruler. His followers were known as Virashaivas (heroes of Shiva) or Lingayats (wearers of the linga). Lingayats continue to be an important community in the region to date. They worship Shiva in his manifestation as a linga, and men usually wear a small linga in a silver case on a loop strung over the left shoulder. The Lingayats challenged the idea of caste and the "pollution" attributed to certain groups by Brahmanas. They also questioned the theory of rebirth. These won them followers amongst those who were marginalised within the Brahmanical social order. The Lingayats also encouraged certain practices disapproved in the Dharmashastras, such as post-puberty marriage and the remarriage of widows. Our understanding of the Virashaiva tradition is derived from vachanas (literally, sayings) composed in Kannada by women and men who joined the movement.

Q.2. Give some detail about the Baba Guru Nanak and his teachings?

Ans. Baba Guru Nanak (1469-1539) was born in a Hindu merchant family in a village called Nankana Sahib near the river Ravi in the predominantly Muslim Punjab. He trained to be an accountant and studied Persian. He was married at a young age but he spent most of his time among sufis and bhaktas. The message of Baba Guru Nanak is spelt out in his hymns and teachings. These suggest that he advocated a form of nirguna bhakti. He firmly repudiated the external practices of the religions he saw around him. He rejected sacrifices, ritual baths, image worship, austerities and the scriptures of both Hindus and Muslims. For Baba Guru Nanak, the Absolute or "rab" had no gender or form. He proposed a simple way to connect to the Divine by remembering and repeating the Divine Name, expressing his ideas through hymns called "shabad" in Punjabi, the language of the region.

TOPIC 2

New Strands in the Fabric Islamic Traditions

Summary

- In 711 an Arab general named Muhammad Qasim conquered Sind, which became part of the Caliph's domain. Later (c. thirteenth century) the Turks and Afghans established the Delhi Sultanate.

- Theoretically, Muslim rulers were to be guided by the ulama, who were expected to ensure that they ruled according to the shari'a. Clearly, the situation was complicated in the subcontinent, where there were populations that did not subscribe to Islam.

- All those who adopted Islam accepted, in principle, the five "pillars" of the faith: that there is one God, Allah, and Prophet Muhammad is his messenger (shahada); offering prayers five times a day (namaz/salat); giving alms (zakat); fasting during the month of Ramzan (sawm); and performing the pilgrimage to Mecca (hajj).

- Historians who have studied Sanskrit texts and inscriptions dating between the eighth and fourteenth centuries point out that the term musalman or Muslim was virtually never used.

- A more general term for these migrant communities was mlechchha, indicating that they did not observe the norms of caste society and spoke languages that were not derived from Sanskrit.

- In the early centuries of Islam a group of religiousminded people called sufis turned to asceticism and mysticism in protest against the growing materialism of the Caliphate as a religious and political institution.

- Institutionally, the sufis began to organise communities around the hospice or khanqah (Persian) controlled by a teaching master known as shaikh (in Arabic), pir or murshid (in Persian). He enrolled disciples (murids) and appointed a successor (khalifa). He established rules for spiritual conduct and interaction between inmates as well as between laypersons and the master.

- Some mystics initiated movements based on a radical interpretation of sufi ideals. Many scorned the khanqah and took to mendicancy and observed celibacy.

- The khanqah was the centre of social life. We know about Shaikh Nizamuddin's hospice (c. fourteenth century) on the banks of the river Yamuna in Ghiyaspur, on the outskirts of what was then the city of Delhi.

- The earliest textual references to Khwaja Muinuddin's dargah date to the fourteenth century. It was evidently popular because of the austerity and piety of its Shaikh, the greatness of his spiritual successors, and the patronage of royal visitors.

- It was not just in sama' that the Chishtis adopted local languages. In Delhi, those associated with the Chishti silsila conversed in Hindavi, the language of the people.

- A major feature of the Chishti tradition was austerity, including maintaining a distance from worldly power. However, this was by no means a situation of absolute isolation from political power.

- The Kabir Bijak is preserved by the Kabirpanth (the path or sect of Kabir) in Varanasi and elsewhere in Uttar Pradesh; the Kabir Granthavali is associated with the Dadupanth in Rajasthan, and many of his compositions are found in the Adi Granth Sahib.

- However, the verses attributed to Kabir use the words guru and satguru, but do not mention the name of any specific preceptor. Historians have pointed out that it is very difficult to establish that Ramananda and Kabir were contemporaries, without assigning improbably long lives to either or both.

Multiple Choice Questions   [1 Mark]

Q.1. An Arab general named Muhammad Qasim conquered Sind, which became part of the Caliph's domain. In which year Muhammad Qasim conquered Sindh?

  (a) 1021

  (b) 711

  (c) 945

  (d) 1226

Ans. (b)

Q.2. A Khojaki manuscript The ginan were transmitted orally before being recorded in the Khojaki script that was derived from the local landa ("clipped" mercantile script) used by the linguistically diverse community of Khojahs. Where was this manuscript found ?

  (a) Punjab

  (b) Sind

  (c) Gujarat

  (d) All of the above

Ans. (d)

Q.3. People were occasionally identified in terms of the region from which they came. So, the Turkish rulers were designated as Turushka, Tajika were people from Tajikistanrm and Parashika were people from Persia. Mlechchha term is used for-

  (a) People from Indonesia

  (b) People from Morocco

  (c) A general term for migrant

  (d) None of the above

Ans. (c)

Q.4. By the eleventh century Sufism evolved into a well developed movement with a body of literature on Quranic studies and sufi practices. Khanqah is related to Sufism which is a ____ word?

(a) Arabic   (b) Persian

(c) Urdu   (d) Hindi

Ans. (b)

Q.5. Shaikh Fariduddin Ganj-i Shakar was a great sufi teacher, who died in 1265. Where was his dargah?

(a) Ajodhan (Pakistan) (b) Ajmer

(c) Delhi   (d) Agra

Ans. (a)

Q.6. In 1039 Abu'l Hasan al Hujwiri, a native of Hujwir near Ghazni in Afghanistan, was forced to cross the Indus as a captive of the invading Turkish army. Where was he buried after death?

(a) Delhi   (b) Ajmer

(c) Lahore   (d) Kabul

Ans. (c)

Q.7. The earliest textual references to Khwaja Muinuddin's dargah date to the fourteenth century. It was evidently popular because of the austerity and piety of its Shaikh, the greatness of his spiritual successors, and the patronage of royal visitors. Who was the frst ruler who visited this place?

(a) Sultan Ghiyasuddin Khalji

(b) Balban

(c) Muhammad bin Tughlaq

(d) None of the above

Ans. (c)

Q.8. His poems survived in several languages and dialects; and some are composed in the special language of nirguna poets, the sant bhasha. For whom these statements are correct?

(a) Raidas   (b) Mirabai

(c) Guru nanak   (d) Kabir

Ans. (d)

Q.9. Kabir drew on to describe the Ultimate Reality. These include Islam: he described the Ultimate Reality as Allah, Khuda, Hazrat and Pir. He also used terms drawn from Vedantic traditions, alakh, nirakar, Brahman, Atman, etc. What is the mwaning of Alakh?

(a) Unseen   (b) Formless

(c) Emptiness   (d) Sound

Ans. (a)

Very Short Answer Type   [1 Mark]

Q.1. Define ginan?

Ans. It derived from the Sanskrit jnana, meaning "knowledge".

Q.2. By whom muslim rulers were guided?

Ans. Muslim rulers were to be guided by the ulama.

Q.3. What is the meaning of sawm?

Ans. Fasting during the month of Ramzan.

Q.4. Where was Shaikh Nizamuddin's hospice stuated?

Ans. Ghiyaspur, Delhi.

Q.5. Where is the Dargah of Shaikh Muinuddin Sijzi?

Ans. Ajmer (Rajasthan).

Q.6. When was the Shaikh Nizamuddin Auliya died?

Ans. 1325

Q.7. Who had written the book Kashful- Mahjub (Unveiling of the Veiled) to explain the meaning of tasawwuf, and those who practised it, that is, the sufi.?

Ans. Abu'l Hasan al Hujwiri.

Q.8. According to an eighteenth-century visitor from the Deccan, Dargah Quli Khan, which shrine is as 'the lamp of entire land'?

Ans. Shrine of Nasiruddin Chiragh-I Dehli.

Q.9. Kabir Granthavali is related to which panth?

Ans. Dadupanth.

Short Answer Type - I [2 Marks]

Q.1. Define ulama regarding Islam?

Ans. Ulama (plural of alim, or one who knows) are scholars of Islamic studies. As preservers of this tradition they perform various religious, juridical and teaching functions.

Q.2. What is the meaning of Matrilocal?

Ans. Matrilocal residence is a practice where women after marriage remain in their natal home with their children and the husbands may come to stay with them.

Q.3. Define the term wali?

Ans. Wali (plural auliya) or friend of God was a sufi who claimed proximity to Allah, acquiring His Grace (barakat) to perform miracles (karamat).

Q.4. Which are the universal features of mosque?

Ans. Mosques have some universal features- such as their orientation towards Mecca, evident in the placement of the mihrab (prayer niche) and the minbar (pulpit).

Q.5. What is the meaning of word Silsilas?

Ans. The word silsila literally means a chain, signifying a continuous link between master and disciple, stretching as an unbroken spiritual genealogy to the Prophet Muhammad.

Q.6. What happened when a sheikh died?

Ans. When the shaikh died, his tomb-shrine (dargah, a Persian term meaning court) became the centre of devotion for his followers.

Q.7. What is the meaning ziyarat?

Ans. Pilgrimage, called ziyarat, to tombs of sufi saints is prevalent all over the Muslim world. This practice is an occasion for seeking the sufi's spiritual grace (barakat).

Q.8. Which shrine was known as "Gharib Nawaz"?

Ans. Amongst these, the most revered shrine is that of Khwaja Muinuddin, popularly known as "Gharib Nawaz" (comforter of the poor).

Short Answer Type - II [3 Marks]

Q.1. Define Sharia?

Ans. The shari'a is the law governing the Muslim community. It is based on the Qur'an and the hadis, traditions of the Prophet including a record of his remembered words and deeds. With the expansion of Islamic rule outside Arabia, in areas where customs and traditions were different, qiyas (reasoning by analogy) and ijma (consensus of the community) were recognised as two other sources of legislation. Thus, the shari'a evolved from the Qur'an, hadis, qiyas and ijma.

Q.2. What is Zimmi? It was imposed on whom?

Ans. zimmi, meaning protected (derived from the Arabic word zimma, protection) developed for people who followed revealed scriptures, such as the Jews and Christians, and lived under Muslim rulership. They paid a tax called jizya and gained the right to be protected by Muslims.

Q.3. What are the five pillars of Islam?

Ans. In principle, the five "pillars" of the Islam: that there is one God, Allah, and Prophet Muhammad is his messenger (shahada); offering prayers five times a day (namaz/salat); giving alms (zakat); fasting during the month of Ramzan (sawm); and performing the pilgrimage to Mecca (hajj).

Q.4. What was khojahs term meaning in initial phase of Islam in India?

Ans. The Khojahs, a branch of the Ismailis (a Shi'a sect), developed new modes of communication, disseminating ideas derived from the Qur'an through indigenous literary genres. These included the ginan (derived from the Sanskrit jnana, meaning "knowledge"), devotional poems in Punjabi, Multani, Sindhi, Kachchi, Hindi and Gujarati, sung in special ragas during daily prayer meetings.

Q.5. What were the features of hospice?

Ans. It comprised several small rooms and a big hall (jama'at khana) where the inmates and visitors lived and prayed. The inmates included family members of the Shaikh, his attendants and disciples. The Shaikh lived in a small room on the roof of the hall where he met visitors in the morning and evening. A veranda surrounded the courtyard, and a boundary wall ran around the complex. On one occasion, fearing a Mongol invasion, people from the neighbouring areas flocked into the khanqah to seek refuge.

Q.6. Describe the main teachings of Baba Guru Nanak.

[CBSE 2019]

Ans. Baba Guru Nanak firmly repudiated the external practices of the religions he saw around him. He rejected sacrifices, ritual bath, image worship, austerities and the scriptures of both Hindu and Muslims. He organise his followers into a community. He set up rules for congregational worship (sangat)' involving collective recitation. For Baba Nanak, the absolute or Rab had no gender form. He proposed a simple way to connect to the Divine by remembering and repeating the Divine's Name through hymns called shabad.

Long Answer Type [5 Marks]

Q.1. Define the term sufism and tasawwuf?

Ans. Sufism is an English word coined in the nineteenth century. The word used for Sufism in Islamic texts is tasawwuf. Historians have understood this term in several ways. According to some scholars, it is derived from suf, meaning wool, referring to the coarse woolen clothes worn by sufis. Others derive it from safa, meaning purity. It may also have been derived from suffa, the platform outside the Prophet's mosque, where a group of close followers assembled to learn about the faith.

Q.2. Give a short note on the spreading of Islam in India in initial phase.

Ans. In 711 an Arab general named Muhammad Qasim conquered Sind, which became part of the Caliph's domain. Later (c. thirteenth century) the Turks and Afghans established the Delhi Sultanate. This was followed by the formation of Sultanates in the Deccan and other parts of the subcontinent; Islam was an acknowledged religion of rulers in several areas. This continued with the establishment of the Mughal Empire in the sixteenth century as well as in many of the regional states that emerged in the eighteenth century. Theoretically, Muslim rulers were to be guided by the ulama, who were expected to ensure that they ruled according to the shari'a. Clearly, the situation was complicated in the subcontinent, where there were populations that did not subscribe to Islam.

Q.3. Give a short note on Khanqahs and silsilas.

Ans. Institutionally, the sufis began to organise communities around the hospice or khanqah (Persian) controlled by a teaching master known as shaikh (in Arabic), pir or murshid (in Persian). He enrolled disciples (murids) and appointed a successor (khalifa). He established rules for spiritual conduct and interaction between inmates as well as between laypersons and the master. Sufi silsilas began to crystallise in different parts of the Islamic world around the twelfth century. The word silsila literally means a chain, signifying a continuous link between master and disciple, stretching as an unbroken spiritual genealogy to the Prophet Muhammad. It was through this channel that spiritual power and blessings were transmitted to devotees.

Q.4. Give some detail about the relation between sufis and state?

Ans. A major feature of the Chishti tradition was austerity, including maintaining a distance from worldly power. However, this was by no means a situation of absolute isolation from political power. The sufis accepted unsolicited grants and donations from the political elites. The Sultans in turn set up charitable trusts (auqaf) as endowments for hospices and granted tax-free land (inam). The Chishtis accepted donations in cash and kind. Rather than accumulate donations, they preferred to use these fully on immediate requirements such as food, clothes, living quarters and ritual necessities (such as sama).

Chapter Practice

Multiple Choice Questions [1 Mark]

Q.1. Kabir Bijak, *one of the* verses ascribed to Kabir, is preserved in which of the following states?

(a) Uttar Pradesh (b) Gujrat (c) Rajasthan (d) Uttrakhand

Q.2. Who among the following authors/historians wrote about Shaikh Nizamuddin's hospice

(a) Amir Hasan Sijzi (b) Amir Khusrau (c) Ziyauddin Barani (d) All of the above

Q.3. The category of the *zimmi*, developed for people who followed revealed scriptures, such as the Jews and Christians, and lived under Muslim rulership.

Zimmi signifies

(a) protected (b) Taxed (c) devoted (d) administration

Very Short Answer Type [1 Mark]

Q.4. Who compiled Baba Guru Nanak's hymns?

Q.5. Differentiate between Shaguna and Nirguna [CBSE 2020]

Short Answer Type - I [2 Marks]

Q.6. Point out any two similarities between the philosophy of Kabir and Guru Nanak Dev ? [CBSE 2016]

Q.7. Kabir Bijak and Kabir Granthavali are the two distinct but overlapping traditions.

How are they preserved? [CBSE 2015]

Q.8. Who initiated Kabir into Bhakti ? Mention his concept of Ultimate Reality. [CBSE 2014]

Q.9. Who was the preceptor of Mirabai ? Mention any one principle of her philosophy. [CBSE 2014]

Q.10. Name the major anthology compiled by the Alvars which is also described as the Tamil Veda. How did various chiefdoms in the Tamil region help them in the early first millennium CE ? [CBSE 2015]

Short Answer Type - II [3 Marks]

Q.11. The message of Guru Nanak Devji was based on divinity." Mention any two aspects of it. [CBSE 2017]

Q.12. Who were called be-shari'a?

Long Answer Type [5 Marks]

Q.13. Discuss the ways in which the Alvars, Nayanars and Virashaivas expressed critiques of the caste system.

[CBSE 2019]

An Imperial Capital Vijayanagara

Political Sequence of Vijayanagara Empire

Summary

- Vijayanagara or "city of victory" was the name of both a city and an empire. The empire was founded in the fourteenth century. In its heyday it stretched from the river Krishna in the north to the extreme south of the peninsula.

- The ruins at Hampi were brought to light in 1800 by an engineer and antiquarian named Colonel Colin Mackenzie. An employee of the English East India Company, he prepared the first survey map of the site.

- According to tradition and epigraphic evidence two brothers, Harihara and Bukka, founded the Vijayanagara Empire in 1336.

- On their northern frontier, the Vijayanagara kings competed with contemporary rulers - including the Sultans of the Deccan and the Gajapati rulers of Orissa - for control of the fertile river valleys and the resources generated by lucrative overseas trade.

- Gajapati literally means lord of elephants. This was the name of a ruling lineage that was very powerful in Orissa in the fifteenth century. In the popular traditions of Vijayanagara the Deccan Sultans are termed as ashvapati or lord of horses and the rayas are called narapati or lord of men.

- Vijayanagara was also noted for its markets dealing in spices, textiles and precious stones. Trade was often regarded as a status symbol for such cities, which boasted of a wealthy population that demanded high-value exotic goods, especially precious stones and jewellery.

- The first dynasty, known as the Sangama dynasty, exercised control till 1485. They were supplanted by the Saluvas, military commanders, who remained in power till 1503 when they were replaced by the Tuluvas. Krishnadeva Raya belonged to the Tuluva dynasty.

- In 1565 Rama Raya, the chief minister of Vijayanagara, led the army into battle at Rakshasi-Tangadi (also known as Talikota), where his forces were routed by the combined armies of Bijapur, Ahmadnagar and Golconda. The victorious armies sacked the city of Vijayanagara.

- In fact the Vijayanagara kings were keen to ensure the stability of the Sultanates and vice versa. It was the adventurous policy of Rama Raya who tried to play off one Sultan against another that led the Sultans to combine together and decisively defeat him.

- The amara-nayaka system was a major political innovation of the Vijayanagara Empire. It is likely that many features of this system were derived from the iqta system of the Delhi Sultanate.

Multiple Choice Questions　　[1 Mark]

Q.1. On their northern frontier, the Vijayanagara kings competed with contemporary rulers - including the Sultans of the Deccan and the Gajapati rulers of Orissa - for control of the fertile river valleys and the resources generated by lucrative overseas trade. In which century Viaynagara Empire was founded?

(a) Eleventh century　(b) Twelfth century

(c) Thirteen century　(d) Fourteen century

Ans. (d)

Q.2. According to tradition and epigraphic evidence two brothers, Harihara and Bukka, founded the Vijayanagara Empire in 1336. In the popular traditions of Vijayanagara the rayas are called______?

(a) Ashvapati　　　(b) Gajapati

(c) Narapati　　　(d) None of the above

Ans. (c)

Q.3. Warfare during these times was depended upon effective cavalry. Where from these horses were imported?

(a) Arab

(b) Central Asia

(c) Russia

(d) Both (a) and (b)

Ans. (d)

Q.4. Krishnadeva Raya (ruled 1509-29), the most famous ruler of Vijayanagara, composed a work on statecraft in Telugu known as the Amuktamalyada. He belongs to which dynasty?

(a) Sangama dynasty

(b) Tuluvas dynasty

(c) Saluvas dynasty

(d) Nayakas

Ans. (b)

Q.5. Among those who exercised power in the empire were military chiefs who usually controlled forts and had armed supporters. These chiefs were known as nayakas and they usually spoke ______ languages?

(a) Telugu　　　　(b) Kannada

(c) Tamil　　　　(d) Both (a) and (b)

Ans. (d)

Q.6. Krishnadeva Raya's rule was characterised by expansion and consolidation. This was the time when the land between the ______and______ rivers was acquired (1512), the rulers of Orissa were subdued (1514) and severe defeats were inflicted on the Sultan of Bijapur (1520).

(a) Tungbhadra and Krishna

(b) Tungbhadra and kaveri

(c) Ghatprabha and Krishna

(d) Hemavati and Krishna

Ans. (a)

Q.7. Who were competed with the Vijayanagara Empire for control of the fertile river valleys and the resources generated by lucrative overseas trade?

(a) Gajapati rulers of Orissa

(b) Sultans of deccan

(c) The cholas

(d) Both (a) and (b)

Ans. (d)

Q.8. Vijayanagara or "city of victory" was the name of both a city and an empire. The empire was founded in the fourteenth century. In its heyday it stretched from the river Krishna in the north to the extreme south of the peninsula. Select the correct option which shows right sequence who ruled Vijayanagara Empire?

(a) Sangama - Tuluva - Aravidu - Saluvas

(b) Salivas - Taluva - Sangama - Aravidu

(c) Sangama - Saluvas - Tuluva - Aravidu

(d) Sangama - Aravidu - Saluvas - Tuluva

Ans. (c)

Q.9. Rama Raya, the chief minister of Vijayanagara, led the army into battle at Rakshasi-Tangadi (also known as Talikota), where his forces were routed by the combined armies of Bijapur, Ahmadnagar and Golconda. In which year this War was happened?

(a) 1454   (b) 1200

(c) 1665   (d) 1565

Ans. (d)

Very Short Answer Type   [1 Mark]

Q.1. Who discovered Hampi in the year 1800?

Ans. Colonel Colin Mackenzie.

Q.2. Who were known as asvapati?

Ans. Deccan Sultans.

Q.3. Who was the successor of Sanagam dynasty?

Ans. Suluvas dynasty

Q.4. The first dynasty, known as the Sangama dynasty, exercised control till?

Ans. They exercised their control till 1485

Q.5. Amuktamalyada book was written by?

Ans. The book was written by Krishnadeva Raya.

Q.6. What was the name of the suburban township near Vijayanagara which was built by krishnadeva raya?

Ans. Nagalapuram township near Vijayanagara was built by krishnadeva raya

Q.7. When was Odisha subdued by krishnadeva raya?

Ans. Odisha was subdued by krishnadeva raya in 1514

Q.8. Who is credited with building some fine temples and adding impressive gopurams to many important south Indian temples?

Ans. Krishnadeva Raya

Short Answer Type - I   [2 Marks]

Q.1. Who was the first Surveyor General of India?

Ans. Born in 1754, Colin Mackenzie became famous as an engineer, surveyor and cartographer. In 1815 he was appointed the first Surveyor General of India, a post he held till his death in 1821.

Q.2. Who founded Vijaynagara Empire?

Ans. According to tradition and epigraphic evidence two brothers, Harihara and Bukka, founded the Vijayanagara Empire in 1336.

Q.3. Who were the Yavana?

Ans. Yavana is a Sanskrit word used for the Greeks and other peoples who entered the subcontinent from the northwest.

Q.4. What was the meaning of amara-nayaka?

Ans. The amara-nayaka system was a major political innovation of the Vijayanagara Empire. It is likely that many features of this system were derived from the iqta system of the Delhi Sultanate. The amara-nayakas were military commanders who were given territories to govern by the raya.

Q.5. Define the word Amara?

Ans. Amara is believed to be derived from the Sanskrit word samara, meaning battle or war. It also resembles the Persian term amir, meaning a high noble.

Q.6. Who prepared the first survey map of Viayanagara Empire?

Ans. The ruins at Hampi were brought to light in 1800 by an engineer and antiquarian named Colonel Colin Mackenzie. An employee of the English East India Company, he prepared the first survey map of the site.

Short Answer Type - II [3 Marks]

Q.1. Who are the rivals of Vijayanagara empire in initial phase?

Ans. According to tradition and epigraphic evidence two brothers, Harihara and Bukka, founded the Vijayanagara Empire in 1336. On their northern frontier, the Vijayanagara kings competed with contemporary rulers - including the Sultans of the Deccan and the Gajapati rulers of Orissa - for control of the fertile river valleys and the resources generated by lucrative overseas trade.

Q.2. Who were the kudirai chettis?

Ans. As warfare during these times depended upon effective cavalry, the import of horses from Arabia and Central Asia was very important for rival kingdoms. This trade was initially controlled by Arab traders. Local communities of merchants known as kudirai chettis or horse merchants also participated in these exchanges.

Q.3. Which trades were flourish in Vijayanagara Empire?

Ans. Vijayanagara was noted for its markets dealing in spices, textiles and precious stones. Trade was often regarded as a status symbol for such cities, which boasted of a wealthy population that demanded high-value exotic goods, especially precious stones and jewellery.

Q.4. What was the result of battle at Rakshasi-Tangadi (also known as Talikota)?

Ans. In 1565 Rama Raya, the chief minister of Vijayanagara, led the army into battle at Rakshasi-Tangadi (also known as Talikota), where his forces were routed by the combined armies of Bijapur, Ahmadnagar and Golconda. The victorious armies sacked the city of Vijayanagara. The city was totally abandoned within a few years.

Q.5. Write sequence of different dynasties in Vijayanagara empire?

Ans. Within the polity, claimants to power included members of the ruling lineage as well as military commanders. The first dynasty, known as the Sangama dynasty, exercised control till 1485. They were supplanted by the Saluvas, military commanders, who remained in power till 1503 when they were replaced by the Tuluvas. By 1542 control at the centre had shifted to another ruling lineage, that of the Aravidu.

Long Answer Type [5 Marks]

Q.1. Give some detail about the discovery of Hampi?

Ans. The ruins at Hampi were brought to light in 1800 by an engineer and antiquarian named Colonel Colin Mackenzie. An employee of the English East India Company, he prepared the first survey map of the site. Much of the initial information he received was based on the memories of priests of the Virupaksha temple and the shrine of Pampadevi. Subsequently, from 1856, photographers began to record the monuments which enabled scholars to study them. As early as 1836 epigraphists began collecting several dozen inscriptions found at this and other temples at Hampi. In an effort to reconstruct the history of the city and the empire, historians collated information from these sources with accounts of foreign travellers and other literature written in Telugu, Kannada, Tamil and Sanskrit.

Q.2. Give a short note on the work of Krishnadeva raya?

Ans. Krishnadeva Raya belonged to the Tuluva dynasty. He ruled 1509-29, the most famous ruler of Vijayanagara, composed a work on statecraft in Telugu knownas the Amuktamalyada. His rule was characterised by expansion and consolidation. This was the time when the land between the Tungabhadra and Krishna rivers (the Raichur doab) was acquired (1512), the rulers of Orissa were subdued (1514) and severe defeats were inflicted on the Sultan of Bijapur (1520). Although the kingdom remained in a constant state of military preparedness, it flourished under conditions of unparalleled peace and prosperity. Krishnadeva Raya is credited with building some fine temples and adding impressive *gopurams* to many important south Indian temples. He also founded a suburban township near Vijayanagara called Nagalapuram after his mother. Some of the most detailed descriptions of Vijayanagara come from his time or just after.

Q.3. What were the reasons behind the falling of Viayanagara Empire?

Ans. Strain began to show within the imperial structure following Krishnadeva Raya's death in 1529. His successors were troubled by rebellious *nayakas* or military chiefs. By 1542 control at the centre had shifted to another ruling lineage, that of the Aravidu, which remained in power till the end of the seventeenth century. In 1565 Rama Raya, the chief minister of Vijayanagara, led the army into battle at Rakshasi-Tangadi (also known as Talikota), where his forces were routed by the combined armies of Bijapur, Ahmadnagar and Golconda. The victorious armies sacked the city of Vijayanagara. The city was totally abandoned within a few years. It was the adventurous policy of Rama Raya who tried to play off one Sultan against another that led the Sultans to combine together and decisively defeat him.

TOPIC 2

Architectural Expansion of Vijaynagara Empire

Summary

- Like most capitals, Vijayanagara, was characterized by a distinctive physical layout and building style.

- A large number of inscriptions of the kings of Vijayanagara and their nayakas recording donations to temples as well as describing important events have been recovered.

- The most striking feature about the location of Vijayanagara is the natural basin formed by the river Tungabhadra which flows in a north-easterly direction. The surrounding landscape is characterized by stunning granite hills that seem to form a girdle around the city.

- The most important such tank was built in the early years of the fifteenth century and is now called Kamalapuram tank. Water from this tank not only irrigated fields nearby but was also conducted through a channel to the "royal centre".

- What was most significant about this fortification is that it enclosed agricultural tracts. Abdur Razzaq noted that" between the first, second and the third walls there are cultivated fields, gardens and houses".

- The fort was entered through well-guarded gates, which linked the city to the major roads. Gateways were distinctive architectural features that often defined the structures to which they regulated access.

- Archaeologists have studied roads within the city and those leading out from it. These have been identified by tracing paths through gateways, as well as by finds of pavements. Roads generally wound around through the valleys, avoiding rocky terrain.

- The royal centre was located in the south-western part of the settlement. Although designated as a royal centre, it included over 60 temples. Clearly, the patronage of temples and cults was important for rulers who were trying to establish and legitimize their authority through association with the divinities housed in the shrines.

- The "king's palace" is the largest of the enclosures but has not yielded definitive evidence of being a royal residence. It has two of the most impressive platforms, usually called the "audience hall" and the "mahanavami dibba".

- Located on one of the highest points in the city, the "mahanavami dibba" is a massive platform rising from a base of about 11,000 sq. ft to a height of 40 ft.

- In terms of temple architecture, by this period certain new features were in evidence. These included structures of immense scale that must have been a mark of imperial authority, best exemplified by the raya gopurams or royal gateways.

- Other distinctive features include mandapas or pavilions and long, pillared corridors that often ran around the shrines within the temple complex. Let us look at two temples more closely - the Virupaksha temple and the Vitthala temple.

- Through the twentieth century, the site was preserved by the Archaeological Survey of India and the Karnataka Department of Archaeology and Museums. In 1976, Hampi was recognised as a site of national importance.

Multiple Choice Questions [1 Mark]

Q.1. The size of this city I do not write here, because it cannot all be seen from any one spot, but I climbed a hill whence I could see a great part of it; I could not see it all because it lies between several ranges of hills. Who gave this description for Vijayanagara Empire?

(a) Domingo Paes

(b) Abdur Razzaq

(c) Duarte Barbosa

(d) Afanasii Nikitin

Ans. (a)

Q.2. The most striking feature about the location of Vijayanagara is the natural basin formed by the river Tungabhadra. In which direction of Vijayanagara Empire this river flowing?

(a) North

(b) South

(c) North-west

(d) North-easterly

Ans. (d)

Q.3. In Vijaynagara Empire number of streams flow down to the river from rocky outcrops. In almost all cases embankments were built along these streams to create reservoirs of varying sizes. As this is one of the most ______ of the peninsula, elaborate arrangements had to be made to store rainwater and conduct it to the city. Fill in the blank?

(a) Arid zone   (b) Semi arid zone

(c) Fertile zone   (d) None of the above

Ans. (a)

Q.4. Abdur Razzaq, an ambassador sent by the ruler of Persia to Calicut (present-day Kozhikode), was greatly impressed by the fortifications, and mentioned lines of forts. How many lines of forts he mentioned?

(a) 6   (b) 8

(c) 9   (d) 7

Ans. (d)

Q.5. The arch on the gateway leading into the fortified settlement as well as the dome over the gate were regarded as typical features. These architecture was introduced by the __________.

(a) Afghan sultans

(b) Mangols

(c) Turkish sultans

(d) Arab merchants

Ans. (c)

Q.6. During the survey of Vijayanagara Empire archaeologists have found fine Chinese porcelain in some areas, including in the north-eastern corner of the urban core. It suggested the residents of?

(a) Rich traders

(b) Muslim traders

(c) Both (a) and (b)

(d) None of the above

Ans. (c)

Q.7. While most temples were located in the sacred centre, there were several in the royal centre as well. One of the most spectacular of these is one known as the Hazara Rama temple. This was probably meant to be used only by?

(a) Rich traders   (b) King and his family

(c) Herdsman   (d) Priests

Ans. (b)

Q.8. Traditions suggest that Pampadevi, the local mother goddess, did penance in these hills in order to marry Virupaksha, the guardian deity of the kingdom, also recognised as a form of ________?

(a) Shiva   (b) Vishnu

(c) Krishna   (d) Rama

Ans. (a)

Q.9. In terms of temple architecture, by this period certain new features were in evidence. These included structures of immense scale that must have been a mark of imperial authority, best exemplified by the raya gopurams. These gopurams are ______?

(a) Place of shrine   (b) Big halls

(c) Royal gateways   (d) None of the above

Ans. (c)

Q.10. Another shrine, the Vitthala temple, is also interesting. Here, the principal deity was Vitthala. He generally worshiped in Maharashtra. He is form of______?

(a) Shiva   (b) Vishnu

(c) Rama   (d) Krishna

Ans. (b)

Very Short Answer Type   [1 Mark]

Q.1. Abdur Razzaq, an ambassador sent by the ruler of Persia to Calicut (present-day Kozhikode). In which century he came to Vijaynagara Empire?

Ans. Abdur Razzaq came to Vijaynagara Empire in Fifteenth century

Q.2. For what second line of fortification was of Vijayanagara Empire?

Ans. Around the inner core of the urban complex.

Q.3. What was the dimension of "mahanavami dibba"?

Ans. The "mahanavami dibba" is a massive platform rising from a base of about 11,000 sq. ft to a height of 40 ft.

Q.4. Who named one of the palace as lotus temple?

Ans. British travellers

Q.5. Who was the local goddess of Vijayanagara Empire?

Ans. Pampadevi was the local goddess of Vijayanagara Empire

Q.6. In the Virupaksha temple the hall in front of the main shrine was built by?

Ans. It was built by Krishnadeva raya.

Q.7. Bahamani kingdom was established in?

Ans. It was established in 1347

Q.8. Establishment of the Gajapati kingdom of Orissa was in?

Ans. The Gajapati kingdom was established in 1435

Short Answer Type - I   [2 Marks]

Q.1. What was the importance of Hiriya canal in Vijayanagara Empire?

Ans. One of the most prominent waterworks to be seen among the ruins is the Hiriya canal. This canal drew water from a dam across the Tungabhadra and irrigated the cultivated valley that separated the "sacred centre" from the "urban core". This was apparently built by kings of the Sangama dynasty.

Q.2. What was the Domingo Paes's observation for fortification of walls of Vijayanagara Empire?

Ans. Domingo Paes observed: "From this first circuit until you enter the city there is a great distance, in which are fields in which they sow rice and have many gardens and much water, in which water comes from two lakes."

Q.3. How the sixteenth-century Portuguese traveller Barbosa described the houses of ordinary people, which have not survived?

Ans. This is how the sixteenth-century Portuguese traveller Barbosa described the houses of ordinary people, which have not survived: "The other houses of the people are thatched, but nonetheless well built and arranged according to occupations, in long streets with many open places."

Q.4. According to rituals what was the word mahanavami contained?

Ans. Rituals associated with the structure probably coincided with Mahanavami (literally, the great ninth day) of the ten-day Hindu festival during the autumn months of September and October, known variously as Dusehra (northern India), Durga Puja (in Bengal) and Navaratri or Mahanavami (in peninsular India). The Vijayanagara kings displayed their prestige, power and suzerainty on this occasion.

Q.5. When was the Virupaksha temple built?

Ans. The Virupaksha temple was built over centuries. While inscriptions suggest that the earliest shrine dated to the ninth-tenth centuries, it was substantially enlarged with the establishment of the Vijayanagara Empire.

Short Answer Type - II   [3 Marks]

Q.1. Give some detail about the Kamalapuram tank?

Ans. A number of streams flow down to the river from these rocky outcrops. In almost all cases embankments were built along these streams to create reservoirs of varying sizes. As this is one of the most arid zones of the peninsula, elaborate arrangements had to be made to store rainwater and conduct it to the city. The most important such tank was built in the early years of the fifteenth century and is now called Kamalapuram tank. Water from this tank not only irrigated fields nearby but was also conducted through a channel to the "royal centre".

Q.2. Why do you think agricultural tracts were incorporated within the fortified area?

Ans. The objective of medieval sieges was to starve the defenders into submission. These sieges could last for several months and sometimes even years. Normally rulers tried to be prepared for such situations by building large granaries within fortified areas. The rulers of Vijayanagara adopted a more expensive and elaborate strategy of protecting the agricultural belt itself.

Q.3. According to Archeologists how was the road structure of Vijayanagara Empire?

Ans. Archaeologists have studied roads within the city and those leading out from it. These have been identified by tracing paths through gateways, as well as by finds of pavements. Roads generally wound around through the valleys, avoiding rocky terrain. Some of the most important roads extended from temple gateways, and were lined by bazaars.

Q.4. Which things were indicate the residents of rich traders and Muslim traders in Vijayanagara Empire?

Ans. Archaeologists have found fine Chinese porcelain in some areas, including in the north-eastern corner of the urban core and suggest that these areas may have been occupied by rich traders. This was also the Muslim residential quarter. Tombs and mosques located here have distinctive functions, yet their architecture resembles that of the mandapas found in the temples of Hampi.

Q.5. Give some detail about the gopuram and mandapas?

Ans. In terms of temple architecture, by this period certain new features were in evidence. These included structures of immense scale that must have been a mark of imperial authority, best exemplified by the raya gopurams or royal gateways that often dwarfed the towers on the central shrines, and signalled the presence of the temple from a great distance. Other distinctive features include mandapas or pavilions and long, pillared corridors that often ran around the shrines within the temple complex. Let us look at two temples more closely - the Virupaksha temple and the Vitthala temple.

Long Answer Type [5 Marks]

Q.1. Give a short note on the water resources of the Vijaynagara Empire?

Ans. The most striking feature about the location of Vijayanagara is the natural basin formed by the river Tungabhadra which flows in a north-easterly direction. The surrounding landscape is characterized by stunning granite hills that seem to form a girdle around the city. A number of streams flow down to the river from these rocky outcrops. In almost all cases embankments were built along these streams to create reservoirs of varying sizes. As this is one of the most arid zones of the peninsula, elaborate arrangements had to be made to store rainwater and conduct it to the city. One of the most prominent waterworks to be seen among the ruins is the Hiriya canal. This canal drew water from a dam across the Tungabhadra and irrigated the cultivated valley that separated the "sacred centre" from the "urban core".

Q.2. Give a short note on the fortification of Vijayanagara Empire?

Ans. Abdur Razzaq, an ambassador sent by the ruler of Persia to Calicut (present-day Kozhikode) in the fifteenth century, was greatly impressed by the fortifications, and mentioned seven lines of forts. These encircled not only the city but also its agricultural hinterland and forests. The outermost wall linked the hills surrounding the city. The massive masonry construction was slightly tapered. No mortar or cementing agent was employed anywhere in the construction. The stone blocks were wedge shaped, which held them in place, and the inner portion of the walls was of earth packed with rubble. Square or rectangular bastions projected outwards.

Q.3. Give a short note on the "mahanavami dibba"?

Ans. Some of the more distinctive structures in the area have been assigned names based on the form of the buildings as well as their functions. The "king's palace" is the largest of the enclosures but has not yielded definitive evidence of being a royal residence. It has two of the most impressive platforms, usually called the "audience hall" and the "mahanavami dibba". The entire complex is surrounded by high double walls with a street running between them. The audience hall is a high platform with slots for wooden pillars at close and regular intervals. It had a staircase going up to the second floor, which rested on these pillars. The pillars being closely spaced, would have left little free space and thus it is not clear what the hall was used for. Located on one of the highest points in the city, the "mahanavami dibba" is a massive platform rising from a base of about 11,000 sq. ft to a height of 40 ft. There is evidence that it supported a wooden structure. The base of the platform is covered with relief carvings.

Q.4. What was the importance of God Virupaksha for the Vijayanagara kingdom?

Ans. According to local tradition, these rocky northern hills sheltered the monkey kingdom of Vali and Sugriva mentioned in the Ramayana. Other traditions suggest that Pampadevi, the local mother goddess, did penance in these hills in order to marry Virupaksha, the guardian deity of the kingdom, also recognised as a form of Shiva. To this day this marriage is celebrated annually in the Virupaksha temple. In fact the Vijayanagara kings claimed to rule on behalf of the god Virupaksha. All royal orders were signed "Shri Virupaksha", usually in the Kannada script. Rulers also indicated their close links with the gods by using the title "Hindu Suratrana". This was a Sanskritisation of the Arabic term Sultan, meaning king, so it literally meant Hindu Sultan.

Chapter Practice

Multiple Choice Questions   [1 Mark]

Q.1. After the death of Krishnadeva Raya the control at the centre had shifted to which of the following rulers?

(a) Aravidu
(b) Rama Raya
(c) *Amara-nayakas*
(d) *Raya*

Q.2. Raichur doab is between which of the following rivers?

(a) Tungabhadra and Krishna rivers

(b) Krishna rivers and Godavari rivers

(c) Tungabhadra and Cauvery rivers

(d) Krishna and Cauvery rivers

Q.3. Military chiefs were known as

(a) *nayakas*
(b) *rayas*
(c) *amara-nayakas*
(d) None of the above

Q.4. Which of the following temples was probably meant to be used only by the king and his family in Vijayanagara?   **[CBSE 2020]**

(a) Lotus temple

(b) Vitthala temple

(c) Virupaksha temple

(d) Hazara Ram temple

Very Short Answer Type   [1 Mark]

Q.5. Who founded Nagalapuram?

Q.6. Who founded the Vijayanagara empire

Short Answer Type - I   [2 Marks]

Q.7. How was the water of the Hiriya canal used in the Vijayanagara Empire?

Q.8. Examine the significance of enclosing agricultural land within the fortified area of the city of Vijaynagar.   **[CBSE 2018]**

Short Answer Type - II   [3 Marks]

Q.9. Which dynasty did Krishnadeva Raya belong to ? Mention any one of his expansion and consolidation policies.   [CBSE 2015]

Q.10. Highlight the contribution of Krishnadeva Raya in the expansion of Vijaynagar Empire.   [CBSE 2014]

Q.11. Why were the water resources of the Vijaynagar Empire developed ? Give reasons.   [CBSE 2015]

Long Answer Type   [5 Marks]

Q.12. Explain why Abdur Razzak, a Persian Ambassador, was greatly impressed by the fortification of Vijaynagar Empire during the, 15th century.   [CBSE 2017]

Q.13. Analyse the rituals associated with Mahanavami Dibba at the Royal Centre in Vijayanagara.

[CBSE 2019]

Q.14. Analyse the main features of Amara-Nayaka System which was introduced in Vijanayagara Empire

[CBSE 2019]

Peasants, Zamindars and the State

Peasants and their Societies

Summary

- The basic unit of agricultural society was the village, inhabited by peasants who performed the manifold seasonal tasks that made up agricultural production throughout the year - tilling the soil, sowing seeds, harvesting the crop when it was ripe.

- One of the most important chronicles was the Ain-i Akbari authored by Akbar's court historian Abu'l Fazl. This text meticulously recorded the arrangements made by the state to ensure cultivation, to enable the collection of revenue by the agencies of the state and to regulate the relationship between the state and rural magnates, the zamindars.

- The term which Indo-Persian sources of the Mughal period most frequently used to denote a peasant was raiyat (plural, riaya) or muzarian. In addition, we also encounter the terms kisan or asami.

- Seldom did the average peasant of north India possess more than a pair of bullocks and two ploughs; most possessed even less.

- Monsoons remained the backbone of Indian agriculture, as they are even today. But there were crops which required additional water. Artificial systems of irrigation had to be devised for this.

- Irrigation projects received state support as well. For example, in northern India the state undertook digging of new canals (nahr, nala) and also repaired old ones like the shahnahr in the Punjab during Shah Jahan's reign.

- During the seventeenth century several new crops from different parts of the world reached the Indian subcontinent.

- There were three constituents of peasants community - the cultivators, the panchayat, and the village headman (muqaddam or mandal).

- Despite the abundance of cultivable land, certain caste groups were assigned menial tasks and thus relegated to poverty.

- There was a direct correlation between caste, poverty and social status at the lower strata of society.

- The village panchayat was an assembly of elders, usually important people of the village with hereditary rights over their property. In mixed-caste villages, the panchayat was usually a heterogeneous body.

- The panchayat was headed by a headman known as muqaddam or mandal. Some sources suggest that the headman was chosen through the consensus of the village elders, and that this choice had to be ratified by the zamindar.

- Village artisans - potters, blacksmiths, carpenters, barbers, even goldsmiths - provided specialized services in return for which they were compensated by villagers by a variety of means.

- Women were considered an important resource in agrarian society also because they were child bearers in a society dependent on labour.

- Amongst the landed gentry, women had the right to inherit property. Instances from the Punjab show that women, including widows, actively participated in the rural land market as sellers of property inherited by them.

- Apart from the intensively cultivated provinces in northern and north-western India, huge swathes of forests - dense forest (jangal) or scrubland (kharbandi) - existed all over eastern India, central India, northern India (including the Terai on the Indo-Nepal border), Jharkhand, and in peninsular India down the Western Ghats and the Deccan plateau.

- The spread of commercial agriculture was an important external factor that impinged on the lives of those who lived in the forests. Forest products - like honey, beeswax and gum lac - were in great demand.

Multiple Choice Questions   [1 Mark]

Q.1. The non-resident cultivators who belonged to some other village, but cultivated lands elsewhere on a contractual basis, they were known as?

(a) pahi-kashta.   (b) khud-kashta.

(c) Sahi-kashta   (d) None of the above

Ans. (a)

Q.2. We often come across the term jins-i kamil (literally, perfect crops) in our sources. Choose the correct option of crop which comes under this-

(a) Rice   (b) Wheat

(c) Potato   (d) Cotton

Ans. (d)

Q.3. The village panchayat was an assembly of elders, usually important people of the village with hereditary rights over their property. In mixed-caste villages, the panchayat was usually a heterogeneous body. What was the different functions panchayat do-

(a) Managed funds

(b) Ensure caste boundaries

(c) Levy fines and punishments

(d) All of the above

Ans. (d)

Q.4. During the seventeenth century several new crops from different parts of the world reached the Indian subcontinent. Vegetables like tomatoes, potatoes and chillies were introduced from the-

(a) Continental world (b) New world

(c) Middle world   (d) Old world

Ans. (b)

Q.5. Our major source for the agrarian history of the sixteenth and early seventeenth centuries are chronicles and documents from the Mughal court. One of the most important chronicles was the Ain-i Akbari. Who was the author of Ain- I-Akbari?

(a) Abdur Razaqq   (b) Ibn Battuta

(c) Abul Fazal   (d) Al-Biruni

Ans. (c)

Q.6. Tobacco, which arrived first in the Deccan, spread to northern India in the early years of the seventeenth century. The Ain does not mention tobacco in the lists of crops in northern India. Which ruler banned this crop?

(a) Akbar   (b) Janhagir

(c) Babur   (d) Aurangjeb

Ans. (b)

Q.7. Deep inequities on the basis of caste and other caste like distinctions meant that the cultivators were a highly heterogeneous group. Which of the following Muslim community was considered menial?

(a) Jangli   (b) Majur

(c) Halalkhoran   (d) Mandal

Ans. (c)

Q.8. Documents from which part of India found that petitions sent by women to the village panchayat, seeking redress and justice?

(a) Eastern India   (b) Western India

(c) Northern India   (d) Southern India

Ans. (b)

Q.9. Being jangli, however, did not mean an absence of "civilisation", as popular usage of the term today seems to connote. Rather, the term described those whose livelihood came from?

(a) Forest produce

(b) Hunting

(c) Shifting agriculture

(d) All of the above.

Ans. (d)

Very Short Answer Type   [1 Mark]

Q.1. During the sixteenth and seventeenth centuries about what per cent of the population of India lived in its villages?

Ans. 85 per cent of the population of India lived in its villages

Q.2. Where were from the crop Maize (makka) was introduced in India?

Ans. It was introduced from Africa and spain.

Q.3. Who were the generally head of grihasthi?

Ans. Male were the generally head of grihasthi

Q.4. Who was the court historian of Akbar?

Ans. Abul Fazal was the court historian of Akbar

Q.5. Ahom kingdom belongs to?

Ans. Ahom kingdom belongs Assam

Q.6. How many daftars of Ain?

Ans. There were three daftars of Ain

Q.7. During the Mughal Empire, what was Jins-i-kamil?

Ans. Jins-i-kamil was Perfect crop.

Q.8. During Mughal time kharbandi term denoted?

Ans. It denoted Scrubland

Short Answer Type - I   [2 Marks]

Q.1. What are our major source for the agrarian history of the sixteenth and early seventeenth centuries?

Ans. Our major source for the agrarian history of the sixteenth and early seventeenth centuries are chronicles and documents from the Mughal court One of the most important chronicles was the Ain-i Akbari authored by Akbar's court historian Abu'l Fazl.

Q.2. For whom the term khud-kashta was used in sixteen century?

Ans. Sources of the seventeenth century refer to two kinds of peasants - khud-kashta and pahi-kashta. The former were residents of the village in which they held their lands.

Q.3. What were the factors that accounted for the constant expansion of agriculture?

Ans. The abundance of land, available labour and the mobility of peasants were three factors that accounted for the constant expansion of agriculture.

Q.4. What is the meaning of do-fasla?

Ans. Agriculture was organised around two major seasonal cycles, the kharif (autumn) and the rabi (spring). This would mean that most regions, except those terrains that were the most arid or inhospitable, produced a minimum of two crops a year which is known as do-fasla.

Q.5. Who are the Patwaris?

Ans. The chief function of the headman was to supervise the preparation of village accounts, assisted by the accountant or patwari of the panchayat.

Q.6. Define the term muzarian?

Ans. The term which Indo-Persian sources of the Mughal period most frequently used to denote a peasant was raiyat (plural, riaya) or muzarian.

Q.7. Define word pargana?

Ans. Pargana was an administrative subdivision of a Mughal province.

Short Answer Type - II [3 Marks]

Q.1. What were the average peasant possessions of Gujarat and Bengal farmers in the sixteen and seventeen centuries?

Ans. Seldom did the average peasant of north India possess more than a pair of bullocks and two ploughs; most possessed even less. In Gujarat peasants possessing about six acres of land were considered to be affluent; in Bengal, on the other hand, five acres was the upper limit of an average peasant farm; 10 acres would make one a rich asami.

Q.2. Who are the muqaddam or mandal?

Ans. The panchayat was headed by a headman known as muqaddam or mandal. Some sources suggest that the headman was chosen through the consensus of the village elders, and that this choice had to be ratified by the zamindar. Headmen held office as long as they enjoyed the confidence of the village elders, failing which they could be dismissed by them.

Q.3. How were Mandals misused their positions?

Ans. The mandals often misused their positions. They were principally accused of defrauding village accounts in connivance with the patwari, and for underassessing the revenue they owed from their own lands in order to pass the additional burden on to the smaller cultivator.

Q.4. What are the jati panchayat? And what they work?

Ans. In addition to the village panchayat each caste or jati in the village had its own jati panchayat. These panchayats wielded considerable power in rural society. In Rajasthan jati panchayats arbitrated civil disputes between members of different castes. They mediated in contested claims on land, decided whether marriages were performed according to the norms laid down by a particular caste group, determined who had

ritual precedence in village functions, and so on. In most cases, except in matters of criminal justice, the state respected the decisions of jati panchayats.

Q.5. Who were the shroff?

Ans. The seventeenth-century French traveller Jean-Baptiste Tavernier found it remarkable that in "India a village must be very small indeed if it has not a moneychanger called a Shroff. (They) act as bankers to make remittances of money (and who) enhance the rupee as they please for paisa and the paisa for these (cowrie) shells".

Long Answer Type [5 Marks]

Q.1. Give a short note on irrigation and technology of agriculture during seventeen century?

Ans. Since the primary purpose of agriculture is to feed people, basic staples such as rice, wheat or millet were the most frequently cultivated crops. Areas which received 40 inches or more of rainfall a year were generally rice-producing zones, followed by wheat and millets, corresponding to a descending scale of precipitation. Monsoons remained the backbone of Indian agriculture, as they are even today. But there were crops which required additional water. Artificial systems of irrigation had to be devised for this. Irrigation projects received state support as well. For example, in northern India the state undertook digging of new canals (nahr, nala) and also repaired old ones like the shahnahr in the Punjab during Shah Jahan's reign. Though agriculture was labour intensive, peasants did use technologies that often harnessed cattle energy.

Q.2. Give a short note on the term jins-I kamil?

Ans. However, the focus on the cultivation of basic staples did not mean that agriculture in medieval India was only for subsistence. We often come across the term jins-i kamil (literally, perfect crops) in our sources. The Mughal state also encouraged peasants to cultivate such crops as they brought in more revenue. Crops such as cotton and sugarcane were jins-i kamil par excellence. Cotton was grown over a great swathe of territory spread over central India and the Deccan plateau, whereas Bengal was famous for its sugar. Such cash crops would also include various sorts of oilseeds (for example, mustard) and lentils. This shows how subsistence and commercial production were closely intertwined in an average peasant's holding.

Q.3. How were the panchayats managed their funds?

Ans. The panchayat was headed by a headman known as muqaddam or mandal. Some sources suggest that the headman was chosen through the consensus of the village elders, and that this choice had to be ratified by the zamindar. The chief function of the headman was to supervise the preparation of village accounts, assisted by the accountant or patwari of the panchayat. The panchayat derived its funds from contributions made by individuals to a common financial pool. These funds were used for defraying the costs of entertaining revenue officials who visited the village from time to time. Expenses for community welfare activities such as tiding over natural calamities (like floods), were also met

from these funds. Often these funds were also deployed in construction of a bund or digging a canal which peasants usually could not afford to do on their own.

Q.4. What ere the conditions of women during sixteen- seventeen century?

Ans. As you may have observed in many different societies, the production process often involves men and women performing certain specified roles. Nonetheless biases related to women's biological functions did continue. Menstruating women, for instance, were not allowed to touch the plough or the potter's wheel in western India, or enter the groves where betel-leaves (paan) were grown in Bengal. Artisanal tasks such as spinning yarn, sifting and kneading clay for pottery, and embroidery were among the many aspects of production dependent on female labour. The more commercialised the product, the greater the demand on women's labour to produce it. In fact, peasant and artisan women worked not only in the fields, but even went to the houses of their employers or to the markets if necessary.

TOPIC 2

Zamindars and their Zamindari Systems

Summary

- Our story of agrarian relations in Mughal India will not be complete without referring to a class of people in the countryside that lived off agriculture but did not participate directly in the processes of agricultural production.

- Caste was one factor that accounted for the elevated status of zamindars; another factor was that they performed certain services (khidmat) for the state.

- The zamindars held extensive personal lands termed milkiyat, meaning property.

- Zamindars spearheaded the colonisation of agricultural land, and helped in settling cultivators

by providing them with the means of cultivation, including cash loans. The buying and selling of zamindaris accelerated the process of monetization in the countryside.

- Revenue from the land was the economic mainstay of the Mughal Empire.

- This apparatus included the office (daftar) of the diwan who was responsible for supervising the fiscal system of the empire. Thus revenue officials and record keepers penetrated the agricultural domain and became a decisive agent in shaping agrarian relations.

- The land revenue arrangements consisted of two stages - first, assessment and then actual collection. The jama was the amount assessed, as opposed to hasil, the amount collected.

- Amin was an official responsible for ensuring that imperial regulations were carried out in the provinces.

- The Mughal Empire was among the large territorial empires in Asia that had managed to consolidate power and resources during the sixteenth and seventeenth centuries. These empires were the Ming (China), Safavid (Iran) and Ottoman (Turkey).

- The Ain-i Akbari was the culmination of a large historical, administrative project of classification undertaken by Abu'l Fazl at the order of Emperor Akbar. It was completed in 1598, the forty-second regnal year of the emperor, after having gone through five revisions.

- The Ain-i Akbari, the third book, was organised as a compendium of imperial regulations and a gazetteer of the empire.

- The Ain is made up of five books (daftars), of which the first three books describe the administration.

- Although the Ain was officially sponsored to record detailed information to facilitate Emperor Akbar govern his empire, it was much more than a reproduction of official papers.

- Another limitation of the Ain is the somewhat skewed nature of the quantitative data. Data were not collected uniformly from all provinces.

- These limitations notwithstanding, the Ain remains an extraordinary document of its times.

Multiple Choice Questions   [1 Mark]

Q.1. Our story of agrarian relations in Mughal India will not be complete without referring to a class of people in the countryside that lived off agriculture but did not participate directly in the processes of agricultural production. These were ______?

(a) Jangali   (b) Peshkash

(c) Mandal   (d) zamindars

Ans. (d)

Q.2. These were the zamindars who were landed proprietors who also enjoyed certain social and economic privileges by virtue of their superior status in rural society. The zamindars held extensive Milkiyat. Milkiyat was stand for?

(a) Army   (b) Land

(c) Cash   (d) chariot

Ans. (b)

Q.3. Thus revenue officials and record keepers penetrated the agricultural domain and became a decisive agent in shaping agrarian relations. Which office was responsible for supervising the fiscal system of the empire?

(a) Zamindar's office   (b) Office of Diwan

(c) Office of Munim   (d) None of the above

Ans. (b)

Q.4. The Emperor Akbar in his profound sagacity classified the lands and fixed different revenue to be paid by each. Land that has lain fallow for three or four years was?

(a) Chachar   (b) Polaj

(c) Parauti   (d) Banjar

Ans. (a)

Q.5. The Mughal Empire was among the large territorial empires in Asia that had managed to consolidate power and resources during the sixteenth and seventeenth centuries. These empires were the Ming, Safavid and Ottoman. The Ming Empire related to-

(a) China   (b) Magnolia

(c) Turkey   (d) Iran

Ans. (a)

Q.6. The period between the sixteenth and eighteenth centuries was also marked by a remarkable stability in the availability of metal currency, particularly the rupya in India. This rupya was made up of which metal?

(a) Gold   (b) Copper

(c) Silver   (d) Lead

Ans. (c)

Q.7. The Ain-i Akbari was the culmination of a large historical, administrative project of classification undertaken by Abu'l Fazl at the order of Emperor Akbar. In which part imperial regulations and a gazetteer of the empire were given?

(a) First   (b) Second

(c) Third   (d) Fourth

Ans. (c)

Q.8. The Ain is made up of five books (daftars), of which the first three books describe the administration. In these three books which book describes administration?

(a) Mulk-abadi   (b) Manjil-abadi

(c) Sipah-abadi   (d) None of the above

Ans. (b)

Very Short Answer Type   [1 Mark]

Q.1. What was khidmat in Mughal period?

Ans. Zamindars perform certain services to state

Q.2. During Mughal period what was the imperial order called?

Ans. Imperial order was called Sanad

Q.3. Zamindars have miliyat and qilachas. Qilachas word used for?

Ans. It was used for Fortress.

Q.4. During Mughal period amil-guzar word is used for?

Ans. Amil-guzar were Revenue collector.

Q.5. Which type of land was called banjar during Akbar time?

Ans. Land uncultivated for five years and more.

Q.6. Define meaning of Kankut?

Ans. In the Hindi language kan signifies grain, and kut, estimates.

Q.7. Safavid Empire was related to which country?

Ans. Safavid Empire was related to Iran

Q.8. When was Ain-I-Akbari completed?

Ans. Ain-I-Akbari was completed in 1598

Q.9. The term which was used during Mughal period for foot-solider was?

Ans. Piyada was used during Mughal period for foot-solider

Short Answer Type - I   [2 Marks]

Q.1. Define the milkiyat?

Ans. The zamindars held extensive personal lands termed milkiyat, meaning property. Milkiyat lands were cultivated for the private use of zamindars, often with the help of hired or servile labour. The zamindars could sell, bequeath or mortgage these lands at will.

Q.2. Who were the Amin?

Ans. Amin was an official responsible for ensuring that imperial regulations were carried out in the provinces.

Q.3. In which mode Mansabdars were paid?

Ans. Some mansabdars were paid in cash (naqdi), while the majority of them were paid through assignments of revenue (jagirs) in different regions of the empire.

Q.4. What was written in Sipah-abadi book of Ain?

Ans. Sipah-abadi, covers the military and civil administration and the establishment of servants. This book includes notices and short biographical sketches of imperial officials (mansabdars), learned men, poets and artists.

Q.5. Define the word Peshkash?

Ans. Peshkash was a form of tribute collected by the Mughal state.

Short Answer Type - II   [3 Marks]

Q.1. What were Jama and Hasil?

Ans. The Mughal state tried to first acquire specific information about the extent of the agricultural lands in the empire and what these lands produced before fixing the burden of taxes on people. The land revenue arrangements consisted of two stages - first, assessment and then actual collection. The jama was the amount assessed, as opposed to hasil, the amount collected.

Q.2. Define Mansabdari system?

Ans. The Mughal administrative system had at its apex a military cum- bureaucratic apparatus (mansabdari) which was responsible for looking after the civil and military affairs of the state. Some mansabdars were paid in cash (naqdi), while the majority of them were paid through assignments of revenue (jagirs) in different regions of the empire. They were transferred periodically.

Q.3. Give a short detail about Ain-I-Akbari? (CBSE 2018)

Ans. The Ain-i Akbari was the culmination of a large historical, administrative project of classification undertaken by Abu'l Fazl at the order of Emperor Akbar. It was completed in 1598, the forty-second regnal year of the emperor, after having gone through five revisions. The Ain was part of a larger project of history writing commissioned by Akbar. This history, known as the Akbar Nama, comprised three books. The first two provided a historical narrative. The Ain-i Akbari,the third book, was organised as a compendium of imperial regulations and a gazetteer of the empire.

Q.4. Which type of information we can get from Ain?

Ans. The Ain gives detailed accounts of the organization of the court, administration and army, the sources of revenue and the physical layout of the provinces of Akbar's empire and the literary, cultural and religious traditions of the people. Along with a description of the various departments of Akbar's government and elaborate descriptions of the various provinces (subas) of the empire, the Ain gives us intricate quantitative information of those provinces.

Long Answer Type   [5 Marks]

Q.1. Who were the Zamindars during Mughal period and from where they got power?

Ans. Our story of agrarian relations in Mughal India will not be complete without referring to a class of people in the countryside that lived off agriculture but did not participate directly in the processes of agricultural production. These were the zamindars who were landed proprietors who also enjoyed certain social and economic privileges by virtue of their superior status in rural society. Milkiyat lands were cultivated for the private use of zamindars, often with the help of hired or servile labour. The zamindars could sell, bequeath or mortgage these lands at will. Zamindars also derived their power from the fact that they could often collect revenue on behalf of the state, a service for which they were compensated financially. Control over military resources was another source of power. Most zamindars had fortresses (qilachas) as well as an armed contingent comprising unit of cavalry, artillery and infantry.

Q.2. What was the classification of land during Akbar?

Ans. The Emperor Akbar in his profound sagacity classified the lands and fixed a different revenue to be paid by each. Polaj is land which is annually cultivated for each crop in succession and is never allowed to lie fallow. Parauti is land left out of cultivation for a time that it may recover its strength. Chachar is land that has lain fallow for three or four years. Banjar is land uncultivated for five years and more. Of the first two kinds of land, there are three classes, good, middling, and bad. They add together the produce of each sort, and the third of this represents the medium produce, one-third part of which is exacted as the Royal dues.

Q.3. What is the difference between the Kankut, Batai and Khet-Batai?

Ans. First, kankut : in the Hindi language kan signifies grain, and kut, estimates … If any doubts arise, the crops should be cut and estimated in three lots, the good, the middling, and the inferior, and the hesitation removed. Often, too, the land taken by appraisement, gives a sufficiently accurate return. Secondly, batai, also called bhaoli, the crops are reaped and stacked and divided by agreement in the presence of the parties. But in this case several intelligent inspectors are required; otherwise, the evil-minded and false are given to deception. Thirdly, khet-batai, when they divide the fields after they are sown. Fourthly, lang batai , after cutting the grain, they form it in heaps and divide it among themselves, and each takes his share home and turns it to profit.

Q.4. Give a short note on the flow of silver during Mughal period?

Ans. The Mughal Empire was among the large territorial empires in Asia that had managed to consolidate power and resources during the sixteenth and seventeenth centuries. Voyages of discovery and the opening up of the New World resulted in a massive expansion of Asia's (particularly India's) trade with Europe. This resulted in a greater geographical diversity of India's overseas trade as well as an expansion in the commodity composition of this trade. An expanding trade brought in huge amounts of silver bullion into Asia to pay for goods procured from India, and a large part of that bullion gravitated towards India. This was good for India as it did not have natural resources of silver. As a result, the period between the sixteenth and eighteenth centuries was also marked by a remarkable stability in the availability of metal currency, particularly the silver rupya in India.

Chapter Practice

Multiple Choice Questions   [1 Mark]

Q.1. Find the correct statement

(a) *Pargana* was an administrative division of a Mughal province.

(b) *Peshkash* was a form of tribute collected by the Zamindars

(c) Both (a) and (b)

(d) None of the above

Q.2. The *Ain* is made up of five books , which of the following is not the part of those five books

(a) zamin-i paimuda   (b) suyurghamanzil-abadi

(c) manzil-abadi   (d) sipah-abadi

Q.3. In the Mughal state, the role of amil-guzar was to

(a) Measure cultivated and cultivable lands   (b) collect revenue

(c) to do administrative service   (d) None of the above

Very Short Answer Type   [1 Mark]

Q.4. Who were the halalkhoran?

Q.5. Milkiyat lands were used for?

Short Answer Type - I   [2 Marks]

Q.6. Why is Al-Biruni is text "Kitab-ul-Hind" considered as a voluminous text ?   [CBSE 2019]

Q.7. Who were khud-kashta and pahi-kashta?

Short Answer Type - II   [3 Marks]

Q.8. State any two features of Akbar Nama.   [CBSE 2019]

Q.9. State the role of Jati Panchayats in the Mughal agrarian society.   [CBSE 2020]

Long Answer Type   [5 Marks]

Q.10. Explain how the chronicle 'Ain-i-Akbari' is the major source to understand agararian history of sixteenth and seventeenth centuries.   [CBSE 2018]

CHAPTER 9

Kings and Chronicles

The Mughals and the Production of Chronicles

Summary

- The name Mughal derives from Mongol. Though today the term evokes the grandeur of an empire, it was not the name the rulers of the dynasty chose for themselves. They referred to themselves as Timurids.

- During the sixteenth century, Europeans used the term Mughal to describe the Indian rulers of this branch of the family.

- The founder of the empire, Zahiruddin Babur, was driven from his Central Asian homeland, Farghana, by the warring Uzbeks. He first established himself at Kabul and then in 1526 pushed further into the Indian subcontinent in search of territories and resources to satisfy the needs of the members of his clan.

- Many consider Jalaluddin Akbar (1556-1605) the greatest of all the Mughal emperors, for he not only expanded but also consolidated his empire, making it the largest, strongest and richest kingdom of his time.

- Akbar succeeded in extending the frontiers of the empire to the Hindukush mountains, and checked the expansionist designs of the Uzbeks of Turan (Central Asia) and the Safavids of Iran. Akbar had three fairly able successors in Jahangir (1605-27), Shah Jahan (1628-58) and Aurangzeb (1658-1707), much as their characters varied.

- Chronicles commissioned by the Mughal emperors are an important source for studying the empire and its court. They were written in order to project a vision of an enlightened kingdom to all those who came under its umbrella.

- Mughal court chronicles were written in Persian. Under the Sultans of Delhi it flourished as a language of the court and of literary writings, alongside north Indian languages, especially Hindavi and its regional variants.

- It was Akbar who consciously set out to make Persian the leading language of the Mughal court.

- All books in Mughal India were manuscripts, that is, they were handwritten. The centre of manuscript production was the imperial kitabkhana.

- Calligraphy, the art of handwriting, was considered a skill of great importance. It was practised using different styles. Akbar's favourite was the nastaliq, a fluid style with long horizontal strokes.

- Paintings served not only to enhance the beauty of a book, but were believed to possess special powers of communicating ideas about the kingdom and the power of kings in ways that the written medium could not.

- The production of paintings portraying the emperor, his court and the people who were part of it, was a source of constant tension between rulers and representatives of the Muslim orthodoxy, the ulama.

- Artists from Iran also made their way to Mughal India. Some were brought to the Mughal court, as in the case of Mir Sayyid Ali and Abdus Samad, who were made to accompany Emperor Humayun to Delhi.

- Beginning in 1589, Abu'lFazl worked on the Akbar Nama for thirteen years, repeatedly revising the draft. The chronicle is based on a range of sources, including actual records of events (waqai), official documents and oral testimonies of knowledgeable persons.

- Court chroniclers drew upon many sources to show that the power of the Mughal kings came directly from God.

- Mughal chronicles present the empire as comprising many different ethnic and religious communities – Hindus, Jainas, Zoroastrians and Muslims.

- Abu'lFazl defined sovereignty as a social contract: the emperor protects the four essences of his subjects, namely, life (jan), property (mal), honour (namus) and faith (din), and in return demands obedience and a share of resources.

Multiple Choice Questions [1 Mark]

Q.1. The name Mughal derives from Mongol. Though today the term evokes the grandeur of an empire, it was not the name the rulers of the dynasty chose for themselves. They referred to themselves as?

(a) Timurids   (b) Mongol

(c) Afghani   (d) Badshah

Ans. (a)

Q.2. During the sixteenth century, Europeans used the term Mughal to describe the Indian rulers of this branch of the family. Babur, the first Mughal ruler, was related to?

(a) Timur

(b) Ghenghiz Khan

(c) Both (a) and (b)

(d) None of the above

Ans. (c)

Q.3. As the Mughals were Chaghtai Turks by origin, Turkish was their mother tongue. Who consciously set out to make Persian the leading language of the Mughal court?

(a) Humayun

(b) Babur

(c) Akbar

(d) Janhagir

Ans. (c)

Q.4. All books in Mughal India were manuscripts, that is, they were hand written. Nastaliq word is related to manuscripts, what was this?

(a) A type of paper

(b) A type of pen

(c) A type of calligraphy style

(d) A type of colour

Ans. (c)

Q.5. Artists from Iran also made their way to Mughal India. Some were brought to the Mughal court, as in the case of Mir Sayyid Ali and Abdus Samad, who were made to accompany Emperor ______ to Delhi. Choose the correct option?

(a) Akbar

(b) Humayun

(c) Janhagir

(d) Shahjahan

Ans. (b)

Q.6. Among the important illustrated Mughal chronicles the Akbar Nama and Badshah Nama (The Chronicle of a King) are the most well known. Who had written Badshah Nama?

(a) Nizamuddin Ahmad

(b) Abu'l Fazl

(c) Abdul Hamid Lahori

(d) Abbas Khan Sarwani

Ans. (c)

Q.7. During the colonial period, British administrators began to study Indian history and to create an archive of knowledge about the subcontinent to help them better understand the people and the cultures of the empire they sought to rule. Who founded the Asiatic Society of Bengal?

(a) Sir William Jones

(b) Henry Thomas

(c) Colebrooke

(d) None of the above

Ans. (a)

Q.8. Court chroniclers drew upon many sources to show that the power of the Mughal kings came directly from God. Who first developed this idea?

(a) Abu'l Fazl

(b) Al Biruni

(c) Abbas khan Sarwani

(d) Shihabuddin Surawadi

Ans. (d)

Very Short Answer Type   [1 Mark]

Q.1. The name Mughal derives from?

Ans. Mongols

Q.2. Which Mughal ruler, was related to Ghenghiz Khan from his mother's side?

Ans. Babur was related to Ghenghiz Khan from his mother's side

Q.3. The name Mowgli, the young hero of Rudyard Kipling's Jungle Book, is derived from?

Ans. Mughal

Q.4. Where was the birth place of the founder of the Mughal empire, Zahiruddin Babur?

Ans. Farghana

Q.5. In which year Humayun defeated the Surs?

Ans. Humayun defeated the Sursin 1555

Q.6. Who was the successor of king Janhagir?

Ans. Shah Jahan was the successor of king Janhagir

Q.7. Mughal chronicles such as the Akbar Nama were written in which language?

Ans. Akbar Nama were written in Persian.

Q.8. In Persian language Mahabharta book was known as?

Ans. In Persian language Mahabharta book was known as Razmnama

Q.9. How many volumes of Badshah Nama?

Ans. There were three volumes of Badshah Nama

Short Answer Type - I   [2 Marks]

Q.1. Who were Chaghtai Turks?

Ans. Chaghtai Turks traced descent from the eldest son of Ghengiz Khan. Mughals were Chaghtai Turks by origin.

Q.2. What was Kitabkhana during Mughal time?

Ans. All books in Mughal India were manuscripts, that is, they were handwritten. The centre of manuscript production was the imperial kitabkhana. Although kitabkhana can be translated as library, it was a scriptorium, that is, a place where the emperor's collection of manuscripts was kept and new manuscripts were produced.

Q.3. Which part of Akbar Nama is Aine-I-Akbari?

Ans. The Akbar Nama is divided into three books of which the first two are chronicles. The third book is the Ain-i Akbari.

Q.4. Who had completed the third volume of Badshah Nama?

Ans. Lahori wrote the first and second daftars comprising the first two decades of the emperor's rule (1627-47); these volumes were later revised by Sadullah Khan, Shah Jahan's wazir.

Q.5. Who translated Akbar Nama into English?

Ans. Edited versions of the Akbar Nama and Badshah Nama were first published by the Asiatic Society in the nineteenth century. In the early twentieth century the Akbar Nama was translated into English by Henry Beveridge after years of hard labour.

Short Answer Type - II — [3 Marks]

Q.1. How was the Urdu language evolve during seventeen century?

Ans. Even when Persian was not directly used, its vocabulary and idiom heavily influenced the language of official records in Rajasthani and Marathi and even Tamil. Since the people using Persian in the sixteenth and seventeenth centuries came from many different regions of the subcontinent and spoke other Indian languages, Persian too became Indianised by absorbing local idioms. A new language, Urdu, sprang from the interaction of Persian with Hindavi.

Q.2. What was the importance of painting?

Ans. Paintings served not only to enhance the beauty of a book, but were believed to possess special powers of communicating ideas about the kingdom and the power of kings in ways that the written medium could not. The historian Abu'l Fazl described painting as a "magical art": in his view it had the power to make inanimate objects look as if they possessed life.

Q.3. How was the transmission of notions of luminosity happened?

Ans. The origins of Suhrawardi's philosophy went back to Plato's Republic, where God is represented by the symbol of the sun. Suhrawardi's writings were universally read in the Islamic world. They were studied by Shaikh Mubarak, who transmitted their ideas to his sons, Faizi and Abu'l Fazl, who were trained under him.

Q.4. What was the meaning of sovereignty as a social contract?

Ans. Abu'l Fazl defined sovereignty as a social contract: the emperor protects the four essences of his subjects, namely, life (jan), property (mal), honour (namus) and faith (din), and in return demands obedience and a share of resources. Only just sovereigns were thought to be able to honour the contract with power and Divine guidance.

Long Answer Type — [5 Marks]

Q.1. Why was Chronicles commissioned by the Mughal emperors?

Ans. Chronicles commissioned by the Mughal emperors are an important source for studying the empire and its court. They were written in order to project a vision of an enlightened kingdom to all those who came under its umbrella. At the same time they were meant to convey to those who resisted the rule of the Mughals that all resistance was destined to fail. Also, the rulers wanted to ensure that there was an account of their rule for posterity. The authors of Mughal chronicles were invariably courtiers. The histories they wrote focused on events centred on the ruler, his family, the court and nobles, wars and administrative arrangements.

Q.2. How was a manuscripts created during Mughal time and which people were involved in this process?

Ans. All books in Mughal India were manuscripts, that is, they were handwritten. The centre of manuscript production was the imperial kitabkhana. The creation of a manuscript involved a number of people performing a variety of tasks. Paper makers were needed to prepare the folios of the manuscript, scribes or calligraphers to copy the text, gilders to illuminate the pages, painters to illustrate scenes from the text, bookbinders to gather the individual folios and set them within ornamental covers. The finished manuscript was seen as a precious object, a work of intellectual wealth and beauty. It exemplified the power of its patron, the Mughal emperor, to bring such beauty into being.

Q.3. Why were Ulamas oppose paintings?

Ans. The production of paintings portraying the emperor, his court and the people who were part of it, was a source of constant tension between rulers and representatives of the Muslim orthodoxy, the ulama. The latter did not fail to invoke the Islamic prohibition of the portrayal of human beings enshrined in the Qur'an as well as the hadis, which described an incident from the life of the Prophet Muhammad. Here the Prophet is cited as having forbidden the depiction of living beings in a naturalistic manner as it would suggest that the artist was seeking to appropriate the power of creation. This was a function that was believed to belong exclusively to God.

Q.4. Give a short note on Akbar Nama?

Ans. The Akbar Nama is divided into three books of which the first two are chronicles. The third book is the Ain-i Akbari. The first volume contains the history of mankind from Adam to one celestial cycle of Akbar's life (30 years). The second volume closes in the fortysixth regnal year (1601) of Akbar. The Akbar Nama was written to provide a detailed description of Akbar's reign in the traditional diachronic sense of recording politically significant events across time, as well as in the more novel sense of giving a synchronic picture of all aspects of Akbar's empire–geographic, social, administrative and cultural – without reference to chronology. In the Ain-i Akbari the Mughal Empire is presented as having a diverse population consisting of Hindus, Jainas, Buddhists and Muslims and a composite culture.

Q.5. What was the sulh-ikul?

Ans. Abu'l Fazl describes the ideal of sulh-ikul (absolute peace) as the cornerstone of enlightened rule. In sulh-ikul all religions and schools of thought had freedom of expression but on condition that they did not undermine the authority of the state or fight among themselves. The ideal of sulh-ikul was implemented through state policies – the nobility under the Mughals was a composite one comprising Iranis, Turanis, Afghans, Rajputs, Deccanis – all of whom were given positions and awards purely on the basis of their service and loyalty to the king. Further, Akbar abolished the tax on pilgrimage in 1563 and jizya in 1564 as the two were based on religious discrimination. Instructions were sent to officers of the empire to follow the precept of sulh-ikul in administration.

TOPIC 2

Administration of Mughal Empire Inside and Outside

Summary

- The heart of the Mughal Empire was its capital city, where the court assembled. The capital cities of the Mughals frequently shifted during the sixteenth and seventeenth centuries.

- Akbar commissioned the construction of a white marble tomb for Shaikh Salim Chishti next to the majestic Friday mosque at Sikri.

- During the 1560s Akbar had the fort of Agra constructed with red sandstone quarried from the adjoining regions. In the 1570s he decided to build a new capital, Fatehpur Sikri.

- In 1648 the court, army and household moved from Agra to the newly completed imperial capital, Shahjahanabad.

- The forms of salutation to the ruler indicated the person's status in the hierarchy: deeper prostration represented higher status. The highest form of submission was sijda or complete prostration.

- Grand titles were adopted by the Mughal emperors at the time of coronation or after a victory over an enemy. High sounding and rhythmic, they created an atmosphere of awe in the audience when announced by ushers (naqib).

- A courtier never approached the emperor empty handed: he offered either a small sum of money (nazr) or a large amount (peshkash).

- The term "harem" is frequently used to refer to the domestic world of the Mughals. It originates in the Persian word haram, meaning a sacred place.

- Both for the Rajput clans as well as the Mughals marriage was a way of cementing political relationships and forging alliances.

- In the Mughal household a distinction was maintained between wives who came from royal families (begams), and other wives (aghas) who were not of noble birth.

- After Nur Jahan, Mughal queens and princesses began to control significant financial resources. Shah Jahan's daughters Jahanara and Roshanara enjoyed an annual income often equal to that of high imperial mansabdars.

- The nobility was recruited from diverse ethnic and religious groups. This ensured that no faction was large enough to challenge the authority of the state.

- The mir bakhshi supervised the corps of court writers (waqianawis) who recorded all applications and documents presented to the court, and all imperial orders (farman).

- The head of the provincial administration was the governor (subadar) who reported directly to the emperor.

- The local administration was looked after at the level of the pargana (sub-district) by three semi-hereditary officers, the qanungo (keeper of revenue records), the chaudhuri (in charge of revenue collection) and the qazi.

- The political and diplomatic relations between the Mughal kings and the neighbouring countries of Iran and Turan hinged on the control of the frontier defined by the Hindukush mountains that separated Afghanistan from the regions of Iran and Central Asia.

- The relationship between the Mughals and the Ottomans was marked by the concern to ensure free movement for merchants and pilgrims in the territories under Ottoman control.

- Europe received knowledge of India through the accounts of Jesuit missionaries, travellers, merchants and diplomats. The Jesuit accounts are the earliest impressions of the Mughal court ever recorded by European writers.

- Akbar's quest for religious knowledge led to interfaith debates in the ibadatkhana at Fatehpur Sikri between learned Muslims, Hindus, Jainas, Parsis and Christians. Akbar's religious views matured as he queried scholars of different religions and sects and gathered knowledge about their doctrines.

Multiple Choice Questions [1 Mark]

Q.1. The capital cities of the Mughals frequently shifted during the sixteenth and seventeenth centuries. Who decided to build a new capital at Fatehpur Sikri?

(a) Humayun   (b) Akbar

(c) Janhagir   (d) Babur

Ans. (b)

Q.2. The Mughal emperors enteredinto a close relationship with sufis of the Chishtisilsila. Who commissioned the construction of a white marble tomb for Shaikh Salim Chishti next to the majestic Friday mosque at Sikri?

(a) Aurangjeb   (b) Janhagir

(c) Humayun   (d) Akbar

Ans. (d)

Q.3. The forms of salutation to the ruler indicated the person's status in the hierarchy: deeper prostration represented higher status. Which is the highest form of submission?

(a) Chahartaslim   (b) Sijda

(c) Zaminbos   (d) Kornish

Ans. (b)

Q.4. Grand titles were adopted by the Mughal emperors at the time of coronation or after a victory over an enemy. The title Mirza Raja was accorded by which ruler to his two highest-ranking nobles, Jai Singh and Jaswant Singh?

Ans. (a) Aurangjeb

(b) Akbar

(c) Janhagir

(d) Shahjahan

Ans. (a)

Q.5. Who could move between the external and internal life of the household as guards, servants,and also as agents for women dabbling in commerce?

(a) Aghacha

(b) Begum

(c) Aghas

(d) Khwajasara

Ans. (d)

Q.6. There were two other important ministers at the centre: the diwan-i ala and sadr-us sudur. Diwan-i-Ala represent the-

(a) Finance minister

(b) Agriculture minister

(c) Minister of grants

(d) Defence minister

Ans. (a)

Q.7. The division of functions established at the centre was replicated in the provinces (subas) where the ministers had their corresponding subordinates. Who was the head of the province?

(a) Qanungo

(b) Faujdars

(c) Subadar

(d) Qaji

Ans. (c)

Q.8. During the mughal time The sarkars, into which each suba was divided, often overlapped with the jurisdiction of faujdars(commandants) who were deployed with contingents of heavy cavalry and musketeers in districts. Who was the keeper of revenue records at pargana level?

(a) Faujdar   (b) Qaji

(c) Bakshi   (d) Qanungo

Ans. (d)

Q.9. Alamgir Nama, a history of the first ten years of Aurangzeb's reign compiled by?

(a) Muhammad Waris

(b) Lahori

(c) Gulbadan Begum

(d) Muhammmad Kazim

Ans. (d)

Very Short Answer Type   [1 Mark]

Q.1. Where is the dargah of Shaikh Muinuddin Chishti?

Ans. The dargah of Shaikh Muinuddin Chishtiis in Ajmer

Q.2. Term 'Diwan-I am' means?

Ans. It means Hall of audience

Q.3. Term Diwan-I khas means?

Ans. Meeting with private members.

Q.4. Humayun Nama book was written by?

Ans. It was written by Gulbadan Begum

Q.5. Who were known as waqianaw is?

Ans. They were Court poets

Q.6. Who was in charge of revenue collection at pargana level?

Ans. Chaudhari was in charge of revenue collection at pargana level

Q.7. The first Jesuit mission reached the Mughal court in which year?

Ans. The first Jesuit mission reached the Mughal court in 1580

Short Answer Type - I [2 Marks]

Q.1. Why Akbar had decided to build new capital at Fatehpur Sikri?

Ans. In the 1570s he decided to build a new capital, Fatehpur Sikri. One of the reasons prompting this may have been that Sikri was located on the direct road to Ajmer, where the dargah of Shaikh Muinuddin Chishti had become an important pilgrimage centre.

Q.2. Why Buland darwaja were made by Mughals?

Ans. The enormous arched gateway (Buland Darwaza) was meant to remind visitors of the Mughal victory in Gujarat.

Q.3. What is Axis mundi?

Ans. Axis mundi is a Latin phrase for a pillar or pole that is visualized as the support of the earth.

Q.4. When Shab-i barat celebrated?

Ans. Shab-i barat is the full moonnight on the 14 Shaban, the eighth month ofthehijri calendar, and is celebrated with prayers and fireworks in the subcontinent. It is the night when the destinies of the Muslims for the coming year are said to be determined and sins forgiven.

Q.5. Who introduced Jharoha darshan and why?

Ans. Jharoka darshan was introduced by Akbar with the objective of broadening the acceptance of the imperial authority as part of popular faith.

Q.6. Define the term Tajwiz?

Ans. Tajwiz was a petition presented by a nobleman to the emperor, recommending that an applicant be recruited as mansabdar.

Short Answer Type - II [3 Marks]

Q.1. Give a short detail about Shahjahanabad?

Ans. In 1648 the court, army and household moved from Agra to the newly completed imperial capital, Shahjahanabad. It was a new addition to the old residential city of Delhi, with the Red Fort, the Jama Masjid, a tree-lined esplanade with bazaars (Chandni Chowk) and spacious homes for the nobility. Shah Jahan's new city was appropriate to a more formal vision of a grand monarchy.

Q.2. Define the term Kornish?

Ans. Kornish was a form of ceremonial salutation in which the courtier placed the palm of his right hand against his forehead and bent his head. It suggested that the subject placed his head – the seat of the senses and the mind – into the hand of humility, presenting it to the royal assembly.

Q.3. Define the term Chahartaslim?

Ans. Chahartaslim is a mode of salutation which begins with placing the back of the right hand on the ground, and raising it gently till the person stands erect, when he puts the palm of his hand upon the crown of his head. It is done four (chahar) times. Taslim literally means submission.

Q.4. What were the differences between aghas and begams?

Ans. In the Mughal household a distinction was maintained between wives who came from royal families (begams), and other wives (aghas) who were not of noble birth. The begams, married after receiving huge amounts of cash and valuables as dower (mahr), naturally received a higher status and greater attention from their husbands than did aghas.

Q.5. Define the term Zat and Sawar?

Ans. All holders of government offices held ranks (mansabs) comprising two numerical designations : zat which was an indicator of position in the imperial hierarchy and the salary of the official (mansabdar), and sawar which indicated thenumber of horsemen he was required to maintain in service. In the seventeenth century, mansabdars of 1,000 zat or above ranked as nobles (umara, which is the plural of amir).

Long Answer Type [5 Marks]

Q.1. Give a short detail about the daily schedule of Mughal kings?

Ans. The emperor began his day at sunrise with personal religious devotions or prayers, and then appeared on a small balcony, the jharoka, facing the east. Below, a crowd of people (soldiers, merchants, crafts persons, peasants, women with sick children) waited for a view, darshan, of the emperor. After spending an hour at the jharoka, the emperor walked to the public hall of audience (diwan-i am) to conduct the primary business of his government. State officials presented reports and made requests. Two hours later, the emperor was in the diwan-ikhas to hold private audiences and discuss confidential matters. High ministers of state placed their petitions before him and tax officials presented their accounts. Occasionally, the emperor viewed the works of highly reputed artists or building plans of architects (mimar). On special occasions such as the anniversary of accession to the throne, Id, Shab-i barat and Holi, the court was full of life.

Q.2. How was the relation between Safavids and Mughals?

Ans. Qandahar was a bone of contention between the Safavids and the Mughals. The fortress-town had initially been in the possession of Humayun, reconquered in 1595 by Akbar. While the Safavid court retained diplomatic relations with the Mughals, it continued to stake claims to Qandahar. In 1613 Jahangir sent a diplomatic envoy to the court of Shah Abbas to plead the Mughal case for retaining Qandahar, but the mission failed. In the winter of 1622 a Persian army besieged Qandahar. The ill-prepared Mughal garrison was defeated and had to surrender the fortress and the city to the Safavids.

Q.3. How was the relation between the Akbar and Jesuit priests?

Ans. The Christian missions to India during the sixteenth century were part of this process of trade and empire building. Akbar was curious about Christianity and dispatched an embassy to Goa to invite Jesuit priests. The first Jesuit mission reached the Mughal court at Fatehpur Sikri in 1580 and stayed for about two years. The Jesuits spoke to Akbar about Christianity and debated its virtues with the ulama. Two more missions were sent to the Mughal court at Lahore, in 1591 and 1595. The Jesuit accounts are based on personal observation and shed light on the character and mind of the emperor. At public assemblies the Jesuits were assigned places in close proximity to Akbar's throne.

Chapter Practice

Multiple Choice Questions　　　　　　　　　　　　　　　[1 Mark]

Q.1. Given below are two statements, one labelled as Assertion (A) and the other labelled as Reason (R).

[CBSE 2020]

Assertion (A) : As the source of peace and stability, Emperor Akbar mediated among religions.

Reason (R) : Akbar allowed freedom of expression to all religions and schools of thought provided they did not undermine the authority of the State.

Which of the following is the correct option ?

(a) Both Assertion (A) and Reason (R) are correct and Reason (R) is the correct explanation of Assertion (A).

(b) Both Assertion (A) and Reason (R) are correct, but Reason (R) is not the correct explanation of Assertion (A).

(c) Assertion (A) is correct, but Reason (R) is not correct.

(d) Reason (R) is correct, but Assertion (A) is not correct.

Q.2. Which one of the following is correctly matched ?　　　　　　　[CBSE 2020]

(a) Humayun Nama	Waris Khan
(b) Akbar Nama	Abu'l -Fazl
(c) Gulbadan Begum	Badshah Nama
(d) Babur Nama	Sadullah Khan

Q.3. Find the true statement about Mughal manuscripts

(a) All books in Mughal India were manuscripts

(b) All the books were handwritten.

(c) The centre of manuscript production was the imperial kitabkhana

(d) All of the above

Q.4. Calligraphy is the art of ________

(a) Painters　　　　　　　　　　　(b) handwriting

(c) Traditional dance　　　　　　　(d) dictation

Very Short Answer Type　　　　　　　　　　　　　　　[1 Mark]

Q.5. Who abolished the tax on pilgrimage and *jizya*

Q.6. Who was the founder of the Mughal empire?

Short Answer Type - I   [2 Marks]

Q.7. Who made Persian, the leading language of the Mughal court?

Q.8. How did the Mughal dynasty fall?

Short Answer Type - II   [3 Marks]

Q.9. Describe the process of manuscript production in the Mughal court.   [CBSE 2019]

Q.10. Discuss the major features of Mughal provincial administration.   [CBSE 2019]

Q.11. How did the centre control the provinces in mughal provincial administration?   [CBSE 2020]

Long Answer Type   [5 Marks]

Q.12. Akbar consciously made Persian the leading language of the Mughal Court." Justify the statement with the efforts made by him.   [CBSE 2019]

PART IIII

Colonialism and Countryside

Relation with Bengal and Zamindars

Summary

- The name Mughal derives from Mongol. Though today the term evoke

- In introducing the Permanent Settlement, British officials hoped to resolve the problems they had been facing since the conquest of Bengal.

- The process, officials hoped, would lead to the emergence of a class of yeomen farmers and rich landowners who would have the capital and enterprise to improve agriculture. Nurtured by the British, this class would also be loyal to the Company.

- After a prolonged debate amongst Company officials, the Permanent Settlement was made with the rajas and taluqdars of Bengal.

- The Company fixed the total demand over the entire estate whose revenue the zamindar contracted to pay. The zamindar collected rent from the different villages, paid the revenue to the Company, and retained the difference as his income. He was expected to pay the Company regularly, failing which his estate could be auctioned.

- By the early nineteenth century, jotedars had acquired vast areas of land – sometimes as much as several thousand acres.

- A large part of their land was cultivated through sharecroppers (adhiyars or bargadars) who brought their own ploughs, laboured in the field, and handed over half the produce to the jotedars after the harvest.

- Within the villages, the power of jotedars was more effective than that of zamindars. Unlike zamindars who often lived in urban areas, jotedars were located in the villages and exercised direct control over a considerable section of poor villagers.

- There were other ways in which zamindars circumvented displacement. When people from outside the zamindari bought an estate at an auction, they could not always take possession.

- It was only during the Great Depression of the 1930s that they finally collapsed and the jotedars consolidated their power in the countryside.

Multiple Choice Questions [1 Mark]

Q.1. In introducing the Permanent Settlement, British officials hoped to resolve the problems they had been facing since the conquest of Bengal. When were the permanent settlement came into operation?

(a) 1717　　　　(b) 1820

(c) 1765　　　　(d) 1793

Ans. (d)

Q.2. The East India Company had fixed the revenue that each zamindar had to pay. The estates of those who failed to pay were to be auctioned to recover the revenue. These statements true for which British policy?

(a) Permanent settlement

(b) Ryotwari system

(c) Mahalwari system

(d) None of the above

Ans. (a)

Q.3. The Company had recognised the zamindars as important, but it wanted to control and regulate them, subdue their authority and restrict their autonomy. When Zamindars lost their power to their "cutcheries" (courts) then who became supervisors of courts?

(a) Taluqdars

(b) Mandals

(c) District collector

(d) Amlah

Ans. (c)

Q.4. In introducing the Permanent Settlement, British officials hoped to resolve the problems they have been facing since the conquest of Bengal. Who was the actual owner of land in this system?

(a) Ryot   (b) Zamindar

(c) Peasant   (d) Company

Ans. (b)

Q.5. In Francis Buchanan's survey of the Dinajpur district in North Bengal we have a vivid description of this class of rich peasants known as jotedars. What were the other names of jotedars?

(a) Gantidars

(b) Haoladars

(c) Mandals

(d) All of the above

Ans. (d)

Q.6. Francis Buchanan was a physician who came to India and served in the Bengal Medical Service. He serve as surgeon which governor general?

(a) William bentick

(b) Rippon

(c) Lord mayo

(d) Lord Wellesley

Ans. (d)

Q.7. Who was the governor-general of Bengal when permanent settlement was implemented in Bengal?

(a) Hector Munro

(b) Charles Cornwallis

(c) William Bentick

(d) Lord Mayo

Ans. (b)

Q.8. By the early nineteenth century, jotedars had acquired vast areas of land – sometimes as much as several thousand acres. A large part of their land was cultivated through sharecroppers. They were known as?

(a) Adhiyars

(b) Bargadars

(c) Both (a) and (b)

(d) Mandals

Ans. (c)

Very Short Answer Type   [1 Mark]

Q.1. What Mahals denote in nineteenth century?

Ans. In 19th century Mahals denote Estates.

Q.2. Which law was known as sunset law?

Ans. Permanent settlement was known as sunset law

Q.3. Who is responsible for collecting revenue which was appointed by zamindars?

Ans. Amla his responsible for collecting revenue

Q.4. In the end of eighteen century village headmen was also known as?

Ans. Gantidars or Mandals.

Q.5. Who were Holdars?

Ans. They were Village Headman.

Short Answer Type - I   [2 Marks]

Q.1. Define the term Raja?

Ans. Raja (literally king) was a term that was often used to designate powerful zamindars.

Q.2. What was the meaning of Taluqdar?

Ans. Taluqdar literally means "one who holds a taluq" or a connection. Taluq came to refer to a territorial unit.

Q.3. What was the meaning of ryot?

Ans. Ryot is the way the term raiyat, used to designate peasants, was spelt in British records. Ryots in Bengal did not always cultivate the land directly, but leased it out to under-ryots.

Q.4. For what were the Zamindars were responsible for?

Ans. Zamindars were responsible for: (a) paying revenue to the company (b) distributing the revenue demand (jama) over villages.

Q.5. Who were the Lathiyals?

Ans. Lathyal, literally one who wields the lathi or stick, functioned as a strongman of the zamindar.

Short Answer Type - II   [3 Marks]

Q.1. What were the reasons behind the failure of permanent settlement?

Ans. The reasons for this failure were various. First: the initial demands were very high. Second: this high demand was imposed in the 1790s, a time when the prices of agricultural produce were depressed, making it difficult for the ryots to pay their dues to the zamindar. Third: the revenue was invariable, regardless of the harvest, and had to be paid punctually. Fourth: the Permanent Settlement initially limited the power of the zamindar to collect rent from the ryot and manage his zamindari.

Q.2. What is the meaning of Benami?

Ans. Benami, literally anonymous, is a term used in Hindi and several other Indian languages for transactions made in the name of a fictitious or relatively insignificant person, whereas the real beneficiary remains unnamed.

Q.3. When were the Zamindars got their power and overcome on jotedars?

Ans. By the beginning of the nineteenth century the depression in prices was over. Thus those who had survived the troubles of the 1790s consolidated their power. Rules of revenue payment were also made somewhat flexible. As a result, the zamindar's power over the villages was strengthened. It was only during the Great Depression of the 1930s that they finally collapsed and the jotedars consolidated their power in the countryside.

Long Answer Type   [5 Marks]

Q.1. What was the objective behind the implementation of permanent settlement?

Ans. In introducing the Permanent Settlement, British officials hoped to resolve the problems they had been facing since the conquest of Bengal. By the 1770s, the rural economy in Bengal was in crisis, with recurrent famines and declining agricultural output. Officials felt that agriculture, trade and the revenue resources of the state could all be developed by encouraging investment in agriculture. This could be done by securing rights of property and permanently fixing the rates of revenue demand. If the revenue demand of the state was permanently fixed, then the Company could look forward to a regular flow of revenue, while entrepreneurs could feel sure of earning a profit from their investment, since the state would not siphon it off by increasing its claim. The process, officials hoped, would lead to the emergence of a class of yeomen farmers and rich landowners who would have the capital and enterprise to improve agriculture. Nurtured by the British, this class would also be loyal to the Company.

Q.2. Who were the Jotedars at the end of eighteenth century?

Ans. While many zamindars were facing a crisis at the end of the eighteenth century, a group of rich peasants were consolidating their position in the villages. In Francis Buchanan's survey of the Dinajpur district in North Bengal we have a vivid description of this class of rich peasants known as jotedars. By the early nineteenth century, jotedars had acquired vast areas of land – sometimes as much as several thousand acres. They controlled local trade as well as moneylending, exercising immense power over the poorer cultivators of the region. A large part of their land was cultivated through sharecroppers (adhiyars or bargadars) who brought their own ploughs, laboured in the field, and handed over half the produce to the jotedars after the harvest.

Q.3. Why Zamindars did not like Jotedars?

Ans. Within the villages, the power of jotedars was more effective than that of zamindars. Unlike zamindars who often lived in urban areas, jotedars were located in the villages and exercised direct control over a considerable section of poor villagers. They fiercely resisted efforts by zamindars to increase the jama of the village, prevented zamindari officials from executing their duties, mobilised ryots who were dependent on them, and deliberately delayed payments of revenue to the zamindar. In fact, when the estates of the zamindars were auctioned for failure to make revenue payment, jotedars were often amongst the purchasers.

TOPIC 2

Revolt in Different Areas

Summary

- In the early nineteenth century, Buchanan travelled through the Rajmahal hills. From his description, the hills appeared impenetrable, a zone where few travellers ventured, an area that signified danger.

- If we look at late-eighteenth-century revenue records, we learn that these hill folk were known as Paharias. They lived around the Rajmahal hills, subsisting on forest produce and practising shifting cultivation.

- From the forests they collected mahua (a flower) for food, silk cocoons and resin for sale, and woodfor charcoal production. The undergrowth that spread like a mat below the trees and the patches of grass that covered the lands left fallow provided pasture for cattle.

- With their base in the hills, the Paharias regularly raided the plains where settled agriculturists lived.

- In the 1770s the British embarked on a brutal policy of extermination, hunting the Paharias down and killing them. Then, by the 1780s, Augustus Cleveland, the Collector of Bhagalpur, proposed a policy of pacification.

- By this time in fact there were newer intimations of danger. Santhals were pouring into the area, clearing forests, cutting down timber, ploughing land and growing rice and cotton. As the lower hills were taken over by Santhal settlers, the Paharias receded deeper into the Rajmahal hills.

- The Santhals were given land and persuaded to settle in the foothills of Rajmahal. By 1832 a large area of land was demarcated as Damin-i-Koh. This was declared to be the land of the Santhals.

- The Santhals, however, soon found that the land they had brought under cultivation was slipping away from their hands. The state was levying heavy taxes on the land that the Santhals had cleared, moneylenders (dikus) were charging them high rates of interest and taking over the land when debts remained unpaid, and zamindars were asserting control over the Damin area.

- According to Ricardian ideas, a landowner should have a claim only to the "average rent" that prevailed at a given time. When the land yielded more than this "average rent", the landowner had a surplus that the state needed to tax. If tax was not levied, cultivators were likely to turn into rentiers, and their surplus income was unlikely to be productively invested in the improvement of the land.

- The revenue system that was introduced in the Bombay Deccan came to be known as the ryotwari settlement. Unlike the Bengal system, the revenue was directly settled with the ryot.

- Before the 1860s, three-fourths of raw cotton imports into Britain came from America. British cotton manufacturers had for long been worried about this dependence on American supplies. What would happen if this source was cut off? Troubled by this question, they eagerly looked for alternative sources of supply.

- While the American crisis continued, cotton production in the Bombay Deccan expanded. Between 1860 and 1864 cotton acreage doubled. By 1862 over 90 per cent of cotton imports into Britain were coming from India.

- The ryots came to see the moneylender as devious and deceitful. They complained of moneylenders manipulating laws and forging accounts. In 1859 the British passed a Limitation Law that stated that the loan bonds signed between moneylenders and ryots would have validity for only three years.

Multiple Choice Questions   [1 Mark]

Q.1. If we look at late-eighteenth-century revenue records, we learn that these hill folk were known as Paharias. They lived around the-

(a) Chotanagpur hill

(b) Garhjat hill

(c) Rajmahal hill

(d) Damodar hill

Ans. (c)

Q.2. With their base in the hills, the Paharias regularly raided the plains where settled agriculturists lived. These raids were necessary for survival. Lije of Paharias of Rajmahal completely dependent upon _______?

(a) River

(b) Permanent agriculture

(c) Forests

(d) Trade

Ans. (c)

Q.3. The battle between the hoe and the plough was a long one. Who represents hoe and the plough in end of eighteenth century?

(a) Paharias and Britishers

(b) Santhals and Britishers

(c) Paharias and Santhals

(d) French and Britishers

Ans. (c)

Q.4. The Santhals were given land and persuaded to settle in the foothills of Rajmahal. When were Santhal people revolted against Britishers?

(a) 1820-21

(b) 1898-99

(c) 1910-15

(d) 1855-56

Ans. (d)

Q.5. Through the nineteenth century, peasants in various parts of India rose in revolt against money lenders and grain dealers. One such revolt occurred in the Deccan. When was this revolt happened?

(a) 1875   (b) 1855

(c) 1905   (d) 1924

Ans. (a)

Q.6. Consider the following options.

1. The fifth report submitted to the British Parliament in 1813 AD.

2. Jotedars were quite powerful.

3. Santhals were a great danger to Paharis.

4. No Zamindari was auctioned in Bengal.

(a) 1, 2 and 3   (b) 1, 2, 3 and 4

(c) 2 and 3   (d) 3 and 4

Ans. (a)

Q.7. Consider the following statements:

1. Permanent settlement was introduced in 1793 AD.

2. Jotedars were quite powerful.

3. All the Zamindars paid their dues very easily.

4. The ryots came to see the moneylenders as devious and deceitful.

(a) 1, 2 and 3   (b) 1, 2, 3 and 4

(c) 1, 2 and 4   (d) 2, 3 and 4

Ans. (c)

Q.8. Consider the following events:

1. Introduction of Permanent settlement

2. American Civil war

3. Fifth report in the British Parliament

4. Santhals arrived in the hilly area of Rajmahal

The correct Chronological order of these events is:

(a) 1, 2, 3, 4   (b) 1, 4, 3, 2

(c) 1, 3, 2, 4   (d) 1, 3, 4, 2

Ans. (b)

Q.1. By 1832 a large area of land was demarcated as Damin-i-Koh. Which place was this?

Ans. Foothills of Rajmahal hills.

Q.2. Who were dikus for the people of Santhals?

Ans. Dikus were Moneylenders.

Q.3. In Ryotwari system the revenue was directly settled with?

Ans. The revenue was directly settled with Ryots

Q.4. When was the Fifth report introduced in the British parliament?

Ans. The Fifth report introduced in the British parliamentin1813

Q.5. Damin-i-koh was formed for?

Ans. Damin-i-koh was formed for Santhals

Q.6. When was the Cotton Supply Association was founded?

Ans. The Cotton Supply Association was foundedin 1857

Q.1. What is called Aquatint?

Ans. Aquatint is a picture produced by cutting into a copper sheet with acid and then printing it.

Q.2. Who proposed a policy of pacification?

Ans. By the 1780s, Augustus Cleveland, the Collector of Bhagalpur, proposed a policy of pacification.

Q.3. Define the tern Sahukars?

Ans. A sahukar was someone who acted as both a moneylender and a trader.

Q.4. Define the term Rentier?

Ans. Rentier is a term used to designate people who live on rental income from property.

Short Answer Type - II   [3 Marks]

Q.1. Why Paharias regularly raided the plains where settled agriculturists lived?

Ans. With their base in the hills, the Paharias regularly raided the plains where settled agriculturists lived. These raids were necessary for survival, particularly in years of scarcity; they were a way of asserting power over settled communities; and they were a means of negotiating political relations with outsiders. The zamindars on the plains had to often purchase peace by paying a regular tribute to the hill chiefs.

Q.2. When was Santhal revolt happened?

Ans. By the 1850s, the Santhals felt that the time had come to rebel against zamindars, moneylenders and the colonial state, in order to create an ideal world for themselves where they would rule. It was after the Santhal Revolt (1855-56) that the Santhal Pargana was created, carving out 5,500 square miles from the districts of Bhagalpur and Birbhum. The colonial state hoped that by creating a new territory for the Santhals and imposing some special laws within it, the Santhals could be conciliated.

Q.3. What was the Recardian idea about the landowner and rent?

Ans. According to Ricardian ideas, a landowner should have a claim only to the "average rent" that prevailed at a given time. When the land yielded more than this "average rent", the landowner had a surplus that the state needed to tax. If tax was not levied, cultivators were likely to turn into rentiers, and their surplus income was unlikely to be productively invested in the improvement of the land.

Q.4. What was the Ryotwari system?

Ans. The revenue system that was introduced in the Bombay Deccan came to be known as the ryotwari settlement. Unlike the Bengal system, the revenue was directly settled with the ryot. The average income from different types of soil was estimated, the revenue-paying capacity of the ryot was assessed and a proportion of it fixed as the share of the state. The lands were resurveyed every 30 years and the revenue rates increased. Therefore the revenue demand was no longer permanent.

Q.5. When was cotton production boom in India? And what was effect on people of this?

Ans. While the American crisis continued, cotton production in the Bombay Deccan expanded. Between 1860 and 1864 cotton acreage doubled. By 1862 over 90 per cent of cotton imports into Britain were coming from India. But these boom years did not bring prosperity to all cotton producers. Some rich peasants did gain, but for the large majority, cotton expansion meant heavier debt.

Long Answer Type   [5 Marks]

Q.1. Give a short note on the paharias of Rajmahal hill?

Ans. If we look at late-eighteenth-century revenue records, we learn that these hill folk were known as Paharias. They lived around the Rajmahal hills, subsisting on forest produce and practising shifting cultivation. They cleared patches of forest by cutting bushes and burning the undergrowth. On these patches, enriched by the potash from the ash, the Paharias grew a variety of pulses and millets for consumption. They scratched the ground lightly with hoes, cultivated the cleared land for a few years, then left it fallow so that it could recover its fertility, and moved to a new area. From the forests they collected mahua (a flower) for food, silk cocoons and resin for sale, and wood for charcoal production.

Q.2. Give a short note on policy of pacification?

Ans. In the 1770s the British embarked on a brutal policy of extermination, hunting the Paharias down and killing them. Then, by the 1780s, Augustus Cleveland, the Collector of Bhagalpur, proposed a policy of pacification. Paharia chiefs were given an annual allowance and made responsible for the proper conduct of their men. They were expected to maintain order in their localities and discipline their own people. Many Paharia chiefs refused the allowances. Those who accepted, most often lost authority within the community. Being in the pay of the colonial government, they came to be perceived as subordinate employees or stipendiary chiefs.

Q.3. When was Deccan revolt happened and how it spread in other region?

Ans. The movement began at Supa, a large village in Poona (present-day Pune) district. It was a market centre where many shopkeepers and moneylenders lived. On 12 May1875, ryots from surrounding rural areas gathered and attacked the shopkeepers, demanding their bahikhatas (account books) and debt bonds. They burnt the khatas, looted grain shops, and in some cases set fire to the houses of sahukars. From Poona the revolt spread to Ahmednagar. Then over the next two months it spread even further, over an area of 6,500 square km. More than thirty villages were affected. Everywhere the pattern was the same: sahukars were attacked, account books burnt and debt bonds destroyed. Terrified of peasant attacks, the sahukars fled the villages, very often leaving their property and belongings behind.

Q.4. In which scenarios cotton production was increases in India in late nineteenth century?

Ans. Before the 1860s, three-fourths of raw cotton imports into Britain came from America. British cotton manufacturers had for long been worried about this dependence on American supplies. What would happen if this source was cut off? Troubled by this question, they eagerly looked for alternative sources of supply. In 1857 the Cotton Supply Association was founded in Britain, and in 1859 the Manchester Cotton Company was formed. Their objective was "to encourage cotton production in every part of the world suited for its growth". India was seen as a country that could supply cotton to Lancashire if the American supply dried up. It possessed suitable soil, a climate favourable to cotton cultivation, and cheap labour.

Chapter Practice

Multiple Choice Questions
[1 Mark]

Q.1. The first Colonial rule was established in __________

(a) Bengal

(b) Madras

(c) Bombay

(d) Surat

Q.2. The East India Company had fixed the revenue that each zamindar had to pay. The estates of those who failed to pay were to be auctioned to recover the revenue.

The above statement best describes which of the following revenue system

(a) Mansabdari System

(b) Permanent Settlement

(c) Ryotwari Settlement

(d) None of the above

Q.3. Find the true statement with reference to Permanent Settlement in Bengal

(a) The zamindars were the landowners in the village

(b) The taluqdar swere the revenue Collector of the state.

(c) There was a single village under each zamindar

(d) The Permanent Settlement was made with the rajas and *taluqdars* of Bengal.

Q.4. In terms of Company calculations, one revenue estate consisted of

(a) villages within a province

(b) villages within the kingdom

(c) villages within one zamindari

(d) none of the above

Q.5. The Permanent Settlement had come into operation in ________

(a) 1893

(b) 1814

(c) 1793

(d) 1799

Very Short Answer Type
[1 Mark]

Q.6. In which area did Jotdars live?

Q.7. The Permanent Settlement was made with the rajas and taluqdars of which region?

Short Answer Type - I
[2 Marks]

Q.8. Who were Paharias?

Q.9. One revenue estate consisted of?

Short Answer Type - II   [3 Marks]

Q.10. How the Deeds and bonds appeared as symbols of the new oppressive system for the Peasants?

[CBSE 2014]

Q.11. How did the Paharias respond to the coming of outsiders?   [CBSE 2017]

Long Answer Type   [5 Marks]

Q.12. What explains the anger of the Deccan ryots against the moneylenders?   [CBSE 2019]

Q.13. Why was jotedar a powerful figure in many areas of rural Bengal ?   [CBSE 2019]

CHAPTER 11

Revels and The Raj

Beginning of Revolt

Summary

- Late in the afternoon of 10 May 1857, the sepoys in the cantonment of Meerut broke out in mutiny. It began in the lines of the native infantry, spread very swiftly to the cavalry and then to the city. The ordinary people of the town and surrounding villages joined the sepoys.

- The sepoys began their action with a signal: in many places it was the firing of the evening gun or the sounding of the bugle. They first seized the bell of arms and plundered the treasury. They then attacked government buildings – the jail, treasury, telegraph office, record room, bungalows – burning all records. Everything and everybody connected with the white man became a target.

- It is clear that there was communication between the sepoy lines of various cantonments.

- To fight the British, leadership and organization were required. For these the rebels sometimes turned to those who had been leaders before the British conquest.

- In Kanpur, the sepoys and the people of the town gave Nana Sahib, the successor to Peshwa Baji Rao II, no choice save to join the revolt as their leader. In Jhansi, the rani was forced by the popular pressure around her to assume the leadership of the uprising. So was Kunwar Singh, a local zamindar in Arrah in Bihar.

- Elsewhere, local leaders emerged, urging peasants, zamindars and tribals to revolt. Shah Mal mobilised the villagers of pargana Barout in Uttar Pradesh; Gonoo, a tribal cultivator of Singhbhumin Chotanagpur, became a rebel leader of the Kol tribals of the region.

- Rumours and prophecies played a part in moving people to action. As we saw, the sepoys who had arrived in Delhi from Meerut had told Bahadur Shah about bullets coated with the fat of cows and pigs and that biting those bullets would corrupt their caste and religion.

- This is one rumour whose origin can be traced. Captain Wright, commandant of the Rifle Instruction Depot, reported that in the third week of January 1857 a "low-caste" khalasi who worked in the magazine in Dum Dum had asked a Brahmin sepoy for a drink of water from his lota.

- This was not the only rumour that was circulating in North India at the beginning of 1857. There was the rumour that the British government had hatched a gigantic conspiracy to destroy the caste and religion of Hindus and Muslims.

- In 1851 Governor General Lord Dalhousie described the kingdom of Awadh as "a cherry that will drop into our mouth one day". Five years later, in 1856, the kingdom was formally annexed to the British Empire.

- Nawab Wajid Ali Shah was dethroned and exiled to Calcutta on the plea that the region was being misgoverned. The British government also wrongly assumed that Wajid Ali Shah was an unpopular ruler.

- The annexation displaced not just the Nawab. It also dispossessed the taluqdars of the region.

- The dispossession of taluqdars meant the breakdown of an entire social order. The ties of loyalty and patronage that had bound the peasant to the taluqdar were disrupted.

- The rebel proclamations in 1857 repeatedly appealed to all sections of the population, irrespective of their caste and creed. Many of the proclamations were issued by Muslim princes or in their names but even these took care to address the sentiments of Hindus.

Multiple Choice Questions   [1 Mark]

Q.1. The sepoys arrived at the gates of the Red Fort early in the morning on 11 May. It was the month of Ramzan, the Muslim holy month of prayer and fasting. Who was the emperor of Delhi in 1857?

(a) Bahadur shah

(b) Akbar 2

(c) Muhammad shah

(d) Farrukshiyar

Ans. (a)

Q.2. To fight the British, leadership and organization were required. For these the rebels sometimes turned to those who had been leaders before the British conquest. Who led the revolt from Kanpur?

(a) Maharani Laxmibai

(b) Nana Sahib

(c) Kunwar Singh

(d) None of the above

Ans. (b)

Q.3. From Meerut, there were reports that a fakir had appeared riding on an elephant and that the sepoys were visiting him frequently during 1857 revolt. Who was that fakir?

(a) Ahmadullah shah

(b) Sikandar shah

(c) Fakir jiyauddin

(d) Hajrat mahal

Ans. (a)

Q.4. Shah Mal belonged to a clan of Jat cultivators whose kinship ties extended over chaura seedes(eighty-four villages). The lands in the region were irrigated and fertile, with rich dark loam soil. He belonged from-

(a) Bihar

(b) Jharkhand

(c) Delhi

(d) Uttar Pradesh

Ans. (d)

Q.5. Maulvi Ahmadullah Shah was jailed in Faizabad. When released, he was elected by the mutinous 22nd Native Infantry as their leader. He fought in the famous Battle of Chinhat against which of the following the British officers?

(a) James neil

(b) John Nicholson

(c) Hennery Lawrence

(d) Hugh rose

Ans. (c)

Q.6. In 1851 for which kingdom Governor General Lord Dalhousie described as "a cherry that will drop into our mouth one day". Five years later, in 1856, the kingdom was formally annexed to the British Empire?

(a) Kanpur

(b) Jhansi

(c) Satara

(d) Awadh

Ans. (d)

Q.7. By the terms of this alliance the king had to disband his military force, allow the British to position their troops within the kingdom, and act in accordance with the advice of the British Resident who was now to be attached to the court. This policy of British was known as?

(a) Ring-fence policy

(b) Doctrine of lapse

(c) Subsidiary alliance

(d) None of the above

Ans. (c)

Q.8. The Subsidiary Alliance had been imposed on Awadh in 1801. Who devised the system of subsidiary alliance?

(a) William Bentick

(b) Lord Canning

(c) Hector Munro

(d) Lord Wellesley

Ans. (d)

Q.9. Not everywhere were the leaders people of the court – ranis, rajas, nawabs and taluqdars. Often the message of rebellion was carried by ordinary men and women and in places by religious men too. Who established 'Hall of Justice' during revolt?

(a) Nana Sahib

(b) Bahadur Shah

(c) Shah Mal

(d) Kunwar Singh

Ans. (c)

Very Short Answer Type [1 Mark]

Q.1. When were the sepoys in the cantonment of Meerut broke out in mutiny?

Ans. The sepoys in the cantonment of Meerut broke out on 10 May 1857

Q.2. Who was popularly known as Danka Shah?

Ans. Maulvi Ahmadullah Shah was popularly known as Danka Shah

Q.3. The Subsidiary Alliance had been imposed on Awadh in?

Ans. The Subsidiary Alliance had been imposed on Awadh in 1801

Q.4. Subsidiary Alliance was a system devised by Lord Wellesley in?

Ans. Subsidiary Alliance was a system devised by Lord Wellesley in 1798

Q.5. Who was the leader of revolt of 1857 from Bihar?

Ans. Kunwar Singh was the leader of revolt of 1857 from Bihar

Q.6. Who led the revolt from Lucknow?

Ans. Begam Hajrat Mahal

Q.7. Who was ruler of Awadh when it annexed in 1856?

Ans. Nawab Wajid Ali Shah

Short Answer Type - I [2 Marks]

Q.1. What was Bell of arms?

Ans. Bell of arms is a storeroom in which weapons are kept.

Q.2. Define the term Firangi?

Ans. Firangi, a term of Persian origin, possibly derived from Frank (from which France gets its name), is used in Urdu and Hindi, often in a derogatory sense, to designate foreigners.

Q.3. Define the term Resident?

Ans. Resident was the designation of a representative of the Governor General who lived in a state which was not under direct British rule.

Q.4. On which ground was Awadh annexed by British?

Ans. Nawab Wajid Ali Shah was dethroned and exiled to Calcutta on the plea that the region was being misgoverned.

Short Answer Type - II   **[3 Marks]**

Q.1. What s the difference between mutiny and revolt?

Ans. Mutiny – a collective disobedience of rules and regulations within the armed forces. Revolt – a rebellion of people against established authority and power. The terms 'revolt' and 'rebellion' can be used synonymously.

In the context of the revolt of 1857 the term revolt refers primarily to the uprising of the civilian population (peasants, zamindars, rajas, jagirdars) while the mutiny was of the sepoys.

Q.2. What was the reason for the similarity in the pattern of the revolt in different places?

Ans. The reason for the similarity in the pattern of the revolt in different places lay partly in its planning and coordination. It is clear that there was communication between the sepoy lines of various cantonments. After the 7th Awadh Irregular Cavalry had refused to accept the new cartridges in early May, they wrote to the 48th Native Infantry that "they had acted for the faith and awaited the 48th's orders". Sepoys or their emissaries moved from one station to another. People were thus planning and talking about the rebellion.

Q.3. How were the common people participated in 1857 revolt?

Ans. Not everywhere were the leaders people of the court – ranis, rajas, nawabs and taluqdars. Often the message of rebellion was carried by ordinary men and women and in places by religious men too. From Meerut, there were reports that a fakir had appeared riding on an elephant and that the sepoys were visiting him frequently. In Lucknow, after the annexation of Awadh, there were many religious leaders and self-styled prophets who preached the destruction of British rule. Elsewhere, local leaders emerged, urging peasants, zamindars and tribals to revolt. Shah Mal mobilised the villagers of pargana Barout in Uttar Pradesh; Gonoo, a tribal cultivator of Singhbhum in Chotanagpur, became a rebel leader of the Kol tribals of the region.

Q.4. Who was Maulavi Ahmadullah Shah?

Ans. Maulvi Ahmadullah Shah was one of the many maulvis who played an important part in the revolt of 1857. Educated in Hyderabad, he became a preacher when young. In 1856, he was seen moving from village to village preaching jehad (religious war) against the British and urging people to rebel. He moved in a palanquin, with drumbeaters in front and followers at the rear. He was therefore popularly called Danka Shah – the maulvi with the drum (danka). British officials panicked as thousands began following the maulvi and many Muslims began seeing him as an inspired prophet. When he reached Lucknow in 1856, he was stopped by the police from preaching in the city. Subsequently, in 1857, he was jailed in Faizabad. When released, he was elected by the mutinous 22nd Native Infantry as their leader. He fought in the famous Battle of Chinhat in which the British forces under Henry Lawrence were defeated.

Q.5. What was the terms of subsidiary alliance?

Ans. The Subsidiary Alliance had been imposed on Awadh in 1801. By the terms of this alliance the Nawab had to disband his military force, allow the British to position their troops within the kingdom, and act in accordance with the advice of the British Resident who was now to be attached to the court. Deprived of his armed forces, the Nawab became increasingly dependent on the British to maintain law and order within the kingdom. He could no longer assert control over the rebellious chiefs and taluqdars.

Q.6. What was the summary settlement of 1857?

Ans. The British land revenue policy further undermined the position and authority of the taluqdars. After annexation, the first British revenue settlement, known as the Summary Settlement of 1856, was based on the assumption that the taluqdars were interlopers with no permanent stakes in land: they had established their hold over land through force and fraud. The Summary Settlement proceeded to remove the taluqdars wherever possible.

Long Answer Type [5 Marks]

Q.1. Who was the target of sepoys and common man during revolt?

Ans. The sepoys began their action with a signal: in many places it was the firing of the evening gun or the sounding of the bugle. They first seized the bell of arms and plundered the treasury. They then attacked government buildings – the jail, treasury, telegraph office, record room, bungalows – burning all records. Everything and everybody connected with the white man became a target. Proclamations in Hindi, Urdu and Persian were put up in the cities calling upon the population, both Hindus and Muslims, to unite, rise and exterminate the firangis. When ordinary people began joining the revolt, the targets of attack widened. In major towns like Lucknow, Kanpur and Bareilly, moneylenders and the rich also became the objects of rebel wrath. Peasants not only saw them as oppressors but also as allies of the British.

Q.2. Give a short detail on the movement of Shah mal?

Ans. Shah Mal mobilised the headmen and cultivators of chaurasee des, moving at night from village to village, urging people to rebel against the British. As in many other places, the revolt against the British turned into a general rebellion against all signs of oppression and injustice. Shah Mals men attacked government buildings, destroyed the bridge over the river, and dug up metalled roads – partly to prevent government forces from coming into the area, and partly because bridges and roads were seen as symbols of British rule. They sent supplies to the sepoys who had mutinied in Delhi and stopped all official communication between British headquarters and Meerut. Locally acknowledged as the Raja, Shah Mal took over the bungalow of an English officer, turned it into a "hall of justice", settling disputes and dispensing judgments. He also set up an amazingly effective network of intelligence. For a period the people of the area felt that firangi raj was over, and their raj had come. Shah Mal was killed in battle in July 1857.

Q.3. What were the consequences of summary settlement of 1857?

Ans. The Summary Settlement proceeded to remove the taluqdars wherever possible. During pre-British times, taluqdars had held 67 per cent of the total number of villages in Awadh; by the Summary Settlement this number had come down to 38 per cent. The taluqdars of southern Awadh were the hardest hit and some lost more than half of the total number of villages they had previously held. The dispossession of taluqdars meant the breakdown of an entire social order. The ties of loyalty and patronage that had bound the peasant to the taluqdar were disrupted. In pre-British times, the taluqdars were oppressors but many of them also appeared to be generous father figures: they exacted a variety of dues from the peasant but were often considerate in times of need. Now, under the British, the peasant was directly exposed to overassessment of revenue and inflexible methods of collection.

Q.4. What were the rumors behind the revolt of 1857?

Ans. Rumors and prophecies played a part in moving people to action. As we saw, the sepoys who had arrived in Delhi from Meerut had told Bahadur Shah about bullets coated with the fat of cows and pigs and that biting those bullets would corrupt their caste and religion. This is one rumors whose origin can be traced. Captain Wright, commandant of the Rifle Instruction Depot, reported that in the third week of January 1857 a "low-caste" khalasi who worked in the magazine in Dum Dum had asked a Brahmin sepoy for a drink of water from his lota. This was not the only rumors that was circulating in North India at the beginning of 1857. There was the rumors that the British government had hatched a gigantic conspiracy to destroy the caste and religion of Hindus and Muslims.

TOPIC 2

Repression of Revolt

Summary

- It is clear from all accounts that we have of 1857 that the British did not have an easy time in putting down the rebellion.

- By a number of Acts, passed in May and June 1857, not only was the whole of North India put under martial law but military officers and even ordinary Britons were given the power to try and punish Indians suspected of rebellion.

- British attempts to recover Delhi began in earnest in early June 1857 but it was only in late September that the city was finally captured. The fighting and losses on both sides were heavy.

- In large parts of present-day Uttar Pradesh, where big landholders and peasants had offered united resistance, the British tried to break up the unity by promising to give back to the big landholders their estates. Rebel landholders were dispossessed and the loyal rewarded.

- As we have seen, we have very few records on the rebels' point of view. There are a few rebel proclamations and notifications, as also some letters that rebel leaders wrote. But historians till now have continued to discuss rebel actions primarily through accounts written by the British.

- One important record of the mutiny is the pictorial images produced by the British and Indians: paintings, pencil drawings, etchings, posters, cartoons, bazaar prints.

- When the rebel forces besieged Lucknow, Henry Lawrence, the Commissioner of Lucknow, collected the Christian population and took refuge in the heavily fortified Residency. Lawrence was killed but the Residency continued to be defended under the command of Colonel Inglis.

- Barker's painting celebrates the moment of Campbell's entry. At the centre of the canvas are the British heroes – Campbell, Outram and Havelock. The gestures of the hands of those around lead the spectator's eyes towards the centre.

- British paintings created a sense that the time of trouble was past and the rebellion was over; the British were the victors.

- Newspaper reports have a power over public imagination; they shape feelings and attitudes to events. Inflamed particularly by tales of violence against wo and children, there were public demands in Britain for revenge and retribution.

- As waves of anger and shock spread in Britain, demands for retribution grew louder. Visual representations and news about the revolt created a milieu in which violent repression and vengeance were seen as both necessary and just.

- A whole world of nationalist imagination was woven around the revolt. It was celebrated as the First War of Independence in which all sections of the people of India came together to fight against imperial rule.

- The leaders of the revolt were presented as heroic figures leading the country into battle, rousing the people to righteous indignation against oppressive imperial rule.

- Rani of Jhansi was represented as a masculine figure chasing the enemy, slaying British soldiers and valiantly fighting till her last. Children in many parts of India grow up reading the lines of Subhadra Kumari Chauhan: "Khoob lari mardani woh to Jhansi wali rani thi" (Like a man she fought, she was the Rani of Jhansi).

Multiple Choice Questions [1 Mark]

Q.1. British attempts to recover Delhi began in earnest in early June 1857 but it was only in late September that the city was finally captured. The fighting and losses on both sides were heavy. Which officer captured Delhi?

(a) Hugh Rose   (b) Hennery Lawrence

(c) John Nicholson   (d) James Neil

Ans. (c)

Q.2. The reason for the similarity in the pattern of the revolt in different places lay partly in its planning and coordination. It is clear that there was communication between the sepoy lines of various cantonments. Apart from ishtahars, the 857 rebels spread their views through?

(a) Speeches

(b) Proclamations

(c) Letters

(d) Newspaper

Ans. (b)

Q.3. Rumours and prophecies played a part in moving people to action. Which of the following was not one of the rumors and prophecies during the 19th century?

(a) British had mixed bone dust of dog in aata and salt.

(b) New cartridges of the enfield rifle were greased with fat of cow and pig

(c) British came to end Hindu and Muslim for spreading Christianity.

(d) None of the above

Ans. (d)

Q.4. Consider the following events:

1. Abolition of sati

2. Passing of Widow Remarriage Act.

3. The beginning of the revolt

4. Queen's Proclamation.

The correct chronological order of these events is-

(a) 2, 1, 3, 4   (b) 3, 4, 1, 2

(c) 1, 2, 3, 4   (d) 2, 3, 4, 1

Ans. (c)

Q.5. Consider the following events:

1. Soldiers revolted at Meerut.

2. Bahadur Shah Zafar declared the leader of Barker.

3. Awadh was captured by the British.

4. Relief of Lucknow was painted by Thomas Jones Barker.

Write these events in correct chronological order-

(a) 1, 2, 3, 4

(b) 2, 1, 3, 4

(c) 3, 1, 2, 4

(d) 4, 3, 2, 1

Ans. (c)

Q.6. In another set of sketches and paintings we see women in a different light. They appear heroic, defending themselves against the attack of rebels. Which English lady defended herself bravely against the Indian rebels in Kanpur?

(a) Miss Olivia

(b) Miss Emma

(c) Miss Wheeler

(d) Miss ulliet

Ans. (c)

Q.7. When the government passed the Hindu property law under which even after converting to Christianity one could inherit one's ancestral property?

(a) 1849

(b) 1850

(c) 1824

(d) 1798

Ans. (b)

Very Short Answer Type [1 Mark]

Q.1. When Delhi was finally captured by Britishers after revolt of 1857?

Ans. Delhi was finally captured by Britishers after revolt of 1857 in September 1857

Q.2. Who was the painter of "Relief of Lucknow"?

Ans. Thomas Jones was the painter of Relief of Lucknow

Q.3. Who was the painter of "In Memoriam"?

Ans. Joseph Noel Paton

Q.4. What is bell of arms?

Ans. Store house of weapons

Q.5. Who was the writer of poem "Khoob lari mardani woh to Jhansi wali rani thi"?

Ans. Subhadra Kumari Chauhan

Q.6. When was Rani Jhansi killed by British army?

Ans. She was killed by British in June 1858

Short Answer Type - I [2 Marks]

Q.1. What was the British plan for conquering Delhi?

Ans. The British thus mounted a two-pronged attack. One force moved from Calcutta into North India and the other from the Punjab – which was largely peaceful – to reconquer Delhi.

Q.2. What was the motive of British pictures during revolt?

Ans. British pictures offer a variety of images that were meant to provoke a range of different emotions and reactions. Some of them commemorate the British heroes who saved the English and repressed the rebels.

Q.3. During the revolt who was the commissioner of Lucknow?

Ans. When the rebel forces besieged Lucknow, Henry Lawrence, the Commissioner of Lucknow, collected the Christian population and took refuge in the heavily fortified Residency. Lawrence was killed but the Residency continued to be defended under the command of Colonel Inglis.

Q.4. According to Barker's painting who were the British heroes of Lucknow?

Ans. Barker's painting celebrates the moment of Campbell's entry. At the centre of the canvas are the British heroes – Campbell, Outram and Havelock.

Short Answer Type - II [3 Marks]

Q.1. How did the British used landholders to suppress the revolt?

Ans. The British used military power on a gigantic scale. But this was not the only instrument they used. In large parts of present-day Uttar Pradesh, where big landholders and peasants had offered united resistance, the British tried to break up the unity by promising to give back to the big landholders their estates. Rebel landholders were dispossessed and the loyal rewarded. Many landholders died fighting the British or they escaped into Nepal where they died of illness or starvation.

Q.2. What was shown in "In Memoriam" painting?

Ans. "In Memoriam" was painted by Joseph Noel Paton two years after the mutiny. In this English women and children huddled in a circle, looking helpless and innocent, seemingly waiting for the inevitable – dishonour, violence and death. "In Memoriam" does not show gory violence; it only suggests it. It stirs up the spectator's imagination, and seeks to provoke anger and fury. It represents the rebels as violent and brutish, even though they remain invisible in the picture. In the background you can see the British rescue forces arriving as saviours.

Q.3. From which sources historians come to know the different angle of the revolt?

Ans. As we have seen, we have very few records on the rebels' point of view. There are a few rebel proclamations and notifications, as also some letters that rebel leaders wrote. But historians till now have continued to discuss rebel actions primarily through accounts written by the British. Official accounts, of course, abound: colonial administrators and military men left their versions in letters and diaries, autobiographies and official histories. One important record of the mutiny is the pictorial images produced by the British and Indians: paintings, pencil drawings, etchings, posters, cartoons, bazaar prints.

Long Answer Type   [5 Marks]

Q.1. How did the British react to suppress the revolt?

Ans. It is clear from all accounts that we have of 1857 that the British did not have an easy time in putting down the rebellion. Before sending out troops to reconquer North India, the British passed a series of laws to help them quell the insurgency. By a number of Acts, passed in May and June 1857, not only was the whole of North India put under martial law but military officers and even ordinary Britons were given the power to try and punish Indians suspected of rebellion.

Armed with these newly enacted special laws and the reinforcements brought in from Britain, the British began the task of suppressing the revolt. They, like the rebels, recognised the symbolic value of Delhi. The British thus mounted a two-pronged attack. One force moved from Calcutta into North India and the other from the Punjab – which was largely peaceful – to reconquer Delhi.

Q.2. How did the Britishers captured Lucknow?

Ans. When the rebel forces besieged Lucknow, Henry Lawrence, the Commissioner of Lucknow, collected the Christian population and took refuge in the heavily fortified Residency. Lawrence was killed but the Residency continued to be defended under the command of Colonel Inglis. On 25 September James Outram and Henry Havelock arrived, cut through the rebel forces, and reinforced the British garrisons. Twenty days later Colin Campbell, who was appointed as the new Commander of British forces in India, came with his forces and rescued the besieged British garrison. In British accounts the siege of Lucknow became a story of survival, heroic resistance and the ultimate triumph of British power.

Chapter Practice

Multiple Choice Questions   [1 Mark]

Q.1. A collective disobedience of rules and regulations within the armed forces called as

(a) Revolt   (b) Mutiny

(c) Rebellion   (d) None of the above

Q.2. One of the first acts of the sepoys of Meerut, was to rush to Delhi and appeal to the old Mughal emperor _______________ to accept the leadership of the revolt.

(a) Hashim ud-Daula   (b) Bahadur Shah

(c) Siraj ud-Daulah   (d) Alivardi Khan

Q.3. Find the incorrect statement with reference to the Pattern of the Rebellion

(a) Only white man was the target of sepoys

(b) Both Hindus and Muslims, united, rose and exterminated the British.

(c) Proclamations in Hindi, Urdu and Persian were put up in the cities calling upon the population

(d) Money- lenders and the rich also became the objects of rebel wrath.

Q.4. In Kanpur, the sepoys and the people of the town gave Nana Sahib, the successor to__________

(a) Peshwa Baji Rao II   (b) Peshwa Baji Rao I

(c) Baji Rao I   (d) None of the above

Q.5. In which of the following regions the people celebrated the fall of British rule by hailing Birjis Qadr, the young son of the Nawab, as their leader.

(a) Lucknow   (b) Ujjain

(c) Buxar   (d) Bareilly

Very Short Answer Type   [1 Mark]

Q.6. In which year did the British establish a law to end the practice of Sati?

Q.7. In which kingdom, the resistance to the British lasted for the longest duration?

Q.8. Gonu, who became the rebel leader of the Kol tribals, belongs to which region?

Short Answer Type - I   [2 Marks]

Q.9. British adopted policies aimed at "reforming" Indian society under the leadership of which Governor general?

Q.10. Which ruler was exiled to Calcutta by the British Empire in 1856?

Q.11. What was Summary Settlement of 1856?

Q.12. With which leader did the Talukdars of Awadh region join to fight against the British?

Q.13. The large majority of the sepoys of the Bengal Army were recruited from which regions?   [CBSE 2013]

Read the extracts given below arid answer the questions that follow : (Q14, Q15 and Q16)

Ordinary life in extraordinary times

What happened in cities during the months of Revolt ? How did people live, through those months of tumult? How was normal life affected ? Reports from different cities tell us about the breakdown in routine activities. Read these reports from the Delhi Urdu Akhbar, 14 June, 1857 :

The same thing is true far vegetables and saag (spinach). People have been found to complain that even kaddu (pumpkin) and baingan (brinjal) cannot be found in the bazars. Potatoes and arvi (yam) when available are of stale and rotten variety, stored from before by farsighted kunjras (vegetable growers). From the gardens inside the city some I produce does reach a few places but the poor and the middle class can only lick their lips and watch them (as they are earmarked for the select).

….. There is something else that needs attention which is causing a lot of damage to the people which is that the water-carriers have stopped filling water. Poor Shurfas (gentility) are seen carrying water in pails on their shoulders and only ther. the necessary household tasks such as cooking, etc. can take place. The halalkhors (righteous) have become haramkhors (corrupt), many mohallas have not been able to earn for several, days and if this situation continues then decay, death and disease will combine together to spoil the city's air and an epidemic will spread all over the city and even to areas adjacent and around.

Q.14. Explair what happened in Delhi city during the months of the 1857 Revolt ?

Q.15. How did the routine activities disturb the people?

Short Answer Type - II

[3 Marks]

Q.16. How did people live through those months of tumult ?

Q.17. How did changes occur in the building pattern of colonial cities after the revolt of 1857 ? Cite any two examples.   [CBSE 2014]

Long Answer Type

[5 Marks]

Q.18. The relationship of the Indian sepoys with their superior white officers underwent a significant change in 1840s and 1850s." Explain.   [CBSE 2013]

Q.19. Explain how rumours and prophecies played an important part in moving people to action during the revolt of 1857.   [CBSE 2015]

CHAPTER 12

Colonial Cities

Towns and Cities in Pre-colonial Time

Summary

- Towns were often defined in opposition to rural areas. They came to represent specific forms of economic activities and cultures.

- Towns dominated over the rural population, thriving on the surplus and taxes derived from agriculture. Towns and cities were often fortified by walls which symbolised their separation from the countryside.

- However, the separation between town and country was fluid. During the sixteenth and seventeenth centuries the towns built by the Mughals were famous for their concentration of populations, their monumental buildings and their imperial grandeur and wealth.

- The presence of the emperor and noblemen in these centres meant that a wide variety of services had to be provided.

- Medieval towns were places where everybody was expected to know their position in the social order dominated by the ruling elite. In North India, maintaining this order was the work of the imperial officer called the kotwal who oversaw the internal affairs and policing of the town.

- Some local notables and officials associated with Mughal rule in North India also used this opportunity to create new urban settlements such as the qasbah and ganj.

- The European commercial Companies had set up base in different places early during the Mughal era: the Portuguese in Panaji in 1510, the Dutch in Masulipatnam in 1605, the British in Madras in 1639 and the French in Pondicherry (present-day Puducherry) in 1673.

- From the mid-eighteenth century, there was a new phase of change. Commercial centres such as Surat, Masulipatnam and Dhaka, which had grown in the seventeenth century, declined when trade shifted to other places.

- Colonial rule was based on the production of enormous amounts of data. The British kept detailed records of their trading activities in order to regulate their commercial affairs.

- From the late nineteenth century the British tried to raise money for administering towns through the systematic annual collection of municipal taxes. To avoid conflict they handed over some responsibilities to elected Indian representatives.

- The census operation, for instance, was a means by which social data were converted into convenient statistics about th population. But this process was riddled with ambiguity.

- For a long while they were suspicious of census operations and believed that enquiries were being conducted to impose new taxes.

- A careful study of censuses reveals some fascinating trends. After 1800, urbanisation in India was sluggish.

- In the forty years between 1900 and 1940 the urban population increased from about 10 per cent of the total population to about 13 per cent.

- The introduction of railways in 1853 meant a change in the fortunes of towns. Economic activity gradually shifted away from traditional towns which were located along old routes and rivers.

Multiple Choice Questions   [1 Mark]

Q.1. Towns were often defined in opposition to rural areas. During the sixteenth and seventeenth centuries the towns built by the Mughals were famous for their-

(a) Concentration of population

(b) Residence of Mansabdars

(c) Imperial grandeur and wealth

(d) All of the above

Ans. (d)

Q.2. Medieval towns were places where everybody was expected to know their position in the social order dominated by the ruling elite. In North India which officer was assigned to maintain these social orders?

(a) Mansabdar   (b) Wajir

(c) Kotwal   (d) Subedar

Ans. (c)

Q.3. Changes in the networks of trade were reflected in the history of urban centres. The European commercial Companies had set up base in different places early during the Mughal era. Choose the correct option from below-

(a) Portuguese in Panaji in 1510

(b) Dutch in Masulipatnam in 1673

(c) British in Madras in 1605

(d) French in Pondicherry 1639

Ans. (a)

Q.4. The growth of cities was monitored through regular head counts. By the mid-nineteenth century several local censuses had been carried out in different regions. The first all-India census was attempted in?

(a) 1881   (b) 1892

(c) 1872   (d) 1905

Ans. (c)

Q.5. A careful study of censuses reveals some fascinating trends. After 1800, urbanisation in India was sluggish. All through the nineteenth century up tothe first two decades of the twentieth, the proportion of the urban population to the total population in India was-

(a) Increased 10%   (b) Decreased 25%

(c) Low and stagnant (d) Data not available

Ans. (c)

Q.6. The introduction of railways meant a change in the fortunes of towns. Economic activity gradually shifted away from traditional towns which were located along old routes and rivers. In which year railway was introduced?

(a) 1754   (b) 1919

(c) 1892   (d) 1853

Ans. (d)

Very Short Answer Type   [1 Mark]

Q.1. In North India, maintaining law and order was the work of the imperial officer called?

Ans. The imperial officer was called Kotwal

Q.2. Define the term Ganj?

Ans. Ganj refers to a small fixed market.

Q.3. In the forty years between 1900 and 1940 the urban population increased from about?

Ans. 10 per cent of the total population to about 13 per cent.

Q.4. Supreme Court setup in Calcutta by East India company was in?

Ans. Supreme Court setup in Calcutta by East India company was in 1773

Q.5. Asiatic society of Bengal was established by?

Ans. Sir William Jones in 1784

Q.6. Cornwallis code was enacted in which year?

Ans. Cornwallis code was enacted in 1793

Q.7. From which year census conducted every ten years?

Ans. From 1881 census conducted every ten years

Short Answer Type - I [2 Marks]

Q.1. In which conditions reverse flow of humans and goods from towns to villages was happened in pre-colonial time?

Ans. There was a reverse flow of humans and goods from towns to villages. When towns were attacked, people often sought shelter in the countryside. Traders and pedlars took goods from the towns to sell in the villages, extending markets and creating new patterns of consumption.

Q.2. What was the difference between principal focus of town of north India and south India?

Ans. The focus of the town was oriented towards the palace and the principal mosque. In the towns of South India such as Madurai and Kanchipuram the principal focus was the temple.

Q.3. What were the effects of political decentralisation in eighteenth century?

Ans. The effects of political decentralisation were uneven. In some places there was renewed economic activity, in other places war, plunder and political uncertainty led to economic decline.

Q.4. Define the term Qasbah?

Ans. Qasbah is a small town in the countryside, often the seat of a local notable.

Q.5. Why were Britishers keen to create the familiar landscape in Bombay ? Give two reasons. (CBSE 2013)

Ans. British were keen to make familiar landscape of Bombay because of the following two reasons

- They wanted to make European style buildings so that they can feel home in the colony.
- The British felt that European styles would best symbolise their superiority, authority and power.

Short Answer Type - II [3 Marks]

Q.1. What were the basic differences between town and rural areas?

Ans. Towns were often defined in opposition to rural areas. They came to represent specific forms of economic activities and cultures. In the countryside people subsisted by cultivating land, foraging in the forest, or rearing animals. Towns by contrast were peopled with artisans, traders, administrators and rulers. Towns dominated over the rural population, thriving on the surplus and taxes derived from agriculture. Towns and cities were often fortified by walls which symbolised their separation from the countryside.

Q.2. How the presence of the emperor and noblemen in the towns provided job opportunities for villagers? **[CBSE 2013]**

Ans. The presence of the emperor and noblemen in these centres meant that a wide variety of services had to be provided. Artisans produced exclusive handicrafts for the households of nobles. Grain from the countryside was brought into urban markets for the town dwellers and the army. The treasury was also located in the imperial capital. Thus the revenues of the kingdom flowed into the capital regularly. The emperor lived in a fortified palace and the town was enclosed by a wall, with entry and exit being regulated by different gates. Within these towns were gardens, mosques, temples, tombs, colleges, bazaars and caravanserais. For all of these required men were fulfilled from rural areas.

Q.3. Why census was necessary?

Ans. The census operation, for instance, was a means by which social data were converted into convenient statistics about the population. But this process was riddled with ambiguity. The census commissioners devised categories for classifying different sections of the population. This classification was often arbitrary and failed to capture the fluid and overlapping identities of people. How was a person who was both an artisan and a trader to be classified? How was a person who cultivated his land and carted produce to the town to be enumerated? Was he a cultivator or a trader? For these all question census was necessary.

Q.4. According to census data of early twentieth century what was trend of population in India? **[CBSE 2017]**

Ans. A careful study of censuses reveals some fascinating trends. After 1800, urbanisation in India was sluggish. All through the nineteenth century up to the first two decades of the twentieth, the proportion of the urban population to the total population in India was extremely low and had remained stagnant. In the forty years between 1900 and 1940 the urban population increased from about 10 per cent of the total population to about 13 per cent. Beneath this picture of changelessness, there were significant variations in the patterns of urban development in different regions.

Q.5. What changes came for towns after introducing railways?

Ans. The introduction of railways in 1853 meant a change in the fortunes of towns. Economic activity gradually shifted away from traditional towns which were located along old routes and rivers. Every railway station became a collection depot for raw materials and a distribution point for imported goods. For instance, Mirzapur on the Ganges, which specialised in collecting cotton and cotton goods from the Deccan, declined when a railway link was made to Bombay. With the expansion of the railway network, railway workshops and railway colonies were established. Railway towns like Jamalpur, Waltair and Bareilly developed.

Long Answer Type [5 Marks]

Q.1. Regarding towns which new changes came in eighteenth century?

Ans. All this started changing in the eighteenth century. With political and commercial realignments, old towns went into decline and new towns developed. The gradual erosion of Mughal power led to the demise of towns associated with their rule. The Mughal capitals, Delhi and Agra, lost their political authority. The growth of new regional powers was reflected in the increasing importance of regional capitals – Lucknow, Hyderabad, Seringapatam, Poona (present-day Pune), Nagpur, Baroda (present day Vadodara) and Tanjore (present-day Thanjavur). Traders, administrators, artisans and others migrated from the old Mughal centres to these new capitals in search of work and patronage. Continuous warfare between the new kingdoms meant that mercenaries too found ready employment there.

Q.2. How map help Britishers to established cities or town in India?

Ans. The British kept detailed records of their trading activities in order to regulate their commercial affairs. To keep track of life in the growing cities, they carried out regular surveys, gathered statistical data, and published various official reports. From the early years, the colonial government was keen on mapping. It felt that good maps were necessary to understand the landscape and know the topography. This knowledge would allow better control over the region. When towns began to grow, maps were prepared not only to plan the development of these towns but also to develop commerce and consolidate power. The town maps give information regarding the location of hills, rivers and vegetation, all important for planning structures for defence purposes. They also show the location of ghats, density and quality of houses and alignment of roads, used to gauge commercial possibilities and plan strategies of taxation.

Q.3. What were the challenges came in front of census official in nineteenth century?

Ans. The census commissioners devised categories for classifying different sections of the population. This classification was often arbitrary and failed to capture the fluid and overlapping identities of people. Often people themselves refused to cooperate or gave evasive answers to the census officials. For a long while they were suspicious of census operations and believed that enquiries were being conducted to impose new taxes. Upper-caste people were also unwilling to give any information regarding the women of their household: women were supposed to remain secluded within the interior of the household and not subjected to public gaze or public enquiry. Census officials also found that people were claiming identities that they associated with higher status. Similarly, the figures of mortality and disease were difficult to collect, for all deaths were not registered, and illness was not always reported, nor treated by licensed doctors.

TOPIC 2

Segregation, Town Planning and Architecture

Summary

- By the eighteenth century Madras, Calcutta and Bombay had become important ports.

- The English East India Company built its factories (i.e., mercantile offices) there and because of competition among the European companies, fortified these settlements for protection.

- Once the British captured political power these racial distinctions became sharper.

- After the 1850s, cotton mills were set up by Indian merchants and entrepreneurs in Bombay, and European-owned jute mills were established on the outskirts of Calcutta.

- Colonial cities reflected the mercantile culture of the new rulers. Political power and patronage shifted from Indian rulers to the merchants of the East India Company.

- The rich Indian agents and middlemen built large traditional courtyard houses in the Black Town in the vicinity of the bazaars.

- The nature of the colonial city changed further in the mid-nineteenth century. After the Revolt of 1857 British attitudes in India were shaped by a constant fear of rebellion.

- Pasturelands and agricultural fields around the older towns were cleared, and new urban spaces called "Civil Lines" were set up. White people began to live in the Civil Lines. Cantonments– places where Indian troops under European command were stationed – were also developed as safe enclaves.

- For the British, the "Black" areas came to symbolise not only chaos and anarchy, but also filt and disease. For a long while the British were interested primarily in the cleanliness and hygiene of the "White" areas.

- As in the case of cantonments, hill stations were a distinctive feature of colonial urban development. The founding and settling of hill stations was initially connected with the needs of the British army.

- The overwhelming presence of the army made these stations a new kind of cantonment in the hills. These hill stations were also developed as sanitariums, i.e., places where soldiers could be sent for rest and recovery from illnesses.

- For the Indian population, the new cities were bewildering places where life seemed always in a flux. There was a dramatic contrast between extreme wealth and poverty.

- There was an increasing demand for clerks, teachers, lawyers, doctors, engineers and accountants. As a result the "middle classes" increased. They had access to new educational institutions such as schools, colleges and libraries.

- Even reformers who supported women's education saw women primarily as mothers and wives, and wanted them to remain within the enclosed spaces of the household.

- In 1639 they constructed a trading post in Madraspatam. This settlement was locally known as Chenapattanam.

- Fort St George became the nucleus of the White Town where most of the Europeans lived. Walls and bastions made this a distinct enclave. Colour and religion determined who was allowed to live within the Fort.

- The new Black Town resembled traditional Indian towns, with living quarters built around its own temple and bazaar. On the narrow lanes that crisscrossed the township, there were distinct caste-specific neighbourhoods.

- As the British consolidated their power, resident Europeans began to move out of the Fort. Garden houses first started coming up along the two main arteries – Mount Road and Poonamalee Road – leading from the Fort to the cantonment. Wealthy Indians too started to live like the English.

- After Wellesley's departure the work of town planning was carried on by the Lottery Committee (1817) with the help of the government.

- Bombay was initially seven islands. As the population grew, the islands were joined to create more space and they gradually fused into one big city. Bombay was the commercial capital of colonial India.

- Another style that was extensively used was the neo-Gothic, characterised by high-pitched roofs, pointed arches and detailed decoration. The Gothic style had its roots in buildings, especially churches, built in northern Europe during the medieval period.

- Towards the beginning of the twentieth century a new hybrid architectural style developed which combined the Indian with the European. This was called Indo-Saracenic. "Indo" was shorthand for Hindu and "Saracen" was a term Europeans used to designate Muslim.

- Architecture reflects the aesthetic ideals prevalent at a time, and variations within those ideals. But, as we have seen, buildings also express the vision of those who build them. Rulers everywhere seek to express their power through buildings.

Multiple Choice Questions   [1 Mark]

Q.1. The English East India Company built its factories (i.e., mercantile offices) there and because of competition among the European companies, fortified these settlements for protection. Fort St George was established in-

(a) Bombay

(b) Madras

(c) Calcutta

(d) Surat

Ans. (b)

Q.2. The nature of the colonial city changed further in the mid-nineteenth century. A new Civil line area develop in countryside. For whom this area was?

(a) For rich merchants

(b) For sepoys

(c) For white people

(d) For Indian people

Ans. (c)

Q.3. As in the case of cantonments, hill stations were a distinctive feature of colonial urban development. The temperate and cool climate of the Indian hills was seen as an advantage. Hill station are used as-

(a) Billeting troops

(b) Launching against enemy

(c) Rest and recovery from illnesses

(d) All of the above

Ans. (d)

Q.4. It became a practice for viceroys to move to hill stations during the summer months. In 1864 which Viceroy officially moved his council to Shimla?

(a) Henery Lawrence

(b) John Lawrence

(c) Rippon

(d) Lord Mayo

Ans. (b)

Q.5. Madras, Calcutta and Bombay gradually developed into the biggest cities of colonial India. The Company had first set up its trading activities in the well-established port of –

(a) Bombay　　　(b) Madras

(c) Surat　　　(d) Cochin

Ans. (c)

Q.6. Subsequently the search for textiles brought British merchants to the east coast. In which year they constructed a trading post in Madraspatam?

(a) 1664　　　(b) 1739

(c) 1704　　　(d) 1639

Ans. (d)

Q.7. The Lottery Committee was so named because funds for townimprovement were raised through public lotteries. When this Lottery Committee came to India?

(a) 1719　　　(b) 1817

(c) 1864　　　(d) 1903

Ans. (b)

Q.8. Towards the beginning of the twentieth century anew hybrid architectural style developed which combined the Indian with the European. This was called Indo-Saracenic. The Saracen word is used for—

(a) Hindu

(b) European

(c) Muslims

(d) Jains

Ans. (c)

Very Short Answer Type　　　**[1 Mark]**

Q.1. Fort William was established by East India Company in which Indian city?

Ans. Fort William was established by East India Company in Calcutta

Q.2. When was the Gurkha war happened?

Ans. Gurkha war happened in 1815-16

Q.3. In which year Lord Wellesley's Minute on Calcutta town improvement was came?

Ans. It came in 1803

Q.4. First spinning and weaving mill in Bombay came in?

Ans. First spinning and weaving mill in Bombay came in 1857

Q.5. In which year capital was shifted from Calcutta to Delhi?

Ans. The capital was shifted from Calcutta to Delhi 1911

Q.6. In which year did elected representatives start in municipalities?

Ans. In 1870 elected representatives participated in municipalities

Q.7. Fort St George was established in?

Ans. It was established in Madras

Short Answer Type - I [2 Marks]

Q.1. Why the factories were fortified?

Ans. The settlements that came up here were convenient points for collecting goods. The English East India Company built its factories (i.e., mercantile offices) there and because of competition among the European companies, fortified these settlements for protection.

Q.2. Which two cities were called proper "industrial cities" in nineteenth century?

Ans. There were only two proper "industrial cities": Kanpur, specialising in leather, woollen and cotton textiles, and Jamshedpur, specialising in steel. India never became a modern industrialised country, since discriminatory colonial policies limited the levels of industrial development.

Q.3. Define the term Ionic?

Ans. Ionic was one of the three orders (organisational systems) of Ancient Greek architecture, the other two being Doric, and Corinthian. One feature that distinguished each order was the style of the capital at the head of the columns. These forms were re-adapted in the Renaissance and Neo-classical forms of architecture.

Q.4. In new urban cities how women express themselves?

Ans. Social changes did not happen with ease. Cities, for instance, offered new opportunities for women. Middle-class women sought to express themselves through the medium of journals, autobiographies and books.

Q.5. Define the term pet?

Ans. Pet is a Tamil word meaning settlement, while puram is used for a village.

Q.6. What was Chenapattanam?

Ans. Subsequently the search for textiles brought British merchants to the east coast. In 1639 they constructed a trading post in Madraspatam. This settlement was locally known as Chenapattanam.

Q.7. Why was the colonial government keen on mapping of Indian cities from the early years ? Give any two reasons. **[CBSE 2013]**

Ans. The colonial government keen on mapping of Indian cities from the early years because

- The maps were essential to understand the landscape and know the topography according to the colonial government

- This knowledge of mapping would allow better control over the region. The maps provided various important information.

Q.8. Name any two hill stations developed during the British period. Why did these hill stations become an ideal destination for the British and Europeans ? Give any one reason. **[CBSE 2015]**

Ans. Hill stations developed during the British period were:

- Shimla in Himachal Pradesh

- Mount-Abu in Rajasthan

The British government developed the hill stations keeping in mind the environment of Shimla and Mount-Abu. The climate of these hill stations were similar to that of Europe and thus was an ideal for holidays and recreation.

Short Answer Type - II [3 Marks]

Q.1. What changes came in new urban settlement after Mughal declined?

Ans. Colonial cities reflected the mercantile culture of the new rulers. Political power and patronage shifted from Indian rulers to the merchants of the East India Company. Indians who worked as interpreters, middlemen, traders and suppliers of goods also had an important place in these new cities. Economic activity near the river or the sea led to the development of docks and ghats. Along the shore were godowns, mercantile offices, insurance agencies for shipping, transport depots, banking establishments. Further inland were the chief administrative offices of the Company. The Writers' Building in Calcutta was one such office. Around the periphery of the Fort, European merchants and agents built palatial houses in European styles.

Q.2. What was the difference between "White Town" and "Black Town"?

Ans. The English East India Company built its factories (i.e., mercantile offices) there and because of competition among the European companies, fortified these settlements for protection. In Madras, Fort St George, in Calcutta Fort William and in Bombay the Fort marked out the areas of British settlement. Indian merchants, artisans and other workers who had economic dealings with European merchants lived outside these forts in settlements of their own. Thus, from the beginning there were separate quarters for Europeans and Indians, which came to be labelled in contemporary writings as the "White Town" and "Black Town" respectively.

Q.3. What were the British thought about Black areas?

Ans. For the British, the "Black" areas came to symbolise not only chaos and anarchy, but also filth and disease. For a long while the British were interested primarily in the cleanliness and hygiene of the "White" areas. But as epidemics of cholera and plague spread, killing thousands, colonial officials felt the need for more stringent measures of sanitation and public health. They feared that disease would spread from the "Black" to the "White" areas. From the 1860s and 1870s, stringent administrative measures regarding sanitation were implemented and building activity in the Indian towns was regulated.

Q.4. Due to which cause middle class population increased in new urban areas?

Ans. Within the cities new social groups were formed and the old identities of people were no longer important. All classes of people were migrating to the big cities. There was an increasing demand for clerks, teachers, lawyers, doctors, engineers and accountants. As a result the "middle classes" increased. They had access to new educational institutions such as schools, colleges and libraries. As educated people, they could put forward their opinions on society and government in newspapers, journals and public meetings.

Q.5. Define the term Bustis?

Ans. Busti (in Bengali and Hindi) originally meant neighbourhood or settlement. However, the British narrowed the sense of the word to mean makeshift huts built by the poor. In the late nineteenth century "bustis" and insanitary slums became synonymous in British records.

Q.6. Explain why some hill stations were developed during the colonial period in India. **[CBSE 2018]**

Ans. Some hill stations like Shimla, Mount Abu, were developed during the colonial period in India as the cold climate of the Indian hills were similar to that of Europe. The British associated the hot weather with epidemics so the hill stations were established mainly for the army, to protect them from diseases like cholera and malaria. They also became strategic places for billeting troops guarding frontiers and launching campaigns against enemy rulers. These hill stations were also developed as Sanatoriums i.e., places where soldiers could be sent for rest.

Long Answer Type [5 Marks]

Q.1. What changes came in colonial city after the revolt of 1857?

Ans. The nature of the colonial city changed further in the mid-nineteenth century. After the Revolt of 1857 British attitudes in India were shaped by a constant fear of rebellion. They felt that towns needed to be better defended, and white people had to live in more secure and segregated enclaves, away from the threat of the "natives". Pasturelands and agricultural fields around the older towns were cleared, and new urban spaces called "Civil Lines" were set up. White people began to live in the Civil Lines. Cantonments– places where Indian troops under European command were stationed – were also developed as safe enclaves. These areas were separate from but attached to the Indian towns. With broad streets, bungalows set amidst large gardens, barracks, parade ground and church, they were meant as a safe haven for Europeans as well as a model of ordered urban life in contrast to the densely builtup Indian towns.

Q.2. How the labour class lived in new urban cities late nineteenth century?

Ans. Another new class within the cities was the labouring poor or the working class. Paupers from rural areas flocked to the cities in the hope of employment. Some saw cities as places of opportunity; others were attracted by the allure of a different way of life, by the desire to see things they had never seen before. To minimise costs of living in the city, most male migrants left their families behind in their village homes. Life in the city was a struggle: jobs were uncertain, food was expensive, and places to stay were difficult to afford. Yet the poor often created a lively urban culture of their own. They were enthusiastic participants in religious festivals, tamashas (folk theatre) and swangs (satires) which often mocked the pretensions of their masters, Indian and European.

Q.3. Who were dubashes and how they lived in cities?

Ans. Madras developed by incorporating innumerable surrounding villages and by creating opportunities and spaces for a variety of communities. Several different communities came and settled in Madras, performing a range of economic functions. The dubashes were Indians who could speak two languages – the local language and English. They worked as agents and merchants, acting as intermediaries between Indian society and the British. They used their privileged position in government to acquire wealth. Their powerful position in society was established by their charitable works and patronage of temples in the Black Town.

Q.4. Give a short detail about the Lottery Committee?

Ans. After Wellesley's departure the work of town planning was carried on by the Lottery Committee (1817) with the help of the government. The Lottery Committee was so named because funds for town improvement were raised through public lotteries. In other words, in the early decades of the nineteenth century raising funds for the city was still thought to be the responsibility of public minded citizens and not exclusively that of the government. The Lottery Committee commissioned a new map of the city so as to get a comprehensive picture of Calcutta. Among the Committee's major activities was road building in the Indian part of the city and clearing the river bank of "encroachments". In its drive to make the Indian areas of Calcutta cleaner, the committee removed many huts and displaced the labouring poor, who were now pushed to the outskirts of Calcutta.

Chapter Practice

Multiple Choice Questions

[1 Mark]

Q.1. *Kotwali* , who oversaw the internal affairs and policing of the town, *was an* imperial officer of _______

(a) Mughals

(b) North India

(c) Provinces

(d) Mansabdars

Q.2. During the sixteenth and seventeenth centuries the towns consisted of

1. artisans

2. traders

3. administrators

4. rulers

Choose the correct answer from the codes given below

(a) 1, 2, 3 only

(b) 1, 2, 3 and 4

(c) 1, 3 and 4 only

(d) 2, 3 and 4 only

Q.3. Which of the following cities was not built by the Mughals

(a) Agra

(b) Delhi

(c) Lahore

(d) Lucknow

Q.4. In Mughal empire, Mansabdars and jagirdars were used to live in

(a) Cities

(b) Villages

(c) Provinces

(d) Emperor palace

Q.5. During the sixteenth and seventeenth centuriesthe focus of the town was oriented towards

(a) the palace

(b) the principal mosque

(c) the temple

(d) All of the above

Q.6. Find the incorrect pair

European l Commercia	Companies Bases Location
(a) Portuguese	Panaji in 1510
(b) Dutch	Masulipatnam in 1605
(c) British	Surat in 1639
(d) The French	Pondicherry in1673.

Q.7. Calcutta had grown from which of the following villages

1. Sutanati

2. Kolkata

3. Govindapur

4. Maidan

Choose the correct answer from the codes given below

(a) 1, 2, 3 only

(b) 1, 2, 3 and 4

(c) 1, 3 and 4 only

(d) 2, 3 and 4 only

Very Short Answer Type   [1 Mark]

Q.8. After which war did the British gradually gain political control?

Q.9. When was the first All India Census attempted?

Q.10. Which were the important port cities of the eighteenth century?

Q.11. What were the new urban settlements that emerged after the Revolt of 1857 called?

Q.12. Vellalars were the rural caste people of which region?

Short Answer Type - I   [2 Marks]

Q.13. Discuss the beginning of modern industrial development in India.

Q.14. How was the Social life in the new cities?

Q.15. Simla was founded during the course of which event?

Q.16. Which viceroy officially moved his council to Simla, setting seal to the practice of shifting capitals during the hot season ?   **[CBSE 2015]**

Q.17. Who were dubashes

Q.18. What was the architectural style of Bombay?   **[CBSE 2017]**

Short Answer Type - II   [3 Marks]

Q.19. What do the terms "White" and "Black" Town signify?   **[CBSE 2019]**

Q.20. How did prominent Indian merchants establish themselves in the colonial city?   **[CBSE 2018]**

Long Answer Type   [5 Marks]

Q.21. 'The colonial cities offered new opportunities to women during the 19th century." Support the statement with facts.   **[CBSE 2013]**

CHAPTER 13

Mahatma Gandhi and The Nationalist Movement

Civil Disobedience and Beyond

Summary

- In January 1915, Mohandas Karamchand Gandhi returned to his homeland after two decades of residence abroad.

Condition when Gandhi arrived India:

- The India that Mahatma Gandhi came back to in 1915 was rather different from the one that he had left in 1893.

- The Indian National Congress now had branches in most major cities and towns. Through the Swadeshi movement of 1905-07 it had greatly broadened its appeal among the middle classes.

- That movement had thrown up some towering leaders – among them Bal Gangadhar Tilak of Maharashtra, Bipin Chandra Pal of Bengal, and Lala Lajpat Rai of Punjab. The three were known as "Lal, Bal and Pal".

- There was a group of "Moderates" who preferred a more gradual and persuasive approach. Among these Moderates was Gandhiji's acknowledged political mentor, Gopal Krishna Gokhale, as well as Mohammad Ali Jinnah, who, like Gandhiji, was a lawyer of Gujarati extraction trained in London.

After Arrival

- On Gokhale's advice, Gandhiji spent a year travelling around British India, getting to know the land

- His first major public appearance was at the opening of the Banaras Hindu University (BHU) in February 1916.

- He had been invited on account of his work in South Africa, rather than his status within India.

- At the annual Congress, held in Lucknow in December 1916, he was approached by a peasant from Champaran in Bihar, who told him about the harsh treatment of peasants by British indigo planters.

The Making and Unmaking of Non-cooperation

- Mahatma Gandhi was to spend much of 1917 in Champaran, seeking to obtain for the peasants security of tenure as well as the freedom to cultivate the crops of their choice. The following year, 1918, Gandhiji was involved in two campaigns in his home state of Gujarat.

- First, he intervened in a labour dispute in Ahmedabad, demanding better working conditions for the textile mill workers. Then he joined peasants in Kheda in asking the state for the remission of taxes following the failure of their harvest.

- During the Great War of 1914-18, the British had instituted censorship of the press and permitted detention without trial. Now, on the recommendation of a committee chaired by Sir Sidney Rowlatt, these tough measures were continued. In response, Gandhiji called for a countrywide campaign against the "Rowlatt Act".

- Gandhiji was detained while proceeding to Punjab, even as prominent local Congressmen were arrested.

- The situation in the province grew progressively tenser, reaching a bloody climax in Amritsar in April 1919, when a British Brigadier ordered his troops to open fire on a nationalist meeting - known as the Jallianwala Bagh massacre.

- Emboldened by the success of Rowlatt Syagrah, Gandhiji called for a campaign of "non-cooperation" with British rule. Indians who wished colonialism to end were asked to stop attending schools, colleges and law courts, and not pay taxes.

- To further broaden the struggle he had joined hands with the Khilafat Movement that sought to restore the Caliphate, a symbol of Pan-Islamism

Knitting a popular movement

- Non-cooperation was negative enough to be peaceful but positive enough to be effective.

- Peasants, workers, and others interpreted and acted upon the call to "non-cooperate" with colonial rule in ways that best suited their interests, rather than conform to the dictates laid down from above.

- As a consequence of the Non-Cooperation Movement the British Raj was shaken to its foundations for the first time since the Revolt of 1857.

A people's leader

- While other nationalist leaders dressed formally, wearing a Western suit or an Indian *bandgala*, Gandhiji went among the people in a simple *dhoti* or loincloth.

- Meanwhile, he spent part of each day working on the *charkha* (spinning wheel), and encouraged other nationalists to do likewise.

- The act of spinning allowed Gandhiji to break the boundaries that prevailed within the traditional caste system, between mental labour and manual labour.

- New branches of the Congress were set up in various parts of India.

- A series of "Praja Mandals" were established to promote the nationalist creed in the princely states. Gandhiji encouraged the communication of the nationalist message in the mother tongue.

- Between 1917 and 1922, a group of highly talented Indians attached themselves to Gandhiji. They included Mahadev Desai, Vallabh Bhai Patel, J.B. Kripalani, Subhas Chandra Bose, Abul Kalam Azad, Jawaharlal Nehru, Sarojini Naidu, Govind Ballabh Pant and C. Rajagopalachari.

- He vouched for removal of untouchability and promotion of Hindu Muslim unity

The Salt Satyagraha A Case Study

- In 1928, there was an all-India campaign in opposition to the all-White Simon Commission, sent from England to enquire into conditions in the colony. Gandhiji did not himself participate in this movement, although he gave it his blessings, as he also did to a peasant satyagraha in Bardoli in the same year.

- In the end of December 1929, the Congress held its annual session in the city of Lahore.

- The meeting was significant for two things: the election of Jawaharlal Nehru as President, signifying the passing of the baton of leadership to the younger generation; and the proclamation of commitment to "Purna Swaraj", or complete independence.

- On 26 January 1930, "Independence Day" was observed, with the national flag being hoisted in different venues, and patriotic songs being sung

Dandi

- The state monopoly over salt was deeply unpopular; by making it his target, Gandhiji hoped to mobilise a wider discontent against British rule.

- Viceroy Lord Irwin, Irwin failed to grasp the significance of the action.

- On 12 March 1930, Gandhiji began walking from his ashram at Sabarmati towards the ocean. He reached his destination three weeks later, making a fistful of salt as he did and thereby making himself a criminal in the eyes of the law.

Dialogues

- Salt March which forced upon the British the realisation that their Raj would not last forever.

- To that end, the British government convened a series of "Round Table Conferences" in London. The first meeting was held in November 1930, but without the pre-eminent political leader in India, thus rendering it an exercise in futility.

- "Gandhi-Irwin Pact", by the terms of which civil disobedience would be called off, all prisoners released, and salt manufacture allowed along the coast.

- A second Round Table Conference was held in London in the latter part of 1931. Here, Gandhiji represented the Congress. However, his claims that his party represented all of India came under challenge from the Muslim League, the Prince and BR Ambedkar.

- After the second round table conference, Gandhiji returned to India and resumed civil disobedience.

- In 1935, however, a new Government of India Act promised some form of representative government. Two years later, in an election held on the basis of a restricted franchise, the Congress won a comprehensive victory.

- In September 1939, two years after the Congress ministries assumed office, the Second World War broke out. Congress promised Congress support to the war effort if the British, in return, promised to grant India independence once hostilities ended.

- The offer was refused. In protest, the Congress ministries resigned in October 1939.

- In the spring of 1942, Churchill was persuaded to send one of his ministers, Sir Stafford Cripps, to India to try and forge a compromise with Gandhiji and the Congress. Talks broke down, however, after the Congress insisted that if it was to help the British defend India from the Axis powers, then the Viceroy had first to appoint an Indian as the Defence Member of his Executive Council.

Quit India

- After the failure of the Cripps Mission, Mahatma Gandhi decided to launch his third major movement against British rule. This was the "Quit India" campaign, which began in August 1942.

- Particularly active in the underground resistance were socialist members of the Congress, such as Jayaprakash Narayan.

- In several districts, such as Satara in the west and Medinipur in the east, "independent" governments were proclaimed.

- Early in 1946 fresh elections were held to the provincial legislatures. The Congress swept the "General" category, but in the seats specifically reserved for Muslims the League won an overwhelming majority.

- A Cabinet Mission sent in the summer of 1946 failed to get the Congress and the League to agree on a federal system that would keep India together while allowing the provinces a degree of autonomy.

- After the talks broke down, Jinnah called for a "Direct Action Day" to press the League's demand for Pakistan. On the designated day, 16 August 1946, bloody riots broke out in Calcutta.

- The violence spread to rural Bengal, then to Bihar, and then across the country to the United Provinces and the Punjab.

- In February 1947, Wavell was replaced as Viceroy by Lord Mountbatten.

- The formal transfer of power was fixed for 15 August. When that day came, it was celebrated with gusto in different parts of India.

Multiple Choice Questions   [1 Mark]

Q.1. After the _________round table conference, Gandhiji returned to India and resumed civil disobedience

(a) First

(b) Second

(c) Third

(d) Fourth

Ans. (b)

Q.2. A second Round Table Conference was held in London in the latter part of 1931. Here, Gandhiji represented _______

(a) India (b) Congress

(c) Backward class (d) All of the above

Ans. (b)

Q.3. The claims of single party representation for the entire India by Gandhi at the Second Round table conference was rejected by who among the following?

(a) The Muslim League

(b) The Princely States

(c) B R Ambedkar

(d) All of the above

Ans. (d) A second Round Table Conference was held in London in the latter part of 1931. Here, Gandhiji represented the Congress. However, his claims that his party represented all of India came under challenge from the Muslim League, the Prince and B R Ambedkar.

Q.4. Which of the following provisions were agreed upon by the Gandhi Irwin Pact?

(a) Calling off of the civil disobedience

(b) Salt manufacture allowed along the coast.

(c) Both (a) and (b)

(d) Release of all prisoners

Ans. (c) "Gandhi-Irwin Pact', by the terms of which civil disobedience would be called off, all prisoners released, and salt manufacture allowed along the coast.

Q.5. Who among the following leaders did no associate themselves with the Gandhian style of politics ?

(a) Subhas Chandra Bose

(b) Govind Ballabh Pant

(c) J.B. Kripalani

(d) None of the above

Ans. (d) Between 1917 and 1922, a group of highly talented Indians attached themselves to Gandhiji. They included Mahadev Desai, Vallabh Bhai Patel, J.B. Kripalani, Subhas Chandra Bose, Abul Kalam Azad, Jawaharlal Nehru, Sarojini Naidu, Govind Ballabh Pant and C. Rajagopalachari.

Q.6. The Praja Mandals were established to promote the nationalist creed in which of the following parts of the pre-independent India?

(a) The southern states

(b) Jammu and Kashmir

(c) Bihar and Bengal

(d) The pricely states

Ans. (d) A series of "Praja Mandals" were established to promote the nationalist creed in the princely states. Gandhiji encouraged the communication of the nationalist message in the mother tongue.

Q.7. The Civil Disobedience Movement was resumed by which of the following event ?

(a) The First Rounf Table Conference

(b) The Second Rounf Table Conference

(c) The Third Rounf Table Conference

(d) None of the above

Ans. (b) After the second round table conference, Gandhiji returned to India and resumed civil disobedience.

Q.8. Identify the incorrect statement with respect to the Round Table Conferences ?

(a) All the conferences were convened by the British Government in London.

(b) The first meeting was held in November 1930,

(c) There was no pre-eminent political leader in India in the First Round Table Conference

(d)   None of the above

Ans. (d) All the statements are correct. The British government convened a series of "Round Table Conferences" in London. The first meeting was held in November 1930, but without the pre-eminent political leader in India, thus rendering it an exercise in futility

Q.9. The people were asked to contribute to the Non-cooperation Movement through which of the following processes?

(a) To stop attending schools

(b) Not resorting to law courts

(c) Not paying the taxes

(d) All of the above

Ans. (d) Emboldened by its success, Gandhiji called for a campaign of "non-cooperation" with British rule. Indians who wished colonialism to end were asked to stop attending schools, colleges and law courts, and not pay taxes.

Q.10. Gandhiji spent a year travelling around British India, getting to know the land, on the advice of who among the following leaders?

(a) J.B. Kripalani

(b) Abul Kalam Azad

(c) Govind Ballabh Pant

(d) Gopal Krishna Gokhale

Ans. (d) On Gokhale's advice, Gandhiji spent a year travelling around British India, getting to know the land

Q.11. Gandhiji joined hands with the Khilafat Movement to further broaden the struggle under which of the following movement?

(a) Swadeshi and Boycott Movement

(b) Rowlatt Satyagrah

(c) Non Cooperation Movement

(d) None of the above

Ans. (c) To further broaden the struggle under the Non Cooperation Movement he had joined hands with the Khilafat Movement that sought to restore the Caliphate, a symbol of Pan-Islamism

Q.12. Identify the correct statements:

(a) Both Gokhale and Mohammad jinnah belonged to the group of Moderates.

(b) Both Gandhi and Jinnah were lawyers by profession who were trained in London.

(c) Both (a) and (b)

(d) None of the above

Ans. (c) There was a group of "Moderates" who preferred a more gradual and persuasive approach. Among these Moderates was Gandhiji's acknowledged political mentor, Gopal Krishna Gokhale, as well as Mohammad Ali Jinnah, who, like Gandhiji, was a lawyer of Gujarati extraction trained in London.

Q.13. Consider the following incidents

1. A Cabinet Mission was sent to get the Congress and the League to agree on a federal system

2. Jinnah called for a "Direct Action Day"

3. Sir Stafford Cripps visited India

Which of the following is the correct chronological order from earliest to latest

(a) 1-2-3   (b) 3-1-2

(c) 1-3-2   (d) 2-1-3

Ans. (b) In the spring of 1942, Churchill was persuaded to send one of his ministers, Sir Stafford Cripps, to India to try and forge a compromise with Gandhiji and the Congress.

A Cabinet Mission sent in the summer of 1946 failed to get the Congress and the League to agree on a federal system that would keep India together while allowing the provinces a degree of autonomy.

After the talks broke down, Jinnah called for a "Direct Action Day" to press the League's demand for Pakistan. On the designated day, 16 August 1946, bloody riots broke out in Calcutta.

Q.14. Which of the following is not the correct statement with difference to the Indian national Congress?

(a) A resolution was passed on "the rights of minorities" at the initiative of Gandhi and Nehru

(b) The party had never accepted the "two-nation theory".

(c) The Congress wished to "assure the minorities in India that it will continue to protect

(d) The party, for the sake of peace, accepted the rightfulness of state religion

Ans. (d) At the initiative of Gandhiji and Nehru, the Congress now passed a resolution on "the rights of minorities". The party had never accepted the "two-nation theory": forced against its will to accept Partition, it still believed that "India is a land of many religions and many races, and must remain so". Whatever be the situation in Pakistan, India would be "a democratic secular State where all citizens enjoy full rights and are equally entitled to the protection of the State, irrespective of the religion to which they belong". The Congress wished to "assure the minorities in India that it will continue to protect, to the best of its ability, their citizen rights against aggression".

Q.15. Which of the following statements is incorrect with reference to the elections of 1946?

(a) The elections were held in the provincial legislatures.

(b) Congress swept the "General" category.

(c) The performance of the Muslim League assured its diminishing importance even among the Muslims.

(d) There was the provision for a separate electorate in the election

Ans. (c) In the seats specifically reserved for Muslims, the Muslim League won an overwhelming majority.

Q.16. Which of the following incidents is/are related to the quit India movement?

(a) Independent governments at Satara in the west and Medinipur in the east.

(b) Underground resistance by socialist members of the Congress, such as Jayaprakash Narayan.

(c) Observation of "Independence Day" throughout the country.

(d) (a) and (b)

Ans. (d) Particularly active in the underground resistance during Qui India movement were socialist members of the Congress, such as Jayaprakash Narayan. In several districts, such as Satara in the west and Medinipur in the east, "independent" governments were proclaimed.

On 26 January 1930, "Independence Day" was observed, with the national flag being hoisted in different venues, and patriotic songs being sung

Q.17. The talks that were initiated in 1942 by Sir Stafford Cripps, broke down on which of the following grounds?

(a) Viceroy had first to appoint an Indian as the Defence Member

(b) Immediate transfer of power

(c) Release of the prisoners of the Indian National Army

(d) Release of the leaders.

Ans. (a) In the spring of 1942, Churchill was persuaded to send one of his ministers, Sir Stafford Cripps, to India to try and forge a compromise with Gandhiji and the Congress. Talks broke down, however, after the Congress insisted that if it was to help the British defend India from the Axis powers, then the Viceroy had first to appoint an Indian as the Defence Member of his Executive Council.

Q.18. Consider the following image

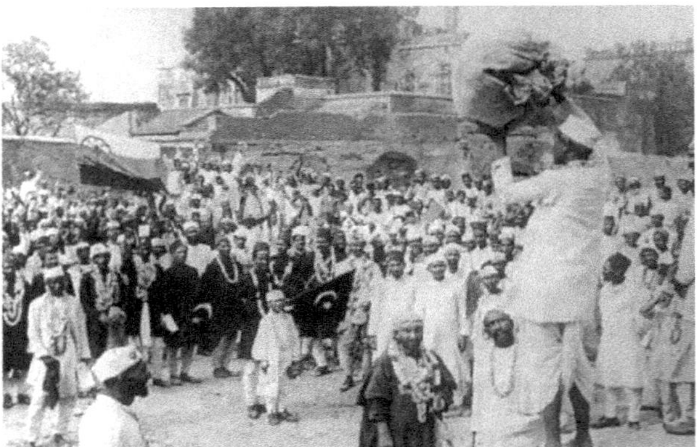

In this image Foreign cloth being collected to be burnt in bonfires.

The above image represents which of the following movements

(a) Non-cooperation Movement

(b) Swaraj movement

(c) Civil disobedient movement

(d) None of the above

Ans. (a)

Very Short Answer Type [1 Mark]

Q.1. What was the objective of Dandi March

Ans. The state monopoly over salt was deeply unpopular; by making it his target, Gandhiji hoped to mobilise a wider discontent against British rule.

Q.2. Who was the Viceroy at the time of Dandi March

Ans. Viceroy Lord Irwin

Q.3. On which date did Gandhiji start walking towards the sea from his ashram at Sabarmati?

Ans. On 12 March 1930, Gandhiji began walking from his ashram at Sabarmati towards the ocean.

Q.4. In which year Lord Mountbatten replaced Wavell as the Viceroy?

Ans. February 1947

Q.5. Jinnah called for a "Direct Action Day" to press the League's demand for Pakistan. On the designated day, 16 August 1946, bloody riots broke out in which city?

Ans. Calcutta.

Q.6. Which mission failed to get the Congress and the League to agree on a federal system that would keep India together while allowing the provinces a degree of autonomy.

Ans. A Cabinet Mission sent in the summer of 1946

Q.7. After the failure of the Cripps Mission, Mahatma Gandhi decided to launch which major movement against British rule?

Ans. After the failure of the Cripps Mission, Mahatma Gandhi decided to launch his third major movement against British rule. This was the "Quit India" campaign, which began in August 1942.

Q.8. Which movement shaken the British Raj foundations for the first time since the Revolt of 1857? **[CBSE 2015]**

Ans. As a consequence of the Non-Cooperation Movement the British Raj was shaken to its foundations for the first time since the Revolt of 1857.

Q.9. Failure of which mission led to the launch of Quit India Movement?

Ans. Failure of Cripps Mission led to the launch of Quit India Movement in August 1942

Q.10. In August 1942, just after the Quit India Movement began, Gandhi was arrested by the British Government. When did he get out of jail?

Ans. In June 1944, Gandhiji was released from jail

Q.11. Emboldened by the success of which movement, Gandhiji called for a campaign of "non-cooperation" with British rule.

Ans. Rowlatt Syagrah

Q.12. Who called for a countrywide campaign against the "Rowlatt Act".

Ans. Gandhiji

Q.13. In which year Mohandas Karamchand Gandhi returned to his homeland after living abroad for two decades?

Ans. January 1915

Short Answer Type - I [2 Marks]

Q.1. Why did the Congress ministries resign in October 1939? **[CBSE 2019]**

Ans. MIn September 1939, two years after the Congress ministries assumed office, the Second World War broke out. Congress promised Congress support to the war effort if the British, in return, promised to grant India independence once hostilities ended.

The offer was refused. In protest, the Congress ministries resigned in October 1939.

Q.2. Why did Mahatma Gandhi spend much of 1917 in Champaran?

Ans. Mahatma Gandhi was to spend much of 1917 in Champaran, seeking to obtain for the peasants security of tenure as well as the freedom to cultivate the crops of their choice.

Q.3. How the socialist members of the Congress contributed in socialist members of the Congress

Ans. Socialist members such as Jayaprakash Narayan were Particularly active in the underground resistance

Q.4. Independent governments were proclaimed in which of the following regions?

Ans. In several districts, such as Satara in the west and Medinipur in the east, "independent" governments were proclaimed.

Q.5. In which two campaigns did Gandhiji join in his home state of Gujarat in 1918?

Ans. In 1918, Gandhiji was involved in two campaigns in his home state of Gujarat. First, he intervened in a labour dispute in Ahmedabad, demanding better working conditions for the textile mill workers. Then he joined peasants in Kheda in asking the state for the remission of taxes following the failure of their harvest.

Q.6. What was Rowlatt Act?

Ans. During the Great War of 1914-18, the British had instituted censorship of the press and permitted detention without trial. Now, on the recommendation of a committee chaired by Sir Sidney Rowlatt, these tough measures were continued

Q.7. What was the role of Praja Mandals?

[CBSE 2014]

Ans. A series of "Praja Mandals" were established to promote the nationalist creed in the princely states. Gandhiji encouraged the communication of the nationalist message in the mother tongue.

Q.8. Who were moderators?

Ans. Moderates preferred a more gradual and persuasive approach. Among these Moderates was Gandhiji's acknowledged political mentor, Gopal Krishna Gokhale, as well as Mohammad Ali Jinnah, who, like Gandhiji, was a lawyer of Gujarati extraction trained in London.

Q.9. Which act of violence prompted Gandhiji to call off the movement altogether ?

Ans. In February 1922, a group of peasants attacked and torched a police station in the hamlet of Chauri Chaura, in the United Provinces (now, Uttar Pradesh) Several constables perished in the conflagration. Thisact of violence prompted Gandhiji to call off the movement altogether.

Short Answer Type - II   [3 Marks]

Q.1. Discuss the events in which Mahatma Gandhi participated after his arrival from South Africa?   [CBSE 2019]

Ans. On Gokhale's advice, Gandhiji spent a year travelling around British India, getting to know the land. His first major public appearance was at the opening of the Banaras Hindu University (BHU) in February 1916. He had been invited on account of his work in South Africa, rather than his status within India. At the annual Congress, held in Lucknow in December 1916, he was approached by a peasant from Champaran in Bihar, who told him about the harsh treatment of peasants by British indigo planters.

Q.2. How have the different kinds of available sources helped the historians in reconstructing the political career of Gandhiji and the history of the national movement that was associated with it ? Explain.   [CBSE 2018]

Ans. The most important source was writings and speeches by Gandhiji, his contemporaries and associates. Example : Gandhiji started magazines such as Harijan etc. Another sources is autobiographies, as they give an account of the past that is often rich in human detail. Example : Story of my experiments with truth. Another vital source is government' records. As these records can be read from archives, these provide information about what was the response of the government to his policies and actions. Newspapers also give details of the movements and presented what ordinary Indians thought of him.

Q.3. What were the conditions when Gandhi arrived India? **[CBSE 2019]**

Ans. The India that Mahatma Gandhi came back to in 1915 was rather different from the one that he had left in 1893. The Indian National Congress now had branches in most major cities and towns. Through the Swadeshi movement of 1905-07 it had greatly broadened its appeal among the middle classes. That movement had thrown up some towering leaders – among them Bal Gangadhar Tilak of Maharashtra, Bipin Chandra Pal of Bengal, and Lala Lajpat Rai of Punjab. The three were known as "Lal, Bal and Pal". There was a group of "Moderates" who preferred a more gradual and persuasive approach. Among these Moderates was Gandhiji's acknowledged political mentor, Gopal Krishna Gokhale, as well as Mohammad Ali Jinnah, who, like Gandhiji, was a lawyer of Gujarati extraction trained in London.

Q.4. Why Gandhiji was a people's leader?

Ans. While other nationalist leaders dressed formally, wearing a Western suit or an Indian *bandgala*, Gandhiji went among the people in a simple *dhoti* or loincloth. Meanwhile, he spent part of each day working on the *charkha* (spinning wheel), and encouraged other nationalists to do likewise. The act of spinning allowed Gandhiji to break the boundaries that prevailed within the traditional caste system, between mental labour and manual labour.

Q.5. What was the significance of the annual session of the 1929 Congress held at Lahore?

Ans. In the end of December 1929, the Congress held its annual session in the city of Lahore. The meeting was significant for two things: the election of Jawaharlal Nehru as President, signifying the passing of the baton of leadership to the younger generation; and the proclamation of commitment to "Purna Swaraj", or complete independence. On 26 January 1930, "Independence Day" was observed, with the national flag being hoisted in different venues, and patriotic songs being sung

Q.6. Describe the role of Mahatma Gandhi in the freedom struggle of India.

Ans. Gandhi transformed the national movement by making it into a mass struggle. Under his leadership the freedom struggle acquired a multi-class umbrella character. By taking up the cause of peasants at Champaran and Kheda, textile workers at Ahmedabad and later launching of the Khilafat Non-Cooperation Movement (1920), Civil Disobedience Movement (1930) and Quit India Movement (1942) Gandhi transformed the national movement. The national movement was no longer a movement limited to professionals and intellectuals but a movement representative of Indian people as a whole. Peasants, workers, artisans, tribals, women and students played an active role. The Non-Cooperation Movement was the hallmark of Hindu-Muslim unity.

Q.7. How Gandhian ideology played a key role in getting Independence

Ans. Satyagraha based on the concepts of truth, non-violence and passive resistance formed the basis of mass mobilisation and mass participation. The non-violent national struggle was based on the courage, strength self-confidence and self-sacrificing spirit of the masses. It enabled participation of mass people who could not have participated in a violent struggle example women. It was based on moral force and posed the best challenge to the mighty British rule, while defining Gandhian principle of means and ends.

Q.8. "The worst is over but Indians need to work collectively for the equality of all classes and creeds." Substantiate the statement of Gandhiji for bringing communal peace after the partition of India. **[CBSE 2013]**

Ans. On 26 January, 1948, at his prayer meeting he said that "the worst is over", that Indians would henceforth work collectively for the "equality of all classes and creeds, never the domination and superiority of the major community over a minor, however insignificant it may be in numbers or influence". He had the hope that geographically and politically India was divided into two but the people will remain friends and brothers forever and respect and help each other. Many scholars have written of the months after Independence as being Gandhiji's "finest hour". After communal harmony. He believed that people's hearts could be changed with Non-Violence. Gandhiji came to Delhi in Sep. 1947 and addressed the Sikhs at Sisganj Gurudwara to bring peace. He started a fast to bring about a change in the hearts of people.

Q.9. What was the Khilafat Movement?

Ans. The Khilafat Movement, (1919-1920) was a movement of Indian Muslims, led by Muhammad Ali and Shaukat Ali, that demanded the following: The Turkish Sultan or Khalifa must retain control over the Muslim sacred places in the erstwhile Ottoman empire; the jazirat-ul-Arab (Arabia, Syria, Iraq, Palestine) must remain under Muslim sovereignty; and the Khalifa must be left with sufficient territory to enable him to defend the Islamic faith. The Congress supported the movement and Mahatma Gandhi sought to conjoin it to the Non-cooperation Movement

Q.10. What were the steps suggested by Gandhiji towards Swaraj?

Ans. Gandhiji told the upper castes that "if you are out for Swaraj you must serve untouchables. You won't get Swaraj merely by the repeal of the salt taxes or other taxes. For Swaraj you must make amends for the wrongs which you did to the untouchables. For Swaraj, Hindus, Muslims, Parsis and Sikhs will have to unite. These are the steps towards Swaraj." The police spies reported that Gandhiji's meetings were very well attended, by villagers of all castes, and by women as well as men. They observed that thousands of volunteers were flocking to the nationalist cause.

Long Answer Type   [5 Marks]

Q.1. "Quit India Movement" was genuinely a mass movement bringing into its ambition hundreds of thousands of ordinary Indians." Analyse the statement.   [CBSE 2018]

Ans. The Quit India movement was launched in August 1942 by Gandhiji. The slogan of the movement was 'Do or Die' and 'British leave India'. In this movement after the arrest of Gandhiji younger activists organised strikes and acts of sabotage all over the country. Students in very large numbers, left their colleges to go to jail. Socialist members such as Jayaprakash Narayan were active in the underground resistance. Independent or Parallel governments were proclaimed in several districts, such as Satara in the west and Medinipur in the east,. A large number of women across the country also participated in the processions. The British responded with much force, yet it took more than a year to suppress the rebellion. Thousands of Indians joined the mass movement. The Congress leaders were sent to jail. Jinnah expanded his influence over Muslims in Punjab and Sind. In 1944, Gandhiji was released from prison. Afterwards the Congress started negotiations with the League.

Q.2. "The India in which Gandhiji came back to in 1915 was rather different than the one he had left in 1893." Substantiate the statement.

[CBSE 2019]

Ans. In January 1915, Gandhiji returned to his homeland after two decades of residence abroad. He went to South Africa as a lawyer, and in time became a leader of the Indian community in that territory. The India that Mahatma Gandhi came back to in 1915 was rather different from the one that he had left in 1893. Although still a colony of the British, it was far more active in a political sense. The Indian National Congress then had branches in most major cities and towns.Through the Swadeshi movement of 1905-07, it had broadened its appeal among the middle classes. That movement had thrown up some towering leaders — Bal Gangadhar Tilak of Maharashtra, Bipin Chandra Pal of Bengal, and Lala Rajpat Rai of Punjab. The trio was famous as Lai, Bal and Pal. Where these leaders advocated militant opposition to colonial rule, there was a group of 'Moderates' who preferred a more gradual and persuasive approach. Among these moderates was Gandhiji's acknowledged political mentor, Gopal

Krishna Gokhale, as well as Mohammad Ali Jinnah, who like Gandhiji, was a lawyer of the Gujarati extraction trained in London.

Q.3. "The initiatives in Champaran, Ahmedabad and Kheda marked Gandhiji out as a nationalist with a deep sympathy for the poor." Substantiate the statement.   **[CBSE 2015]**

Ans. Gandhiji in the last month of the year 1916 was presented with an opportunity to put his precepts into practice. At the annual Congress held in Lucknow, Gandhiji was approached by a peasant from Champaran in Bihar, who told about the harsh treatment by the British indigo planters. After this information, Mahatma Gandhi had to spend much of 1917 in Champatan, seeking to obtain freedom for the peasants, security of tenure as well as the freedom to cultivate the crops of their choice. The following year, 1918, Gandhiji was involved in two campaigns in his home state of Gujarat. First, he intervened better working conditions for the textile mill workers in Ahmedabad. Then he joined the peasants in Kheda, in asking the state for the remission of taxes following the failure of their harvest. These initiatives in Champarari, Ahmedbad and Kheda marked Gandhiji out as a nationalist with a deep sympathy for the poor.

Q.4. "It was the Rowlatt Satyagraha that made Gandhiji a truly national leader." Substantiate the statement.   **[CBSE 2014]**

Ans. In 1919, Gandhiji gave a call Satyagraha against the Rowlatt Act, passed by the British. The Act restricted the freedom of expression and strengthened police powers. It was the Rowlatt Satyagraha that made Gandhiji a true national leader. Encouraged by its success, Gandhiji called for a campaign of Non-Cooperation with British rule. Indians who wished colonialism to end were asked to stop attending schools, colleges and law courts, and not pay taxes. In sum, they were asked to adhere to a 'renunciation of (all) voluntary association with the (British) Government'. Gandhiji said that if non-cooperation was effectively carried out, India would win swaraj within a year. To further broaden the struggle, he had joined hands with Khilafat Movement.

Q.5. The Non-Cooperation Movement was training for self rule." Analyze the statement of American biographer Louis Fisher in the context of Indian Nationalism.   **(CBSE 2015)**

Ans. Gandhiji hoped that by coupling Non-cooperation with Khilafat, the Hindus and Muslims collectively will bring an end to the British rule. These movements were a surge of popular action that was unprecedented in colonial rule. The people were asked to stop attending schools, colleges and law courts, and not pay taxes. In sum, they were asked' to adhere to a "renunciation of (all) voluntary association with the (British) Government". If non-cooperation was effectively carried out, said Gandhiji, India would win swaraj within a year.

Consequently, students stopped going to schools and colleges run by the government. Lawyers refused to attend court. The working class went on strike in many towns and cities. According to official figures, there were 396 strikes in 1921, involving 600,000 workers and a loss of seven million workdays. The countryside was filled with discontent too. Hill tribes in Northern Andhra violated the forest laws. Farmers in Awadh did not pay taxes and peasants refused to carry loads for colonial officials. These protest movements were sometimes carried out in defiance of the local nationalist leadership. Peasants, workers, and others interpreted and acted upon the call to "non-cooperate" with colonial rule in ways that best suited their interests. The main ideas behind the movement were Satya, Satyagraha, Ahimsa, Self discipline. The British Raj was shaken to its foundation. The non cooperation movement brought people from different parts of the country to fight against the British. People of all castes , creeds and from all classes of society participated in the movement. Khadi, promotion of village industries, Hindu-Muslim unity, abolition of untouchability, boycott of British goods and social reforms were an important part of the movement. Chauri Chaura incident forced Gandhi to call off the Non-Cooperation Movement.

Chapter Practice

Multiple Choice Questions [1 Mark]

Q.1. He was the Viceroy of India during the Dandi March carried by Gandhi. He is known for having made a declaration that Britain would be committed to the eventual dominion status of India.

The above description is related to who among the following?

(a) Lord Linlithgow   (b) Lord Wavell

(c) Lord Mountbatten   (d) Lord Irwin

Q.2. The session of the Indian National Congress was significant for two things: the election of Jawaharlal Nehru as President, signifying the passing of the baton of leadership to the younger generation; and the proclamation of commitment to "Purna Swaraj", or complete independence. The session was held in which year?

(a) 1926   (b) 1929

(c) 1930   (d) 1936

Q.3. During the course of Indian Freedom struggle, a group of peasants attacked and torched a police station in the hamlet of Chauri Chaura, in the United Provinces (now, Uttar Pradesh and Uttaranchal). Several constables perished in the conflagration. As a response to this, which of the following movements was called off?

(a) Rowlatt Satyagrah   (b) Quit India Movement

(c) Non Cooperation Movement   (d) Civil Disoedience Movement

Q.4. After the return form South Africa, the first major public appearance was at the opening of which of the following Universities?

(a) Patna University   (b) Banaras Hindu University

(c) Madras College   (d) College of Engineering, Pune

Q.5. Which of the following events had already happened before the return of Gandhi from South Africa?

(a) Expansion of the Indian National Congress in most major cities and towns.

(b) Swadeshi movement broadened its appeal among the middle classes.

(c) Emergence of leaders like Lala Lajpat Rai of Punjab.

(d) All of the above

Q.6. Which of the following incidents led to the censorship of the press and permission to detention without trial in India for the first time?

(a) Formation of the Indian National Army

(b) The Great War of 1914-18

(c) The recommendation of the committee chaired by Sir Sidney Rowlatt

(d) None of the above

Very Short Answer Type [1 Mark]

Q.7. How did Indians participate in the Quit India Movement?

Q.8. To further broaden the struggle under the Non Cooperation Movement Mahatma Gandhi had joined hands with which movement?

Short Answer Type - I [2 Marks]

Questions (Q9, Q10 and Q11): [CBSE 2017]

Read the following extract carefully and answer the questions that follow

"Tomorrow we shall break the salt tax law"

On 5 April, 1930 Mahatma Gandhi spoke at Dandi :

When I left Sabarmati with my companions for this seaside hamlet of Dandi, I was not certain in my mind that we would be allowed to reach this place.

Even while I was at Sabarmati there was a rumour that I might be arrested. I had thought that the Government might perhaps let my party come as far as Dandi, but not me certainly. If someone says that this betrays imperfect faith on my part, I shall not deny the charge. That I have reached here is in no small measure due to the power of peace and non-violence : that power is universally felt. The Government may, if it wishes, congratulate itself on acting as it has done, for it could have arrested every one of us. In saying that it did not have the courage to arrest this army of peace, we praise it. It felt ashamed to arrest such an army. He is a civilised man who feels ashamed to do anything which his neighbours would disapprove. The Government deserves to be congratulated on not arresting us, even if it desisted only from fear of world opinion.

Tomorrow we shall break the salt tax law. Whether the Government will tolerate that is a different question. It may not tolerate it, but it deserves congratulations on the patience and forbearance it has displayed in regard to this party......

What if I and all the eminent leaders in Gujarat and in the rest of the country are arrested ? This movement is based on the faith that when a whole nation is roused and on the march no leader is necessary.

Q.9. What were the apprehensions of Mahatma Gandhi when he started his Dandi March ?

Q.10. Why did Gandhiji say that the Government deserve to be congratulated ?

Q.11. Why was the 'Salt March' very significant ?

Short Answer Type - II [3 Marks]

Q.12. Discuss the first and second Round Table Conferences"

Long Answer Type [5 Marks]

Q.13. "The Salt Satyagraha was one of the most successful campaigns in Gandhiji's non-violent struggle against Britishers." Analyse the statement. [CBSE 2018]

CHAPTER 14

Understanding Partition

Understanding Partition/Withdrawal of Law and Order/Politics, Memories, Experiences

Summary

Why and How Did Partition Happen?

- Scholars suggest that separate electorates for Muslims, created by the colonial government in 1909 and expanded in 1919, crucially shaped the nature of communal politics.

- Separate electorates created a temptation for politicians working within this system to use sectarian slogans and gather a following by distributing favours to their own religious groups.

- Communal identities were consolidated by a host of other developments in the early twentieth century. Muslims were angered by "music-before-mosque", by the cow protection movement, and by the efforts of the Arya Samaj to bring back to the Hindu fold (*shuddhi*) those who had recently converted to Islam.

- Hinds were angered by the rapid spread of *tabligh* (propaganda) and *tanzim*(organisation) after 1923.

What is Communalism?

- Communalism refers to a politics that seeks to unify one community around a religious identity in hostile opposition to another community. It seeks to define this community identity as fundamental and fixed. It attempts to consolidate this identity and present it as natural – as if people were born into the identity, as if the identities do not evolve through history over time.

- In order to unify the community, communalism suppresses distinctions within the community and emphasises the essential unity of the community against other communities.

- Communalism, then, is a particular kind of politicisation of religious identity, an ideology that seeks to promote conflict between religious communities.

The Lucknow Pact

- The Lucknow Pact of December 1916 was an understanding between the Congress and the Muslim League (controlled by the UP-based "Young Party") whereby the Congress accepted separate electorates. The pact provided a joint political platform for the Moderates, Radicals and the Muslim League

Arya Samaj

- A North Indian Hindu reform organisation of the late nineteenth and early twentieth centuries, particularly active in the Punjab, which sought to revive Vedic learning and combine it with modern education in the sciences.

The Muslim League

- Initially floated in Dhaka in 1906, the Muslim League was quickly taken over by the U.P.-based Muslim elite. The party began to make demands for autonomy for the Muslim-majority areas of the subcontinent and/or Pakistan in the 1940s.

Hindu Mahasabha

- Founded in 1915, the Hindu Mahasabha was a Hindu party that remained confined to North India. It aimed to unite Hindu society by encouraging the Hindus to transcend the divisions of caste and sect. It sought to define Hindu identity in opposition to Muslim identity.

The provincial elections of 1937 and the Congress ministries

- In 1937, elections to the provincial legislatures were held for the first time.

- Only about 10 to 12 per cent of the population enjoyed the right to vote.

- The Congress did well in the elections, winning an absolute majority in five out of eleven provinces and forming governments in seven of them. It did badly in the constituencies reserved for Muslims, but the Muslim League also fared poorly

- The League failed to win a single seat in the North West Frontier Province (NWFP) and could capture only two out of 84 reserved constituencies in the Punjab and three out of 33 in Sind.

- In the United Provinces, the Muslim League wanted to form a joint government with the Congress. The Congress had won an absolute majority in the province, so it rejected the offer. Some scholars argue that this rejection convinced the League for a separate nation for Muslims.

- But Jinnah's insistence that the League be recognised as the "sole spokesman" of Muslims could convince few at the time. Though popular in the United Provinces, Bombay and Madras, social support for the League was still fairly weak in three of the provinces from which Pakistan was to be carved out just ten years later – Bengal, the NWFP and the Punjab.

- The Congress ministries also contributed to the widening rift. In the United Provinces, the party had rejected the Muslim League proposal for a coalition government partly because the League tended to support landlordism, which the Congress wished to abolish, although the party had not yet taken any concrete steps in that direction.

- Nor did the Congress achieve any substantial gains in the "Muslim mass contact" programme it launched.

- Maulana Azad, an important Congress leader, pointed out in 1937 that members of the Congress were not allowed to join the League

- Only in December 1938 did the Congress Working Committee declare that Congress members could not be members of the Mahasabha.

The "Pakistan" Resolution

- On 23 March 1940, the League moved a resolution demanding a measure of autonomy for the Muslim-majority areas of the subcontinent. This ambiguous resolution never mentioned partition or Pakistan

- Sikandar Hayat Khan, Punjab Premier and leader of the Unionist Party, who had drafted the resolution, declared in a Punjab assembly speech on 1 March 1941 that he was opposed to a Pakistan that would mean "Muslim Raj here and Hindu Raj elsewhere

- He reiterated his plea for a loose (united), confederation with considerable autonomy for the confederating units.

- The origins of the Pakistan demand have also been traced back to the Urdu poet Mohammad Iqbal, the writer of *"Sare Jahan Se Achha Hindustan Hamara"*. However he only visualized reorganisation of Muslim-majority areas in north-western India into an autonomous unit within a single, loosely structured Indian federation.

Post-War developments

- When negotiations were begun again in 1945, the British agreed to create an entirely Indian central Executive Council, except for the Viceroy and the Commander-in-Chief of the armed forces, as a preliminary step towards full independence.

- Provincial elections were again held in 1946. The Congress swept the general constituencies, capturing 91.3 per cent of the non-Muslim vote. The League's success in the seats reserved for Muslims was equally spectacular: it won all 30 reserved constituencies in the Centre with 86.6 per cent of the Muslim vote and 442 out of 509 seats in the provinces.

- However, franchise was extremely limited. About 10 to 12 per cent of the population enjoyed the right to vote in the provincial elections and a mere one per cent in the elections for the Central Assembly.

A possible alternative to Partition

- In March 1946 the British Cabinet sent a three- member mission to Delhi to examine the League's demand

- Recommendation by the Cabinet Mission: India was to remain united. It was to have a weak central government controlling only foreign affairs, defence and communications with the existing provincial assemblies being grouped into three sections while electing the constituent assembly: Section A for the Hindu- majority provinces, and Sections B and C for the Muslim-majority provinces of the north-west and the north-east (including Assam) respectively.

- They would have the power to set up intermediate-level executives and legislatures of their own

- Initially all the major parties accepted this plan. But the agreement was short-lived because it was based on mutually opposed interpretations of the plan.

- Initially all the major parties accepted this plan. But the agreement was short-lived because it was based on mutually opposed interpretations of the plan.

- Ultimately, therefore, neither the League nor the Congress agreed to the Cabinet Mission's proposal.

- This made the idea of partition even more inevitable. Only Mahatma Gandhi and Khan Abdul Ghaffar Khan of the NWFP continued to firmly oppose the idea of partition.

Towards Partition

- After withdrawing its support to the Cabinet Mission plan, the Muslim League decided on "Direct Action" for winning its Pakistan demand. It announced 16 August 1946 as "Direct Action Day".

- It was in March 1947 that the Congress high command voted for dividing the Punjab into two halves, one with Muslim majority and the other with Hindu/Sikh majority; and it asked for the application of a similar principle to Bengal.

Multiple Choice Questions   [1 Mark]

Q.1. Find the incorrect statement with reference to Partition

(a) Over 10 million people were uprooted from their homelands and forced to migrate

(b) The Partition of British India into the sovereign states of India and Pakistan (with its western and northern wings) led to many sudden developments.

(c) The boundaries between the two new states were not officially known until two days *after* formal independence

(d) None of the above

Ans. (b) The Partition of British India into the sovereign states of India and Pakistan (with its western and eastern wings) led to many sudden developments.

Q.2. Rukka is ________

(a) Encrypted message

(b) Punjabi ritual

(c) short handwritten note

(d) official documents

Ans. (c) a short handwritten note

Q.3. The________ that characterised the partition of India was carried out by self-styled representatives of religious communities rather than by state agencies.

(a) Holocaust

(b) ethnic cleansing

(c) sixteen- month civil war

(d) Genocide

Ans. (b)

Q.4. Pakistan was craved out of

1. Bengal

2. NWFP

3. Punjab

4. Sindh

Codes

(a) 1, 3 and 4

(b) 2, 3 and 4

(c) 1, 2 and 3

(d) 1, 2, 3 and 4

Ans. (c)

Q.5. In which of the following areas the Congressmen were active in the Hindu Mahasabha?

(a) Madhya Pradesh

(b) Odisha

(c) Bihar

(d) United Province

Ans. (a)

Q.6. Find the incorrect statement with reference to the origin of Pakistan demand

(a) The Pakistan demand was formalised gradually.

(b) In 1930, Urdu poet Mohammad Iqbalvisualises the emergence of a new country

(c) On 23 March 1940, the League moved a resolution demanding a measure of autonomy for the Muslim

(d) All of the above

Ans. (b)

Q.7. Pethick Lawrence, Stafford Cripps and A.V alexander the members of which of the following missions

(a) Cabinet Mission

(b) Cripps Mission

(c) Wavell Plan

(d) Constituent Assembly

Ans. (a)

Q.8. The elections to the provincial legislatures were held for the first time in __

(a) 1919   (b) 1925

(c) 1937   (d) 1946

Ans. (c) In 1937, elections to the provincial legislatures were held for the first time

Q.9. The "Muslim mass contact" was launched by which of the following organizations?

(a) The Indian National Congress

(b) The Muslim League

(c) The Ahmadiya Movement followers

(d) None of the above

Ans. (b) The "Muslim mass contact" was launched by Congress but it did not achieve any substantial gains in the "Muslim mass contact" programme it launched.

Q.10. Which of the following is the reason that contributed to communalism in the colonial India?

(a) Separate electorates created by the colonial government in 1919.

(b) Suddhi efforts by the members of the Arya Samaj

(c) Cow Protection Movements

(d) Both (b) and (c)

Ans. (d)

Q.11. Which of the following led to the breakdown of talks for the transfer of power under the Cabinet Mission?

(a) Different interpretations

(b) Reluctance and violence by communal groups

(c) The demand of the League to choose all Muslim members of the executive council

(d) None of the above

Ans. (c) Discussions about the transfer of power broke down due to Jinnah's unrelenting demand that the League had an absolute right to choose all the Muslim members of the Executive Council and that there should be a kind of communal veto in the Council

Very Short Answer Type   [1 Mark]

Q.1. Who was the Urdu poet who spoke of the need for a North-West Indian Muslim state in the Presidential speech of the Muslim League in 1930?

Ans. Mohammad Iqbalspoke of the need for a North-West Indian Muslim state in the Presidential speech of the Muslim League in 1930

Q.2. When people attach greater significance to certain chosen aspects of their identity such as religion. This is defined as

Ans. It is defined as Communalism

Q.3. Any attempt to see a religious community as a nation would mean sowing the seeds of antagonism against some other religion is defined as

Ans. It is defined as Religious nationalism

Q.4. Who wrote 'Sare Jahan Se Achha Hindustan Hamara'?

Ans. Urdu poet Mohammad Iqbal

Q.5. In which provincial election the Congress won an absolute majority in five of the eleven provinces and formed governments in seven of them?

Ans. 1937

Q.6. In which Province the Muslim League wanted to form a joint government with the Congress.?

Ans. United Provinces

Q.7. What percentage of people had the right to vote in the provincial elections of 1937?

Ans. 10 to 12 percent

Q.8. In which year the Congress Working Committee declared that members of Congress could not be members of the General Assembly?

Ans. 1938

Q.9. Hindu Mahasabha and the Rashtriya Swayamsevak Sangh (RSS) were based on the ideology of?

Ans. Hindu nationalism

Q.10. The "Pakistan" Resolution was drafted by?

Ans. Sikandar Hayat Khan

Q.11. The name 'Pakistan was coined by ?

Ans. Choudhry Rehmat Ali

Q.12. Which freedom struggle movement compelled the British officials to open a dialogue with Indian parties regarding a possible transfer of power?

Ans. Quit India Movement

Q.13. Siyah Hashiye was written by

Ans. Siyah Hashiye was written bySaadat Hasan Manto

Q.14. Who are the political leaders who strongly oppose the idea of partition?

Ans. Mahatma Gandhi and Khan Abdul Ghaffar Khan

Q.15. Who moved from the villages of Noakhali in East Bengal (present-day Bangladesh) to the villages of Bihar and then to the riot-torn slums of Calcutta and Delhi, in a heroic effort to stop the riots during partition?

Ans. Mahatma Gandhi

Q.16. Meghe Dhaka Tara, Subarnarekha, Garam Hawa and Tamas are films based on?

Ans. These films are based on Partition

Short Answer Type - I   [2 Marks]

Q.1. Define Confederation

Ans. In modern political language confederation refers to a union of fairly autonomous and sovereign states with a central government with delimited powers

Q.2. When and why was the Lucknow pact signed?

Ans. The Lucknow Pact was signed on December 1916between the Congress and the Muslim League whereby the Congress accepted separate electorates. The pact provided a joint political platform for the Moderates, Radicals and the Muslim League.

Q.3. Define Civil War

Ans. A civil war or intrastate war is a war between organized groups within the same state. The aim of one side may be to take control of the country or a region, to achieve independence for a region, or to change government policies.

Q.4. Define the term Holocaust

Ans. It is primarily meaning destruction or slaughter on a mass scale and it is a state-driven extermination

Q.5. Discuss the objectives of Arya Samaj

Ans. It was a Northern Indian Hindu reform organisation of the late nineteenth and early twentieth centuries, particularly active in Punjab region. It sought to revive vedic learning and combine it with modern education in the sciences.

Q.6. Who were muhajirs?

Ans. They were Urdu – speaking migrants. Most of these Urdu-speaking people, known as *muhajirs* (migrants) in Pakistan moved to the Karachi-Hyderabad region in Sind.

Q.7. What did Bengali Muslims do to East Pakistan?

Ans. Bengali Muslims (East Pakistanis) rejected Jinnah's two-nation theory through political action, breaking away from Pakistan and creating Bangladesh in - 1971-72.

Q.8. What was the position of Muslim League in the provincial elections of 1937

Ans. The Muslim League fared poorly as it failed to win a single seat in the North West Frontier Province (NWFP). They won two out of 84 reserved constituencies in the Punjab and three out of 33 in Sind.

Q.9. Why did the Congress reject the proposal to form a joint government with the Muslim League in the United Provinces?

Ans. The Muslim League tended to support land lordism, which the Congress wished to abolish

Short Answer Type - II   **[3 Marks]**

Q.1. Discuss the objectives of Hindu Mahasabha

Ans. Founded in 1915, the Hindu Mahasabha was a Hindu party that remained confined to North India. It aimed to unite Hindu society by encouraging the Hindus to transcend the divisions of caste and sect. It sought to define Hindu identity in opposition to Muslim identity.

Q.2. What was the objective of Pakistan Resolution

Ans. On 23 March 1940, the Muslim League moved a resolution demanding a measure of autonomy for the Muslim- majority areas of the subcontinent. This ambiguous resolution never mentioned partition or Pakistan.

Q.3. What do you understand by ethnic cleansing

Ans. "Ethnic cleansing" has been defined as the attempt to get rid of (through deportation, displacement or even mass killing) members of an unwanted ethnic group in order to establish an ethnically homogenous geographic area.

Q.4. Discuss about Unionist Party

Ans. It was a political party representing the interests of landholders – Hindu, Muslim and Sikh – in the Punjab. The party was particularly powerful during the period 1923-47.Unionists controlled the Punjab government and had been consistently loyal to the British. Members of the Unionist Party were largely Muslims.

Q.5. Did the political parties accept the Cripps Mission's plan?

Ans. Initially all the major parties accepted this plan but the agreement was short-lived as the League wanted the right to secede from the Union in the future but the Congress wanted that provinces be given the right to join a group. Neither the League nor the Congress agreed to the Cabinet Mission's proposal.

Q.6. What were the steps taken by the British after World War II as a preliminary step towards complete independence?

Ans. British agreed to create an entirely Indian central Executive Council, except for the Viceroy and the Commander-in-Chief of the armed forces, as a preliminary step towards full independence. It broke down due to Jinnah's unrelenting demand largely Muslims.

Q.7. Discuss the role of Urdu poet Mohammad Iqbal in the establishment of Pakistan.

Ans. In his presidential address to the Muslim League in 1930, the poet spoke of a need for a "North-West Indian Muslim state". Iqbal, however, was not visualising the emergence of a new country in that speech but a reorganisation of Muslim-majority areas in north-western India into an autonomous unit within a single, loosely structured Indian federation

Q.8. Define Communalism

Ans. It seeks to unify one community around a religious identity in hostile opposition to another community. It nurtures a politics of hatred for an identified "other"– "Hindus" in the case of Muslim communalism, and "Muslims" in the case of Hindu communalism. It nurtures a politics of hatred and politicisation of religious identity .It also promotes conflict between religious communities.

Q.9. What do you understand by the ownership of *zan* and *zamin?*

Ans. Scholars have shown how ideas of preserving community honour came into play in the partition period. This notion of honour drew upon a conception of masculinity defined as ownership of *zan* and *zamin*, a notion of considerable antiquity in North Indian peasant societies. It was believed, lay in the ability to

protect your possessions – *zan* and *zamin*– from being appropriated by outsiders.

Q.10. What was the role of separate electorates in nurturing the role of communal politics.

[CBSE 2019]

Ans. Separate electorates for Muslims, created by the colonial government in 1909 and expanded in 1919, crucially shaped the nature of communal politics. Separate electorates created a temptation for politicians working within this system to use sectarian slogans and gather a following by distributing favours to their own religious groups. Communal identities were consolidated by a host of other developments in the early twentieth century

Long Answer Type [5 Marks]

Q.1. What was the objective of he "Pakistan" Resolution? **[CBSE 2018]**

Ans. On 23 March 1940, the League moved a resolution demanding a measure of autonomy for the Muslim- majority areas of the subcontinent. This ambiguous resolution never mentioned partition or Pakistan. Sikandar Hayat Khan, Punjab Premier and leader of the Unionist Party, who had drafted the resolution, declared in a Punjab assembly speech on 1 March 1941 that he was opposed to a Pakistan that would mean "Muslim Raj here and Hindu Raj elsewhere. He reiterated his plea for a loose (united), confederation with considerable autonomy for the confederating units. The origins of the Pakistan demand have also been traced back to the Urdu poet Mohammad Iqbal, the writer of *"Sare Jahan Se Achha Hindustan Hamara"*. However he only visualized reorganisation of Muslim-majority areas in north-western India into an autonomous unit within a single, loosely structured Indian federation.

Q.2. What are the events that led to the communal politics and Partition of India.   **[CBSE 2014]**

Ans. Events that led to the communal politics and Partition of India

- During the 1920s and early 1930s tension grew around a number of issues. Muslims were angered by 'music-before-mosque', by the cow protection movement formation of the Hindu Mahasabha in 1915 and by the efforts of the Arya Samaj to bring back to the Hindu fold (shuddhi) those who had recently converted to Islam.

- Hindus were angered by the rapid spread of tabfigh (propaganda) and tanzim (organisation) after 1923.

- Failure of the Cabinet Mission (March 1946)

- Direct Action Day : After withdrawing its support to the Cabinet Mission plan, the Muslim League decided on 'Direct Action' for winning its demand for Pakistan.

- Withdrawal of law and order from 1946 to 1947

Q.3. Discuss the highlights of Provincial elections of 1946.

Ans. The Congress swept the general constituencies, capturing 91.3 per cent of the non-Muslim vote. The League won all 30 reserved constituencies in the Centre with 86.6 per cent of the Muslim vote and 442 out of 509 seats in the provinces. League establish itself as the dominant party among Muslim voters, seeking to vindicate its claim to be the "sole spokesman" of India's Muslims. About 10 to 12 per cent of the population enjoyed the right to vote in the provincial elections and a mere one per cent in the elections for the Central Assembly.

Q.4. Discuss the Post-War developments.

Ans. When negotiations were begun again in 1945, the British agreed to create an entirely Indian central Executive Council, except for the Viceroy and the Commander-in-Chief of the armed forces, as a preliminary step towards full independence.

Provincial elections were again held in 1946. The Congress swept the general constituencies, capturing 91.3 per cent of the non-Muslim vote. The League's success in the seats reserved for Muslims was equally spectacular: it won all 30 reserved constituencies in the Centre with 86.6 per cent of the Muslim vote and 442 out of 509 seats in the provinces.

However, franchise was extremely limited. About 10 to 12 per cent of the population enjoyed the right to vote in the provincial elections and a mere one per cent in the elections for the Central Assembly.

Q.5. There was collapse of the institutions of governance during the period the partition. Discuss

Ans. Muslim League announced 16 August 1946 as "Direct Action Day". On this day, riots broke out in Calcutta, lasting several days and leaving several thousand people dead. By March 1947 violence spread to many parts of northern India. The bloodbath continued for about a year from March 1947 onwards. One main reason for this was the collapse of the institutions of governance as there was a complete breakdown of authority. British officials were unwilling to take decisions, as they were busy preparing to quit India. Nobody knew who could exercise authority and power. Indian soldiers and policemen came to act as Hindus, Muslims or Sikhs.

Chapter Practice

Multiple Choice Questions [1 Mark]

Q.1. Which of the following statements correctly represent the idea of communalism?

(a) It is the politics that seeks to unify one community around a religious identity in hostile opposition to another community.

(b) It attempts to consolidate religious identity and present it as natural

(c) It suppresses distinctions within the community and emphasises the essential unity.

(d) All of the above

Q.2. Find the incorrect statement with respect to the Lucknow pact:

(a) Congress accepted separate electorates under the pact.

(b) The pact provided a joint political platform for the Moderates, the Muslim League but not the radicals.

(c) Both (a) and (b)

(d) None of the above

Q.3. The terms tabligh and tanzim refer to which of the following ?

(a) Religious pilgrimage paid by the particular community

(b) Propaganda and organization

(c) Forms of offering prayers

(d) Institutions for religious ceremonies

Q.4. The elections to the provincial legislatures were held for the first time in __

(a) 1919 (b) 1925

(c) 1937 (d) 1946

Very Short Answer Type [1 Mark]

Q.5. Who opposed the idea of partition?

Q.6. In which province the Muslim League wanted to form a joint government with the Congress?

Short Answer Type - I [2 Marks]

Q.7. What were the final events that led towards Partition?

Q.8. What was the Lucknow Pact?

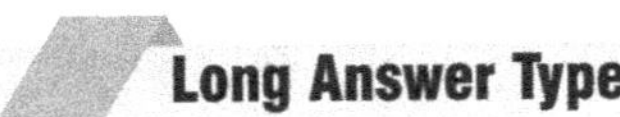

Short Answer Type - II [3 Marks]

Q.9. What was the plan presented by the Cripps Mission [CBSE 2020]

Q.10. What were the repercussions of Direct Action Day [CBSE 2018]

Long Answer Type [5 Marks]

Q11. Explain how Indian partition was a culmination of communal politics that started developing in the opening decades of the 20th century. [CBSE 2015]

CHAPTER 15

Framing the Constitution

Framing the Constitution /Rights, Powers of the State and Language of the Nation

Summary

The making of the Constituent Assembly

- The members of the Constituent Assembly were not elected on the basis of universal franchise.

- In the winter of 1945-46 provincial elections were held in India.

- The Provincial Legislatures then chose the representatives to the Constituent Assembly.

- The Constituent Assembly that came into being was dominated by one party: the Congress.

- The Congress swept the general seats in the provincial elections, and the Muslim League captured most of the reserved Muslim seats.

- But the League chose to boycott the Constituent Assembly, pressing its demand for Pakistan with a separate constitution.

- 82 per cent of the members of the Constituent Assembly were also members of the Congress.

- The Congress however was not a party with one voice. Its members differed in their opinion on critical issues.

- The discussions within the Constituent Assembly were also influenced by the opinions expressed by the public.

- As the deliberations continued, the arguments were reported in newspapers, and the proposals were publicly debated.

- Important issues of cultural rights and social justice raised in these public discussions were debated on the floor of the Assembly.

The dominant voices

- The Constituent Assembly had 300 members.

- Of these, six members played particularly important roles.

- Three were representatives of the Congress, namely, Jawaharlal Nehru, Vallabh Bhai Patel and Rajendra Prasad.

- Nehru -moved the crucial "Objectives Resolution", as well as the resolution proposing that the National Flag of India be a "horizontal tricolour of saffron, white and dark green in equal proportion", with a wheel in navy blue at the centre.

- Patel - worked mostly behind the scenes, playing a key role in the drafting of several reports

- Rajendra Prasad - As President of the Assembly, he had to steer the discussion

- Besides this Congress trio, a very important member of the Assembly was the lawyer and economist B. R. Ambedkar.

- He served as Chairman of the Drafting Committee of the Constitution.

- Serving with him were two other lawyers, K.M. Munshi and Alladi Krishnaswamy Aiyar

- Ambedkar himself had the responsibility of guiding the Draft Constitution through the Assembly.

- This took three years in all, with the printed record of the discussions taking up eleven bulky volumes.

The Vision of the Constitution

- On 13 December 1946, Jawaharlal Nehru introduced the "Objectives Resolution" in the Constituent Assembly.

- It was a momentous resolution that outlined the defining ideals of the Constitution of Independent India, and provided the framework within which the work of constitution-making was to proceed.

- It proclaimed India to be an "Independent Sovereign Republic", guaranteed its citizens justice, equality and freedom, and assured that "adequate safeguards shall be provided for minorities, backward and tribal areas, and Depressed and Other Backward Classes

- The Constituent Assembly was expected to express the aspirations of those who had participated in the movement for independence.

- The British had been forced to introduce a series of constitutional reforms.

- A number of Acts were passed (1909, 1919 and 1935), gradually enlarging the space for Indian participation in provincial governments.

- When elections were held in 1937, under the 1935 Act, the Congress came to power in eight out of the 11 provinces.

Defining Rights

The problem with separate electorates

- On 27 August 1947, B. Pocker Bahadur from Madras made a powerful plea for continuing separate electorates.

- This demand for separate electorates provoked anger and dismay amongst most nationalists.

- Not all Muslims supported the demand for separate electorates.

- Some felt that separate electorates were self-destructive since they isolated the minorities from the majority.

- By 1949, most Muslim members of the Constituent Assembly were agreed that separate electorates were against the interests of the minorities.

- Instead Muslims needed to take an active part in the democratic process to ensure that they had a decisive voice in the political system.

Rights of the Depressed Castes

- Numerically the Depressed Castes were not a minority: they formed between 20 and 25 per cent of the total population.

- Their suffering was due to their systematic marginalisation, not their numerical insignificance. They had no access to education, no share in the administration.

- The Constituent Assembly finally recommended that untouchability be abolished, Hindu temples be thrown open to all castes, and seats in legislatures and jobs in government offices be reserved for the lowest castes.

The Powers of the State

- One of the topics most vigorously debated in the Constituent Assembly was the respective rights of the Central Government and the states

- The Draft Constitution provided for three lists of subjects: Union, State, and Concurrent.

- The subjects in the first list were to be the preserve of the Central Government, while those in the second list were vested with the states.

- As for the third list, here Centre and state shared responsibility.

- The Union also had control of minerals and key industries.

- Besides, Article 356 gave the Centre the powers to take over a state administration on the recommendation of the Governor.

- In the case of some taxes (for instance, customs duties and Company taxes) the Centre retained all the proceeds; in other cases (such as income tax and excise duties) it shared them with the states; in still other cases (for instance, estate duties) it assigned them wholly to the states.

- The states, meanwhile, could levy and collect certain taxes on their own: these included land and property taxes, sales tax, and the hugely profitable tax on bottled liquor.

- Ambedkar had declared that he wanted "a strong and united Centre, much stronger than the Centre we had created under the Government of India Act of 1935".

The Language of the Nation

- By the 1930s, the Congress had accepted that Hindustani ought to be the national language. Hindustani – a blend of Hindi and Urdu – was a popular language of a large section of the people of India

- From the end of the nineteenth century, however, Hindustani as a language had been gradually changing.

- As communal conflicts deepened, Hindi and Urdu also started growing apart.

A plea for Hindi

- The Language Committee of the Constituent Assembly decided, but not yet formally declared, that Hindi in the Devanagari script would be the official language, but the transition to Hindi would be gradual. For the first fifteen years, English would continue to be used for all official purposes. Each province was to be allowed to choose one of the regional languages for official work within the province.

- By referring to Hindi as the official rather that the national language, the Language Committee of the Constituent Assembly hoped to placate ruffled emotions and arrive at a solution that would be acceptable to all.

Multiple Choice Questions [1 Mark]

Q.1. On one central feature of the Constitution there was substantial agreement. This was on the granting of the

(a) Fundamental rights

(b) Legal rights

(c) vote to every adult Indian

(d) Citizen's rights

Ans. (c)

Q.2. A important feature of the Constitution was its emphasis on

(a) Socialism   (b) Secularism

(c) Sovereignty   (d) Communalism

Ans. (b) This was done through the carefully drafted series of Fundamental Rights to "freedom of religion" (Articles 25-28), "cultural and educational rights" (Articles 29, 30), and "rights to equality" (Articles 14, 16, 17).

Q.3. Which of the following member of the Constituent Assembly was a member of Congress?

(a) K.M. Munshi

(b) Alladi Krishnaswamy Aiyar

(c) Rajendra Prasad

(d) S. N. Mukherjee

Ans. (c)

Q.4. ___________ of the members of the Constituent Assembly were also members of the Congress.

(a) 82 percent   (b) 85 percent

(c) 75 percent   (d) 90 percent

Ans. (a)

Q.5. Which of the following person joined the Union Cabinet as law minister?

(a) B. N. Rau   (b) S. N. Mukherjee

(c) B.R. Ambedkar   (d) None of the following

Ans. (c)

Consider the following image (for question Q6 and Q7)

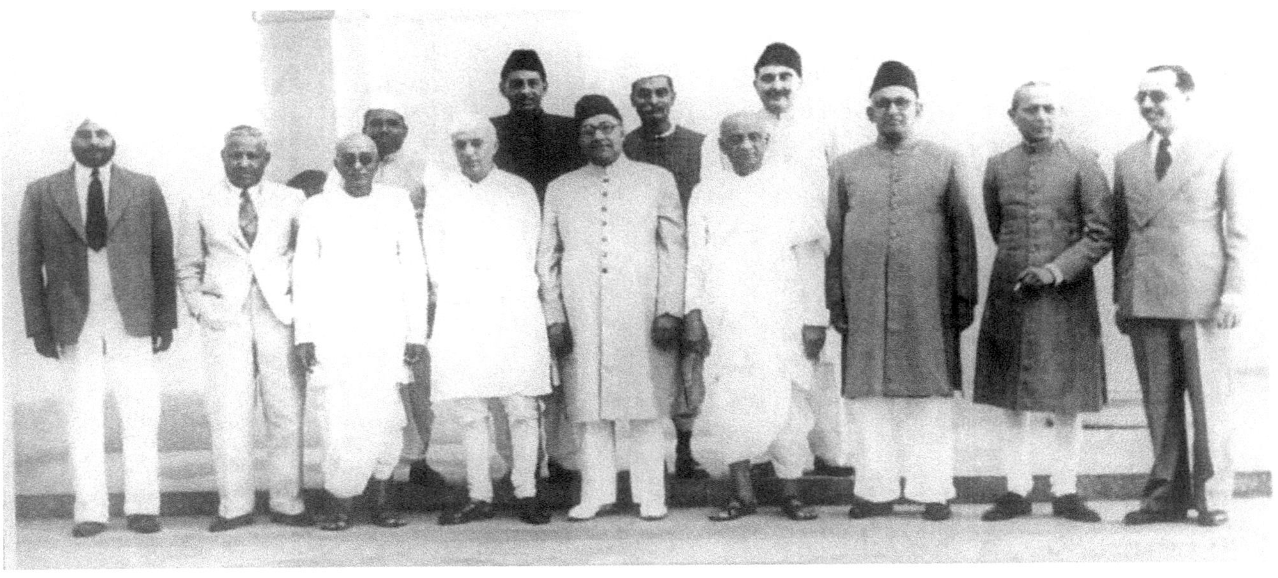

Q.6. These are the members of

(a) Interim Government

(b) Cabinet Committee

(c) Constituent Assembly

(d) Cabinet Assembly

Ans. (a) Members of the Interim Government

Q.7. Which of the following leader is not in the picture

(a) C Rajagopalachari

(b) B.R Ambedkar

(c) Jawaharlal Nehru

(d) Liaquat Ali

Ans. (b)

Q.8. The executive was made almost entirely responsible to the provincial legislature under the

(a) Government of India Act of 1935

(b) Government of India Act of 1947

(c) Government of India Act 1919

(d) Morley Minto Reforms (1909)

Ans. (a)

Q.9. On 27 August 1947, which of the following leaders made a powerful plea for continuing separate electorates in the constituent assembly

(a) B. Pocker Bahadur

(b) Govind Ballabh Pant

(c) Liaquat Ali

(d) Mohammad Ali Jinnah

Ans. (a)

Q.10. The executive was made partly responsible to the provincial legislature in

(a) 1909   (b) 1919

(c) 1935   (d) 1937

Ans. (a) A number of Acts were passed (1909, 1919 and 1935), gradually enlarging the space for Indian participation in provincial governments.

Q.11. Consider the following statement given by Sardar Vallabh Bhai Patel in the constituent assembly debate.

Therefore, I say, it is not for my good alone, it is for your own good that I say it, forget the past. One day, we may be united ... The British element is gone, but they have left the mischief behind.

We do not want to perpetuate that mischief. (Hear, hear). When the British introduced this element they had not expected that they will have to go so soon. They wanted it for their easy administration. That is all right. But they have left the legacy behind. Are we to get out of it or not?

Sardar Vallabh Bhai Patel saying against

(a) Princely States

(b) Separate electorates

(c) Two Nation Theory

(d) Partition

Ans. (b)

Q.12. _____________gave the Centre the powers to take over a state administration on the recommendation of the Governor.

(a) Article 356   (b) Article 355

(c) Article 357   (d) Article 358

Ans. (a)

Q.13. If the Centre was overburdened with responsibilities, it could not function effectively. By relieving it of some of its functions, and transferring them to the states, the Centre could, in fact, be made stronger.

The above statement was given by

(a) K. Santhanam

(b) Ramaswamy Mudaliar

(c) Gopalaswami Ayyangar

(d) Balakrishna Sharma,

Ans. (c)

Q.14. Arrange the following events in chronological order

1. Muslim League announces Direct action day

2. Muslim League Joined the Interim Government

3. Muslim League demanded dissolution of constituent assembly

4. Muslim League accepts Cabinet Mission Constitutional scheme

Choose the most appropriated sequence from the options given below

(a) 4, 1, 2, 3   (b) 3, 1, 2, 4

(c) 1, 2, 3, 4   (d) 2, 1, 3, 4

Ans. (a) • Muslim League announces Direct action day – 16 August 1946

• Muslim League Joined the Interim Government – 13 October 1946

• Muslim League demanded dissolution of constituent assembly – January 1947

• Muslim League accepts Cabinet Mission Constitutional scheme – June 1946

Q.15. Which of the following term was not used by Jawaharlal Nehru in the Objectives Resolution

(a) Democratic   (b) Republic

(c) Sovereign   (d) Both (a) and (b)

Ans. (a) Jawaharlal Nehru didn't use the term "democratic" in the Objectives Resolution

Q.16. The executive was made entirely responsible to the provincial legislature through which of the following acts?

(a) Government of India Act of 1935

(b) Indian Councils Act 1909

(c) Indian Councils Act 1909

(d) The 1947 Indian Independence Act

Ans. (a) The executive was made partly responsible to the provincial legislature in 1919, and almost entirely so under the Government of India Act of 1935.

Q.17. The legislatures elected under the 1935 Act operated within the framework of colonial rule, and were responsible to the _____________ appointed by the British

(a) Governor   (b) Governor General

(c) Viceroy   (d) Interim governor

Ans. (a) The legislatures elected under the 1935 Act operated within the framework of colonial rule, and were responsible to the Governor appointed by the British.

Q.18. Direct action day was announced by which of the following organisations/leaders?

(a) Muslim League   (b) Mahatma Gandhi

(c) Hindu Mahasabha (d) Rajputanas

Ans. (a)

Q.19. Find the correct statement with reference to the central features of the Constitution

(a) One central feature of the Constitution was to grant the vote to every adult Indian

(b) All religions were guaranteed equal treatment by the State and given the right to maintain charitable institutions.

(c) In the Indian variant of political secularism, then, there has been no absolute separation of State from religion, but a kind of judicious distance between the two.

(d) All of the above

Ans. (d)

Q.20. Consider the following statement with reference to the draft presented by the Language Committee of the Constituent Assembly

1. Hindi in the Devanagari script would be the national language

2. The transition from official language to National language would be gradual.

3. For the first fifteen years, English would continue to be used for all official purposes.

4. Each province was to be allowed to choose one of the regional languages for official work within the province.

Find the correct statement from the codes given below

(a) 1, 3 and 4   (b) 1, and 2

(c) 3 and 4   (d) 1, 2 and 3

Ans. (b) • Hindi in the Devanagari script would be the official language, but the transition to Hindi would be gradual.

• For the first fifteen years, English would continue to be used for all official purposes.

• Each province was to be allowed to choose one of the regional languages for official work within the province.

• By referring to Hindi as the official rather that the national language, the Language Committee of the Constituent Assembly hoped to placate ruffled emotions and arrive at a solution that would be acceptable to all.

Very Short Answer Type   [1 Mark]

Q.1. Constitution of India Came into effect on

Ans. Constitution of India Came into effect on 26 January 1950

Q.2. Which member of the constituent assembly worked mostly behind the scenes and played a key role in the drafting of several reports?

Ans. Vallabh Bhai Patel worked mostly behind the scenes and played a key role in the drafting of several reports?

Q.3. Constitution of India framed between

Ans. December 1946 and November 1949.

Q.4. Who was the Constitutional Advisor to the Government of India

Ans. B. N. Rau was the Constitutional Advisor to the Government of India

Q.5. On what basis were the members of the Constituent Assembly elected?

Ans. The members of the Constituent Assembly were elected on the basis of universal franchise.

Q.6. Who were the two lawyers who served with BR Ambedkar on the drafting committee of the Constitution?

Ans. K.M. Munshi and Alladi Krishnaswamy Aiyar

Q.7. In which year were the provincial elections held in India?

Ans. The provincial elections held in India in 1945-46

Q.8. Which party dominated the Constituent Assembly that came into existence?

Ans. Congress party dominated the Constituent Assembly

Q.9. In which year does the Labor government come to power in the UK?

Ans. The Labor government come to power in the UK on 20 July 1945

Q.10. Which was the date when the Muslim League declared Direct Action Day?

Ans. The Muslim League declared Direct Action Dayon 16 August 1946

Q.11. The last meeting of the constituent assembly was held on?

Ans. The last meeting of the constituent assembly was held on 24 January 1950

Q.12. The last meeting of the Interim Government was held on?

Ans. The last meeting of the Interim Government was held on16 July 1947

Q.13. Who was the Chief Draughtsman, who had the ability to put complex proposals in clear legal language

Ans. S. N. Mukherjee had the ability to put complex proposals in clear legal language

Q.14. Name the two political parties which were initially not ready to join the Constituent Assembly

Ans. Muslim League and the Socialists

Q.15. How many members were there in the Constituent Assembly before partition?

Ans. 389 members (before partition)

Q.16. Who had the responsibility of guiding the Draft Constitution through the Assembly.

Ans. B. R Ambedkar had the responsibility of guiding the Draft Constitution through the Assembly

Q.17. Who moved the crucial "Objectives Resolution", as well as the resolution proposing that the National Flag of India be a "horizontal tricolour of saffron, white and dark green in equal proportion", with a wheel in navy blue at the centre.?

Ans. Jawaharlal Nehru moved the crucial "Objectives Resolution", as well as the resolution proposing that the National Flag of India

Q.18. Which article gave the Centre the powers to take over a state administration on the recommendation of the Governor.

Ans. Article 356 gave the Centre the powers to take over a state administration on the recommendation of the Governor.

Q.19. Chairman of the ad-hoc flag committee was

Ans. Dr. Rajendra Prasad was the chairman of the ad-hoc flag committee

Q.20. Who presided the first meeting of the constituent assembly?

Ans. Dr. Sachchindanand Sinha presided the first meeting of the constituent assembly

Short Answer Type - I   [2 Marks]

Q.1. Who won the provincial election of 1945-46?

Ans. The Congress swept the general seats in the provincial elections, and the Muslim League captured most of the reserved Muslim seats.

Q.2. Define Hindustani language

Ans. Hindustani language- a blend of Hindi and Urdu was a popular language of a large section of the people of India, and it was a composite language enriched by the interaction of diverse cultures.

Q.3. What were the real causes of the suffering of the Depressed castes?

Ans. Numerically the Depressed Castes were not a minority: they formed between 20 and 25 per cent of the total population. Their suffering was due to their systematic marginalisation, not their numerical insignificance. They had no access to education, no share in the administration.

Q.4. What measures were taken by the Constituent Assembly to eradicate social discrimination?

Ans. The Constituent Assembly finally recommended that untouchability be abolished, Hindu temples be thrown open to all castes, and seats in legislatures and jobs in government offices be reserved for the lowest castes.

Q.5. Can social discrimination be eradicated through constitutional law?

Ans. Social discrimination could not be erased only through constitutional legislation, there had to be a change in the attitudes within society. But the measures were welcomed by the democratic public.

Q.6. What was Ambedkar's view of a strong government?

Ans. Ambedkar had declared that he wanted "a strong and united Centre (hear, hear) much stronger than the Centre we had created under the Government of India Act of 1935

Q.7. What was the significance of the Constituent Assembly debates

Ans. The Constituent Assembly debates help us understand the many conflicting voices that had to be negotiated in framing the Constitution, and the many demands that were articulated. They tell us about the ideals that were invoked and the principles that the makers of the Constitution operated with.

Q.8. Why is 'objectives resolution' of Nehru considered a momentous resolution ? Give any two reasons.   **[CBSE 2017]**

Ans. Objectives resolution was a momentous resolution because :

1. It outlined the defining ideals of the Constitution of Independent India, and provided the framework within which the work of constitution-making was to proceed.

2. It proclaimed India to be an Independent Sovereign Republic which guaranteed its citizens justice, equality and freedom and safeguards for depressed classes.

Q.9. What were depressed Castes?

Ans. Numerically the Depressed Castes were not a minority: they formed between 20 and 25 per cent of the total population. Their suffering was due to their systematic marginalisation, not their numerical insignificance. They had no access to education, no share in the administration. The Constituent Assembly finally recommended that untouchability be abolished, Hindu temples be thrown open to all castes, and seats in legislatures and jobs in government offices be reserved for the lowest castes.

Short Answer Type - II   [3 Marks]

Q.1. What provisions were recommended by the Language Committee of the Constituent Assembly with reference to Hindi as the official language?

Ans. The Languages Committee recommended that for the first fifteen years, English would continue to be used for all official purposes. Hindi in the Devanagari script would be the official language, but the transition to Hindi would be gradual. Each province was to be allowed to choose one of the regional languages for official work within the province.

Q.2. Who were the six members who played an important roles in the Constituent Assembly

Ans. Jawaharlal Nehru, Vallabh Bhai Patel and Rajendra Prasad played particularly important roles.Besides this Congress trio, a very important member of the Assembly was the lawyer and economist B.R. Ambedkar. He served as Chairman of the Drafting Committee of the Constitution. Serving with him were two other lawyers, K.M. Munshi from Gujarat and Alladi Krishnaswamy Aiyar from Madras

Q.3. The British Government had a "hand in its birth". What do you understand by the term "hand in its birth"?

Ans. Nehru admitted that most nationalist leaders had wanted a different kind of Constituent

Assembly. It was also true, in a sense, that the British Government had a "hand in its birth", and it had attached certain conditions within which the Assembly had to function. "But," emphasised Nehru, "you must not ignore the source from which this Assembly derives its strength."

Q.4. Discuss Begum Aijas Rasool's idea for a separate electorate

Ans. Begum Aizaas Rasul felt that separate electorates were self- destructive since they isolated the minorities from the majority. By 1949, most Muslim members of the Constituent Assembly were agreed that separate electorates were against the interests of the minorities. Instead Muslims needed to take an active part in the democratic process to ensure that they had a decisive voice in the political system.

Q.5. Why did Mahatma Gandhi think Hindustani should be the national language?

Ans. Mahatma Gandhi felt that everyone should speak in a language that common people could easily understand. Hindustani – a blend of Hindi and Urdu – was a popular language of a large section of the people of India, and it was a composite language enriched by the interaction of diverse cultures. Over the years it had incorporated words and terms from very many different sources, and was therefore understood by people from various regions.

Q.6. What provisions were made by the Constituent Assembly with respect to the respective rights of the Central Government and the States?

Ans. The respective rights of the Central Government and the states was one of the most vigorously debated topic in the Constituent Assembly . The Draft Constitution provided for three lists of subjects: Union, State, and Concurrent. The subjects in the first list were to be the preserve of the Central Government, while those in the second list were vested with the states. As for the third list, here Centre and state shared responsibility.

Q.7. The problem of the "Untouchables" could not be resolved through protection and safeguards alone. Discuss

Ans. Some members of the Depressed Castes emphasised that the problem of the "Untouchables" could not be resolved through protection and safeguards alone. Their disabilities were caused by the social norms and the moral values of caste society. Society had used their services and labour but kept them at a social distance, refusing to mix with them or dine with them or allow them entry into temples.

Q.8. The Constitution also mandated for a complex system of fiscal federalism. Substantiate

Ans. In the case of some taxes (for instance, customs duties and Company taxes) the Centre retained all the proceeds; in other cases (such as income tax and excise duties) it shared them with the states; in still other cases (for instance, estate duties) it assigned them wholly to the states. The states, meanwhile, could levy and collect certain taxes on their own: these included land and property taxes, sales tax, and the hugely profitable tax on bottled liquor.

Q.9. Give a brief note about Objectives Resolution.

Ans. On 13 December 1946, Jawaharlal Nehru introduced the "Objectives Resolution" in the Constituent Assembly. It outlined the defining ideals of the Constitution of Independent India. It provided the framework within which the work of constitution-making was to proceed. It proclaimed India to be an "Independent Sovereign Republic", guaranteed its citizens justice, equality and freedom, and assured that "adequate safeguards shall be provided for minorities, backward and tribal areas, and Depressed and Other Backward Classes

Q.10. What were the mandates mentioned in the constitution with respect to fiscal federalism?

Ans. The Constitution mandated for a complex system of fiscal federalism. In the case of some taxes (for instance, customs duties and Company taxes) the Centre retained all the proceeds; in other cases (such as income tax and excise duties) it shared them with the states; in still other cases (for instance, estate duties) it assigned them wholly to the states. The states, meanwhile, could levy and collect certain taxes on their own: these included land and property taxes, sales tax, and the hugely profitable tax on bottled liquor.

Long Answer Type [5 Marks]

Q.1. An important feature of the Constitution was its emphasis on Secularism. Discuss its constitutional provisions

Ans. Emphasis on Secularism was done through the carefully drafted series of Fundamental Rights to "freedom of religion" (Articles 25-28), "cultural and educational rights" (Articles 29, 30), and "rights to equality" (Articles 14, 16, 17). All religions were guaranteed equal treatment by the State and given the right to maintain charitable institutions. The State also sought to distance itself from religious communities, banning compulsory religious instructions in State-run schools and colleges, and declaring religious discrimination in employment to be illegal. In the Indian variant of political secularism, then, there has been no absolute separation of State from religion, but a kind of judicious distance between the two

Q.2. How did the constituent assembly dealt with the problem of separate electorates ?

Ans. On 27 August 1947, B. Pocker Bahadur from Madras made a powerful plea for continuing separate electorates. This demand for separate electorates provoked anger and dismay amongst most nationalists. Not all Muslims supported the demand for separate electorates. Some felt that separate electorates were self- destructive since they isolated the minorities from the majority. By 1949, most Muslim members of the Constituent Assembly were agreed that separate electorates were against the interests of the minorities. Instead Muslims needed to take an active part in the democratic process to ensure that they had a decisive voice in the political system.

Q.3. How the rights of the states were defended by K. Santhanam in the Constituent assembly?

Ans. According to K. Santhanam reallocation of powers was necessary to strengthen not only the states but also the Centre. There was a misconception that by adding all kinds of powers to the Centre we can make it strong. If the Centre was overburdened with responsibilities, it could not function effectively. By relieving it of some of its functions, and transferring them to the states, the Centre could, in fact, be made stronger. The fiscal provisions would impoverish the provinces since most taxes, except land revenue, had been made the preserve of the Centre. Without finances how could the states undertake any project of development?

Q.4. What were the ideals expressed in the Objectives Resolution?

Ans. Jawahar Lai Nehru presented the Objectives Resolution in the Constituent Assembly on 13 December, 1946. It gave a brief account of the ideals and objectives of the Constitution.

These are following:

- India was declared an independent sovereign republic.

- Justice, equality and fraternity were assured to all the citizens of India.

- Adequate safeguards were provided to minorities. It also referred to the well-being of the backward and depressed classes.

- It was made an objective that India would combine the liberal ideas of democracy with the socialist idea of economic justice.

- India would adopt that form of government which would be acceptable to its people. No imposition from the British would be acceptable by the people of India.

- India would work for peace and human welfare.

Q.5. How did the Constituent Assembly seek to resolve the language controversy?

Ans. The Language Committee of the Constituent Assembly produced a compromise formula to resolve the deadlock between those who advocated Hindi as the national language and those who opposed it. It had decided, but not yet formally declared, that Hindi in the Devanagari script would be the official language, but the transition to Hindi would be gradual. For the first fifteen years, English would continue to be used for all official purposes. Each province was to be allowed to choose one of the regional languages for official work within the province. By referring to Hindi as the official rather that the national language, the Language Committee of the Constituent Assembly hoped to placate ruffled emotions and arrive at a solution that would be acceptable to all.

Q.6. Why did Dr. B. R. Ambedkar argue for Strong Centre in the Constituent Assembly ? Explain.

[CBSE 2018]

Ans. The need for a strong centre in the Constituent Assembly was important to save the nation from the riots and violence. Many members had repeatedly stated that the powers of the Centre had to be greatly strengthened to enable, it to stop the communal frenzy. Ambedkar had declared that he wanted "a strong and united Centre much stronger than the Centre we had created under the Government of India Act of 1935". One member from the United Provinces, Balakrishna Sharma, reasoned at length that only a strong centre could plan for the well-being of the country, mobilise the available economic resources, establish a proper administration, and defend the country against foreign aggression..

Chapter Practice

Multiple Choice Questions   [1 Mark]

Q.1. Find the correct statement about the Constituent assembly

(a) 60 per cent of the members of the Constituent Assembly were also members of the Congress.

(b) Muslim League and The Socialists chose to boycott the Constituent Assembly

(c) Constituent Assembly was a creation of the British

(d) None of the above

Q.2. The executive was made entirely responsible to the provincial legislature through which of the following acts?   **[CBSE 2019]**

(a) Government of India Act of 1935   (b) Indian Councils Act 1909

(c) Indian Councils Act 1909   (d) The 1947 Indian Independence Act

Q.3. The legislatures elected under the 1935 Act operated within the framework of colonial rule, and were responsible to the ______________appointed by the British

(a) Governor   (b) Governor General

(c) Viceroy   (d) Interim governor

Q.4. Find the correct statement with reference to the Elections of 1937

(a) The elections were held in 1937, under the 1935 Act

(b) In this election the Congress came to power in eight out of the 11 provinces.

(c) There was no universal adult franchise.

(d) All of the above

Very Short Answer Type   [1 Mark]

Q.5. What was Hindustani language?

Q.6. On the advice of Mahatma Gandhi, which Political leader was asked to join the Union Cabinet as law minister after independence?

Short Answer Type - I   [2 Marks]

Question. (Q7, Q8 and Q9)   [CBSE 2015]

Read the following paragraph carefully and answer the questions that follow

"British element is gone but they have left the mischief behind".

Sardar Vallabh Bhai Patel said :

It is no use saying that we ask for separate electorates, because it is good for us. We have heard it long enough. We have heard it for years, and as a result of this agitation we are now a separate nation… Can you show me one free country where there are separate . electorates ? If so, I shall be prepared to accept it. But in this unfortunate country if this separate electorate is going to be persisted in, even after the division of the country, woe betide the country; it is not worth living in. Therefore, I say, it is not for my good alone, it is for your own good that I say it, forget the past. One day, we may be united … The British element is gone, but they have left the mischief behind. We do not want to perpetuate that mischief. (Hear, hear). When the British introduced this element they had not expected that they will have to go so soon. They wanted it for their easy administration. That is all right. But they have left the legacy behind. Are we to get out of it or not ? (CAD, VOL.V)

Q.7 . Why are separate electorates considered as a mischief ?

Q.8. State the arguments given by Sardar Vallabh Bhai Patel for building political unity and forging a nation.

Q.9. How did the philosophy of separate electorates result in a separate nation ?

Q.10. Explain the ideals expressed in 'Objectives Resolution' introduced by Jawaharlal Nehru.   **[CBSE 2019]**

Short Answer Type - II   [3 Marks]

Q.11. How does the Language Committee of the Constituent Assembly quell the raging sentiments and arrive at a solution that is acceptable to all?

Q.12. Discuss the making of the Constituent Assembly?

Q.13. Why did Jaipal Singh plead for the protection of tribes in the Constituent Assembly ? Explain any two reasons.   **[CBSE 2019]**

Q.14. Why did B. Pocker Bahadur from Madras make a powerful plea for continuing separate electorate in the Constituent Assembly ? Explain.   **[CBSE 2015]**

Long Answer Type   [5 Marks]

Q.15. The most vigorous debate took place in the Constituent Assembly on the respective rights of the central government and the states. Discuss   **[CBSE 2019]**

Q.16. Why did N. G. Ranga urge to interpret minorities in the economic terms in the Constituent Assembly ? Explain.   **[CBSE 2018]**

ANSWERS & SOLUTIONS

(Chapter Practice)

CHAPTER-1

Bricks, Beads and Bones
The Harappan Civilisation

1. (c)

2. (a)

- The settlement is divided into two sections, one smaller but higher and the other much larger but lower.
- Archaeologists designate these as the Citadel and the Lower Town respectively.
- The Citadel owes its height to the fact that buildings were constructed on mud brick platforms.
- It was walled, which meant that it was physically separated from the Lower Town.

3. (a) Traces of canals have been found at the Harappan site of Shortughai in Afghanistan, but not in Punjab or Sind.

4. Magan, perhaps a name for Oman

5. Terracotta toy models of bullock carts suggest that this was one important means of transporting goods and people across land routes.

6. It is used for grinding cereals. They were roughly made of hard, gritty, igneous rock or sandstone and mostly show signs of hard usage. As their bases are usually convex, they must have been set in the earth or in mud to prevent their rocking.

7. Canals and wells were constructed for irrigation. Traces of canals eg., Shortugai in Afghanistan and water reservoirs eg, Dholavira.

8. Exchanges were regulated by a precise system of weights usually made of a stone called chert and generally cubical with no markings. Lower denominations of weights were binary (1, 2, 4, 8, 16, 32, etc. up to 12,800), while the higher denominations followed the decimal system.

9. John Marshall, the Director General of the Archaeological Survey of India, from 1902 - 1928 has marked a major change in Indian Arphaeology as he was the first professional archaeologist to work in India, and brought his experience of working in Greece and Crete to the field. He was very much interested in spectacular finds and equally keen to look for patterns of everyday life. He even announced in 1924 the discovery of a new civilization in the Indus Valley, to the world.

10. The Lower Town at Mohenjondaro provides examples of residential buildings. Many were centred on a courtyard, with rooms on all sides. The courtyard was probably the centre for activities such as cooking and weaving, particularly during hot and dry weather. There were no windows in the walls along the ground level. Besides, the main entrance did not give a direct view of the interior or the courtyard. Every house had its own bathroom paved with bricks, with drains connected through the wall to the street drains. Some houses still have remains of staircases to reach a second storey or the roof. Many houses had wells, often in a room that could be reached from the outside and perhaps used by passers-by.

CHAPTER-2

Kings, Farmers and Towns
Early States and Economies (c. 600 BCE-600 CE)

1. (b) The Prayaga Prashasti (also known as the Allahabad Pillar Inscription) composed in Sanskrit by Harishena, the court poet of Samudragupta, arguably the most powerful of the Gupta rulers (c. fourth century CE)

2. (b)

- The Sudarshana lake was an artificial reservoir.

- The inscription mentions that the lake, with embankments and water channels, was built by a local governor during the rule of the Mauryas.

- Rudradaman, repaired the lake using his own resources, without imposing any tax on his subjects.

- Another inscription on the same rock (c. fifth century) mentions how one of the rulers of the Gupta dynasty got the lake repaired once again.

3. (b) Evidence of pastoral populations in the Deccan and further south.

4. Gahapati

5. Prakrit

6. An *agrahara* was land granted to a Brahmana, who was usually exempted from paying land revenue and other dues to the king, and was often given the right to collect these dues from the local people.

7. Inscriptions are writings engraved on hard surfaces such as stone, metal or pottery. They usually record the achievements, activities or ideas of those who commissioned them .Inscriptions are virtually permanent records, some of which carry dates

8. Historians use a variety of sources to reconstruct the lives of the common people during the ancient times.

Some important sources are:

1. Remains of houses and pottery give an idea of the life of common men.

2. Some inscriptions and scriptures talk about the relation between monarchs and the subject. Some talks about taxes and happiness and unhappiness of the common men.

3. Changing tools of craftsmen and farmers talk about the lifestyle of the people.

4. Historians also depend upon folklores to reconstruct the lives of the people during the ancient times.

9. Historians have used many sources to reconstruct the history of the Mauryan Empire.

- The archaeological finds like sculptures.

- Valuable contemporary work such as Magasthene's Indica who was a Greek ambassador to the court of Chandragupta Maurya.

- The book of Arthashastra, parts of which were probably composed by Kautilya or Chanakya.

10. In the post-Mauryan age, the idea of kingship got associated with divine theory of state. Now, the monarchs began to talk about divine sanction to rule the people. Kushan rulers propagated the idea of the same at the unprecented scale. They ruled from central Asia to western India.

kingship based on the dynasties.

1. Kushan Kings: Kushan Kings called themselves Devputra and hence, godly status. They built great statues of themselves in temples.

2. Gupta Rulers: Second development of kingship is found during Gupta dynasty. It was a period of large-sized states. Such states were dependent on Samantas who sometimes became powerful enough to usurp the power of kings too.

3. Literature, coins and inscriptions helped us in creating history of those days. Very often poets would describe the monarch often to praise them but giving insight into the history and kingship too. A good example is of Harisena who praised Samudragupta, the great Gupta ruler.

CHAPTER-3

Kinship, Caste and Class
Early Societies (c. 600 BCE-600 CE)

1. (d)

1. The Shungas and Kanvas, the immediate successors of the Mauryas, were Brahmanas.

2. The Shakas came from Central Asia, were regarded as outsiders by the Brahmanas.

2. (a)

1. It was based on birth.

2. However, while the number of varnas was fixed at four, there was no restriction on the number of jatis.

3. Endogamy refers to marriage within a unit and Exogamy refers to marriage outside the unit.

4. The two occupations to be performed by the Kshatriyas were to engage in warfare, protect people and administer justice.

5. The Brihadaranyaka Upanishad, one of the earliest Upanishads contains a list of successive generations of teachers and students, many of whom were designated by metronymics.

6. Brahmanas used to study and teach the Vedas, perform sacrifices and get sacrifices perform ed, and give and receive gifts.

7. Gender Differences (Patrilineal succession, Claim of resources, Gotra System)

1. Under patriliny, sons could clairJi the resources (including the throne in the case of kings) of their fathers when the latter died.

2. According to the Manusmriti, the paternal estate was to be divided equally amongst sons after the death of the parents, with a special share for the eldest.

8. Mahabharata is a dynamic text:

1. The growth of the Mahabharata did not stop with the Sanskrit version.

2. Over the centuries, versions of the epic were written in a variety of languages through an ongoing process of dialogue between peoples, communities, and those who wrote the texts.

3. Several stories that originated in specific regions or circulated amongst certain people found their way into the epic. At the same time, the central story of the epic was often retold in different ways.

4. Episodes of Mahabharata were depicted in sculpture and painting.

5. They also provided themes for a wide range of performing arts-plays, dance and other kinds of narrations.

9. Mahabharata is one of the major epics. It was originally written in Sanskrit. There are versions in other languages as well i.e., Prakrit ,Pali, Tamil etc. The content of the Mahabharata is broadly divided into two sections : narrative and didactic.

1. The 'narrative section' includes social messages.

2. Generally historians agree that Mahabharata was meant to be a dramatic, moving story and that the didactic portion was probably added later.

3. The 'didactic section' contains prescriptions about social norms and stories.

4. Didactic refers to something that's meant for purposes of instruction.

10. It is believed that the original story was written by the charioteer-bards known as Sutas. They originally accompanied Kshatriya warriors to the battlefield and composed poems celebrating their victories and other achievements. It is also believed that the beginning text of Mahabharata was orally circulated. Scholars and priests carried it from one generation to another. From the 5th century BCE, the Brahmanas took over the story and started writing. This was the time when Kurus and Panchals were gradually becoming Kingdoms. Some parts of the story reflect that old social values were replaced by the new ones. c. 200 BCE and 200 CE is another phase in the composition of the Mahabharata. During this period worship of Vishnu was gaining ground. Krishna came to be identified as Vishnu. Large didactic sections resembling Manusmriti were added during the period between C 200 and 400 CE. These interpretations made the Mahabharata an epic consisting of 100,000 verses. This enormous composition is traditionally attributed to a sage named Vyasa.

CHAPTER-4

Thinkers, Beliefs and Buildings

Cultural Developments (c. 600 BCE - 600 CE)

1. (b)

2. (a)

   The French sought Shahjehan Begum's permission to take away the eastern gateway, which was the best preserved, to be displayed in a museum in France.

3. (d)

4. The meaning of life, the possibility of life after death, and rebirth.

5. It was a hut with a pointed roof

6. Mahavira and the Buddha

7. Mahayana and Hinayana are the sects of Buddhism

8. Buddha attained Nirvana at Bodh Gaya.

9. As Buddhism travelled to new regions such as Sri Lanka, other texts such as the Dipavamsa (literally, the chronicle of the island) and Mahavamsa (the great chronicle) were written, containing regional histories of Buddhism. Many of these works contained biographies of the Buddha. Some of the oldest texts are in Pali, while later compositions are in Sanskrit.

10. The Buddha taught orally - through discussion and debate. Men and attended these discourses and discussed what they heard. None of the Buddha's speeches were written down during his lifetime. After his death his teachings were compiled by his disciples at a council of "elders" or senior monks at Vesali (Pali for Vaishali in present-day Bihar).

11. Buddha's teachings were compiled by his disciples after his death .These compilations were known as Tipitaka - literally, three baskets to hold different types of texts. They were first transmitted orally and then written and classified according to length as well as subject matter. The Vinaya Pitaka included rules and regulations for those who joined the sangha or monastic order; the Buddha's teachings were included in the Sutta Pitaka; and the Abhidhamma Pitaka dealt with philosophical matters. Each pitaka comprised a number of individual texts. Later, commentaries were written on these texts by Buddhist scholars.

12. Gautam Buddha founded Buddhism in the 6th century BCE. The religion became popular during the lifetime of Buddha and continue to spread beyond India after his death. The reason for the popularity and propagation of Buddhism was its message and its simplicity. Local language was used by the Sangh to spread it.People found it easy to follow this philosophy. Buddha did not believe in caste system and treated everyone equally which meant the people of the lower caste were happy. Buddhism attached importance to conduct and values rather than claims of superiority based on birth. A body of followers of Buddha was founded in an organization known as 'Sangha.' Followers came from many social groups which included kings, wealthy men gahapatis and humbler folk.The teachings of Buddha were written in Tripitakas, or the Three Baskets. Buddhist Sangha was quick to spread the message of Buddha to different parts of India and abroad.

CHAPTER-5

Through The Eye of Travelers

(c. 600 BCE - 600 CE)

1. (a) The term "Hindu" was derived from an Old Persian word, used c. sixth-fifth centuries BCE, to refer to the region east of the river Sindhu (Indus). The Arabs continued the Persian usage and called this region "al-Hind" and its people "Hindi"

2. (d) Both the books Al-Biruni and Ibn Batuta were written in Arabic. Al-Biruni had written Kitab-ul-Hind while Rihla was written by Ibn Batuta.

   These were the travelogue that gave an account of their travels to India

3. (a) Ibn Batuta travelled extensively in China, going as far as Beijing, but did not stay for long, deciding to return home in 1347. His account is often compared with that of Marco Polo, who visited China

4. Unlike the accounts in Arabic and Persian, which circulated as manuscripts, Bernier's work was reprinted many times.

5. Al-Biruni disapproved of the notion of pollution.

6. The categories defined as *antyaja* (literally, born outside the system) were often expected to provide inexpensive labour to both peasants and zamindars

7. Two inherent problems that were faced by Al-Baruni were:

   1. Language : Al-Baruni was familiar only with Arabic and Persian and could not understand Sanskrit Language.

   2. Difference in religious beliefs and practices.

   Two sources that provided him the support were:

   a. Vedas and Puranas

   b. The Bhagwad Geeta and Manusmriti.

8. Rihla was called a remarkable hook of Ibn Battuta because :

   1. It provides rich details about the social and cultural life of the fourteenth century, in the Indian subcontinent.

   2. It provides an extensive scholarly account of his travel expeditions across various countries like Syria, Iraq, Persia, Yemen, Oman, India and a few trading ports on the coast of East Africa.

9. Bernier noticed how a child widow were forcefully burnt screaming on the funeral pyre while many of the older women were resigned their fate.

   The following elements drew his attention.

   1. Under this cruel practices an alive widow was forcibly made to sit on the pyre of her husband.

   2. People had no sympathy for her.

   3. The widow was an unwilling victim of the sati-practice. She was forced to be a Sati.

10. According to Bernier, there was no private property during Mughal India. He was a firm believer in the virtues of private property, and saw crown ownership of land as being harmful for both the state and its people. He thought that in the Mughal Empire, the emperor owned all the land and distributed it among his nobles, and that this had disastrous consequences for the economy and society. Owing to crown ownership the land holders could not pass the property to their children. They were averse to long term investment in the sustenance and expansion of production. This had led to uniform ruination of agriculture. Bernier's descriptions influenced Western theorists from the 18th century onwards. The French philosopher Montesquieu, for instance, used this account to develop the idea of oriental despotism, according to which rulers in Asia (the Orient or the East) enjoyed absolute authority over their subjects, who were kept in conditions of subjugation and poverty, arguing that all land belonged to the king and that private property was non-existent.

11. Al-Biruni spent years in the company of Brahmana priests and scholars, learning Sanskrit, and studying religious and philosophical texts. He discussed several 'barriers' that he felt obstructed understanding. The first amongst these was language, Sanskrit was different from Arabic and Persia. The second barrier he identified was the difference in religious beliefs and practices. The self-absorption and consequent insularity of the local population according to him, constituted the third barrier. He tried to explain the caste system by looking for parallels in other societies for example in Ancient Persia. Al-Biruni's description of the caste-system was deeply influence by the Brahamanical point of view, which in real life was not quite as rigid. He wrote about the system of Varna.

12. Ibn Batuta arrived India in the 14th century. He was much impressed by the Postal System of India. Two kinds of postal system were prevalent in the society. These two systems, the horse-post called the Uluq and foot-post called the Dawa. Uluq had their station at every four miles, while the foot-post had three stations per mile and a dawa meant one-third of a mile. The foot system was much spread than the horse system and was prevalent in the entire subcontinent. It is because of this efficient postal system the rulers were able to keep

a strict watch over the vast empire. The ruler used to get all the information about all the events in the minimum possible time. It took nearly 50 days to travel from Sindh to Delhi, whereas, the spies of the king were able to send their news reports in just five days through this efficient system of post. This also proved beneficial for the traders since it enabled them to despatch their goods in a short period of time.

CHAPTER-6

Bhakti-Sufi Traditions

1. (a) The *Kabir Bijak* is preserved by the Kabirpanth (the path or sect of Kabir) in Varanasi and elsewhere in Uttar Pradesh

2. (d) Poets such as Amir Hasan Sijzi and Amir Khusrau and the court historian Ziyauddin Barani, all of whom wrote about the Shaikh.

3. (a) The category of the *zimmi*, meaning protected (derived from the Arabic word *zimma*, protection) developed for people who followed revealed scriptures, such as the Jews and Christians, and lived under Muslim rulership.

4. Guru Arjan, compiled Baba Guru Nanak's hymns along with those of his four successors and other religious poets like Baba Farid, Ravidas (also known as Raidas) and Kabir in the *Adi Granth Sahib.*

5. At a different level, historians of religion often classify bhakti traditions into two broad categories: saguna (with attributes) and nirguna (without attributes).

6. Kabir and Guru Nanak Dev both believed in practice of Nam-Simran. Both were against the polytheism and idol worships.

7. Kabir Bijak and Kabir Granthavali are preserved as :
   1. Kabir Bijak is preserved by the Kabir Panth (the path or sect of Kabir) in Varanasi and elsewhere in U.P.
   2. Kabir Granthavali is associated with the Dadupanth in Rajasthan.

8. He was initiated into bhakti by a guru, Ramananda. Ultimate Reality is that which is the primal cause of the existence of the universe and all beings. He says that we think of that reality as the God and have different names but we know that God is beyond forms and attributes that we can ascribe to Him.

9. Guru Raidas, a low caste leather worker was the preceptor of Mirabai. One main principle of her philosophy was that one should abandon the comforts of life and devote fully to her God for attainment of peace and salvation.

10. 1. The major anthology compiled by the Alvars was the Nalayira Divya prabandham, it is also describe as the Tamil Veda.
    2. There were many significant chiefdoms in the Tamil region in the early first millennium CE. They got occasional royal patronage.

11. Guru Nanak Dev's Divinity:
    1. He advocated nirguna bhakti.
    2. He rejected sacrifices, ritual baths, image worship, austerities and the scriptures of both Hindus and Muslims.
    3. For him the Absolute or 'rab' had no gender or form.
    4. He proposed a simple way to connect to the divine by remembering and repeating the divine name.
    5. He expressed his ideas through hymns called 'Shabad'.

12. Some mystics initiated movements based on a radical interpretation of sufi ideals. Many scorned the khanqah and took to mendicancy and observed celibacy. They ignored rituals and observed extreme forms of asceticism. They were known by different names - Qalandars, Madaris, Malangs, Haidaris, etc. Because of their deliberate defiance of the shari'a they were often referred to as be-shari'a, in contrast to the ba-shari'a sufis who complied with it.

13. The early Bhakti Movement was led by Alvars and Nayanars. It was the period of the 6th Century. Alvars are those who were disciples of Vishnu and Nayanars were those who claimed themselves the followers of Lord Shiva. They travelled place to place and would sing devotional songs in Tamil in the name of Shiva or Vishnu as the case may be. Many historians are of the view that Alvars and Nayanars gave a blow to the caste system and Brahminism. This is corroborated by the fact that the movement was open to people from diverse background. The Bhaktas came from the castes of Brahmin to artisans to even those that were considered untouchables.

Virashaivas was a movement of the 12th Century that took place in Karnataka. The movement was led by a Brahmin named Basavanna (1106-68), who was a minister in the court of Chalukya king. The followers of Basavanna are called Virashaivas and they worshipped Shiv. They were also called and perhaps more often Lingayats, which literary means wearer of Lingas. They challenged the caste system and they challenged the idea of any caste being pollutant. This helped them grow support among marginalised sections of the society.

CHAPTER-7

An Imperial Capital Vijayanagara

1. (a)
   - After the death of Krishnadeva Raya in 1529 the control at the centre had shifted to another ruling lineage, that of the Aravidu
   - Aravidu remained in power till the end of the seventeenth century.

2. (a)

3. (a)
   - Military chiefs exercised power in the empire
   - These chiefs were known as *nayakas* and they usually spoke Telugu or Kannada.

4. (d)

5. Krishnadeva Raya founded a suburban township near Vijayanagara called Nagalapuram after his mother.

6. The kingdom of Vijayanagar was founded by **Harihara and Bukka,**

7. One of the most prominent waterworks to be seen among the ruins is the Hiriya canal. This canal drew water from a dam across the Tungabhadra and irrigated the cultivated valley that separated the "sacred centre" from the "urban core".

8. Agricultural tracts were incorporated within the fortified area. The objective of medieval sieges was to starve the defenders into submission. These sieges could last for several months and sometimes even years. Normally rulers tried to be prepared for such situations by building large granaries within fortified areas.

9. Krishnadeva Raya belonged to the Tuluva dynasty.

   His main policy was that state remained in a constant state of military preparedness but still flourished under conditions of unparalleled peace and prosperity.

   Eg: During his rule the land between the Tungabhadra and Krishna rivers was acquired, the rulers of Odisha were subdued and severe defeats were inflicted on the Sultan of Bijapur yet there was peace in the empire.

10. Krishnadeva Raya was the most powerful of the Vijayanagara kings. He defeated the Adilshah of Bijapur, Golkonda and the Raja of Odisha. He was a kind but ruthless administrator and a very able general who fought along with his soldiers. He's credited with building so as well fine temples and Gopurams. He was a poet. He encouraged artists and expanded trade. The great mathematician Nilkantha was encouraged by him. Vijaynagar was at its peak in his times.

11. Water resources of Vijaynagar
    - The natural basin formed by the Tungabhadra which flows in a north-easterly direction hills surrounds this and a number of streams flow down to the river from these hills.
    - Embankments were built along the streams to create reservoirs of varying sizes.

- As Vijaynagar was in one of the most arid zones of the peninsula, elaborate water arrangements had to be made to store rain water and conduct it to the city.

- Kamalapuram tank not only irrigated fields nearby but water was also conducted through a channel to the "royal centre".

- One of the most prominent was the Hiriya canal. It drew water from a dam across the Tungabhadra and irrigated the cultivated valley which separated the sacred centre from the urban core.

12. Abdur Razzak who was an ambassador from Persia visited Vijaynagar empire in the 15th century. He explains that Vijaynagar was constructed with lot of planning and the best example is fortification structure. He revealed that the Vijaynagar empire created its cities primarily for protection against invasion. The city itself was a fortress and designed as such in every possible way. It was built of massive stone , and earthen walls, with hilltop fortresses and watch towers scattered across its length and breadth. The vijayanagara fort not only encircled the palace; but it also encircled agricultural tracts, river streams, forests etc. This was especially done to survive sieges of the fort by any powerful enemy. There were seven , lines of forts. Between the first, second and the third walls there are cultivated fields, gardens and houses. The water channelized from river Tungabhadra was used for cultivation of agricultural tracts. Therefore, Razzak was impressed by the intelligence, splendid planning and technology used in making the fort.

13. Rituals associated with the structure probably coincided with Mahanavami of the ten-day Hindu festival during the autumn season. The Vijayanagara kings displayed their prestige, power and suzerainty on this occasion. The ceremonies performed on the occasion included image worship, worship of the state horse, and the sacrifice of buffaloes and other animals. Dances, wrestling matches, and processions of caparisoned horses, elephants and chariots and soldiers, as well as ritual presentations before the king and his guests by the chief nayakas and subordinate kings marked the occasion. These ceremonies were imbued with deep symbolic meanings. On the last day of the festival the king inspected his army and the armies of the nayakas in a grand ceremony in an open field. On this occasion the kings accepted rich gifts from the nayakas.

14. The Amara-Nayaka System was a major political innovation of the Vijayanagara Empire. It is likely that many features of this system were derived from the Iqta system of the Delhi Sultanate. The Amara-Nayakas were military commanders who were given territories to govern by the Raya. They collected taxes and other dues from peasants, craftspersons and traders in the area. They retained a part of the revenue for personal use and for maintaining a stipulated contingent of horses and elephants. These contingents provided the Vijayanagara kings with an effective fighting force with which they brought the entire southern peninsula under their control. Some of the revenue was also used for the maintenance of temples and irrigation works. They sent tribute to the king annually and personally appeared in the royal court with gifts to express their loyalty.

CHAPTER-8

Peasants, Zamindars and the State

1. (d)
   - *Pargana* was an administrative subdivision of a Mughal province.
   - *Peshkash* was a form of tribute collected by the Mughal state.

2. (b)
   - The first book, called *manzil-abadi*
   - The second book, *sipah-abadi*
   - The third book, *mulk-abadi*
   - The fourth and fifth books (*daftars*) deal with the religious, literary and cultural traditions of the people of India

3. (b)

- The land revenue arrangements consisted of two stages - first, assessment and then actual collection. The *jama* was the amount assessed, as opposed to *hasil*, the amount collected. In his list of duties of the *amil-guzar* or revenue collector, Akbar decreed that while he should strive to make cultivators pay in cash, the option of payment in kind was also to be kept open.

4. In Muslim communities menials like the *halalkhoran* (scavengers) were housed outside the boundaries of the village

5. *Milkiyat* lands were cultivated for the private use of zamindars, often with the help of hired or servile labour.

6. Al-Biruni's Kitab-ul-Hind comprises 80 chapters on subjects such as religion and philosophy, festivals, astronomy, alchemy, manners and customs social life, weights and measures, iconography, laws and metrology. Al-Biruni adopted a distinctive structure in each chapter, beginning with a question, followed by a description based on Sanskritic traditions, and concluding with a comparison with other cultures.

7. Sources of the seventeenth century refer to two kinds of peasants - khud-kashta and pahi-kashta.

- khud-kashta -   were residents of the village in which they held their lands.

- pahi-kashta - were non-resident cultivators who belonged to some other village, but cultivated lands elsewhere on a contractual basis.

8. The Akbar Nama(the chronicle of a King) was written by Abu'l Fazl who was a court historian in the reign of Akbar. The Mughal chronicle is based on a range of sources including actual records of events, official documents and oral testimonies of knowledgeable person. The Akbar Nama is divided into three books of which the first two are chronicles and the third book is the Ain-i-Akbari. The Akbar Nama provides a detailed description of Akbar's reign in the traditional diachronic sense of recording politically significant events as well as synchronic picture of all aspects of Akbar's empire-geographic social administrative and cultural without reference to chronology.

9. Panchayats had a very important role during the Mughal agrarian society. In addition to the village panchayat, each caste or jati in the village had its own Jati Panchayat. These panchayats wielded I' considerable power in rural society. They mediated in contested claims on lands, decided whether marriages were performed according to the norms laid down by a particular caste group, determined who had rituals precedence in village functions, and so on.The state respected the decisions of Jati Panchayats in most of the cases.

10. 'Ain-i-Akbari' can be supplemented by descriptions contained in sources emanating from regions away from the Mughal capital. These include detailed revenue records from Gujarat, Maharashtra and Rajasthan dating from seventeenth and eighteenth centuries. Ain-i-Akbari is a mine of information regarding agricultural aspects of Mughal rule. It recorded meticulously the arrangements made by the state to ensure cultivation. The aim of Ain was to present a vision of Akbar's empire where social harmery prevailed record instances of conflicts between peasants, zamindars and the state. In the process, they give us an insight into the peasants' perception and their expectations of fairness from the State.

CHAPTER-9

Kings and Chronicles

1. (d)

2. (b)

3. (d)

- All books in Mughal India were manuscripts, that is, they were handwritten.

- The centre of manuscript production was the imperial *kitabkhana.*

- It is, a place where the emperor's collection of manuscripts was kept and new manuscripts were produced.

4. (b)

- Calligraphers and painters held a high social standing
- Calligraphy, the art of handwriting, was considered a skill of great importance.
- It was practised using different styles.

5. Akbar abolished the tax on pilgrimage in 1563 and *jizya* in 1564 as the two were based on religious discrimination.

6. The founder of the empire, Zahiruddin Babur, was driven from his Central Asian homeland, Farghana, by the warring Uzbeks. He first established himself at Kabul and then in 1526 pushed further into the Indian subcontinent

7. It was Akbar who consciously set out to make Persian the leading language of the Mughal court. Persian was elevated to a language of empire, conferring power and prestige on those who had a command of it. It was spoken by the king, the royal household and the elite at court.

8. After 1707, following the death of Shah Jahan, the power of the dynasty diminished. Regional powers acquired greater autonomy. In 1857 the last scion of this dynasty, Bahadur Shah Zafar II, was killed by the British.

9. Process of manuscript production in the Mughal court included the following:

- Paper-maker's responsibility was to prepare the folios of the manuscript.
- Skill writer, i.e. scribes or calligrapher copied the texts.
- Guilders, illuminated the pages of the manuscript.
- Miniature painter illustrated the scene from the text.
- The book binders gathered the folio and gave it to the original shape of a book.

10. The Mughal provincial administration was like the central administration as mentioned below :

- There were diwan, bakhshi and sadr corresponding the central ministers – Diwan-i ala, mir-bakshi and sadr-us sudur.
- The head of the provincial administration was the governor (subadar) who directly reported to the emperor.
- A suba was divided into sarkars.
- Faujdars were deployed with contingents of heavy cavalry and musketeers in districts.
- At the local level were parganas which were looked after by the qanungo (keeper of revenue records), the chaudhuri (in charge of revenue collection) and the qazi.
- There was clerks, accountants, auditors, messengers and other functionaries who were technically qualified officials. They functioned with standardised rules and procedures.
- Persian was the language of the administration but local languages were used for village accounts.

11. The Mughal emperor and his court controlled the entire administrative apparatus down to the village level. However, the relationship between local landed magnates, the zamindars, and the representatives of the Mughal emperor was sometimes marked by conflicts over authority and a share of the resources. Moreover, after the death of Aurangzeb the provincial governors became powerful and this led to the downfall of the Mughal Empire.

12. The Mughal had cultural and intellectual contacts with Iran. Persian was used in the Court of Iran. The Iranians and Central Asian migrants sought positions in the Mughal Courts.

Efforts made by Akbar

- Persian was elevated to a language of empire, conferring power and prestige on those who had acommand of it. It was spoken by the king, the royal household and the elite at court.
- It became the language of administration at all levels so that accountants, clerks and other functionaries also learnt it.
- Its vocabulary and idiom heavily influenced the language of official records in Rajasthani and Marathi and even Tamil urdu sprang from Persian and Persian too became Indianised by absorbing local idioms.

- Mughal chronicles such as the Akbar Nama' were written in Persian, others, like Babur's memoirs, were translated from the Turkish into the Persian 'Babur Nama'.

- Translations of Sanskrit texts such as the Mahabharata and the Ramayana into Persian were commissioned by the Mughal emperors.

CHAPTER-10

Colonialism and Countryside

1. (a)

2. (b)

3. (d)

- The Permanent Settlement was made with the rajas and *taluqdars* of Bengal.

- They were now classified as zamindars, and they had to pay the revenue demand that was fixed in perpetuity.

- In terms of this definition, the zamindar was not a landowner in the village, but a revenue Collector of the state.

- Zamindars had several (sometimes as many as 400) villages under them.

4. (c)

- In Company calculations the villages within one zamindari formed one revenue estate.

- The zamindar collected rent from the different villages, paid the revenue to the Company, and retained the difference as his income.

5. (c)

6. Unlike zamindars who often lived in urban areas, *jotedars* were located in the villages and exercised direct control over a considerable section of poor villagers.

7. The Permanent Settlement was made with the rajas and *taluqdars* of Bengal.

8. They lived around the Rajmahal hills, subsisting on forest produce and practising shifting cultivation. They cleared patches of forest by cutting bushes and burning the undergrowth. On these patches, they grew a variety of pulses and millets for consumption.

9. In Company calculations the villages within one zamindari formed one revenue estate. The zamindar collected rent from the different villages, paid the revenue to the Company, and retained the difference as his income.

10. Moneylenders used a variety of other means to short-change the *ryot*: they refused to give receipts when loans were repaid, entered fictitious figures in bonds, acquired the peasants' harvest at low prices, and ultimately took over peasants' property. Deeds and bonds appeared as symbols of the new oppressive system. Over time, peasants came to associate the misery of their lives with the new regime of bonds and deeds. They were made to sign and put thumb impressions on documents, but they did not know what they were actually signing.

11. Paharias live in the hills of Rajmahal. The British people began to interact with them and later Santhals began to settle down there.

How the Pahariasresponded?

- Paharias resisted the settlement of Santhals initially but had to accommodate them in course of time.

- The Paharias shifted to deeper areas into the hills.

- They were confined to more barren and rocky areas of the hills in course of time.

- The paharias did shifting cultivation. Now shifting cultivation was becoming more and more difficult as proper and stable settlements.

- As forest began to be cleared, the paharis could not depend on it for livelihood. Thus, the lifestyle and living of Paharias underwent change due to coming of outsiders.

12. During the civil war in USA, Indian merchants hoped to capture the world market in raw cotton, but they failed to do so. After the civil war cotton production in America revived and the Indian cotton exports to British steadily declined. Export merchants and sahukars in Maharashtra refused to give long-term credit. They restricted the advances to peasants and demanded repayment of outstanding debts. At the same time as the term of first revenue settlement was over, the demand for revenue was increased from 50 to 100 per cent.

As a result of above, the ryots were not in position to pay the inflated demand because the prices were also falling. Thus, they had no option except to take a further loan from the moneylender who also refused to loans. This enraged the ryots. The moneylenders became insensitive to their plight. They were violating the customary norms of the countryside. They were not charging fair interest. A new law – Limitation Law – was passed in 1859 where validity of loan bonds was fixed for three years but the money lenders manipulated new systems to exploit the ryots. Under these circumstances, the ryots' anger against the moneylenders increased.

13. Jotedars were rich peasants in Bengal. They owned big plots of land sometimes running into thousand of acres of land. They controlled local trade and commerce including the money lending business. They had great influence on the local village population. They were regarded more powerful than the Zamindars even.

Reasons for the high status of Jotedars.

- The Jotedars controlled trade and commerce including money lending business at the local level.In order to weaken the Zamindars, Jotedars would mobilise ryots not to pay or delay payment towards land revenue.

- The Jotedars opposed the moves of Zamindars to increase the Jama of a village.

    The Jotedars lived in villages only. Hence they were in a better position to interact with and influence the peasants.

- Jotedars were rich and owned big areas of land under cultivation. Many a time they would buy estates of Zamindar. That would be auctioned due to failure to pay up land revenue.

CHAPTER-11

Revels and The Raj

1. (b) Mutiny– a collective disobedience of rules and regulations within the armed forces

2. (b)

3. (a)
   - Signals used by the sepoys to began their action: firing of the evening gun or the sounding of the bugle.
   - They first seized the bell of arms and plundered the treasury.
   - They then attacked government buildings – the jail, treasury, telegraph office, record room, bungalows – burning all records.
   - Everything and everybody connected with the white man became a target.

4. (a) In Kanpur, the sepoys and the people of the town gave Nana Sahib, the successor to Peshwa Baji Rao II

5. (a) In Awadh, the people, in Lucknow celebrated the fall of British rule by hailing Birjis Qadr, the young son of the Nawab, as their leader.

6. The British established laws to abolish customs like sati (1829) and to permit the remarriage of Hindu widows.

7. In Awadh, where resistance to the British lasted longest

8. Gonoo, a tribal cultivator of Singhbhum in Chotanagpur, became a rebel leader of the Kol tribals of the region. The Kol tribal people belongs to Jharkhand region.

9. British adopted policies aimed at "reforming" Indian society by introducing Western education, Western ideas and Western institutions under the leadership of Governor General Lord William Bentinck

10. In 1856, the Awadh kingdom was annexed to the British Empire and Nawab Wajid Ali Shah dethroned and exiled to Calcutta The removal of the Nawab led to the dissolution of the court and its culture

11. Immediately after the annexation of Awadh , the *taluqdars* were disarmed and their forts destroyed. After annexation, the first British revenue settlement, known as the Summary Settlement of 1856. The Summary Settlement proceeded to remove the *taluqdars* wherever possible.

12. The *taluqdars* were loyal to the Nawab of Awadh, and they joined Begum Hazrat Mahal (the wife of the Nawab) in Lucknow to fight the British; some even remained with her in defeat.

13. The large majority of the sepoys of the Bengal Army were recruited from the villages of Awadh and eastern Uttar Pradesh.

14. As Delhi was the main center of revolt of 1857 there was a lot of political action during the revolt for example Bahadur Shah Jafar was declared as emperor of India Due to all these activities the routine life of people was disturbed during this war time.

15. The routine activities of Delhi people was at total halt. The vegetables and grains which used to come from outside Delhi was disrupted therefore prices soared up and the local people could not find the vegetables of daily use . Some people left their daily activities and many households did not get wages because the economic activities were at halt.

16. During this time period People had to face lot of difficulties. Most of the revolt was being carried out by sepoys and princely states but peasants in some places also took part in the revolt. This resulted shortage of grains and vegetables. The condition of poor and middle class was all the more worse because they could not get vegetables from the gardens inside the city and they were siphoned off by elites only. The city was not cleaned for months and the reporter fears that there might be outbreak of Mahamaari due to deaths, rotten vegetables and polluted air.

17. After the revolt of 1857 the British felt that cities needed to be better defended and white people had to live in more secure and segregated enclaves. To ward off the threat of the "natives" pasture lands and agricultural fields around the older towns were cleared and new urban spaces known as "Civil Lines" were set up.

18. The relationship of the sepoys with their superior white officers underwent a significant change in the years preceding the uprising of 1857.In the 1820s, white officers made it a point to keep cordial relations with the sepoys. They would participate in their leisure activities—they wrestled with them, fenced with them and went out hawking with them. In fact several white officers could speak and understand Hindustani language fluently. And they were also familiar with the local customs and culture. But in the 1840s, this fabric of friendly relationship began to change very fast. The white officers started considering the sepoys as their racial inferiors . After 1840 abuse and physical violence became common. These events widen the distance between sepoys and officers. Trust was replaced by doubt. The event of the greased cartridges was a classic example of this increasing suspicion.

19. Rumours and prophecies played an important part in moving people to action in the revolt of 1857 as these rumours touched people's religion and caste

    Following were the rumours touched people's religion and caste

    • There were rumours among sepoys that the newly introduced cartridges of enfield rifles were greased with fat of cow and pigs and that the sepoys will have to open these with their mouth thus defiling the religion of Hindus and Muslims respectively.

    • There were rumours that British wanted to destroy the religion of Indians and convert them to Christianity. Thus, they had mixed the bone dust of cows and pigs into the flour that was sold in the market. The response to the call for action was reinforced by the prophecy that British rule would come to an end on the centenary of the Battle of Plassey, on 23 June, 1857.

CHAPTER-12

Colonial Cities

1. (a) The imperial officer of North India – *kotwali*, who oversaw the internal affairs and policing of the town.

2. (b) Towns were peopled with artisans, traders, administrators and rulers.

3. (d) During the sixteenth and seventeenth centuries the towns built by the Mughals like Agra, Delhi and Lahore were important centres of imperial administration and control.

4. (a) *Mansabdars* and *jagirdars* who were assigned territories in different parts of the empire usually maintained houses in these cities

5. (d)
   - The focus of the town was oriented towards the palace and the principal mosque.
   - In the towns of South India such as Madurai and Kanchipuram the principal focus was the temple.

6. (c)

7. (a) Calcutta had grown from three villages called Sutanati, Kolkata and Govindapur.

8. The British gradually acquired political control after the Battle of Plassey in 1757, and the trade of the English East India Company expanded

9. By the mid-nineteenth century several local censuses had been carried out in different regions. The first all-India census was attempted in 1872. Thereafter, from 1881, decennial (conducted every ten years) censuses became a regular feature.

10. By the eighteenth century Madras, Calcutta and Bombay had become important ports. The settlements that came up here were convenient points for collecting goods.

11. New urban spaces (Safe enclaves) called "Civil Lines" were set up. White people began to live in the Civil Lines.

12. Madras

13. After the 1850s, cotton mills were set up by Indian merchants and entrepreneurs in Bombay, and European-owned jute mills were established on the outskirts of Calcutta. This was the beginning of modern industrial development in India. India never became a modern industrialised country, since discriminatory colonial policies limited the levels of industrial development.

14. Within the cities new social groups were formed and the old identities of people were no longer important. All classes of people were migrating to the big cities. A new public sphere of debate and discussion emerged. Social customs, norms and practices came to be questioned. Another new class within the cities was the labouring poor or the working class.

15. Simla was founded during the course of the Gurkha War (1815-16); the Anglo-Maratha War of 1818 led to British interest in Mount Abu; and Darjeeling was wrested from the rulers of Sikkim in 1835.

16. In 1864 the Viceroy John Lawrence officially moved his council to Simla, setting seal to the practice of shifting capitals during the hot season.

17. The *dubashes* were Indians who could speak two languages – the local language and English. They worked as agents and merchants, acting as intermediaries between Indian society and the British.

18. As Bombay's economy grew, many new buildings were constructed at this time. The architectural style was usually European. Initially, these buildings were at odds with the traditional Indian buildings.Gradually, Indians too got used to European architecture and made it their own

19. The area where Europeans lived was known as White. These areas had broad streets, bungalows set amidst large gardens, barracks, parade ground and church. They were safe heaven for the Europeans. For example in Madras Fort St. George was the nucleus of the White Town where most of the Europeans lived.

The Black Town were meant for Indians – the Indian agents, middlemen, weavers, artisans and interpreters. In Madras, the Black Town was developed outside the Fort. A Black Town generally resembled traditional Indian town, with living quarters built around its own temple and bazaar. There were narrow lanes and distinct caste-specific neighbourhoods.

20. The prominent Indian merchants and traders settled in colonial cities like Bombay, Calcutta and Madras. They served as agents or middlemen for the British and lived traditionally built courtyard houses in the Black Town. They centred over large tracts of land in these cities and heavily made investments for the future. They wanted to impress their British masters or colonial ruler or white people living in white towns by giving lavish parties during festivals seasons and built temples to establish their supremacy and prestige in society.

21. Developments such as bazaars, horse-cards, motors, roads etc and new transport facilities such as horse- drawn carriages and, subsequently, trams and buses in colonial cities offered new opportunities to women. It meant that women could visit long distance places from the city centre. These were used not only by the English women but also upper class Indian women. Though lower class women still did not have access to such facilities. The new urban cities had centers for shopping, theatres etc. Though there was resistance but upper class wives of educated Indians used to go for watching movies occasionally.The social reformers also pressed for education of women and thus they opened women's colleges in the new urban centers during nineteenth century for example Madras Medical college in 1835 the Women's Christian Medical College, an exclusive medical school for women, was established in Ludhiana in Punjab in 1894.Some women expressed themselves through journals, books and autobiographies.

Though, this opportunity was enjoyed by only a fraction of women. Many people resented these attempts to change traditional patriarchal norms.

CHAPTER-13

Mahatma Gandhi and The Nationalist Movement
Civil Disobedience and Beyond

1. (d) Lord Irwin was the Viceroy of India during the Dandi March carried by Gandhi. Viceroy Lord Irwin, Irwin failed to grasp the significance of the action.

2. (b) In the end of December 1929, the Congress held its annual session in the city of Lahore. The meeting was significant for two things: the election of Jawaharlal Nehru as President, signifying the passing of the baton of leadership to the younger generation; and the proclamation of commitment to "Purna Swaraj", or complete independence.

3. (c) In February 1922, a group of peasants attacked and torched a police station in the hamlet of Chauri Chaura, in the United Provinces (now, Uttar Pradesh and Uttaranchal). Several constables perished in the conflagration. On this, Gabdhi called off the NCM.

4. (b) His first major public appearance was at the opening of the Banaras Hindu University (BHU) in February 1916.

5. (d) The India that Mahatma Gandhi came back to in 1915 was rather different from the one that he had left in 1893. The Indian National Congress now had branches in most major cities and towns. Through the Swadeshi movement of 1905-07 it had greatly broadened its appeal among the middle classes.

   That movement had thrown up some towering leaders – among them Bal Gangadhar Tilak of Maharashtra, Bipin Chandra Pal of Bengal, and Lala Lajpat Rai of Punjab. The three were known as "Lal, Bal and Pal"

6. (b) During the Great War of 1914-18, the British had instituted censorship of the press and permitted detention without trial. The committee chaired by Sir Sidney Rowlatt recommended only its continuation.

7. Indians who wished colonialism to end were asked to stop attending schools, colleges and law courts, and not pay taxes.

8. To further broaden the struggle under the Non Cooperation Movement he had joined hands with the Khilafat Movement that sought to restore the Caliphate, a symbol of Pan-Islamism

9. He was not certain that he would be allowed to reach Dandi. Gandhiji suspected he might be arrested, as he said, "Government might perhaps let my party come as far as Dandi but not me certainly".

10. According to Gandhi, the Government deserved to be congratulated on not arresting them, even if it desisted only because of the fear of world opinion.

11. The salt march was significant because it brought Gandhi into limelight and attracted the world's attention. The Women participation was very high.It forced the British to think that their British Raj will not continue further.Gandhi mobilized a wider discontent against British rule.

12. The British government convened a series of "Round Table Conferences" in London. The first meeting was held in November 1930, but without the pre-eminent political leader in India, thus rendering it an exercise in futility."Gandhi-Irwin Pact', by the terms of which civil disobedience would be called off, all prisoners released, and salt manufacture allowed along the coast.A second Round Table Conference was held in London in the latter part of 1931. Here, Gandhiji represented the Congress. However, his claims that his party represented all of India came under challenge from the Muslim League, the Prince and BR Ambedkar.After the second round table conference, Gandhiji returned to India and resumed civil disobedience.

13. In the wake of the Salt Law March, nearly 60,0002 Indians were arrested, among them, of course, Gandhiji himself. The progress of Gandhiji's march to the seashore can be traced from the secret reports filed by the police officials deputed to monitor his movements.Gandhiji persuaded the citizens to stand united. The police spies reported that Gandhiji's meetings were very well attended, by villagers of all castes. They observed thousands of volunteers flocking to the ' nationalist cause. Among them were many officials, who had resigned from their posts with the colonial government.The progress of the Salt March can also be traced from another source: the American Hews magazine, 'Time'. Earlier it despised Gandhiji's looks, writing disdainfully, of his "spindly frame" and his "spidery loins". Thus in its first report, Time was deeply sceptical of the Salt March reaching its destination. It claimed that Gandhiji "sank to the ground" at the end of the second day's walking; the magazine did not believe that "the emaciated saint would be physically able to go much further".The Salt March gained the world's attention. The march was widely covered by the European and American press. It was the first nationalist activity in which women participated in large numbers. The march made the British realize that their dominance would not last forever and that they would have to devolve some power to the Indians.

CHAPTER-14

Understanding Partition

1. (d) Communalism refers to a politics that seeks to unify one community around a religious identity in hostile opposition to another community. It seeks to define this community identity as fundamental and fixed. It attempts to consolidate this identity and present it as natural – as if people were born into the identity, as if the identities do not evolve through history over time.

In order to unify the community, communalism suppresses distinctions within the community and emphasises the essential unity of the community against other communities.

Communalism, then, is a particular kind of politicisation of religious identity, an ideology that seeks to promote conflict between religious communities.

2. (b) The Lucknow Pact

The Lucknow Pact of December 1916 was an understanding between the Congress and the Muslim League (controlled by the UP-based "Young Party") whereby the Congress accepted separate electorates. The pact provided a joint political platform for the Moderates, Radicals and the Muslim League

3. (b) There were many reasons that aggravated the Muslims and indus and pushed them further towards communal extremes. Hindus were angered by the rapid spread of *tabligh* (propaganda) and *tanzim* (organisation) after 1923.

4. (c) In 1937, elections to the provincial legislatures were held for the first time

5. Only Mahatma Gandhi and Khan Abdul Ghaffar Khan of the NWFP continued to firmly oppose the idea of partition.

6. In the United Provinces, the Muslim League wanted to form a joint government with the Congress.

7. After withdrawing its support to the Cabinet Mission plan, the Muslim League decided on "Direct Action" for winning its Pakistan demand. It announced 16 August 1946 as "Direct Action Day". It was in March 1947 that the Congress high command voted for dividing the Punjab into two halves, one with Muslim majority and the other with Hindu/Sikh majority; and it asked for the application of a similar principle to Bengal.

8. The Lucknow Pact of December 1916 was an understanding between the Congress and the Muslim League (controlled by the UP-based "Young Party") whereby the Congress accepted separate electorates. The pact provided a joint political platform for the Moderates, Radicals and the Muslim League

9. Cripps Mission suggested a suitable political framework for a free India by recommending a loose three-tier confederation. It was to have a weak central government controlling only foreign affairs, defence and communications. Provincial assemblies being grouped into three sections. Section A for the Hindu majority provinces, Section B and C for Muslim-majority provinces of the north-west – Punjab , NWFP, Sindh and provinces of the north-east (Bengal, Assam) respectively

10. Muslim League decided on "Direct Action" for winning its Pakistan demand. It announced 16 August 1946 as "Direct Action Day". On this day, riots broke out in Calcutta, lasting several days and leaving several thousand people dead. By March 1947 violence spread to many parts of northern India. It was in March 1947 that the Congress high command voted for dividing the Punjab into two halves, and it asked for the application of a similar principle to Bengal.

11. The British followed a divide-and-rule policy in India and started categorised people according to religion .They viewed and treated them as separate from each other. By the end of the 19th century, several nationalist movements had emerged in India and there were communal conflicts and movements in the country that were based on religious identities rather than class or regional ones.Scholars suggest that separate electorates for Muslims, created by the colonial government in 1909 and expanded in 1919, crucially shaped the nature of communal politics.Communal identities were consolidated by a host of other developments in the early twentieth century. Muslims were angered by "music-before-mosque", by the cow protection movement, and by the efforts of the Arya Samaj to bring back to the Hindu fold (*shuddhi*) those who had recently converted to Islam.Hinds were angered by the rapid spread of *tabligh* (propaganda) and *tanzim* (organisation) after 1923. Though communal divide is a major factor in the partition of India but there were several other factors and especially what all transpired in the last decade before independence.

CHAPTER-15

Framing the Constitution

1. (d)

- Muslim League chose to boycott the Constituent Assembly, pressing its demand for Pakistan with a separate constitution.
- The Socialists too were initially unwilling to join, for they believed the Constituent Assembly was a creation of the British, and therefore incapable of being truly autonomous.
- 82 per cent of the members of the Constituent Assembly were also members of the Congress.

2. (a) The executive was made partly responsible to the provincial legislature in 1919, and almost entirely so under the Government of India Act of 1935.

3. (a) The legislatures elected under the 1935 Act operated within the framework of colonial rule, and were responsible to the Governor appointed by the British.

4. (d)

5. Hindustani – a blend of Hindi and Urdu – was a popular language of a large section of the people of India, and it was a composite language enriched by the interaction of diverse cultures.

6. B.R Ambedkar was asked to join the Union Cabinet as law minister after independence

7. Separate electorate was considered as a mischief because it divided the nation. It was like a poison that had entered into politics. Separate electorates demand had turned one community against another and caused bloodshed, civil war riots.

8. Arguments given by Sardar Vallabh Bhai Patel for building political unity and forging a nation.

- In order to build a strong nation every individual must be moulded as a citizen and assimilated within the nation.
- He considered separate electorate as a poison and for the goodness of the country it should not be followed.

9. Separate electorate turned one community against another and caused lot of bloodshed. Separatist feelings were cultivated by the British for their selfish ends. Communal hatred led to the tragic partition and it further led to the isolation of minorities

10. On 13th December 1946, Jawaharlal Nehru introduced the 'Objectives Resolution' in the Constituent Assembly. It proclaimed India to be an 'Independent Sovereign Republic', and guaranteed its citizens justice, equality and freedom, and assured that adequate safeguards shall be provided for minorities, backward and tribal areas, and Depressed and Other Backward Classes.

11. The Language Committee of the Constituent Assembly decided, but not yet formally declared, that Hindi in the Devanagari script would be the official language, but the transition to Hindi would be gradual. For the first fifteen years, English would continue to be used for all official purposes. Each province was to be allowed to choose one of the regional languages for official work within the province.

12. The members of the Constituent Assembly were not elected on the basis of universal franchise. In the winter of 1945-46 provincial elections were held in India. The Provincial Legislatures then chose the representatives to the Constituent Assembly. The Constituent Assembly that came into being was dominated by one party: the Congress. The Congress swept the general seats in the provincial elections, and the Muslim League captured most of the reserved Muslim seats. But the League chose to boycott the Constituent Assembly, pressing its demand for Pakistan with a separate constitution. 82 per cent of the members of the Constituent Assembly were also members of the Congress.

13. Jaipal Singh plead for the protection of tribes in the Constitutional Assembly because the tribes had been dispossessed of the land they had settled, deprived of their forests and pastures, and forced to move in search of new homes. Perceiving them as primitive and backward, the rest of society had spurned them

Through these points Jaipal Singh wanted the society to mix with the tribes and was not asking for separate electorates, but he felt that reservation of seats in the legislature was essential to allow tribals to represent themselves.

14. B. Pocker Bahadur argued that the Minorities exist in all lands ; they could not be wished away, they could not be erased out of existence. The need was to create a political fabric in which minorities could live in harmony with others, and the differences between communities could be minimised. This was possible only if minorities were well represented within the political system, their voices heard, and their views taken into account. The needs of the Muslims could not be understood by Non-Muslims. Therefore he demanded separate Electorate for Muslims.

15. The Draft Constitution provided for three lists of subjects: Union, State, and Concurrent. The subjects in the first list were to be the preserve of the Central Government, while those in the second list were vested with the states. As for the third list, here Centre and state shared responsibility. The Union also had control of minerals and key industries. Besides, Article 356 gave the Centre the powers to take over a state administration on the recommendation of the Governor. In the case of some taxes (for instance, customs duties and Company taxes) the Centre retained all the proceeds; in other cases (such as income tax and excise duties) it shared them with the states; in still other cases (for instance, estate duties) it assigned them wholly to the states. The states, meanwhile, could levy and collect certain taxes on their own: these included land and property taxes, sales tax, and the hugely profitable tax on bottled liquor. Ambedkar had declared that he wanted "a strong and united Centre , much stronger than the Centre we had created under the Government of India Act of 1935".

16. N.G. Ranga, a socialist who had been a leader of the peasant movement, urged that the term minorities be interpreted in economic terms. The real minorities were the poor and the downtrodden. He said that the people were so depressed and oppressed that they were not able to take advantage of the ordinary civil rights. He welcomed the legal rights the Constitution was granting to each individual but pointed to its limits. In his opinion it was meaningless for the poor people in the villages to know that they now had the fundamental right to live, and to have full employment, or that they could have their meetings, their conferences, their associations and various other civil liberties. It was essential to create conditions where these constitutionally enshrined rights could be effectively enjoyed. The tribal traditional laws are violated and their lands are snatched by merchants. The tribals are treated like slaves. The money lenders exploited the poor tribals. The zamindars exploited poor villagers. The poor peasant and the tribals do not get even basic education. For this they needed protection.

CUET UG

Solved Paper 2022

HISTORY

Class XII

1. At which Harappan settlement, the town was separated by walls?

   (a) Harappa

   (b) Mohenjodaro

   (c) Lothal

   (d) Rakhigarhi

2. The remains of which of the following crop are rarely found at the Harappan site?

   (a) Chickpea

   (b) Lentil

   (c) Rice

   (d) Sesame

3. Terracotta models of plough have been reported from:

   A. Kalibangan

   B. Banawali

   C. Cholistan

   D. Rakhigarhi

   E. Lothal

   Choose the correct answer from the options given below:

   (a) A and B only

   (b) B and C only

   (c) C and D only

   (d) D and E only

4. The new kingdoms that emerged in the Deccan during Sangam period includes which of the followings :

   A. Cholas

   B. Chera

   C. Pandyas

   D. Satvahanas

   E. Vakatakas

   Choose the correct answer from the options given below:

   (a) A, B, C

   (b) B, C, D

   (c) A, B, D

   (d) C, D, E

5. Match the composition with the writers

List I – Compositions	List II – Writers
A. Arthashastra	I. Banabhatta
B. Harshacharita	II. Megasthenese
C. Prayag Prashashti	III. Kautilya
D. Indica	IV. Harishena

Choose the correct answer from the options given below:

(*a*) A-III, B-IV, C-I, D-II   (*b*) A-III, B-I, C-IV, D-II

(*c*) A-IV, B-III, C-II, D-I   (*d*) A-I, B-II, C-III, D-IV

6. Whom did Asoka appointed to spread the message of 'Dhamma'?

(*a*) Dhamma Dandadhikari   (*b*) Dhamma Mahamatya

(*c*) Amatya Pradhan   (*d*) Dhamma Pradhan

7. According to Dharmashastras and Dharmasutras ideal occupation performed by Kshatriya was ______.

(*a*) To teach and study Vedas   (*b*) To engage in warfare and protect others

(*c*) To engage in trade   (*d*) To perform sacrifices

8. Point out the differences between Endogamy and Exogamy from the below given options.

(*a*) Endogamy is practice of a man having several wives and Exogamy is practice of a woman having several husbands.

(*b*) Endogamy is practice of woman having several husbands and Exogamy is practice of a man having several wives.

(*c*) Endogamy is marriage within a unit and Exogamy is marriage outside the unit.

(*d*) Endogamy is marriage outside the unit and Exogamy is marriage within a unit.

9. The term used when descent from father to son, grandson and so on:

(*a*) Patriliny   (*b*) Matriliny

(*c*) Polygyny   (*d*) Polyandry

10. Match List I with List II

List I – Religion/sects	List II – Founder
A. Buddhism	I. Vardhamana
B. Jainism	II. Makkhali Gosala
C. Ajivikas	III. Ajita Kesakambalin
D. Lokayatas	IV. Siddhartha

Choose the correct answer from the options given below:

(*a*) A-I, B-III, C-IV, D-II   (*b*) A-I, B-IV, C-III, D-II

(*c*) A-IV, B-I, C-II, D-III   (*d*) A-IV, B-I, C-III, D-II

11. Out of the given options, choose the most appropriate information above the Ajivikas.

A. Ajivikas are also known as fatalists   B. Ajita Kesakambalin belonged to Ajivika sect

C. Ajivika monks and nuns took five vows   D. Ajivikas believed that everything is predetermined

Choose the correct answer from the options given below:

(*a*) A and D only   (*b*) B and C only

(*c*) A and C only   (*d*) A and B only

12. Choose the most appropriate explanation for the reason Buddhism grew rapidly both during the lifetime of Buddha and after his death.

(*a*) He was very handsome and people flocked to see him

(*b*) There was absence of other religions at that time

(*c*) It appealed to many people who were dissatisfied with religious practices and rituals

(*d*) The king told his subjects to follow Buddha

13. Arrange the travellers who left written accounts in chronological order.

A. Ibn Batuta
B. Al-Biruni
C. Francois Bernier
D. Duarte Barbosa
E. Marco Polo

Choose the correct answer from the options given below:

(*a*) B, E, A, D, C
(*b*) A, B, C, D, E
(*c*) C, B, A, D, E
(*d*) B, E, D, A, C

14. To describe the Ultimate Reality, Kabir used the terms – Alakh (unseen) and Nirakar (formless). These philosophy belongs to :

(*a*) Yogic Tradition
(*b*) Tantric Tradition
(*c*) Vedantic Tradition
(*d*) Buddhist Tradition

15. Name the poet saints who belonged to Nirgun Bhakti tradition.

A. Mirabai
B. Kabir
C. Guru Nanak
D. Surdas
E. Ravidas

Choose the correct answer from the options given below:

(*a*) A, B and C only
(*b*) B, C and E only
(*c*) A, C and E only
(*d*) C, D and E only

16. Which of the following term given below is not related to Sufism?

(*a*) Qalandar
(*b*) Khanqah
(*c*) Ziyarat
(*d*) Mlechchha

17. The Portuguese travellers who visited the Vijayanagara city in 16th century are _______.

A. Abdur Razzaq
B. Fernao Nuniz
C. Nicolo Conti
D. Domingo Paes
E. Duarte Barbosa

Choose the correct answer from the options given below:

(*a*) A, B and C only
(*b*) B, D and E only
(*c*) A, B and D only
(*d*) C, D and E only

18. Arrange the following events of Indian history in chronological order.

    A. Vijayanagara Empire

    B. Gajapati Kingdom

    C. Conquest of Goa by the Portuguese

    D. Establishment of Delhi Sultanate

    E. Emergence of the Sultanate of Golconda

Choose the correct answer from the options given below:

    (*a*) A, B, C, D, E

    (*b*) D, A, B, C, E

    (*c*) C, D, E, A, B

    (*d*) B, E, A, D, C

19. Krishnadeva Raya the most famous ruler of the Vijayanagara Empire belonged to _____ dynasty.

    (*a*) Tuluva Dynasty

    (*b*) Sangam Dynasty

    (*c*) Aravidu Dynasty

    (*d*) Saluva Dynasty

20. The Emperor Akbar classified the lands and fixed a different revenue to be paid by each. Find out the incorrect match below.

    (*a*) **Polaj :** Annually cultivated for each crop in succession and never allowed to be left fallow

    (*b*) **Chachar :** Is a land that has lain fallow for three or four years

    (*c*) **Parauti :** Never allowed to lie fallow for cultivation

    (*d*) **Banjar :** A land uncultivated for five years and more

21. The British encouraged forest clearance for a number of reasons. Which of the following is incorrect?

    (*a*) To enlarge sources of land revenue

    (*b*) To acquire animals from forests

    (*c*) To produce crops for export

    (*d*) To tame and civilize forest dwellers.

22. Arrange the following events in chronological order.

    A. Acquiring of Diwani of Bengal by English East India Company

    B. Santhal Rebellion

    C. Rebellion by peasents in Deccan villages

    D. Permanent Settlement in Bengal

    E. Regulating Act passed by the British Parliament

Choose the correct answer from the options given below:

    (*a*) B, D, C, A, E

    (*b*) C, D, B, E, A

    (*c*) D, E, B, A, C

    (*d*) A, E, D, B, C

23. The Summary Settlement undermined the position and authority of the Taluqdars. Find out the other information from the below given options, which support undermining the position and authority of the Taluqdars under the summary settlement.

    A. Taluqdars were not having any permanent stakes in land

    B. British wanted to remove Taluqdars whenever possible

    C. British wanted to settle the land with actual land owners

    D. Revenue was fixed by the Britisher

    E. The Summary Settlement later helped Taluqdars

Choose the correct answer from the options given below:

    (*a*) B, C and D only

    (*b*) A, C and E only

    (*c*) A, B and C only

    (*d*) E, B and D only

24. The Santhals led their revolt against 'Dikus'. The term dikus was used for which of the following people?

(a) Paharias

(b) Settled peasants

(c) Nationalist leaders

(d) Money lenders

25. In Francis Buchanan's survey of Dimajpur district, the class of rich peasants is reported as:

(a) Mansabdars

(b) Jotedars

(c) Subedars

(d) Lathyals

26. 'In Memoriam' is a painting dedicated by the artist to the Christian heroism of British ladies in India during the revolt of 1857. Select the correct name of the artist from the given options.

(a) Henry Lawrence

(b) Thomas Jones Barker

(c) Joseph Noel Paton

(d) Francie Grant

27. Arrange the following historical incidents in chronological order:

A. Sepoys of Meerut Cantonment started mutiny

B. Annexation of Awadh by East India Company

C. Sati custom was abolished

D. Subsidiary Alliance had been imposed on Awadh

Choose the correct answer from the options given below:

(a) A, B, C, D

(b) D, C, B, A

(c) B, C, A, D

(d) D, B, C, A

28. Match The Rebel leader with their region

List I – Rebel Leaders	**List II – Regions**
A. Shah Mal	I. Singhbhoom
B. Kunwar Singh	II. Chinhat
C. Gonoo	III. Barout
D. Maulavi Ahmadullah Shah	IV. Arrah

Choose the correct answer from the options given below:

(a) A-I, B-III, C-IV, D-II

(b) A-II, B-I, C-IV, D-III

(c) A-III, B-IV, C-II, D-I

(d) A-III, B-IV, C-I, D-II

29. Rumours of greased cartridges spread like wild fire across cantonments As:

(a) Cantonments were connected through telegraphic lines

(b) Cantonments published their own newspapers

(c) News was broadcasted on television

(d) News spread through British officials

30. Which one is not a correct cause for the Revolt of 1857?

(a) Import of British manufactures into India

(b) Disrespect of Indians on public places

(c) Recognition of the Right to adopt an heir

(d) conversion of Indians to Christianity

31. The close link existed between the Sepoys and the rural world of North India during 1850s as the large number of Sepoys were being recruited in Bengal Army. Name the region which is called as the 'Nursery of the Bengal Army'.

(a) Bareilly

(b) Kanpur

(c) Awadh

(d) Jhansi

32. Name the ruler who had been defeated in the Battle of Plassey in 1757 by the British Officer Robert Clive?

(*a*) Mir Jafar

(*b*) Mir Bakshi

(*c*) Mir Qasim

(*d*) Sirajuddaula

33. Correctly match leader with their countries.

List I – Nationalist Leaders	List II – Countries
A. Mahatma Gandhi	I. America
B. Garibaldi	II. Vietnam
C. Ho chi Minh	III. India
D. George Washington	IV. Italy

Choose the correct answer from the options given below:

(*a*) A-III, B-IV, C-I, D-II

(*b*) A-II, B-IV, C-III, D-I

(*c*) A-III, B-II, C-IV, D-I

(*d*) A-III, B-IV, C-II, D-I

34. related to Provincial elections of 1937 in India, choose the **incorrect** options.

(*a*) There were fifteen provinces where the elections were held

(*b*) Only 10-12% Indians were eligible to vote

(*c*) Muslim League performed poorly

(*d*) Congress won absolute majority in five provinces

35. Which NWFP leader was known as "Frontier Gandhi'?

(*a*) Abdul Kalam Azad

(*b*) M. A. Jinnah

(*c*) Abdul Ghaffar Khan

(*d*) Abdul Latif

36. Match the personalities with their roles/responsibility.

List I – Personalities	List II – Their role/responsibility
A. K. M. Munshi	I. Lawyer from Madras
B. B. N. Rao	II. Chief Draughtsman
C. Alladi Krishnaswamy Aiyar	III. Constitutional Advisor to the Government of India
D. S. N. Mukherjee	IV. Lawyer from Gujarat

Choose the correct answer from the options given below:

(*a*) A-II, B-I, C-IV, D-III

(*b*) A-III, B-IV, C-I, D-II

(*c*) A-IV, B-III, C-I, D-II

(*d*) A-IV, B-III, C-II, D-I

37. Who proposed that the National Flag of India should be in horizontal tricolor of saffron, white and green in equal proportion with a wheel in Navy blue at the Centre?

(*a*) Vallabh Bhai Patel

(*b*) Rajendra Prasad

(*c*) Mahatma Gandhi

(*d*) Jawahar Lal Nehru

38. ______ of Bombay demanded justice for women, not reserved seats or separate electorate.

  (*a*) Dakshayani Velayudhan

  (*b*) A. Ramaswamy Mudaliar

  (*c*) Balakrishna Sharma

  (*d*) Hansa Mehta

39. Name the Constituent Assembly member who played vital role in reconciling different opposing points of view in assembly.

  (*a*) Jawahar Lal Nehru

  (*b*) Sardar Vallabh Bhai Patel

  (*c*) B. N. Rao

  (*d*) Dr. B. R. Ambedkar

40. The Constitution of India was framed and signed between:

  (*a*) November 1946 to December 1949

  (*b*) November 1946 to December 1950

  (*c*) December 1946 to November 1949

  (*d*) December 1946 to December 1949

Passage

Read the Passage and answer the questions the follows

For several years after the Non-cooperation Movement ended, Mahatma Gandhi focused on his social reform work. In 1928, however he began to think of re-entering politics. That year there was an all India campaign in opposition to the all-White Simon Commission, sent from England to enquire into conditions in the colony. Gandhiji did not himself participate in this movement, although he gave it his bleassings, as he also didi to a peasant satyagraha in Bardoli in the same year.

In the end of December 1929, the Congress held its annual session in the city of Lahore. The meeting was significant for two things; the election of Jawaharlal Nehru as President, signifying the passing of the baton of leadership to the younger generation; and the proclamation of commitment to 'Purna Swaraj', or complete independence. Now the pace of politics picked up once more. On 26 January 1930, 'Independence Day' was observed, with the national flage being hoisted in different venues, and patriotic songs being sung. Gandhiji himself issued precise instructions as to how the days should be observed. "It would be good," he says "if the declaration of Independence is made by whole villages, whole cities even.... It would be well if all the meetings were held at the identical minute in all the places."

41. In December 1929, who was appointed as the President of the Indian National Congress?

  (*a*) Dr. Rajendra Prasad

  (*b*) Sardar Vallabh Bhai Patel

  (*c*) Dr. B. R. Ambedkar

  (*d*) Jawahar Lal Nehru

42. The Purna Swaraj was observed on:

  (*a*) 26 January 1930

  (*b*) 29 January 1930

  (*c*) 28 January 1930

  (*d*) 27 January 19030

43. The annual session of the Indian National Congress was held at which place in December 1929?

  (*a*) Delhi

  (*b*) Lucknow

  (*c*) Lahore

  (*d*) Bombay

44. What proclamation of commitment had been taken in Indian National Congress session in December 1929?

    (*a*) Equality

    (*b*) Liberty

    (*c*) Purna Swaraj

    (*d*) Simon Go Back

45. There was an all India campaign to oppose the all-white Simon Commission, sent from England in ______.

    (*a*) 1927

    (*b*) 1928

    (*c*) 1929

    (*d*) 1930

Passage

Read the Passage and answer the questions that follows

The author of the Akbar Nama, Abu'l Fazl grew up in the Mughal capital of Agra. He was widely read in Arabic, Persian, Greek philosophy and Sufism. Moreover, he was a forceful debater and independent thinker who consistently opposed the views of the conservative ulama. These qualities impressed Akbar, who found Abu'l Fazl ideally suited as an adviser and a spokesperson for his policies. One major objective of the emperor was to free the state from the control of religious orthodoxy. In his role as court historian, Abu's Fazl both shaped and articulated the ideas associated with the reign of Akbar.

Beginning in 1589, Abu'l Fazl worked on the Akbar Nama for thirteen years, repeatedly revising the draft. The chronicle is based on a range of sources, including actuall records of events (waqai), official documents and oral testimonies of knowledgeable person.

The Akbar Name is divided into three books of which the first two are chronicles. The third book is the Ain-i-Akbari. The first volume contains the history of mankind from Adam to one celestial cycle of Akbar's life (30 years). The second volumes closes in the forty-sixth regnal year (1601) of Akbar, The very next year Abu'l Fazl fell victim to a conspiracy hatched by Prince Salim, and was murdered by his accomplice, Bir Singh Bundela.

46. The central purpose of Ain-i-Akbari was related to which ruler?

    (*a*) Jahangir's Vision

    (*b*) Akbar's vision

    (*c*) Humayun's vision

    (*d*) Shah Jahan's vision

47. Name the prince who was involves in the conspiracy against AbulFazl, a court writer of Akbar.

    (*a*) Prince Dara Shikoh

    (*b*) Prince Khurram

    (*c*) Prince Azam

    (*d*) Prince Salim

48. Point out the difference between Ain-i-Akbari and Akbar Nama.

    (*a*) One is biography while another is autobiography

    (*b*) Both the treatises written by two different writers

    (*c*) The first two portions are known as Akbar Nama and the last as Ain-i-Akbari

    (*d*) One text belongs to Akbar while another during Jahangir period

49. The first volume of Akbar Nama contained the information about:

    (*a*) Forty sixth regnal year fo Akbar

    (*b*) Early life of Akbar

    (*c*) Bureaucratic system only

    (*d*) Adam to one celestial cycle of Akbar's life

50. Abu'l Fazl, a great court writer of Akbar began his journey of writing in 1589 and took ____ years to complete Akbar Nama.

    (*a*) 11

    (*b*) 13

    (*c*) 12

    (*d*) 14

Answer Keys

1. (C)	**2.** (C)	**3.** (B)	**4.** (A)	**5.** (B)	**6.** (B)	**7.** (B)	**8.** (C)	**9.** (A)	**10.** (C)
11. (A)	**12.** (C)	**13.** (A)	**14.** (C)	**15.** (B)	**16.** (D)	**17.** (B)	**18.** (B)	**19.** (A)	**20.** (C)
21. (B)	**22.** (D)	**23.** (A)	**24.** (D)	**25.** (B)	**26.** (C)	**27.** (D)	**28.** (D)	**29.** (D)	**30.** (C)
31. (C)	**32.** (D)	**33.** (D)	**34.** (A)	**35.** (C)	**36.** (C)	**37.** (D)	**38.** (D)	**39.** (B)	**40.** (A)
41. (D)	**42.** (A)	**43.** (C)	**44.** (C)	**45.** (B)	**46.** (B)	**47.** (D)	**48.** (C)	**49.** (D)	**50.** (B)

Solution

1. (c) While most Harappan settlements have a small high western part and a larger lower eastern section, there are variations. At sites such as Dholavira and Lothal (Gujarat), the entire settlement was fortified, and sections within the town were also separated by walls. The Citadel within Lothal was not walled off, but was built at a height.

2. (c) Grains found at Harappan sites include wheat, barley, lentil, chickpea and sesame. Millets are found from sites in Gujarat. Finds of rice are relatively rare.

3. (b) Terracotta models of the plough have been found at sites in Cholistan and at Banawali (Haryana).

4. (a) The new kingdoms that emerged in the Deccan and further south, including the chiefdoms of the Cholas, Cheras and Pandyas in Tamilakam (the name of the ancient Tamil country, which included parts of present-day Andhra Pradesh and Kerala, in addition to Tamil Nadu), proved to be stable and prosperous.

5. (b)
    - The *Prayaga Prashasti* (also known as the Allahabad Pillar Inscription) composed in Sanskrit by Harishena, the court poet of Samudragupta, arguably the most powerful of the Gupta rulers

    - The Harshacharita is a biography of Harshavardhana, the ruler of Kanauj (see Map 3), composed in Sanskrit by his court poet, Banabhatta

    - *Arthashastra*, was composed by Kautilya or Chanakya

    - Megasthenes (a Greek ambassador to the court of Chandragupta Maurya) - Indica

6. (b) Special officers, known as the *dhamma mahamatta*, were appointed to spread the message of *dhamma*.

7. (b) Brahmanas began composing Sanskrit texts known as the Dharmasutras. These laid down norms for rulers (as well as for other social categories), who were ideally expected to be Kshatriyas

8. (c)
    - Endogamy refers to marriage within a unit - this could be a kin group, caste, or a group living in the same locality.

    - Exogamy refers to marriage outside the unit.

9. (a) *Patriliny* means tracing descent from father to son, grandson and so on.

10. (c) Ajivika, an ascetic sect that emerged in India about the same time as Buddhism and Jainism and that lasted until the 14th century; the name may mean "following the ascetic way of life." It was founded by Goshala Maskariputra

11. (a) The first teacher belonged to the tradition of the Ajivikas. They have often been described as fatalists: those who believe that everything is predetermined.

12. (c)

13. (a)

- Al-Biruni who came from Uzbekistan (eleventh century), Ibn Battuta who came from Morocco, in northwestern Africa (fourteenth century) and the Frenchman Franccois Bernier (seventeenth century).
- Ibn Battuta travelled between 1333 and 1347
- Ibn Battuta account is often compared with that of Marco Polo, who visited China (and also India) from his home base in Venice in the late thirteenth century.

14. (c) Kabir used terms drawn from Vedantic traditions, *alakh* (the unseen), *nirakar* (formless), Brahman, Atman, etc.

15. (b) Nirguna represented those poet-saints who extolled god without and beyond all attributes or form. They are also known as Monotheistic Bhakti saints. Tulsidas, Chaitanya, Surdas and Meera were the main proponents of Saguna. **Nanak and Kabir** were the main proponents of Nirguna.

16. (d) Some mystics initiated movements based on a radical interpretation of sufi ideals. Many scorned the khanqah and took to mendicancy and observed celibacy. They ignored rituals and observed extreme forms of asceticism. They were known by different names - Qalandars, Madaris, Malangs, Haidaris, etc. Because of their deliberate defiance of the *shari'a* they were often referred to as *be-shari'a*, in contrast to the *ba-shari'asufis* who complied with it

17. (b) Duarte Barbosa, Domingo Paes and FernaoNuniz from Portugal, came in the sixteenth century.

18. (b)

- Establishment of the Delhi Sultanate (1206)
- Establishment of the Vijayanagara Empire (1336)
- Establishment of the Gajapati kingdom of Orissa (1435)
- Conquest of Goa by the Portuguese (1510)

19. (a) Krishnadeva Raya belonged to the Tuluva dynasty

20. (c) The Emperor Akbar in his profound sagacity classified the lands and fixed a different revenue to be paid by each. Polaj is land which is annually cultivated for each crop in succession and is never allowed to lie fallow. Parauti is land left out of cultivation for a time that it may recover its strength. Chachar is land that has lain fallow for three or four years. Banjar is land uncultivated for five years and more.

21. (b) To acquire animals from forest

22. (d)

TIMELINE	
1765	English East India Company acquires Diwani of Bengal
1773	Regulating Act passed by the British Parliament to regulate the activities of the East India Company
1793	Permanent Settlement in Bengal
1800s	Santhals begin to come to the Rajmahal hills and settle there
1818	First revenue settlement in the Bombay Deccan
1820s	Agricultural prices begin to fall
1840s-50s	A slow process of agrarian expansion in the Bombay Deccan
1855-56	Santhal rebellion
1861	Cotton boom begins
1875	*Ryots* in Deccan villages reber

23. (a)

- The British land revenue policy further undermined the position and authority of the *taluqdars*. After annexation, the first British revenue settlement, known as the Summary Settlement of 1856, was based on the assumption that the *taluqdarswere* interlopers with no permanent stakes in land: they had established their hold over land through force and fraud. The Summary Settlement proceeded to remove the *taluqdars wherever* possible. Figures show that in pre-British times, *taluqdarshad* held 67 per cent of the total number of villages in Awadh; by the Summary Settlement this number had come down to 38 per cent. The *taluqdars* of southern Awadh were the hardest hit and some lost more than half of the total number of villages they had previously held.

- British land revenue officers believed that by removing *taluqdars they* would be able to settle the land with the actual owners of the soil and thus reduce the level of exploitation of peasants while increasing revenue returns for the state.

24. (d) moneylenders (*dikus*)

25. (b) Jotedars were "wealthy peasants" who comprised one layer of social strata in agrarian Bengal during Company rule in India.

26. (c) In Memoriam" was painted by Joseph Noel Paton two years after the mutiny.

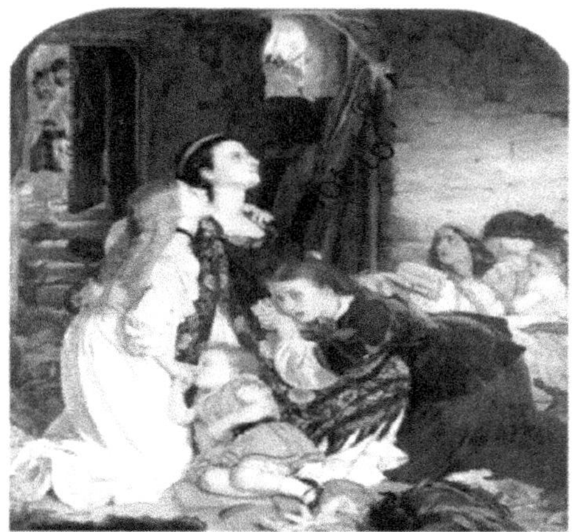

"In Memoriam", by Joseph Noel Paton, 1859

27. (d)

1801	Subsidiary Alliance introduced by Wellesley in Awadh
1856	Nawab Wajid Ali Shah deposed; Awadh annexed
1856-57	Summary revenue settlements introduced in Awadh by the British
1857 10 May	Mutiny starts in Meerut

28. (d)

- Shah Mal mobilised the villagers of pargana Barout in Uttar Pradesh.

- Gonoo, a tribal cultivator of Singhbhum in Chotanagpur, became a rebel leader of the Kol tribals of the region.

29. (d) The British tried to explain to the sepoys that this was not the case but the rumour that the new cartridges were greased with the fat of cows and pigs spread like wildfire across the sepoy lines of North India.

30. (c) On a variety of pleas, like misgovernment and the refusal to recognise adoption, the British annexed not only Awadh, but many other kingdoms and principalities like Jhansi and Satara.

31. (c) Awadh was, called the "nursery of the Bengal Army".

32. (d) The Battle of Plassey was a decisive victory of the British East India Company over the Nawab of Bengal and his French allies on 23 June 1757, under the leadership of Robert Clive. The victory was made possible by the defection of Mir Jafar, who was Nawab Siraj-ud-Daulah's commander in chief.

33. (d)
- Garibaldi - Italy

- Ho Chi Minh - Vietnam

34. (a) In 1937, elections to the provincial legislatures were held for the first time. Only about 10 to 12 per cent of the population enjoyed the right to vote. The Congress did well in the elections, winning an absolute majority in five out of eleven provinces and forming governments in seven of them. It did badly in the constituencies reserved for Muslims, but the Muslim League also fared poorly, polling only 4.4 per cent of the total Muslim vote cast in this election.

35. (c) Abdul Ghaffar Khan, also known as Bacha Khan or Badshah Khan, and honourably addressed as Fakhr-e-Afghan, was a Pashtun, Indian freedom fighter, independence activist, and founder of the KhudaiKhidmatgar resistance movement against British colonial rule in India.

36. (c)
- K.M. Munshi from Gujarat and Alladi Krishnaswamy Aiyar from Madras
- Chief Draughtsman - S. N. Mukherjee
- B. N. Rau - Constitutional Advisor to the Government of India

37. (d) It was Nehru who moved the crucial "Objectives Resolution", as well as the resolution proposing that the National Flag of India be a "horizontal tricolour of saffron, white and dark green in equal proportion", with a wheel in navy blue at the centre.

38. (d) Hansa Mehta of Bombay demanded justice for women, not reserved seats, or separate electorates.

39. (b) Patel worked mostly behind the scenes, playing a key role in the drafting of several reports, and working to reconcile opposing points of view.

40. (a) The Constitution was signed in December 1949 after three years of debate.

41. (d) Jawahar lal Nehru

42. (a) 26 Jan 1930

43. (c) Lahore

44. (c) Purna Swaraj

45. (b) For several years after the Non-cooperation Movement ended, Mahatma Gandhi focused on his social reform work. In 1928, however, he began to think of re-entering politics. That year there was an all-India campaign in opposition to the all-White Simon Commission, sent from England to enquire into conditions in the colony.

46. (b) Akbar's vision

47. (d) Prince Salim

48. (c)

49. (d)

50. (b)

CBSE

HISTORY

Class XII

Time Allowed: 90 minutes   **Maximum Marks: 40**

General Instructions

(i) This question paper contains **60** questions out of which **50** questions are to be attempted. All questions carry **equal marks.**

(ii) This question paper consists **four** Sections – **Section A, B, C** and **D.**

(iii) **Section – A** contains **24** questions. Attempt any **20** questions from Q. No. **1 to 24.**

(iv) **Section – B** contains **22** questions. Attempt any **18** questions from Q. No. **25 to 46.**

(v) **Section – C** contains **12** questions. (Case based study questions). Attempt any **10** questions from Q. No. **47** to **58.**

(vi) **Section – D** contains 2 MAP based questions. Attempt both the questions- Q.No. **59** and **60.**

(vii) The first **20** questions in **Section - A, 18** questions in **Section - B** and **10** questions in **Section - C** attempted by a candidate will be evaluated.

(viii) There is only **one** correct option for every Multiple Choice Question (MCQ). Marks will not be awarded for answering more than one option.

(ix) There is no negative marking.

Section A

Attempt any 20 questions from this section.

1. Which of the following artefact of the Harappa civilization was mainly used for long distance communication?

   (A) Shells   (B) Stone

   (C) Seals   (D) Steatite

2. Which one of the following mature Harappan sites is located in present day Gujarat?

   (A) Rakhi Garhi   (B) Dholavira

   (C) Kot Diji   (D) Amri

3. Which one of the following was a centre of craft production during Harappan Culture?

(A) Banawali

(B) Kalibangan

(C) Chanhudaro

(D) Manda

4. Which one of the following Buddhist Stupas was preserved with the funds provided by the rulers of Bhopal?

(A) Bharhut Stupa

(B) Shravasti Stupa

(C) Amravati Stupa

(D) Sanchi Stupa

5. Harishena, who composed 'Pragya Prashasti' was a court poet of which of the following rulers?

(A) Chandra Gupta

(B) Samudra Gupta

(C) Ashoka

(D) Chandra Gupta Maurya

6. Buddha's foster mother was the first to be ordained as Bhikhuni into the Sangha. Identify her name from the following:

(A) Punna

(B) Yashodhra

(C) Mahaprajapati Gotmi

(D) Maya

7. 'Mahanavami dibba was the centre of elaborate rituals.' Which of the following rituals were performed here?

(A) Lohri Celebration

(B) Holi Celebration

(C) Navratri Celebration

(D) Vaisakhi Celebration

8. Which of the following rulers belonged to Tuluva dynasty?

(A) Sadasiva Raya

(B) Rama Raya

(C) Harihara

(D) Krishan Deva Raya

9. Which one of the following incidents made Budha's first journey into the outside world traumatic?

(A) He saw a young boy praying to god.

(B) He saw a divine message on inscription.

(C) He saw a sick man and corpse.

(D) He saw a saint meditating.

10. Who of the following 'Guru' consolidated the sikh community into socio-religious and military force?

(A) Guru Arjan Sahib

(B) Guru Hargobind Sahib

(C) Guru Gobind Singh Sahib

(D) Guru Tegh Bahadur Sahib

11. Which one of the following is a reason to call Harappan script as enigmatic?

(A) It is written from right to left

(B) It has sign and alphabets.

(C) It has large number of signs, more than 375

(D) It has not been deciphered so far.

12. Who among the following Gupta rules was the most powerful and popular ruler?

(A) Chandra Gupta

(B) Samudra Gupta

(C) Kumara Gupta

(D) Sikanda Gupta

13. Fill in the blank space from the options given below :

When Buddhism spread to east Asia pilgrims such as .... travelled all the way from China to India in search of Buddhist texts.

(A) Chen Hui

(B) Fa-Xian

(C) Nelli-bly

(D) Tao-Te-Cheng

14. The hall in front of which of the following shrines was built by Krishna Deva Raya to mark his accession?

(A) Vitthla temple

(B) Virupaksha temple

(C) Hazara Ram temple

(D) Jaina temple

15. Which one of the following books was written by Chanakya?

(A) Patanjali

(B) Raj tringani

(C) Arthshastra

(D) Harshcharita

16. Which one of the following townships was founded by Krishna Deva Raya near Vijayanagara?

(A) Nagapattnam

(B) Naglapuram

(C) Raichur

(D) Kannanur Kupam

17. Which one of the following battles brought the downfall of Vijayanagara Empire?

(A) Battle of Mysore

(B) Battle of Trichinopoly

(C) Battle of Rakshasi-Tangdi

(D) Battle of Arcot

18. Which of the following foreign powers wanted to take away the eastern gateway of Sanchi Stupa to their own country?

(A) Norwegians

(B) French

(C) Scottish

(D) Portuguese

19. Which one among the following pairs is correctly matched?

	List - I	List - II
(A)	Birth of Buddha	Bodhgaya
(B)	Budha's enlightenment	Sarnath
(C)	Budha's first sermon	Lumbini
(D)	Budha's attained nirvana	Kushinagar

20. Identify the text with the help of the following information

- It is one of the best known legal texts of early India.
- Written in Sanskrit.
- Compiled between 2nd century BCE and 2nd century CE.

Choose appropriate option.

(A) Dharamashastra

(B) Upnishads

(C) Mahabharata

(D) Manusmiriti

21. Which one among the following is a correct pair regarding the teachings of Buddha ?

	Teaching	Essence
(A)	Metta	Sorrow
(B)	Dukkha	Soulless
(C)	Karuna	Compassion
(D)	Anatta	Fellow Feeling

22. Read the following statements regarding Alvar Saints of Medieval India and choose the correct option.

(i) Alvars were devoted to Lord Shiva.

(ii) The hymns of Alvars were compiled in Nalayara Divya Prabhandham.

(iii) Andal was from Alvar tradition.

Option:

(A) i and iii are correct

(B) ii and iii are correct

(C) i and ii are correct

(D) only iii is correct

23. Which one of the following empires issued gold coins for the first time in first century CE in India?

(A) Maurya Empire

(B) Gupta Empire

(C) Kushana Empire

(D) Vakataka Empire

24. Which one among the following is a part of Tipitika?

(A) Dipavamsa

(B) Dhamma Sutta

(C) Mahavamsa

(D) Abhidhammapitaka

Section B

Attempt any 18 questions from this section.

25. Arrange the following in Chronological order and choose the correct option.

(i) Invasion of Alexander

(ii) Reign of Ashoka

(iii) Beginning of Gupta rule

(iv) Rulers of Magadh Consolidated Power

Options:

(A) iv, ii, iii and i

(B) ii, iii, i and iv

(C) iii, ii, iv and i

(D) iv, i, ii, and iii

26. Which one of the following books was written by Ernest Mackay?

(A) The Indus

(B) Ancient India

(C) Early Indus Civilization

(D) Early Indians

27. Which of the following statements prove that there was some authority to take decision and implement them in the Harappan society?

(i)   The extraordinary uniformity of Harappan artefacts.

(ii) Bricks not produced at one centre but were uniform in size.

(iii) Settlements were not strategically set up.

(iv) Entire Harappan society had one ruler.

Options:

(A) i and ii   (B) ii and iii

(C) iii and iv   (D) i and iv

28. Identify the character of Mahabharata with the help of following information

• Ruler of Hastinapur • Pre-mature death • Brother of Dhritrashtra

Options:

(A) Duryodhna   (B) Dronacharya

(C) Pandu   (D) Arjuna

29. Which of the following are the major literary sources to reconstruct the history of Mauryan Empire?

(i)   Work of Magasthanese, a Greek ambassador.

(ii) Arthshastra of Kautilya.

(iii) Buddhist, Jaina and Pauranic literature.

(iv) Meghaduta of Kalidasa.

Choose the correct option from following:

(A) i, ii and iv   (B) ii, iii and iv

(C) i, ii and iii   (D) i, iii and iv

30. Two statements are given below as **Assertion (A)** and **Reason (R)**. Read the statements and choose the appropriate option.

Assertion (A) : Between 6th and 4th centuries BCE, Magadh became the most powerful mahajanpada.

Reason (R) : Magadh had agricultural productive area, Iron mines and vast forest area.

(A) Both (A) and (R) are correct and (R) is the correct explanation of (A).

(B) Both (A) and (R) are correct but (R) is not the correct explanation of (A).

(C) (A) is correct but (R) is incorrect.

(D) (A) is incorrect but (R) is correct.

31. Which one of the following statements regarding Buddhist sect is correct?

(A) Mahayana sect of Buddhism is the old way of thinking.

(B) Followers of Mahayana were regarded as Theravadins.

(C) Hinayana worship the image of Buddha and Boddhisattas.

(D) Hinayana described themselves as Theravadins.

32. Consider the following statements and select the ones that are true.

(i)   John Marshal was the first professional archaeologist to work in India.

(ii) He got the experience while working in Greece and Crete.

(iii) He was an ex-army Brigadier.

(iv) He announced the discovery of new civilization in the Indus Valley to the people.

Choose the correct option:

(A) i, ii and iii

(B) ii, iii and iv

(C) i, iii and iv

(D) i, ii and iv

33. Read the following statements and identify the character of Mahabharata.

> • She declared her love for Bhima.
> • She told Kunti that she liked her tiger like son.
> • She gave birth to a Rakshas boy.

Options :

(A) Drupadi

(B) Ghandhari

(C) Hidimba

(D) Subhadra

34. "The domestic architecture of Mohenjodaro along the ground level meant for privacy of the residents." Identify which of the following statements prove it.

(i)   Houses were centred on a courtyard.

(ii) There were no windows in the walls.

(iii) The main entrance did not give direct view.

(iv) Many houses had wells often in room for passers by.

Options :

(A) i and ii

(B) ii and iii

(C) iii and iv

(D) i and iv

35. Match the following correctly :

	List -I (Archaeologists)		List - II (Work)
(a)	Rakhal Das Bannerjee	i.	First Director General of ASI (Archaeological Survey of India)
(b)	S.N. Roy	ii.	Discovered seals in Harappa
(c)	Daya Ram Sahni	iii.	Discovered seals at Mohenjodara similar to Harappa
(d)	Alexander Cunningham	iv.	Authored "The Story of Civilisation"

Choose the correct option :

(A) (a)-iii, (b)-iv, (c)-ii, (d)-i

(B) (a)-ii, (b)-i, (c)-iii, (d)-iv

(C) (a)-i, (b)-ii, (c)-iv, (d)-iii

(D) (a)-iv, (b)-iii, (c)-i, (d)-ii

36. Which of the following statements are correct regarding Vijayanagara? Choose the correct option.

(i) Vijayanagara Empire was founded in 11th century.

(ii) The empire was routed out in 1565 and subsequently deserted.

(iii) The ruins of Hampi was brought to light by Colin Mackenzie.

(iv) Krishna Deva Raya founded Vijayanagara.

Option:

(A) ii and iv

(B) ii and iii

(C) i and iv

(D) iii and iv

37. Which one of the following statement is correct about Kabir?

(A) Kabir's verses are compiled in 'Kabir Bijak' only.

(B) Kabir was and is a source of inspiration to many.

(C) He advocated only saguna bhakti.

(D) Kabir believed in Polytheism.

38. Find out which of the following is a correct pair.

	Foreign Visitors in Vijayanagara	Countries
(A)	Abdur Razak	Russia
(B)	Duarte Barbossa	Portugal
(C)	Nicolo-de-conti	Persia
(D)	Afanasii Nikitin	Italy

39. Read the following information:

> • It is fourteen century dargah.
> • Mohd. Bin Tuglaq was the first sultan to visit this shrine.
> • It is located in Ajmer.

Identify whose dargah is this?

(A) Shaikh Salim Chishti

(B) Khwaja Muinundin Chishti

(C) Shaikh Nizam-ud-din Auliya

(D) Khwaja Qutbuddin Bakhtiar Kaki

40. Which of the following statements regarding Coin Mackenzie are true?

(i) He became famous as Engineer, Surveyor and Cartographer.

(ii) He became first Surveyor General of India.

(iii) He remained Surveyor General till his death.

(iv) By studying Vijayanagara East India Company could not get useful information.

Choose the correct option :

(A) only i

(B) i and ii

(C) i, ii and iii

(D) ii, iii and iv

41. Fill in the blank.

Archaeologists have been able to reconstruct dietary practices from finds of charred grains and seeds. These are studied by ....

Choose the correct option from the following :

(A) Archaeo-astronomy

(B) Archaeo-geologist

(C) Archaeo-botanist

(D) Archaeo-zoologist

42. Which of the following teachings in not associated with the traditions of Jainism?

(A) The entire world is animated.

(B) Non-injury to animals, plants and insects.

(C) The cycle of birth and rebirth is shaped by worshipping dieties.

(D) Monastic existence is necessary condition of salvation.

43. Which of the following statements are true regarding Mahabharata?

(i) The Sanskrit version of Mahabharata is far simpler than Vedas.

(ii) Historians classified Mahabharata into two broad heads as the narrative and the didactic.

(iii) Mahabharata is a dynamic text.

(iv) Didactic portion was first to be written.

Options:

(A) i, ii and iii

(B) i, iii and iv

(C) ii, iii and iv

(D) i, ii and iv

44. Read the information given below.

> • It is one of the most spectacular shrine.
> • It is probably meant to be used by king and his family.
> • The images in the central shrine are missing

With this information identify the shrine of Vijayanagara from the following:

(A) Jaina temple

(B) Virupaksha temple

(C) Vitthala temple

(D) Hazara Ram temple

45. Given below are two statements, labelled as **Assertion (A)** and **Reason (R)**.

Read them and choose the correct option.

Assertion (A) : It is likely that the very choice of the site of Vijayanagara was inspired by the existence of the shrines of Virupaksha and Pampadevi.

Reason (R) : The Vijayanagara kings claimed to rule on behalf of the god Virupaksha.

(A) Both (A) and (R) are true and (R) is the correct explanation of (A)

(B) Both (A) and (R) are true but (R) is not the correct explanation of (A).

(C) Both (A) and (R) are incorrect

(D) (A) is incorrect but (R) is correct.

46. Look at the figure and find out which school of art is evident on this image of Buddha.

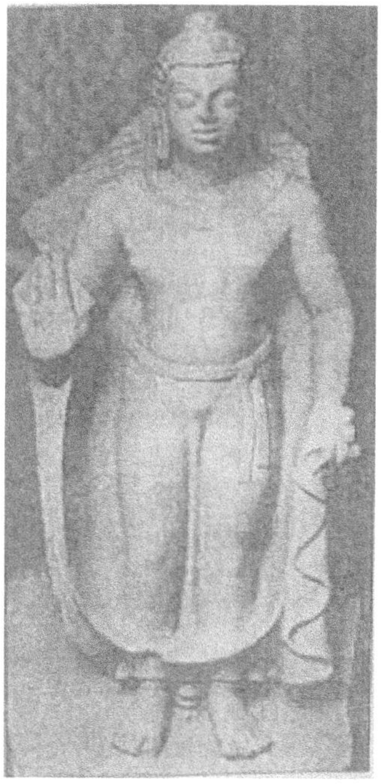

Choose the correct option from the following:

(A) Gandhara school of Art

(B) Mathura school of Art

(C) Karnataka school of Art

(D) Amravati school of Art

Note : The following question is meant for the visually impaired candidiates only in lieu of Q. No. 46.

Fill in the blank :

Buddha founded .... an organisation for monks.

Choose the correct option from the following.

(A) Temples

(B) Sangha

(C) Khanqah

(D) Dharamshala

Section C

(Case Based Questions)

This section contains 12 questions in total. Attempt any 10 questions.

Read the following source carefully and answer the following MCQs by Choosing the most appropriate option:

Draupadi's marriage

Drupada, the king of Panchala, organized a competition where the challenge was to string a bow and hit a target; the winner would be chosen to marry his daughter Draupadi. Arjuna was victorious and was garlanded by Draupadi. The Pandavas returned with her to their mother Kunti, who even before she saw them, asked them to share whatever they had got. She realized her mistake when she saw Draupadi, but her command could not be violated. After much deliberation, Yudhisthira decided that Draupadi would be their common wife.

When Drupada was told about this, he protested. However, the seer Vyasa arrived and told him that the Pandavas were in reality incarnations of Indra, whose wife had been reborn as Draupadi, and they were thus destined for each other.

Vyasa added that in another instance a young women had prayed to Shiva for a husband, and in her enthusiasm, had prayed five times instead of once. This women was now reborn as Draupadi, and Shiva had fulfilled her prayers. Convinced by these stories, Drupada consented to the marriage.

47. Why did King of Panchala organize a Competition?

(A) For popularizing the game.

(B) For providing patronage to the skilled ones.

(C) For the marriage of his daughtr.

(D) For popularizing himself.

48. What was the form of Draupadi's marriage during Mahabharat Era?

(A) Polyandry   (B) Polygyny

(C) Brahma Marriage   (D) Gandharva

49. Why didn't Kunti take her words back?

(A) Kunti's command had been given and it could not be violated.

(B) Kunti wanted to dominate on her children.

(C) Pandavas wanted to marry Draupadi.

(D) Kunti saw Draupadi as the saviour of Pandavas.

50. How does this story strengthen Pandava's brotherhood?

(A) Showed the fraternity of the Pandavas.

(B) Pandavas showed respect towards Kuru.

(C) Pandavas wanted to marry in consent of brothers

(D) Pandavas did all things in consent of King.

51. Analyse the role of the seer Vyasa in the Mahabharat.

(A) Vyasa was a seer, composer and farsighted rishi

(B) Vyasa dictated Mahabharat to his disciples.

(C) Vyasa was the teacher of Kauravas.

(D) Vyasa inspired Draupadi for marriage.

52. How did Vyasa justify the marriage of five brothers with Draupadi?

(A) Vyasa told Draupadi about her reincarnation.

(B) Vyasa mentioned all about his life in the previous birth.

(C) Vyasa explained Draupadi about her life.

(D) Vyasa narrated the story of Sita Mata to them.

Read the following carefully and answer the following MCQs by choosing the most appropriate option:

Shankaradeva

In the late fifteenth century, Shankaradeva emerged as one the loading proponents of Vaishnavism in Assam. His teachings, often known as the Bhagavati dharma because they were based on the *Bhagavad Gita* and the *Bhagavata Purana*, focused on absolute surrender to the supreme deity, in this case Vishnu. He emphasised the need for naam kirtan, recitation of the names of the Lord in *satsanga* or congregations of pious devotees. He also encouraged the establishment of satra or monasteries for the transmission of spiritual knowledge and naam ghar or prayer halls. Many of these institutions and practices continue to flourish in the region. His major compositions include the *Kirtana-ghosha*.

53. Who among the following was the contemporary of Shankaradeva ?

(A) Kabir   (B) Vardhaman Mahavir

(C) Chanakya   (D) Buddha

54. Why do we consider Shankaradeva as supreme saint-scholar?

(A) He was a poet, playwright and writer.

(B) He was a musician and social-religious reformer.

(C) He transmitted spiritual knowledge.

(D) He was a learnt person to save from negativity.

55. Which of the following cult Shankaradeva followed?

(A) Advaita Vedanta   (B) Brahmanism

(C) Mimansa Darshan   (D) Vaishnavism

56. How was Shankaradeva as a person?

(A) Geographer   (B) Historian

(C) Socialist   (D) Religious

57. Which of the following are the major work of Shankaradeva?

(A) Gita Gyan   (B) Harshcharita

(C) Shaiv Darshan   (D) Kirtana Ghosha

58. Why had Shankaradeva given emphasis on Bhagvat Puran?

(A) For the surrender of self in the devotion to Lord.

(B) For the grace of Lord in material things.

(C) For knowing the world in large.

(D) For getting blessings of Lord Vishnu.

SECTION - D
Map skill based questions.

Q. nos. 59 and 60 both are compulsory.

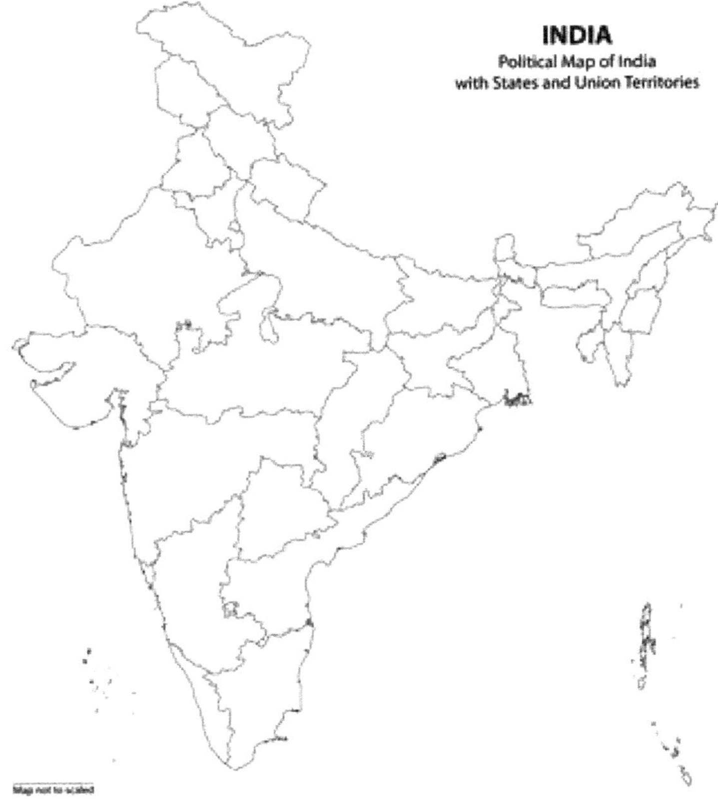

59. On the given outline political map of India a major Buddhist site has been marked as 'A'. Identify this place with the help of the following options.

(A) Shravasti   (B) Sanchi

(C) Bharhut   (D) Nagarjun Konda

60. On the given map an important city of 14th century has been marked as 'B'. Identify this place with the help of following options.

(A) Bidar   (B) Chandragiri

(C) Vijayanagara   (D) Tirunelveli

Note : The following questions are for the visually impaired candidates only in lieu of Question Nos. 59 and 60.

59. Which of the following sites is known for ancient stupa in Madhya Pradesh? Identify from the given information.

(A) Shravasti   (B) Sanchi

(C) Bharhut   (D) Nagarjun Konda

60. Which of the following was an important empire of 14th and 15th centry. Identify with the help of the given information.

(A) Bidar   (B) Chandragiri

(C) Vijayanagara   (D) Tirunelveli

Answer Keys

1. (C)   2. (B)   3. (D)   4. (D)   5. (B)   6. (C)   7. (C)   8. (D)   9. (C)   10. (C)

11. (D)   12. (B)   13. (B)   14. (B)   15. (C)   16. (B)   17. (C)   18. (B)   19. (D)   20. (D)

21. (C)   22. (B)   23. (C)   24. (D)   25. (D)   26. (C)   27. (A)   28. (C)   29. (C)   30. (A)

31. (D)   32. (D)   33. (C)   34. (B)   35. (A)   36. (B)   37. (B)   38. (B)   39. (B)   40. (C)

41. (C)   42. (C)   43. (A)   44. (D)   45. (A)   46. (B)   47. (C)   48. (A)   49. (A)   50. (C)

51. (D)   52. (A)   53. (A)   54. (C)   55. (D)   56. (D)   57. (D)   58. (A)   59. (B)   60. (C)

Solution

1. • The Harappan seal is possibly the most distinctive artefact of the Harappan or Indus valley civilization.

   • It is made of a stone called steatite, seals like this one often contained animal motifs and signs from a script that remains undeciphered.

   • Seals and sealings were used to facilitate long-distance communication.

2. • Dholavira, a mature Harappan site, is located in present-day Gujarat.

3. • Chanhudaro is an archaeological site belonging to the Indus Valley Civilization.

   • The site is located 130 kilometres south of Mohenjo-Daro, in Sindh, Pakistan.

4. • Among the best-preserved monuments of the time is the stupa at Sanchi, Bhopal.

   • The rulers of Bhopal, Shahjehan Begum, and her successor Sultan Jehan Begum provided money for the preservation of this ancient site.

5. • Harishena composed the famous 'Pragya Prashasti' in praise of Samudragupta.

   • He was the court poet of Gupta king Samudragupta.

6. • Mahapajapati Gotami was the foster-mother of the Buddha. She became the first bhikkhuni (Buddhist nun).

7. • The king's palace was the largest enclosure in Royal Residence and had two platforms called the - Audience Hall and the Mahanavami Dibba

   • It is believed that Mahanavami Dibba was used by the kings as a stage to watch the celebration of the nine-day-long splendid Mahanavami festival, also known as the Dusshera festival.

8. • Krishnadeva Raya was the most famous king of the Tuluva Dynasty.

9. • Buddha, saw in succession an old man, a sick person and a corpse being carried to cremation and a monk in meditation beneath a tree.

   • He began to think about old age, disease, and death and decided to follow the way of the monk.

10. • The tenth and the last Guru, Guru Gobind Singh organized the Sikhs into a military sect called Khalsa.

11. • Most of the inscriptions were short, the longest contained about 26 signs, each sign stood for a vowel or a consonant.

    • It contained wider space, sometimes shorter, had no consistency.

    • The script remains undeciphered.

12. • The most powerful ruler of the Gupta Dynasty was Samudragupta. His military achievements earned him the title of - The Indian Napoleon.

13. • Fa-Xian was a Chinese Buddhist monk and translator who travelled from China to India in search of the Buddhist texts.

14. • The hall in front of the main shrine was built by Krishnadera Raya to mark his accession. It has a unique shrine designed as a chariot.

15. • Arthashastra- significant Indian manual on the art of politics, economics, military strategy, the function of the state, and social organization

    • It is attributed to Kautilya or Chanakya

    • He was the chief minister to the emperor Chandragupta, the founder of the Mauryan dynasty.

16. • Krishna Deva Raya founded a suburban township called Naglapuram near Vijayanagar.

17. • The Vijaynagar kingdom suffered a defeat in the battle fought near the villages of Rakshasa and Tangdi. It is also known as the Battle of Talikota.

18. • The French sought the permission of Shahjehan Begum to take away its eastern gateway. They wanted to display it in a museum in France.

19. • Kushinagar is an important Buddhist pilgrimage site, where Buddhists believe Gautam Buddha attained Mahaparinirvana after his death

    • Birth of Buddha - Lumbini

    • Budha's enlightenment - Bodhgaya

    • Budha's first sermon - Sarnath

20. • The Manusmriti is one of the best-known legal texts of early India in Sanskrit and it is compiled between second century BCE and second century CE.

21. • In Buddhism, compassion is called karuna. Buddhists believe that they should show compassion to everyone.

    • Metta - Fellow Feeling

    • Dukkha - Sorrow

    • Anatta - Soulless

22. • The hymns of the Alvars were gathered in the 10th century by Nathamuni, a leader of the Shrivaishnava sect, who introduced the regular singing of the hymns in Vaishnava temples of South India. The collection is called Nalayira Prabandham. Andal was the only woman among the twelve Alvars.

23. • Emperor Kanishka of the Kushana Empire introduced gold coins alongside existing copper and silver coins for the first time in the first century CE in India.

24. • Tripitaka includes the Vinaya Pitaka, the Sutta Pitaka, and the Abhidhamma Pitaka.

    • Together these Three Baskets make up the sacred Buddhist texts known as the Tripitaka.

25. • 325 BCE - Chandragupta overthrew the Nanda Dynasty and ascended to the throne of the Magadha kingdom

    • 326 BC - Alexander invaded India

    • 270 to 232 BCE - Ashoka, the grandson of Chandragupta, led the Maurya Empire

    • 4th century CE to the late 6th century CE - Gupta Empire

26. Early Indus Civilization

27. i and ii

28. • Pandu was a ruler of Hasthinapur and brother of Dhritarashtra. He died a pre- mature death.

29. • The literary sources to reconstruct the history of Mauryan Empire include Kautilya's Arthasastra, Megasthenese's Indica and Buddhist literature and Puranas.

30. Both (A) and (R) are correct and (R) is the correct explanation of (A).

31. • Early Buddhist teachings gave importance to self-efforts in achieving nirvana and Buddha was regarded as a human being, who attained enlightenment and nirvana through his own efforts. This was known as Hinayana or 'Lesser Vehicle'.

• The followers of the old tradition of Buddhism called themselves Theravadins.

32. • John Marshall's stint as Director-General of the ASI marked a major change in Indian archaeology. He was the first professional archaeologist to work in India, and brought his experience of working in Greece and Crete to the field.

33. Hidimba

34. • The Lower Town at Mohenjodaro provides examples of residential buildings. Many were centred on a courtyard, with rooms on all sides.

• The courtyard was probably the centre of activities such as cooking and weaving, particularly during hot and dry weather.

36. • In 1565, Rama Raya, the chief minister of Vijayanagar, led the empire to the fatal battle at Talikota, in which its army was routed by the combined forces of the Muslim states of Bijapur, Ahmadnagar, and Golconda and the city of Vijayanagar was destroyed. It was Colin Mackenzie who discovered the ruins of Hampi in 1800.

37. Kabir was and is a source of inspiration to many.

38. • Duarte Barbosa was a Portuguese writer and officer from Portuguese India.

• Abdur Razak - Persian

• Nicolo-de-conti - Italian

• Afanasy Nikitin - Russian

39. • Khwaja Moinundin Chishti - It is in Ajmer, also called Hazrat Khwaja Gharib Nawaz Dargah or Ajmer Sharif.

40. i, ii and iii.

41. • Archaeologists have been able to reconstruct dietary practices from finds of grains and seeds. These are studied by archaeo-botanists, who are specialists in ancient plant remains.

42. • According to Jaina teachings, the cycle of birth and rebirth is shaped through karma.

43. i, ii and iii

44. • **Hazara Ram Temple** is dedicated to Lord Shri Rama. Hazara Ramaswami temple was the private place of worship for kings and the royal family of Vijayanagara in the 15th century.

45. Both (A) and (R) are true and (R) is the correct explanation of (A).

46. • The main feature of the Mathura School of Art is that includes both standing and seated statues of the Buddha.

• They are represented with broad shoulders, large chest, legs apart, and feet firmly planted, conveying a sense of enormous energy.

• The Buddha's right arm is raised in a gesture of reassurance called abhaya-mudra.

47. • Drupada, the king of Panchala, organised a competition where the challenge was to string a bow and hit a target; the winner would be chosen to marry his daughter Draupadi.

48. • It is a custom of a woman being married to more than one man at the same time.

49. • The Pandavas returned with Draupadi to their mother Kunti, who, even before she saw them, asked them to share whatever they had got.

   • She realised her mistake when she saw Draupadi, but her command could not be violated

50. • Pandas wanted to marry with the consent of the brothers.

51. • Vyasa inspired Drapadi that in another instance a young woman had prayed to Shiva for a husband, and in her enthusiasm, had prayed five times instead of once. This woman was now reborn as Draupadi, and Shiva had fulfilled her prayers.

52. • Vyasa told Drupada that the Pandavas were in reality incarnations of Indra, whose wife had been reborn as Draupadi, and they were thus destined for each other.

53. Kabir

54. He transmitted spiritual knowledge.

55. • In the late fifteenth century, Shankaradeva emerged as one of the leading proponents of Vaishnavism in Assam.

56. Religious

57. Kirtana-Ghosha

58. For the surrender of self in the devotion to Lord.

59. Sanchi

60. Vijayanagara

CBSE

Solved Paper 2022 (Term II)

HISTORY

Class XII

Time Allowed : 2 Hours   Maximum Marks : 40

General Instructions

Please read the following instructions carefully and strictly follow them.

(i) *This question paper contains 10 questions. Marks have been indicated against each question.*

(ii) *All questions are compulsory.*

(iii) *This question paper is divided into FOUR Sections - Section A, B, C and D.*

(iv) ***Section A*** *- Question Nos. 1 to 4 are Short answer type questions of **3 marks** each. Answer to each question should not exceed 80 words.*

(v) ***Section B*** *- Question Nos. 5 to 7 are Long answer type questions, carrying **6 marks** each. Answer to each question should not exceed 150 to 200 words.*

(vi) ***Section C*** *- Question Nos. 8 and 9 are Case Based questions, carrying **4 marks** each.*

(vii) ***Section D*** *- Question No. 10 is MAP based question, carrying **2 marks**.*

(viii) *There is no overall choice in the question paper. However, an internal choice has been provided in some questions. Only one of the choices in such questions have to be attempted.*

SECTION A

(Short Answer Type Questions)

1. How has the art helped in keeping alive the memory of Rani of Jhansi ? Explain.   (3)

2. (a) Explain the reasons of initiating the Non-Cooperation Movement by Gandhiji.   (3)

OR

  (b) Explain the reasons that led to the Civil Disobedience Movement of 1930.

3. Examine the role of Gobind Ballabh Pant on the Unified Nation in the Constituent Assembly.   (3)

4. Why did British introduce the Permanent Settlement in Bengal ? Explain.   (3)

SECTION B

(Long Answer Type Questions)

5. Explain the stages of conquest of Awadh by the British from 1801 onwards. (6)

6. (a) "In the Constituent Assembly, issues over 'national language' were intensely debated." Explain the statement with examples. (6)

OR

(b) "Issues of 'division of power of the government' at the Centre and State level were intensely debated in the Constituent Assembly." Explain the statement with examples.

7. (a) Who was Abul - Fazal ? Why is Akbarnama considered as his one of the important contributions ? Explain. (6)

OR

(b) Why were the imperial officers in the Mughal Empire described by the court historians as a 'bouquet of flowers' ? Explain.

SECTION C

(Case Based Questions)

8. Read the case given below and answer the questions that follow : (1 + 1 + 2 = 4)

Travels of the Badshah Nama

Gifting of precious manuscripts was an established diplomatic custom under the Mughals. In emulation of this, the Nawab of Awadh gifted the illustrated Badshah Nama to King George III in 1799. Since then it has been preserved in the English Royal Collections, now at Windsor Castle.

In 1994, conservation work required the bound manuscript to be taken apart. This made it possible to exhibit the paintings, and in 1997 for the first time, the Badshah Nama paintings were shown in exhibitions in New Delhi, London and Washington.

8.1 Explain the diplomatic practice of Mughals. (1)

8.2 Why did Nawab of Awadh share a common ground of diplomatic gift giving practice with King George III? (1)

8.3 How have the precious work of Mughals preserved? (2)

9. Read the case given below and answer the questions that follow: (1 + 1 + 2 = 4)

Charkha

Mahatma Gandhi was profoundly critical of the modern age in which machines enslaved humans and displaced labour. He saw the charkha as a symbol of a human society that would not glorify machines and technology. The spinning wheel, moreover, could provide the poor with supplementary income and make them self-reliant.

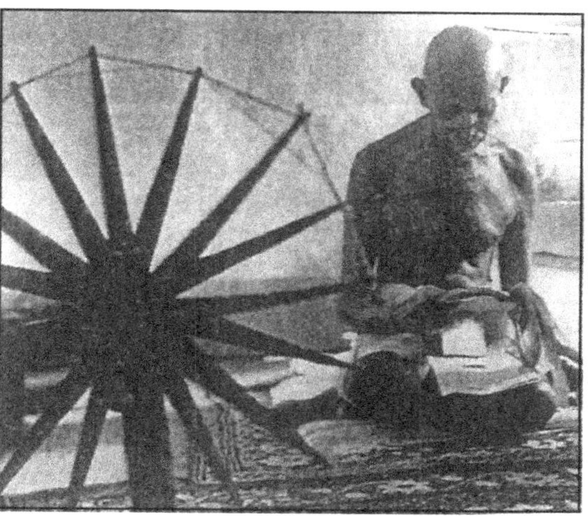

What I object to, is the craze for machinery as such. The craze is for what they call labour-saving machinery. Men go on "saving labour", till thousands are without work and thrown on the open streets to die of starvation. I want to save time and labour, not for a fraction of mankind, but for all; I want the concentration of wealth, not in the hands of few, but in the hands of all. *Young India, 13 November, 1924*

Khaddar does not seek to destroy all machinery but it does regulate its use and check its weedy growth. It uses machinery for the service of the poorest in their own cottages. The wheel is itself an exquisite piece of machinery. *Young India, 17 March, 1927*

9.1 Why was Charkha considered sacred by Gandhiji? (1)

9.2 Why did Gandhiji give importance to Khaddar? (1)

9.3 How had Gandhiji related Charkha with the spirit of service and foundation of sound village life? (2)

SECTION D

(Map Based Questions)

10. On the given political outline Map of India, locate and label any one of the following with appropriate symbol.

(I) (a) The State where Gandhiji withdrew Non-Cooperation Movement. (1)

OR

(b) The State where Gandhiji started Satyagraha for the Kheda peasants.

(II) On the same outline Map of India, a place related to the Capital city of Mughal Empire is marked as A. Identify it and write its name on the lines drawn near them. (1)

Note : The following questions are for the Visually Impaired Candidates only in lieu of Q. No. 10.

(I) Name any one capital city of Mughal Empire. (1)

(II) (a) Mention any one centre related to the Revolt of 1857. (1)

OR

(b) Name the State where Jallianwala Bagh event took place.

Outline Map of India (Political)

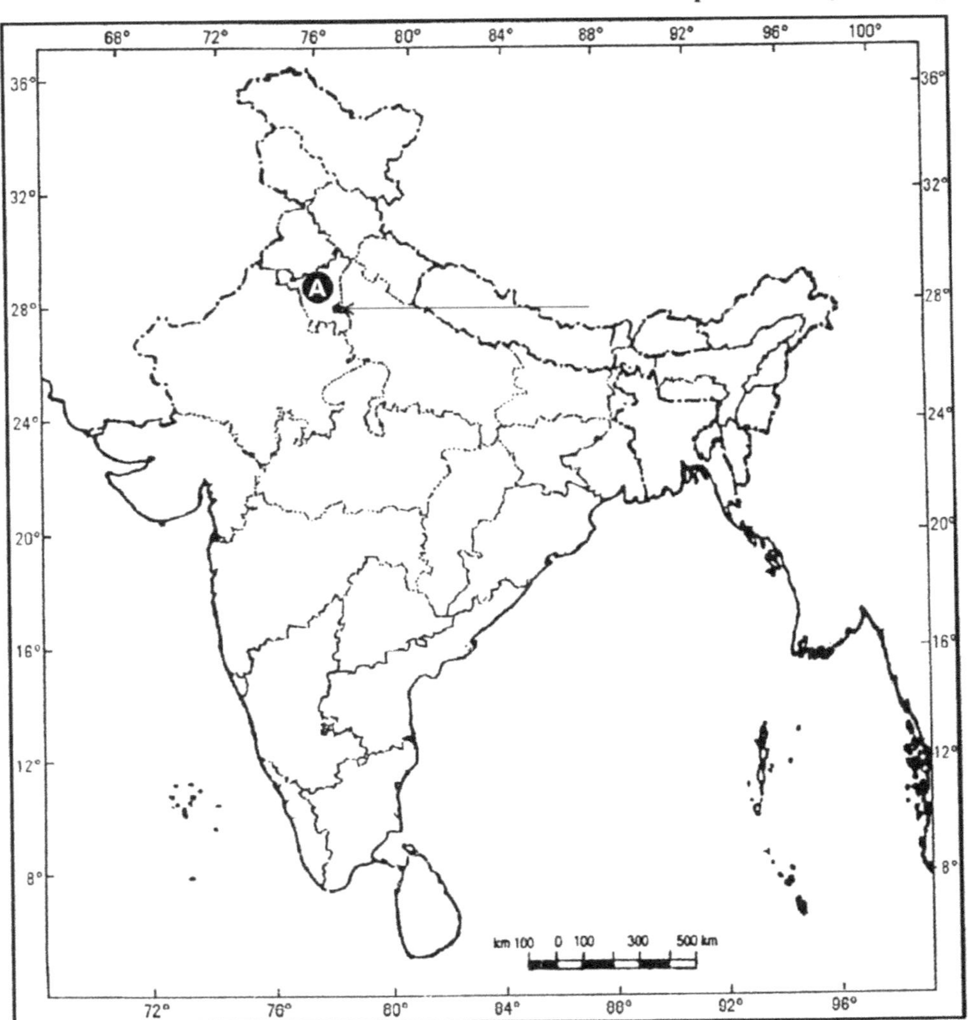

EXPLANATIONS

SECTION A

(Short Answer Type Questions)

1. Art, literature and imageries have helped in keeping the memory of Revolt of 1857 alive. Poems have helped to keep the valour and courage of heroic fighters of 1857 alive. Like many children have grown up reading the poems about Rani of Jhansi, Lakshmi Bai. Books and other media have helped in conveying the stories of these brave fighters, fighting against the atrocities of Britishers. Many images and poster were made to represent the valour of these heroes.

2. (a) The growing resentment against the British rule led to the launch of the Khilafat and Non-Cooperation movement.

    Gandhi ji launched Non-Cooperation Movement due to following reasons :

    - The discriminatory Rowlatt Act attracted large scale protest

    - The Jalianwalla Bagh Massacre and killing of innocents by General Dyer.

    - Gandhi ji wanted to withdraw all cooperation available to Britishers in India.

    - He wanted to eradicate the adverse impact of First World War casted upon Indians.

    - To implement Swaraj/self rule.

    OR

    (b) The Civil Disobedience Movement was launched under the leadership of Gandhiji. It began with the famous Dandi March where The Salt Satyagraha was initiated by Mahatma Gandhi against the salt tax imposed by the British government in India. Gandhi led a large group of people from Sabarmati Ashram to Dandi, a coastal village in Gujarat on 12th March 1930, to break the salt law by producing salt from seawater.

3. Govind Ballabh Pant is remembered as one of the country's **most prominent freedom fighters and an administrator** who played a key role in shaping modern India.

    He unified the Nation in the Constituent assembly by opposing the demand for separate electorates in the Constituent Assembly because he was of the view that separate electorates would isolate the minorities permanently and Minorities would become vulnerable.

    The ruling government will not give them an opportunity to have a voice in the government and it was also against the concept of a unified nation state

4. The Permanent Settlement of Bengal was brought into effect by the East India Company headed by the Governor-General Lord Cornwallis in 1793. This was basically an agreement between the company and the Zamindars to fix the land revenue. Cornwallis thought of this system inspired by the prevailing system of land revenue in England where the landlords were the permanent masters of their holdings and they collected revenue from the peasants and looked after their interests. He envisaged the creation of a hereditary class of landlords in India. This system was also called the Zamindari System.

SECTION B

(Long Answer Type Questions)

5. In 1798 AD, the fifth Nawab Wazir Ali Khan (1797AD–1798 AD) was accused by the British to be unfaithful and uncaring towards his own people. Subsequently he was forced to abdicate and replaced by his uncle Saadat Ali Khan II with the help from the British. The assassination of a British Resident in 1798 AD in Benares by the deposed Wazir Ali gave the British further excuse for interference in internal affairs of Awadh. Lord Wellesley exploited it to the best possible extent by virtue of treaty of 1801 AD. Saadat Ali Khan II was reduced to a mere puppet king   under the provisions of the treaty. He was forced to disband his own troops and agreed to bear the huge expense of the British army.

The final moment came and Awadh was annexed to the English East India Company under the terms of the Doctrine of Lapse on the grounds of internal misrule on 7 February 1856 AD by the order of the Governor General of the British East India Company, Lord Dalhousie.

6. (a) Constituent Assembly was constituted by the British Government in 1946 to solve the political problems and to draft a Constitution for India. From the very beginning of the Assembly, the language question became very controversial. Some members of the Assembly were in favour of Hindi while some others were in favour of Hindustani.

During many sessions of the Assembly there were many heated discussions on the question of Hindi and Hindustani, for Congress had adopted Hindustani language at the instance of Mahatma Gandhi. Acharya J.P. Kripalani, Mr. R.V. Bulekar and Mr. Ran Nath Gbnkar wanted that the proceedings of the Assembly should be in Hindustani, and the Constitution should be drafted in it and it should be authoritative one.

The Constitutional Assembly accepted Hindi written in Devanagari script as the official language of the union and as regards numerals, international (Roman} numerals were accepted. Thus a long-standing issue of official language was ultimately resolved and the integration of the country was saved.

OR

(b) One of the salient features of the Indian Constitution is that it lays down the structure of a federation just like various other western states. The exact nature of the federation of states that India has been is up for debate for a very long time. Federalism was also part of intense debate in the Constituent Assembly. JB Kriplani, who was the President at the historic Meerut Session, 1946 of the Indian National Congress, while outlining the proposed Constitution stated that it must be federal in character with maximum autonomy given to the states.

Dr. Ambedkar described the Constitution proposed to be federal, even though the word used in Article 1 was Union and the word "federal" was never mentioned in the Preamble or any other provision.

7. (a) Ab'ul Fazal was the author of the Akbar Nama, an adviser and a spokesperson for Akbar Policies.In his role as court historian, Ab'ul Fazal both shaped and articulated the ideas associated with the reign of Akbar.

Abul Fazl who was one of the nine jewels of Akbar's court and also one of his closest allies wrote a three-volume history of the reign of Akbar. It was titled as Akbar Nama. It was written in the Persian language which was the literary language of the Mughals and included a vivid description of Akbar and his empire. Akbar Nama is a very useful source of literary information for the historians as it provides an authentic record of the period during the reign of Akbar. It gave a detailed account of all the aspects of the Mughal empire.

OR

(b) The officer corps of the Mughals was described as a bouquet of flowers (guldasta) held together by loyalty to the emperor. In Akbar's imperial service, Turani and Iranian nobles were present from the earliest phase of carving out a political dominion. Many had accompanied Humayun; others migrated later to the Mughal court. The most important pillar of the Mughal state was the nobility. The nobility was recruited from diverse ethnic and religious group which ensured that no faction was large enough to challenge the authority of the state.

SECTION C

(Case Based Questions)

8. 8.1 Humayun's exile in **Persia established diplomatic ties between the Safavid and Mughal Courts,** and led to increasing Persian cultural influence. The Mughal emperors established viable diplomatic relations not only with neighboring regions but also with many European powers. Theses relations were multi-faceted and ranged from military and economic to cultural and familial.

8.2 Gifting of precious manuscripts was an established diplomatic custom under the Mughals. In emulation of this, the Nawab of Awadh gifted the illustrated Badshah Nama to King George III in 1799. Since then it has been preserved in the English Royal Collections, now at Windsor Castle.

8.3 In 1994, conservation work required the bound manuscript to be taken apart. This made it possible to exhibit the paintings, and in 1997 for the first time, the Badshah Nama paintings were shown in exhibitions in New Delhi, London and Washington.

9. 9.1 Gandhiji saw the charkha as a symbol of a human society that would not glorify machines and technology. The spinning wheel, moreover, could provide the poor with supplementary income and make them self-reliant.

9.2 Khaddar does not seek to destroy all machinery but it does regulate its use and check its weedy growth. It uses machinery for the service of the poorest

9.3 The **Charkha** supplemented the agriculture of the **villagers** and gave it dignity. It **was** the friend and solace of the widow. It kept the **villagers** from idleness.

SECTION D

(Map Based Questions)

10. (I) (a) Uttar Pradesh

OR

    (b) Gujarat

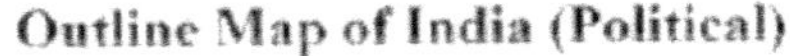

Outline Map of India (Political)

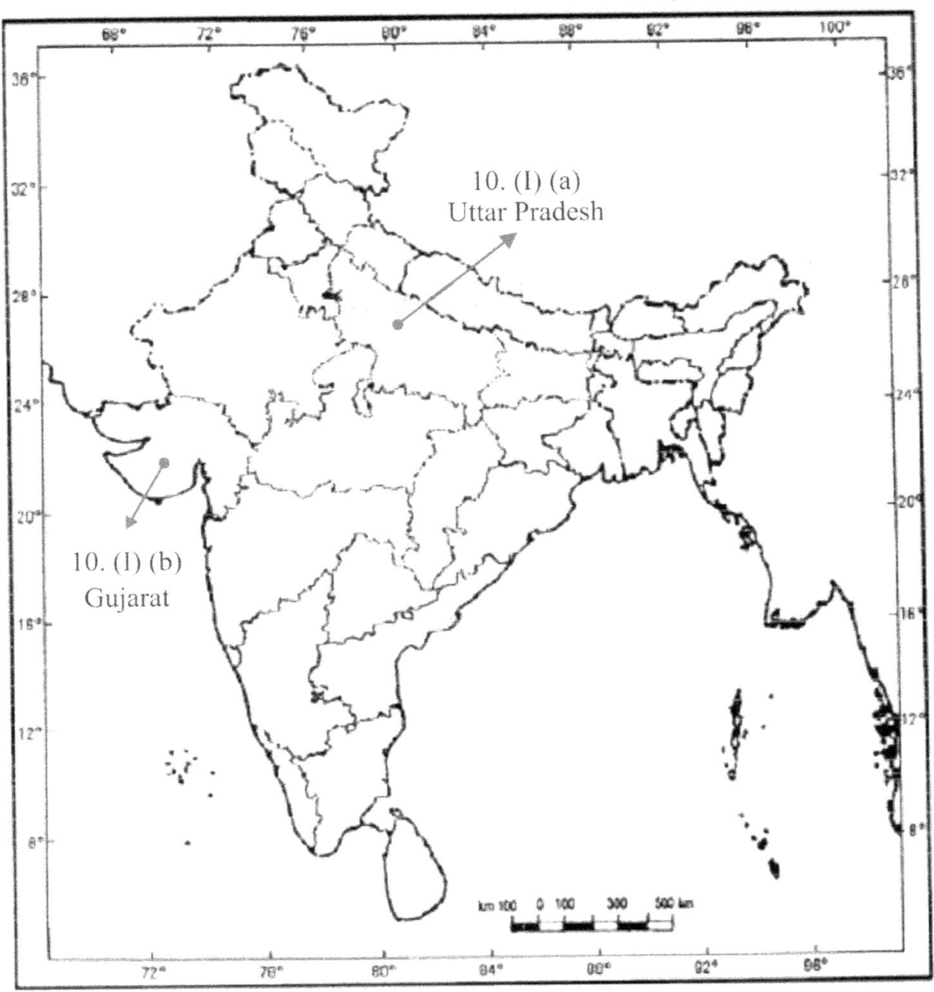

(II) Delhi

Visually impaired

(I) Delhi

(II) (a) Lucknow

OR

    (b) Punjab